An Economic History of Ireland Since Independence

This book provides a cogent summary of the economic history of the Irish Free State/Republic of Ireland. It takes the Irish story from the 1920s right through to the present, providing an excellent case study of one of a number of European states that obtained independence during and after the First World War. This book covers the transition to protectionism and import substitution between the 1930s and the 1950s and the second major transition to trade liberalization from the 1960s. In a wider European context, the Irish experience since EEC entry in 1973 was the most extreme European example of the achievement of industrialization through foreign direct investment (FDI). The eager adoption in recent decades of a neo-liberal economic model by successive governments, more particularly de-regulation in banking and construction, has recently led the Republic of Ireland to the most extreme economic crash of any Western society since the Great Depression.

The book is divided into three sections: the first examines economic policy; the second provides a summary of the core developments in agriculture, industry and services; the third focuses more on the factors of production, capital and labour, in addition to a chapter on trade since this has been a particularly important factor in Irish economic performance.

The Irish experience has followed a pattern evident in many of the more successful micro economies globally, in which policy was flexible and trade was open. This helped the Republic of Ireland to achieve convergence with the rest of Europe between the 1960s and 2007, but the political elite was subject to regulatory capture in policy terms, with disastrous consequences.

Andy Bielenberg is the Statutory Lecturer in Economic History at University College Cork, Republic of Ireland.

Raymond Ryan was a Post-Doctorate research fellow in Modern Irish History at University College Cork, Republic of Ireland.

Routledge studies in the history of economics

1 **Economics as Literature**
Willie Henderson

2 **Socialism and Marginalism in Economics 1870–1930**
Edited by Ian Steedman

3 **Hayek's Political Economy**
The socio-economics of order
Steve Fleetwood

4 **On the Origins of Classical Economics**
Distribution and value from William Petty to Adam Smith
Tony Aspromourgos

5 **The Economics of Joan Robinson**
Edited by Maria Cristina Marcuzzo, Luigi Pasinetti and Alesandro Roncaglia

6 **The Evolutionist Economics of Léon Walras**
Albert Jolink

7 **Keynes and the 'Classics'**
A study in language, epistemology and mistaken identities
Michel Verdon

8 **The History of Game Theory, Vol 1**
From the beginnings to 1945
Robert W. Dimand and Mary Ann Dimand

9 **The Economics of W. S. Jevons**
Sandra Peart

10 **Gandhi's Economic Thought**
Ajit K. Dasgupta

11 **Equilibrium and Economic Theory**
Edited by Giovanni Caravale

12 **Austrian Economics in Debate**
Edited by Willem Keizer, Bert Tieben and Rudy van Zijp

13 **Ancient Economic Thought**
Edited by B. B. Price

14 **The Political Economy of Social Credit and Guild Socialism**
Frances Hutchinson and Brian Burkitt

15 **Economic Careers**
Economics and economists in Britain 1930–1970
Keith Tribe

16 **Understanding 'Classical' Economics**
Studies in the long-period theory
Heinz Kurz and Neri Salvadori

17 **History of Environmental Economic Thought**
E. Kula

18 **Economic Thought in Communist and Post-Communist Europe**
Edited by Hans-Jürgen Wagener

19 **Studies in the History of French Political Economy**
From Bodin to Walras
Edited by Gilbert Faccarello

20 **The Economics of John Rae**
Edited by O. F. Hamouda, C. Lee and D. Mair

21 **Keynes and the Neoclassical Synthesis**
Einsteinian versus Newtonian macroeconomics
Teodoro Dario Togati

22 **Historical Perspectives on Macroeconomics**
Sixty years after the 'General Theory'
Edited by Philippe Fontaine and Albert Jolink

23 **The Founding of Institutional Economics**
The leisure class and sovereignty
Edited by Warren J. Samuels

24 **Evolution of Austrian Economics**
From Menger to Lachmann
Sandye Gloria

25 **Marx's Concept of Money: The God of Commodities**
Anitra Nelson

26 **The Economics of James Steuart**
Edited by Ramón Tortajada

27 **The Development of Economics in Europe since 1945**
Edited by A. W. Bob Coats

28 **The Canon in the History of Economics**
Critical essays
Edited by Michalis Psalidopoulos

29 **Money and Growth**
Selected papers of Allyn Abbott Young
Edited by Perry G. Mehrling and Roger J. Sandilands

30 **The Social Economics of Jean-Baptiste Say**
Markets and virtue
Evelyn L. Forget

31 **The Foundations of Laissez-Faire**
The economics of Pierre de Boisguilbert
Gilbert Faccarello

32 **John Ruskin's Political Economy**
Willie Henderson

33 **Contributions to the History of Economic Thought**
Essays in honour of R. D. C. Black
Edited by Antoin E. Murphy and Renee Prendergast

34 **Towards an Unknown Marx**
A commentary on the manuscripts of 1861–63
Enrique Dussel

35 **Economics and Interdisciplinary Exchange**
Edited by Guido Erreygers

36 **Economics as the Art of Thought**
Essays in memory of G. L. S. Shackle
Edited by Stephen F. Frowen and Peter Earl

37 **The Decline of Ricardian Economics**
Politics and economics in post-Ricardian theory
Susan Pashkoff

38 **Piero Sraffa**
His life, thought and cultural heritage
Alessandro Roncaglia

39 **Equilibrium and Disequilibrium in Economic Theory**
The Marshall–Walras divide
Michel de Vroey

40 **The German Historical School**
The historical and ethical approach to economics
Edited by Yuichi Shionoya

41 **Reflections on the Classical Canon in Economics**
Essays in honour of Samuel Hollander
Edited by Sandra Peart and Evelyn Forget

42 **Piero Sraffa's Political Economy**
A centenary estimate
Edited by Terenzio Cozzi and Roberto Marchionatti

43 **The Contribution of Joseph Schumpeter to Economics**
Economic development and institutional change
Richard Arena and Cecile Dangel

44 **On the Development of Long-run Neo-Classical Theory**
Tom Kompas

45 **F. A. Hayek as a Political Economist**
Economic analysis and values
Edited by Jack Birner, Pierre Garrouste and Thierry Aimar

46 **Pareto, Economics and Society**
The mechanical analogy
Michael McLure

47 **The Cambridge Controversies in Capital Theory**
A study in the logic of theory development
Jack Birner

48 **Economics Broadly Considered**
Essays in honour of Warren J. Samuels
Edited by Steven G. Medema, Jeff Biddle and John B. Davis

49 **Physicians and Political Economy**
Six studies of the work of doctor-economists
Edited by Peter Groenewegen

50 **The Spread of Political Economy and the Professionalisation of Economists**
Economic societies in Europe, America and Japan in the nineteenth century
Massimo Augello and Marco Guidi

51 **Historians of Economics and Economic Thought**
The construction of disciplinary memory
Steven G. Medema and Warren J. Samuels

52 **Competing Economic Theories**
Essays in memory of Giovanni Caravale
Sergio Nisticò and Domenico Tosato

53 **Economic Thought and Policy in Less Developed Europe**
The nineteenth century
Edited by Michalis Psalidopoulos and Maria-Eugenia Almedia Mata

54 **Family Fictions and Family Facts**
Harriet Martineau, Adolphe Quetelet and the population question in England 1798–1859
Brian Cooper

55 **Eighteeth-century Economics**
Peter Groenewegen

56 **The Rise of Political Economy in the Scottish Enlightenment**
Edited by Tatsuya Sakamoto and Hideo Tanaka

57 **Classics and Moderns in Economics, Volume I**
Essays on nineteenth and twentieth century economic thought
Peter Groenewegen

58 **Classics and Moderns in Economics, Volume II**
Essays on nineteenth and twentieth century economic thought
Peter Groenewegen

59 **Marshall's Evolutionary Economics**
Tiziano Raffaelli

60 **Money, Time and Rationality in Max Weber**
Austrian connections
Stephen D. Parsons

61 **Classical Macroeconomics**
Some modern variations and distortions
James C. W. Ahiakpor

62 **The Historical School of Economics in England and Japan**
Tamotsu Nishizawa

63 **Classical Economics and Modern Theory**
Studies in long-period analysis
Heinz D. Kurz and Neri Salvadori

64 **A Bibliography of Female Economic Thought to 1940**
Kirsten K. Madden, Janet A. Sietz and Michele Pujol

65 **Economics, Economists and Expectations**
From microfoundations to macroeconomics
Warren Young, Robert Leeson and William Darity Jnr.

66 **The Political Economy of Public Finance in Britain, 1767–1873**
Takuo Dome

67 **Essays in the History of Economics**
Warren J. Samuels, Willie Henderson, Kirk D. Johnson and Marianne Johnson

68 **History and Political Economy**
Essays in honour of
P. D. Groenewegen
Edited by Tony Aspromourgos and John Lodewijks

69 **The Tradition of Free Trade**
Lars Magnusson

70 **Evolution of the Market Process**
Austrian and Swedish economics
Edited by Michel Bellet, Sandye Gloria-Palermo and Abdallah Zouache

71 **Consumption as an Investment**
The fear of goods from Hesiod to Adam Smith
Cosimo Perrotta

72 **Jean-Baptiste Say and the Classical Canon in Economics**
The British connection in French classicism
Samuel Hollander

73 **Knut Wicksell on Poverty**
No place is too exalted
Knut Wicksell

74 **Economists in Cambridge**
A study through their correspondence 1907–1946
Edited by M. C. Marcuzzo and A. Rosselli

75 **The Experiment in the History of Economics**
Edited by Philippe Fontaine and Robert Leonard

76 **At the Origins of Mathematical Economics**
The Economics of A. N. Isnard (1748–1803)
Richard van den Berg

77 **Money and Exchange**
Folktales and reality
Sasan Fayazmanesh

78 **Economic Development and Social Change**
Historical roots and modern perspectives
George Stathakis and Gianni Vaggi

79 **Ethical Codes and Income Distribution**
A study of John Bates Clark and Thorstein Veblen
Guglielmo Forges Davanzati

80 **Evaluating Adam Smith**
Creating the wealth of nations
Willie Henderson

81 **Civil Happiness**
Economics and human flourishing in historical perspective
Luigino Bruni

82 **New Voices on Adam Smith**
Edited by Leonidas Montes and Eric Schliesser

83 **Making Chicago Price Theory**
Milton Friedman–George Stigler correspondence, 1945–1957
Edited by J. Daniel Hammond and Claire H. Hammond

84 **William Stanley Jevons and the Cutting Edge of Economics**
Bert Mosselmans

85 **A History of Econometrics in France**
From nature to models
Philippe Le Gall

86 **Money and Markets**
A doctrinal approach
Edited by Alberto Giacomin and Maria Cristina Marcuzzo

87 **Considerations on the Fundamental Principles of Pure Political Economy**
Vilfredo Pareto (Edited by Roberto Marchionatti and Fiorenzo Mornati)

88 **The Years of High Econometrics**
A short history of the generation that reinvented economics
Francisco Louçã

89 **David Hume's Political Economy**
Edited by Carl Wennerlind and Margaret Schabas

90 **Interpreting Classical Economics**
Studies in long-period analysis
Heinz D. Kurz and Neri Salvadori

91 **Keynes's Vision**
Why the Great Depression did not return
John Philip Jones

92 **Monetary Theory in Retrospect**
The selected essays of Filippo Cesarano
Filippo Cesarano

93 **Keynes's Theoretical Development**
From the tract to the general theory
Toshiaki Hirai

94 **Leading Contemporary Economists**
Economics at the cutting edge
Edited by Steven Pressman

95 **The Science of Wealth**
Adam Smith and the framing of political economy
Tony Aspromourgos

96 **Capital, Time and Transitional Dynamics**
Edited by Harald Hagemann and Roberto Scazzieri

97 **New Essays on Pareto's Economic Theory**
Edited by Luigino Bruni and Aldo Montesano

98 **Frank Knight and the Chicago School in American Economics**
Ross B. Emmett

99 **A History of Economic Theory**
Essays in honour of Takashi Negishi
Edited by Aiko Ikeo and Heinz D. Kurz

100 **Open Economics**
Economics in relation to other disciplines
Edited by Richard Arena, Sheila Dow and Matthias Klaes

101 **Rosa Luxemburg and the Critique of Political Economy**
Edited by Riccardo Bellofiore

102 **Problems and Methods of Econometrics**
The Poincaré lectures of Ragnar Frisch 1933
Edited by Olav Bjerkholt and Ariane Dupont-Keiffer

103 Criticisms of Classical Political Economy
Menger, Austrian economics and the German historical school
Gilles Campagnolo

104 A History of Entrepreneurship
Robert F. Hébert and Albert N. link

105 Keynes on Monetary Policy, Finance and Uncertainty
Liquidity preference theory and the global financial crisis
Jorg Bibow

106 Kalecki's Principle of Increasing Risk and Keynesian Economics
Tracy Mott

107 Economic Theory and Economic Thought
Essays in honour of Ian Steedman
John Vint, J. Stanley Metcalfe, Heinz D. Kurz, Neri Salvadori and Paul Samuelson

108 Political Economy, Public Policy and Monetary Economics
Ludwig von Mises and the Austrian tradition
Richard M. Ebeling

109 Keynes and the British Humanist Tradition
The moral purpose of the market
David R. Andrews

110 Political Economy and Industrialism
Banks in Saint-Simonian economic thought
Gilles Jacoud

111 Studies in Social Economics
Leon Walras
Translated by Jan van Daal and Donald Walker

112 The Making of the Classical Theory of Economic Growth
Anthony Brewer

113 The Origins of David Hume's Economics
Willie Henderson

114 Production, Distribution and Trade
Edited by Adriano Birolo, Duncan Foley, Heinz D. Kurz, Bertram Schefold and Ian Steedman

115 The Essential Writings of Thorstein Veblen
Edited by Charles Camic and Geoffrey Hodgson

116 Adam Smith and the Economy of the Passions
Jan Horst Keppler

117 The Analysis of Linear Economic Systems
Father Maurice Potron's pioneering works
Translated by Christian Bidard and Guido Erreygers

118 A Dynamic Approach to Economic Theory: Frisch
Edited by Olav Bjerkholt and Duo Qin

119 Henry A. Abbati: Keynes' Forgotten Precursor
Serena Di Gaspare

120 Generations of Economists
David Collard

121 **Hayek, Mill and the Liberal Tradition**
Edited by Andrew Farrant

122 **Marshall, Marshallians and Industrial Economics**
Edited by Tiziano Raffaelli

123 **Austrian and German Economic Thought**
Kiichiro Yagi

124 **The Evolution of Economic Theory**
Edited by Volker Caspari

125 **Thomas Tooke and the Monetary Thought of Classical Economics**
Matthew Smith

126 **Political Economy and Liberalism in France**
The contributions of Frédéric Bastiat
Robert Leroux

127 **Stalin's Economist**
The economic contributions of Jenö Varga
André Mommen

128 **E. E. Slutsky as Economist and Mathematician**
Crossing the limits of knowledge
Vincent Barnett

129 **Keynes, Sraffa, and the Criticism of Neoclassical Theory**
Essays in Honour of Heinz Kurz
Edited by Neri Salvadori and Christian Gehrke

130 **Crises and Cycles in Economic Dictionaries and Encyclopaedias**
Edited by Daniele Bensomi

131 **General Equilibrium Analysis: A Century After Walras**
Edited by Pascal Bridel

132 **Sraffa and Modern Economics, Volume I**
Edited by Roberto Ciccone, Christian Gehrke and Gary Mongiovi

133 **Sraffa and Modern Economics, Volume II**
Edited by Roberto Ciccone, Christian Gehrke and Gary Mongiovi

134 **The Minor Marshallians and Alfred Marshall: An Evaluation**
Peter Groenewegen

135 **Fighting Market Failure: Collected Essays in the Cambridge Tradition of Economics**
Maria Cristina Marcuzzo

136 **The Economic Reader**
Edited by Massimo M. Augello and Marco E. L. Guido

137 **Classical Political Economy and Modern Theory**
Essays in Honour of Heinz Kurz
Edited by Neri Salvadori and Christian Gehrke

138 **The Ideas of Ronald H. Coase**
Lawrence W. C. Lai

139 **Anticipating the Wealth of Nations**
Edited by Maren Jonasson and Petri Hyttinen, with an Introduction by Lars Magnusson

140 **Innovation, Knowledge and Growth**
Edited by Heinz D. Kurz

141 **A History of *Homo Economicus***
The nature of the moral in economic theory
William Dixon and David Wilson

142 **The Division of Labor in Economics: A History**
Guang-Zhen Sun

143 **Keynes and Modern Economics**
Ryuzo Kuroki

144 **Macroeconomics and the History of Economic Thought: *Festschrift* in Honour of Harald Hagemann**
Edited by Hagen M. Krämer, Heinz D. Kurz and Hans-Michael Trautwein

145 **French Liberalism in the 19th Century: An Anthology**
Edited by Robert Leroux

146 **Subjectivisim and Objectivism in the History of Economic Thought**
Edited by Yukihiro Ikeda and Kiichiro Yagi

147 **The Rhetoric of the Right**
Language change and the spread of the market
David George

148 **The Theory of Value and Distribution in Economics: Discussions between Pierangelo Garegnani and Paul Samuelson**
Edited by Heinz Kurz

149 **An Economic History of Ireland Since Independence**
Andy Bielenberg and Raymond Ryan

An Economic History of Ireland Since Independence

Andy Bielenberg and
Raymond Ryan

Routledge
Taylor & Francis Group
LONDON AND NEW YORK

First published 2013
by Routledge
2 Park Square, Milton Park, Abingdon, Oxon OX14 4RN

Simultaneously published in the USA and Canada
by Routledge
711 Third Avenue, New York, NY 10017

Routledge is an imprint of the Taylor & Francis Group, an informa business

British Library Cataloguing in Publication Data
A catalogue record for this book is available from the British Library

Library of Congress Cataloging in Publication Data
Bielenberg, Andy, 1959–
An economic history of Ireland since independence / Andy Bielenberg and Raymond Ryan.
p. cm.
1. Ireland—Economic conditions—1918–1949. 2. Ireland—Economic conditions—1949– 3. Ireland—Economic policy. I. Ryan, Raymond.
II. Title.
HC260.5.B54 2012
330.9417—dc23
2012011989

ISBN: 978-0-415-56694-0 (hbk)
ISBN: 978-0-203-09495-2 (ebk)

Typeset in Times New Roman
by Book Now Ltd, London

Printed and bound in the United States of America
by Edwards Brothers Malloy

Contents

List of tables xv
Acknowledgements xix
List of abbreviations xxi

Introduction 1

PART I 7

1 From dependent free state to EEC member-state: economic policies 1922–73 9

2 A new frontier: the EEC/EU and economic governance: 1973–2011 26

PART II 47

3 Nature's bounty: agriculture and natural resources 49

4 Late industrialization: from import substitution to foreign direct investment 71

5 From good haircuts to bad bankers: the services sector in the Irish economy 96

PART III 121

6 International trade and Irish economic development 123

7 Investment and credit in Irish economic development 145

8 A European outlier?: Demography and the labour force 165

Conclusion 189

Statistical appendix 200
Notes 210
Bibliography 246
Index 272

Tables

1.1 Total ERP funding extended to Ireland, 1949–52 18
2.1 EU transfers to Ireland, 1973–2008 27
2.2 Budgetary stance and government debt, 1976–2007 32
2.3 Government expenditure, 1983–2009 36
3.1 Area planted of selected crops at five-year intervals, 1925–70 54
3.2 Number of livestock for each decade, 1930–70 56
3.3 Percentage distribution of gross agricultural output, 1943–70 61
3.4 Livestock and poultry numbers at five-year intervals, 1975–2009 63
3.5 Percentage distribution of gross agricultural output (excluding direct payments) at three-year intervals, 1998–2007 64
3.6 Acreage of state-owned forestry at three-year intervals, 1927–78 65
3.7 Private and state-owned forestry at three-year intervals, 1981–2008 66
3.8 Agriculture and fisheries employment as a percentage of total employment, 1926–2009 69
4.1 Distribution of employment in transportable goods sectors, 1929–47 79
4.2 Value of transportable goods net output for three-year intervals, 1951–72 84
4.3 Distribution of employment in transportable goods sectors at three-year intervals, 1951–72 85
4.4 Total number of dwellings completed in Republic of Ireland, 1970–2010 92
5.1 Distribution of service employment (by occupational sub-sector), 1926–66 97
5.2 Railway lines and railway freight traffic at three-year intervals, 1945–2008 99
5.3 Earnings from foreign tourists and expenditure by overseas Irish tourists at three-year intervals, 1953–2007 and 2009 105
5.4 Distribution of service employment (by occupational sub-sector), 1971–2006 107
5.5 Percentage distribution of service employment (by occupational sub-sector), 1926–2006 108

5.6 Number, total sales and percentage of food /drink sales accounted for by supermarkets, 1966–87 110
5.7 Number of retail establishments, 1951–88 111
5.8 Percentage distribution of retail sales by sub-sector, 1951/54–87 113
5.9 Percentage distribution of service exports by sub-sector, 1999–2010 117
5.10 Percentage distribution of service imports by sub-sector, 1999–2010 117
5.11 Contribution of services to Net Domestic Product at three-year intervals, 1947–2007 and 2009 118
6.1 Geographic distribution exports and imports (value) by percentage, 1925–45 126
6.2 Geographic distribution of exports and imports (value) by percentage, 1946–63 129
6.3 Selected industrial commodities as a percentage of all exports, 1974–89 131
6.4 Geographic distribution of exports (value) by percentage, 1964–94 134
6.5 Geographic distribution of Irish exports (value) by percentage, 1995–2010 135
6.6 Percentage composition of mercantile exports (value) by broad commodity groups, 1990–2010 136
6.7 Selected industrial commodities as a percentage of all exports (value), 1990–2010 137
6.8 Percentage distribution of imports (value) by usage at three-year intervals, 1952–2007 138
6.9 Geographic distribution of merchandize imports (value) by percentage, 1967–94 139
6.10 Geographic distribution of merchandize imports (value) by percentage, 1995–2010 140
6.11 Service imports and exports at three-year intervals, 1953–2010 142
6.12 International trade as a percentage of GNP at five-year intervals, 1950–2010 143
7.1 Global Foreign Direct Investment inflows to selected countries and regions, 1970–2009 151
7.2 Financial account balances, 1998–2010 153
7.3 Gross Domestic Physical Capital Formation as a percentage of GNP for three-year intervals, 1953–2009 154
7.4 Percentage composition of Gross Domestic Fixed Capital Formation for four-year averages, 1953–2010 157
7.5 Percentage distribution of private sector credit, 1991–2009 159
7.6 House price indices for March of each year, 1996–2008 161
7.7 Value of loans transferred to NAMA by institution, September 2010 163
8.1 Birth rates, death rates and natural increase for inter-censal periods, 1926–2011 166
8.2 Population summary, 1911–2011 169
8.3 Estimated annual net migration rates, 1926–2011 172

8.4 Unemployment rate (percentage of labour force not gainfully employed), 1985–2011 173
8.5 Female labour force participation rate (percentage of total female population in the labour force), 1926–2009 174
8.6 Percentage female share of employment in different sectors, 1926–2009 175
8.7 Dependency ratios, 1926–2009 176
8.8 Number and percentage of population (14 years and over 1926–66, 15 years and over 1971–2009) employed, 1926–2009 177
8.9 Annual migration rates, 1987–2010 180
8.10 Persons in secondary and tertiary-level education, 1965–2009 181
8.11 Research and development expenditure as a percentage of GDP in Ireland and selected countries at four-year intervals, 1991–2008 185
9.1 Sectional distribution of employment, 1926–2009 191
9.2 Composition of net domestic product (NDP) at current factor prices, 1947–2009 192

Acknowledgements

This general survey draws heavily upon the various works cited in the bibliography. It is essentially a stock-taking exercise, which takes into account work in different disciplines touching on Irish economic development, so we must first acknowledge the important contribution of all of the authors and researchers cited in the bibliography. We also owe a debt to colleagues and family who read and commented on individual chapters; these include, in alphabetical order, Frank Barry, Nick Bielenberg, Linda Connolly, Louis Cullen, Mary Daly, Liam Kennedy, Edward Lahiff, Joe Lee, Cormac Ó Gráda, Eoin O' Leary, Joe Ruane, Ray Ryan, Peter Solar and David Stead. We would like to thank Jayne Barry, Kinsale, for understanding the photography of the cover image and Donna Romano of the National Irish Visual Arts Library at NCAD for her help in identifying the image by Guus Melai (NIVAL/PRC/1/1/ which dates *c.* 1954–6) and her permission to use the same.

This book is the result a three-year funded research project on Irish economic development since independence, which formed part of PRLTI (funded by the Higher Education Authority, the Department of Enterprise, Trade and Innovation, Ireland's EU Structural Funds Programmes, 2007–13 and the European Regional Development Fund) and which was organized under the auspices of the Irish National Institute for Historical Research, UCC. We wish to express our gratitude to the above mentioned stakeholders, whose funding made this project possible. Our thanks is also due to the Principal Investigator of the project, Dr. Hiram Morgan, School of History, UCC, and to Professor Geoff Roberts, Head of the School of History, for their support for the project.

As part of the PRLTI project, we also organized the 2010 Annual Conference of the Economic and Social History Society, whose theme was 'Cycles in Irish economic history and the current downturn'. We thank the many contributors to the conference, who provided many stimulating ideas that helped influence aspects of the book and whose publications derived from the conference we have cited repeatedly (they appear in IESH volume xxxvii: 2010). We would like to thank the President of the society, Neal Garnham, for supporting the conference held in UCC and Sean Connolly, for his role as editor of the journal.

We also express our appreciation to Cormac O' Sullivan, ESRI, who supplied National Income figures from the ESRI Databank and all of the fantastic staff in the Boole Library, UCC, who assisted us in tracing articles, books and much other statistical data. The CSO has also been very helpful in providing statistical data. Last but not least we would like to thank our respective families.

Abbreviations

ACC	Agricultural Credit Corporation
ATGWU	Amalgamated Transport and General Workers' Union
BES	Business Expansion Scheme
BGE	Bord Gáis Éireann
BIM	Bord Iascaigh Mhara
CAP	Common Agricultural Policy
CIE	Coras Iompair Éireann
CSO	Central Statistics Office
DCL	Distillers Company Limited
DDC	Dairy Disposal Company
ECB	European Central Bank
EEC	European Economic Community
EETPU	Electrical, Electronic, Telecommunications and Plumbing Union
EFTA	European Free Trade Association
EMS	European Monetary System
EMU	European Monetary Union
EPTR	Export Profits Tax Relief
ERM	Exchange Rate Mechanism
ERP	European Recovery Program
ESB	Electricity Supply Board
EU	European Union
FDI	Foreign Direct Investment
FEOGA	European Agricultural Guidance and Guarantee Fund
FWUI	Federated Workers' Union of Ireland
GATT	General Agreement on Trade and Tariffs
GDP	Gross Domestic Product
GNP	Gross National Product
GSR	Great Southern Railways
GVA	Gross Added Value
IBM	International Business Machines
ICC	Industrial Credit Corporation
ICT	Information Computer Technology
IDA	Industrial Development Association

IFSC	International Financial Services Centre
ISI	Import Substitution Strategy
IT	Information Technology
ITGWU	Irish Transport and General Workers' Union
NAMA	National Asset Management Agency
NDP	Net Domestic Product
NESC	National Economic and Social Council
NET	Nítrigin Éireann Teoranta
OECD	Organization for Economic Cooperation and Development
OEEC	Organization for European Economic Cooperation
PC	Personal Computer
REPS	Rural Environment Protection Scheme
RTC	Regional Technical College
RTE	Raidio Teilifis Éireann
TDB	Turf Development Board
TFP	Total Factor Productivity
UCC	University College Cork
UCD	University College Dublin
UK	United Kingdom
USA	United States of America
VHI	Voluntary Health Insurance

Introduction

The economic history of Ireland since independence attracted limited scholarly interest prior to the early 1970s. Some important specialized monographs were published, including Raymond Crotty's *Irish Agricultural Production*[1] and Kieran Kennedy's *Productivity and industrial growth: The Irish experience*,[2] which marked a more sophisticated turn in the historiography. Irish economic history gained a wider audience with the publication of two landmark surveys in 1972; Louis Cullen's *An economic history of Ireland since 1660*,[3] which traced the economic history of the island back to the seventeenth century, and James Meenan's *The Irish economy since 1922*,[4] which focused more specifically on the decades since independence. These works provided a synthesis at a time when economic history and material culture in general were becoming more fashionable academic topics both in Ireland and internationally, providing an alternative to the traditional focus on political history.

Since then a number of important works have been published on the period in question by economic historians, such as David Johnson's *The Irish economy in the inter war years* and Liam Kennedy's *The modern industrialization of Ireland*.[5] From a more mainstream historical perspective, Joseph Lee's *Ireland 1912–1985* contains much of value in relation to the role of the state in economic development.[6] The 1988 survey by Kieran Kennedy, Thomas Giblin and Deirdre McHugh, *The economic development of Ireland in the twentieth century*, was a more specialized treatment dealing specifically with economic development.[7] Cormac Ó Gráda's *A rocky road: The Irish economy since the 1920s*,[8] published in 1997 is the most recent comprehensive general survey of the twentieth century. This was written at a time when the Republic of Ireland was only in the early stages of the major boom that lasted until 2007 (now remembered fondly as 'the Celtic Tiger'). Subsequently, Ireland suffered a cataclysmic economic crash in 2008 and was subject to a bailout funded by the European Commission, the European Central Bank (ECB) and the International Monetary Fund (IMF) in 2010. In the wake of the 2008 economic collapse, a somewhat more sober perspective on recent growth and decline emerged, which can now be placed in an appropriate historical context going back to the 1920s using Maddison's data for GDP per capita and the ESRI historical series for GDP and GNP (see appendices). The dramatic events that have come to pass since O'Grada's 1997 survey provide as good a pretext as any to update the story of the Irish economy, which in the intervening years has attracted somewhat greater international attention than its small size might otherwise merit.

How have economists conceptualized Irish economic development? Two competing perspectives emerged in particular by the end of the first phase of the Celtic Tiger (c. 2002). The first argued that Ireland had experienced 'delayed convergence', in other words it underperformed in a European context until the late 1980s, when the appropriate policy measures were finally adapted and the significant potential for catching up with the rest of Europe was finally realized during the 1990s.[9] Convergence theory assumes that with a free flow of capital and the free operation of markets, capital will migrate to contexts where there is an existing scarcity of capital and returns are higher. Therefore, poorer countries will exhibit relatively higher rates of economic growth than wealthier ones. Those economists who adhere to the neo-classical growth model argue that inappropriate economic policies retarded the convergence trend that otherwise would have occurred automatically. Economists such as Brendan Walsh, Patrick Honohan and John Fitzgerald argue that Ireland experienced a process of delayed convergence, due to the inappropriate fiscal policies of the 1970s and the deflationary measures adopted in the 1980s to correct their negative impact. Once economic stability was achieved, convergence resumed and accelerated dramatically in the 1990s. In addition to a deferred process of macro-economic convergence, Fitzgerald argues that the delayed expansion of second-level educational attainment relative to other continental European countries provides one explanation for the differential between economic growth rates between Ireland and other small European countries in the post-Second World War era.[10] Cormac Ó Gráda and Kevin O'Rourke also argue that Irish economic growth between 1945 and 1990 was an example of sub-optimal convergence, which they attributed to investment in unproductive sectors, such as transport, and market-distorting government interventions.[11]

More recently, Frank Barry has argued that the regional economy model is more appropriate for use in describing the process of Irish economic development than delayed convergence. A regional economy is one with unusually mobile factors of production, such as labour and capital. Regional economies experience periods of prolonged growth and protracted recessions. Barry argues that both the expansion of the Irish economy during the Celtic Tiger and the previous recessionary periods, where the labour market was cleared through emigration, provide evidence that Ireland is a regional economy. Due to the historical tendency for labour to migrate, industrial development could not occur under prevailing market conditions, as unemployment could not rise sufficiently to reduce wages that would have stimulated the emergence of more competitive industries. Therefore government intervention was necessary to promote capital accumulation in sectors that could employ labour that would otherwise emigrate.[12] Barry critiques the convergence model on the basis that convergence theory literature does not describe or allow for the 'delay' mechanism advanced by its Irish advocates. Moreover, prior to the 1970s Ireland was not converging with the rest of Europe. Ireland, he argues, is better seen as a 'peripheral regional economy' than a national economy, more particularly in the 1960s when it was effectively operating as a region of the UK economy.[13]

Over-dependence on the slow-growing UK economy was a clear weakness of the economy until the 1970s, but the regional economy model becomes somewhat less compelling as one moves forward through the last third of the twentieth century. The critical relationships of the Republic of Ireland economy became much more triadic, incorporating core influences from three different economic zones; the UK, the US and the continental EEC/EU member– states, so that by 2002 its economy could no longer be described as dependent on any one of these zones. The regional economy and delayed convergence models both place more emphasis on exogenous than endogenous factors. Economic sociologist Denis O' Hearn also argues that periods of economic growth in Ireland are broadly derivative in nature, resulting from adaptation to wider economic trends that occur in Great Britain and the United States of America.[14]

The concept of economic dependency, whereby economic growth in countries occurs only as a result of economic development in more advanced and politically powerful countries has had a strong influence on the literature on Irish economic development. J. K. Jacobsen for example characterizes the expansion of foreign direct investment (FDI) based manufacturing in Ireland from the 1960s as a highly dependent form of development.[15] International competition created many structural problems for developing economies; Eoin O' Malley suggests that the sub-optimal economic growth performance of the Irish economy, prior to the 1990s, was due to *barriers to entry* faced by latecomer industrial nations such as Ireland to world export markets.[16]

Lars Mjøset has argued that while Ireland may have experienced economic growth, it did not experience economic development, due to the combination of high birth rates and the failure to develop viable industries based on existing resource endowments.[17] Seán Ó Riain's concept of a *developmental state network* is influenced by Mjøset's analysis, arguing that both the protectionist industrialization strategy between the 1930s and 1950s, and the attraction of FDI in the 1960s and 1970s, did not generate economic development, but during the 1980s, a coalition of previously marginal state bodies that promoted science and technology succeeded in shifting development policy towards the promotion of high-technology industries. The Irish state and its agencies then operated as a developmental network, similar to the experience of other high-growth small economies such as Israel and Taiwan, linking foreign industries with domestic firms and local authorities. This in his view generated sufficient innovation to cause economic development.[18]

The theories of the political scientist, Mancur Olson, have also been applied to describe the nature of Irish economic development. Olson argued that economic growth could be retarded by the activities of special interest groups, who distort economic activity. The more stable a society, the greater the possibility that such groupings could emerge.[19] He also argued that greater awareness within society as a whole of economic ideas and criteria could diminish the influence of special interest groups. Eoin O'Leary has suggested that the adverse effect on economic

lue to success of the construction sector in securing tax exemptions dur-
1990s and 2000s, along with the strength of anti-competitive forces in the
s sector, validated Olson's concept of distributional coalitions in the Irish
t.[20] The soft and ineffectual regulation of banking by the state in the lead up to the recent crash and the over generous treatment of the banks in the recent bailout at the expense of tax payers provides another example. Tom Garvin applied Olsonian theory in analyzing how cultural values influenced Irish economic development. Garvin argues that the combination of non-materialistic values, promoted by both the Catholic church and nationalist political thought, and a dysfunctional education system that was characterized by a neglect of scientific subjects and limited accessibility, reduced the prospect of economic growth until the policy changes introduced in the 1960s.[21] Such an approach places more emphasis on entrenched interest groups or institutions such as the Catholic church, or specific economic and political agents, with less emphasis on wider international influences.

Rapid Irish growth and improved economic performance from the mid-1990s witnessed the emergence of more optimistic interpretations of Ireland's international economic performance and relationships, which moved away from an emphasis on a combination of economic failings and dependency that figured strongly in the recessionary conditions that prevailed in the 1980s. In contrast, in the decade or more from the mid-1990s, globalization was frequently invoked as something the Irish economy was benefiting from. Nicola Jo-Anne Smith has cogently critiqued the nebulous nature of the assumptions relating to globalization, and demonstrated that while the Irish economy was small and open, it was most certainly not becoming more globalized. She argues that instead it is more focused within the European and US sphere, which collectively accounted for 80 percent of Irish trade in 1980, rising to 82 per cent by 2005, with the relative share of trade with the rest of the world actually declining in the interim. What Ireland was experiencing, she argues, was deeper European integration with closer links to both Boston and Berlin, but politicians have utilized the discursive power of globalization (characterized as inevitable and unavoidable) to legitimate policies that facilitated more neo-liberal market-driven agendas and greater competitiveness to sustain economic development.[22]

Highlighting the work of Harvey Armstrong and his co-authors on 'micro-states' globally, O'Leary has alluded to a wider potential comparative framework in which the Irish development experience could be usefully contextualized. Although historically many micro-states were considered to be particularly vulnerable to exogenous shocks, recent research has identified a number of positive factors enjoyed by micro-states including greater adaptive capacity and flexibility than larger countries. Many micro-states actually performed better in economic terms than their larger neighbours, thus challenging traditional assumptions about core-periphery relationships; island status for example made virtually no difference to economic performance.[23] The 'micro-state' model affords more responsibility to the agency of local political and economic actors in the positive performance of the Irish economy than convergence and regional economy models. Conversely, poor political decision making and nepotism for example can also be held more accountable for much of the dramatic downturn in Irish economic fortunes from 2008. The crash since then has invariably marked a return to more pessimistic perspectives, identifying a series of weaknesses with the Irish development model.[24]

While all of these conceptual models can usefully contribute to the analysis of economic development in different epochs, none of them satisfactorily explain the multiple phases of the Irish experience since independence in its entirety. This work will argue that the economic history of the Irish state is best understood as an interlinking process of structural change in which economic development can be most readily explained in *historical* terms, rather than adhering to conceptual models that have a tendency to be undermined by new directions in the national and international economy. Moreover, while policies developed in the 1930s held back development in the 1950s, part of the success of the economy in the decade from the mid-1990s was based on policies developed many decades earlier, so we argue that historical perspective is absolutely vital, in spite of the dramatic effects of recent economic growth and the subsequent crash.

Since the state constitutes a core variable in our interpretation of Irish economic history, the opening section of this book will trace the evolution of government economic policy since independence, with the first chapter dealing with years prior to EEC entry in 1973 and the second dealing with the period since. In order to examine the structure and changing nature of the economy during the entire period in question, the second section of this book constitutes three chapters focusing on agriculture, industry and services respectively. The third section will examine the role played by factors of production in Irish economic development, with reference to how labour and capital were harnessed more effectively through government intervention to promote economic development. Finally, the conclusion will assess the performance of the Irish economy from a comparative European perspective.

Part I

1 From dependent free state to EEC member-state

Economic policies 1922–73

The Irish Free State acquired full fiscal autonomy from the United Kingdom (UK) as a consequence of the Treaty signed in December 1921. This enabled the new state to pursue independent trade and fiscal policies that came into effect from 1 April 1923, with the first tariffs introduced that year. Gradually more were added so that by 1931 there were 59 categories of goods subject to duty, which influenced the development of certain industrial sectors. There was a greater degree of continuity with pre-independence monetary arrangements. The pro-Treaty Cumann na nGaedheal government relied strongly on the economic establishment for political support. Although tariffs and customs duties were introduced on certain goods entering Ireland from the UK, the trading, financial and farming establishment sought continuity and opposed any prospect of wide-scale protectionism, which they feared would raise costs and reduce trade. Irish trade was conducted predominantly with the UK; the labour and capital markets in both countries were strongly integrated. Significantly, interest rates in Ireland continued to be governed by the London bank rate; the major Irish banks established a standing committee in 1920, which set overdraft and deposit rates with reference to British rates. The Irish banks assumed that if domestic interest rates were set lower than British rates funds would be re-deposited in the UK.[1]

The hallmark of policy relating to monetary, banking and currency issues in the inter war years was caution. There was a general reluctance to change the traditional relationship between the Irish banks and the UK, where they invested a significant share of their balances in the London money market. Continuity was reassuring for business and trade, particularly for Anglo-Irish interests within the new state. The Bank of Ireland retained its predominant position within the Irish banking sector, having already acted as a financial agent for the provisional government on the one hand, while simultaneously retaining many aspects of its special relationship with the Bank of England that lasted until the eve of the Second World War. It was only deemed necessary to establish the Central Bank in 1942.[2]

The Currency Commission was brought into being by the Currency Act of 1927, which marked the first tentative step towards central banking. The formation of the commission had been recommended by the Parker-Willis Commission in 1926. The Currency Commission, chaired by Joseph Brennan, who had previously served as Secretary of the Department of Finance,[3] produced and managed the new currency, the Irish pound. As a consequence the new state acquired seigniorage and the new currency accounted for about two thirds of legal tender by the end of the 1930s. The Irish pound remained firmly linked to sterling, which linked it in turn to the Gold Standard until sterling went off it in the 1930s, even though the government held no gold reserves. Essentially, the Irish pound was backed by sterling assets, which were sufficient to meet any potential demands on the currency until 1955. The economic advantage of this arrangement was that sterling was a relatively stable currency. Moreover, it was highly convenient since most Irish trade and external transactions took place within the sterling area.[4]

The Irish Department of Finance after 1922 was closely modeled upon the system of administration of the British Treasury; it had premier position within the civil service that subsequently emerged within the new state, retaining control of the financial activities of all other departments. Arguably these traits, inherited from its predecessor, were highly negative, inhibiting developmental innovation in the new state. The fundamental principles of the British financial system were adopted and the new government seldom questioned the decisions made by the Department of Finance, which advocated rigid economy in all areas. However, the department failed to block the Shannon Hydroelectricity Scheme, the largest capital investment by the state during its first 40 years. Finance ultimately had to conform to the government's decision to proceed with the scheme.[5] But this was one of the few exceptions to the general pattern.

In the immediate aftermath of independence, some strong protectionist advocates emerged in the Department of Industry and Commerce, including its Secretary, Gordon Campbell. Not only did he argue for a protectionist policy to encourage industrial development; he was of the opinion that an exclusive reliance on agriculture had a detrimental effect on the economic and social progress of the nation.[6] Campbell's concept of industrial development was radical and anticipated policies that were to be implemented many years later. Rather than developing heavy industry, Campbell argued that the Irish Free State should develop sectors in advanced technological areas. To this end, he argued that foreign investment should be encouraged and technological skills should be developed within the education system.[7] But the Department of Industry and Commerce had little success in changing the general stance of government economic policy. The departure of Joe McGrath as Minister for Industry and Commerce in 1924, followed by the resignation of J. J. Walsh as a minister in 1927 reduced potential support for a more developmental approach to industrial policy.[8] However, selective tariff measures in certain industries had resulted in new British investment in the Irish Free State, often by companies who wished to defend or expand their existing interests in the Irish market. As a result, the tobacco sector was largely in British control by the end of the 1920s, with companies such as Wills establishing branch factories in Dublin; Lever Bros had taken over much of the soap industry through takeovers of native firms and about half of all output in the confectionary sector was produced by British companies.[9] The early influence of the state in such developments through customs and excise duties and tariffs should not be overlooked as it was already shaping the pattern of development in certain industries, such as tobacco.

Nonetheless, nationalist developmental polices made limited initial advances against the weight of traditional economic thought. Classical economic theory, as evident in the report of the Fiscal Inquiry Committee of 1923, the Agricultural Commission of 1924 and the 1926 Parker-Willis Commission on the banking system, recommended the continuation of free trade. Government institutions, influenced by British practices, emphasized fiscal rectitude and a broadly orthodox approach, which was all firmly underwritten by the Department of Finance.[10] Coleman and Considine observe that 'the desire to impress British doubters of the Irish capacity for self-development and to reassure skeptical British and Anglo-Irish observers of the attitude of the infant government' reinforced a cautious approach to economic policies.[11]

Cumann na nGaedheal fiscal policy was based on indirect taxation; namely excise duties on alcoholic beverages and other mass consumption items such as tobacco, which were broadly regressive in nature, since lower income groups spent a relatively higher share of household income on these items. The government had to fund the costs of Civil War damages and compensation claims arising from distress suffered during the War of Independence.[12] Yet this was offset by some advantages. The Irish Free State's external liabilities were removed in 1926, as a consequence of the agreement reached with the British government concerning the Boundary Commission (which had been established as part of the Treaty agreement in order to revise the boundaries between the Irish Free State and Northern Ireland). The Irish Free State was at that point relieved of its share of the British National Debt. Moreover, overseas assets held by Irish citizens amounting to some £200 million yielded some income from abroad, which was augmented by emigrants' remittances, assisting the balance of payments.[13]

Despite adherence to conservative macro-economic policies and a professed commitment to laissez-faire, Cumann na nGaedheal intervened in the economy in a number of ways; the Dairy Disposal Company (DDC), which contrary to popular opinion was the first semi-state company established in 1927 (a few hours prior to the Electricity Supply Board (ESB), was given the responsibility of rationalizing the dairy sector and reducing the number of creameries. Other examples of intervention included legislation in 1924 that forced the amalgamation and restructuring of all the hard-pressed railway companies into the Great Southern Railway (GSR) and subsequent acts passed in 1927 permitting railways and tramways to operate road services, with the GSR taking over the Irish Omnibus Company in 1929.[14] Intervention was also evident in the imposition of experimental tariffs and the continuation of land reform. The formation of the ESB as a semi-state company provided a template for many state enterprises subsequently; by the early 1960s there were no less than 55 semi-state companies. These pioneering interventions were indicative of a rather reluctant commitment towards developmental policies in the early years of the Irish Free State,[15] with the Department of Finance using its powers to quash many potential initiatives that might incur short-term costs to the state, but could have been of long-term economic value.

The prevailing ideology of the new state in the 1920s strongly supported the family farm as the basis of social stability, with the objective of having as many people engaged in the agricultural sector as possible. The policy of land transfer to occupying tenants (under the land acts passed since the 1880s) continued with further land legislation passed in 1923. This earlier initiative indicated that land reform was an important priority for the government, with some allowance in the 1920s made for stud farms and larger farms that provided significant employment. The new regime gave priority to the improvement of agriculture for export as it was believed that the well being of the rest of the economy depended on the income of the farming community.[16]

Government policy in the 1920s encouraged farmers to concentrate on areas where Ireland had comparative advantage, more notably in the livestock and dairying sectors, which had long been the traditional pillars of Irish agriculture. The government concentrated on attempting to improve quality by creating farm advisory services and improving credit by establishing the Agricultural Credit Corporation (ACC) in 1927. It also attempted to consolidate the work that had been carried out by the Department of Agriculture since the turn of the century.[17] The department's influence was arguably at its greatest in the 1920s when Patrick Hogan held sway as the Minister for Agriculture. Out of every 1000 men at work in the new state by 1926, 571 worked in farming. At this point agriculture produce, food and drink accounted for about 86 per cent of all exports, so the economy of Irish Free State was overwhelmingly dependent on agriculture in terms of employment and exports. Moreover, most of the major industries in the Irish Free State, such as brewing, distilling, milling, bacon curing, biscuits and (from the 1930s) sugar production, were basically processing raw materials derived from agriculture.[18] So the central significance that agriculture assumed in state policy was hardly surprising.

Following the wider international pattern, the scope of economic policy widened somewhat in response to the crash of 1929 and the deep international depression that followed. Fianna Fáil came to power for the first time in 1932 and made a decisive break with free trade, introducing far stronger protectionist measures. Ó Gráda and O' Rourke argue that 'in a context of world depression, low farm prices and a political imperative to reduce unemployment, this strategy (protectionism) had its logic'.[19] Economic historians and economists in general have traditionally been more critical of the new government's engagement in a trade dispute with the state's major trading partner, Great Britain. When the Fianna Fáil government in 1932 refused to hand over the land annuities to Great Britain under the terms of the land acts and the Treaty settlement, this led to the so-called 'economic war'. The British Treasury sought to recoup losses by imposing tariffs on Irish imports such as live animals, butter, cream, eggs, bacon, pork, poultry, game and other meat. In retaliation, the Irish government placed heavy duties on imports from Britain of coal, cement, electrical goods, iron and steel manufactures and sugar. This dispute, which had political rather than economic origins, dramatically curtailed trade between the two states until it was finally resolved in 1938.[20] Moves towards reconciliation with the British in the economic war started in 1935 with the Coal–Cattle Pact, whereby coal and cattle were exchanged on a pound for pound basis. This increased cattle exports by about 33 per cent, reducing its impact on farmers. The economic war finally came to an end in 1938 when the two governments signed the Anglo-Irish Trade Agreement. Neville Chamberlain, in return for a lump sum of £10 million, agreed to waive all further British claims to Irish land annuities, while tariff restrictions were relaxed.[21]

When Fianna Fáil came to power in 1932, some financial matters such as the preparation of the budget, which had been previously left in the hands of the Department of Finance, became the business of the Minister for Finance and the Cabinet. Conflict emerged in financial and economic policy during the 1930s between the Department of Finance and the Department of Industry and Commerce. The more vigorous policy of protectionism and industrial development pursued from 1932 by the new government marked a watershed in the economic history of the state; the influence of the Department of Industry and Commerce in directing economic policy increased, while conversely the Department of Finance lost its premier status.[22]

Fianna Fáil's policy of industrialization through protectionism was significant as it was the first effort by an Irish administration to change the structure of the southern Irish economy and to escape from the developmental trap posed by its over dependence on Britain and its inability to industrialize under free market conditions.[23] The Department of Industry and Commerce acquired the authority to impose tariffs, of which there were in the region of 1,900 in operation by 1936.[24] The Control of Manufactures Acts were passed in 1932 and 1934 to control the growth of foreign enterprises and investment by obliging new entrants to take out licenses and establish a majority shareholding among native citizens, with a view initially at least to reserve more investment opportunities (with less risk) for native entrepreneurs. But a significant conflict of interests quickly emerged between nationalist ideological demands for native control and restrictions on foreign enterprise, and the more pragmatic proponents of utilizing all available opportunities to achieve greater economic development and employment expansion through maximizing foreign capital inputs, expertise, and marketing capacity through well known British brand names. The government therefore increasingly tempered the initial objectives of the acts, giving more priority to expanding employment growth and achieving greater productive self sufficiency, and many British firms were easily able to circumvent or even completely evade much of the spirit of these acts.[25]

The protectionist economic policies of the 1930s allowed, in theory, for some limited dispersal of industrial development. While many individuals throughout the country lobbied the Department of Industry and Commerce to locate industries in their localities, in reality Dublin's share of national industrial employment actually increased from under 36 per cent in 1926 to almost 40 per cent by 1936, while all other regions, with the exception of a marginal increase in the rest of Leinster, experienced a relative decline in employment share.[26] Moreover, Dublin was the premier choice for most enterprises since it accounted for a substantial share of the home market, had good communications infrastructure and the biggest pool of skilled labour and services in addition to access to government.[27]

A number of state owned companies were set up with varying degrees of success and failure. The Irish Sugar Company was established in 1933 and by 1938 it produced 80 per cent of domestic sugar demand, thus displacing the large amount of imported cane sugar. Aer Lingus, the Irish Tourist Board, Irish Life Assurance Board, Chemici Teo (which produced industrial alcohol) and the Irish Turf Board were all set up in the 1930s, in addition to the Industrial Credit Company, which provided finance for industrial concerns. This investment by the state in both the industrial and service sectors took place in areas where specific social goals were seen to be important and for which private investment was deemed inadequate or non-existent. Overall, however, most of the development in the industrial sector during the 1930s was carried out by private companies, who benefited from favourable tariffs that eliminated foreign competition.[28] Protectionism therefore became the new cornerstone of government economic policy. In the four years from 1932, the Irish Free State rapidly changed from being one of the least to one of the most protected economies in the world.

While Fianna Fáil was willing to alter the structure of Irish output, by for example expanding the industrial sector and encouraging tillage over pasture in agriculture, it made no attempt to radically alter fiscal or monetary policy.[29] Government expenditure increased and a more expansionary domestic credit policy was pursued to increase capital investment. Fianna Fáil also increased the national debt to fund capital expenditure, yet the bulk of the increase in the national debt, from £16.1 million in 1932 to £30.9 million by 1939, was due the 1938 financial agreement with Britain, where the land annuities were waived by the United Kingdom in return for a lump-sum payment by the Irish government. The outcome was generally deemed to have been highly favourable to the Irish side.[30]

The establishment of the Commission of Inquiry into Banking, Currency and Credit, in 1934, posed an apparent threat to orthodox monetary policy. Yet, Joseph Brennan, the chairman of the committee, and the expert economist members who included George O' Brien, Theodore Gregory and Per Jacobsson, collectively ensured that the commission would recommend the continuance of conservative economic policies, while opposing any break with sterling. However, the commission's report was not completely negative in tone. It recommended expanded powers for the Currency Commission regarding monetary market intervention and for the establishment of an economic research facility within the commission.[31] The commission argued that a floating currency, if adopted by a small country, would be victim to volatile international capital funds, and an interest rate 'risk' premium would have arisen, with consequent risks to economic activity.[32] The close correlation between Irish and British price levels during the periods 1922 to 1940 and 1945 to 1979[33] reflects the currency link.

The position of Lemass became much more prominent during the Second World War as at the outset he left the Department of Industry and Commerce and was put in charge of the newly established Department of Supplies. The Emergency Powers Act was passed in 1939, which provided the state with the authority to take over essential supplies and services, controlling imports and exports and the storage, movement, sale and distribution of goods.[34] The railways increasingly assumed a central position once again, as road transport was restricted by petrol shortages. Despite the reduction of coal supplies and the reduction of passenger services, goods traffic actually increased from 2.45 million tons in 1939 to 2.95 million in 1944, while passenger traffic in contrast fell from 11.58 million journeys to 8.75 million. The GSR, a quasi-monopolist private transport operator, assumed considerable importance in moving freight. As a consequence, the government resorted to emergency powers early in 1942 to take control, but not ownership, of the company. This enabled the government to prioritize the transport of strategic commodities, notably turf, wheat, sugar beet, coal and livestock.[35]

Supplies of coal for heating and cooking were drastically curtailed as the war progressed and what precious little came through from Britain was kept for what were deemed to be essential services. As a result, turf began to assume even greater importance in the fuel supply and was extensively used as a substitute for coal as a household fuel. The bogs were extensively harvested by large teams of young men and soldiers. By 1942, according to Ferriter, the government had 26,000 people out on the bogs cutting turf. Overall employment figures were probably significantly higher than this since the county production schemes alone employed 33,000 in 1941 and 29,000 in 1942. Turf production rose from about 3 million tons per annum to about 5 million during the Second World War.[36] Great ricks of turf were built up along the roads in the Phoenix Park, for example, to supply Dublin. By 1943 even turf was rationed to half a ton a month per household outside the major turf districts.[37] To transport turf from the bogs in increasing quantities, the GSR converted cattle wagons and old passenger carriages for that purpose, by removing roofs. Horse drawn turf barges were pressed back into service on the canals for transportation from midland bogs.[38] In the cities and many towns the acrid smell of British coal began to be replaced by the smell of burning turf.

State intervention in the economy intensified during the Second World War. The government placed a freeze on wages introducing a trade union bill in 1941, which curtailed the right to strike and a wages standstill order was passed, which contributed to a general fall in living standards.[39] The war dramatically reduced the kind of staple Irish imports that had been handled by British merchant shipping before the war, so that certain vital foodstuffs and fuel were in short supply. It was in response to this situation that in 1941, Lemass decided to establish Irish Shipping to maintain such essential supplies. From March 1941 to the end of the war, Irish Shipping carried 750,000 tons of wheat, 63,000 tons of phosphates and 178,000 tons of coal, which kept vital supply routes open and maintained some degree of energy and food security.[40] To keep up food supplies the government also imposed compulsory tillage orders, which more than doubled native wheat output between 1939 and 1944. All of these actions by the state secured the vital bread supply.

Raymond argues that one of the consequences of the war from an economic perspective was the introduction of economic planning. A Cabinet Committee on Economic Planning met some 58 times between 1942 and 1945. This did not result in any overall government plan but a series of piecemeal measures in response to particular adverse economic circumstances as they arose. In 1944, a document had been drawn up, which collated the suggestions from each department, including likely costs, but it could not be described (nor was it activated) as a coherent economic plan. It was effectively a form of crisis management to deal with the severe economic problems of the war while also attempting to anticipate and deal with problems that might emerge after the war when over a quarter of a million ex-servicemen and war workers were expected to return.[41] If Raymond slightly overstates his case with regard to economic planning, it is true nonetheless that the impact of the Second World War contributed to greater state intervention both during and after the conflict. State intervention during the war was driven by absolute necessity. In the decades that followed the war, a far wider range of economic policy instruments were utilized to achieve economic growth, which became a matter of far greater political priority.

Another legacy of the war was the Central Bank, which came into operation from 1943, inheriting the function of the Currency Commission. In contrast to its predecessor, the Central Bank was a more proactive authority, demonstrating its independence from the government by a willingness to criticize economic policy and 'through a growing tendency from the 1950s onwards' to advise the Irish Banks Standing Committee on the setting of interest rates.[42]

Rural electrification finally got underway in 1946, which was to transform rural life and play an important role in the consumer revolution of the 1960s and beyond.[43] However, poor economic prospects and social conditions in the wake of the war reduced the popularity of a tired Fianna Fáil government, which lost the election in 1948, opening the way for five different parties to form the first inter-party government. The disparate composition of the inter-party government represented a mixture of old and new economic ideas, but fundamentally they remained committed to tariff protection.

Post war European reconstruction resulted in some important new departures for the state in the economic sphere, as it engaged in a number of new multilateral organizations. From July 1947, Ireland became a founding member of the Organization for European Economic Cooperation (OEEC) and the Council of Europe. The former organization (which later became the OECD) was established to distribute European Recovery Programme funding (ERP), more often referred to as Marshall Aid. These initiatives marked the beginning of a greater degree of co-operation between many European countries. The inability to fund dollar imports provided one of the contexts for American intervention in the economic problems facing post-war Europe. The US government, concerned at the food and fuel shortages prevalent across Europe during 1947 and the consequent reduction in European economic activity, embarked on an ambitious plan of financial aid; the ERP.

While primarily aimed at continental Europe, Ireland was assigned a role in the ERP, since the US administration believed it was advantageous to provide economic assistance to enable Ireland to increase food supplies, especially to Britain.[44] This resulted in some tentative Irish engagement with the economic affairs of Europe. A requirement of ERP funding was the submission of economic data by potential applicants. Assembled by the Department of External Affairs, the 'Long-Term Recovery Programme' was in some respects the first exercise undertaken by an Irish government in economic planning, though its long-term impact was fairly limited. The provision of the requisite economic data for this exercise at least provided the impetus for the establishment of the Central Statistics Office (CSO) in 1949,[45] which was one of the more important outcomes. The consequent improvement in data collection facilitated a general improvement in economic analysis, most notably in developing a more refined comparative international perspective, which brought the weaknesses in the Irish economy relative to the rest of Europe into stark relief during the 1950s.

O'Mahony argues that the most notable feature of policy during the late 1940s and early 1950s was the great increase in state capital expenditure. Much of this investment was directed towards social aims, including housing, hospitals, roads and arterial drainage, while some elements were directed towards economic goals, including the lime subsidy in agriculture and the development of the turf industry and water supply. It was intended that capital investment would alleviate unemployment and reduce emigration.[46] The establishment of the Public Capital Programme in 1950 was also connected to some degree with the demands of the ERP. The separation of capital and current expenditure, and the willingness of the state to borrow for capital purposes, already apparent in the budgets of the outgoing Fianna Fáil administration, became more formalized in 1950 with the presentation of separate capital and current expenditure accounts.[47] In his budget speech of that year, Patrick McGilligan (Minister for Finance) announced that the state now had a role in undertaking capital expenditure as a means of increasing employment and output, and provision was explicitly made for this in the budget. Costello (the new Taoiseach), Mac Bride (the leader of Clann na Poblachta) and the Labour Party as a whole, also favoured a general increase in state capital expenditure, no longer believing that the current volume of investment could be left entirely in private hands.[48]

Over a four-year period, from 1948 to 1952, Ireland obtained over £47 million in ERP funding, the majority of which was in the form of low interest loans; Ireland got the second lowest level of grant aid within the ERP (see Table 1.1). The loans and grants were used to a large degree to fund projects in the agricultural sector, reflecting the intention of the US authorities that Ireland would increase agricultural exports, and to fund the importation of US goods, alleviating the balance of payments deficit.

The significance of Ireland's participation in the ERP is disputed among historians. Early works by D. J. Maher and Miriam Hederman have tended to trace these early engagements through the OEEC and ERP as the genesis of the Republicof Ireland's subsequent entry to Europe, which they trace in a somewhat

Table 1.1 Total ERP funding extended to Ireland, 1949–52

Year	*Loans (£m)*	*Grants (£m)*	*Total funding (£m)*
1949	16.087	1.071	17.158
1950	20.836	–	20.836
1951	3.775	4.968	8.743
1952	–	0.357	0.357
Total	40.698	6.396	47.094

Source: *Statistical abstract 1953–54,* Dublin, CSO.

linear fashion forward to EEC entry in 1973.[49] More recent work has not supported this appraisal. Geiger for example argues that participation did little to break the paramount importance attached to trade with Britain, and Ireland's stated commitment was merely to secure the funding; once secured, the emphasis on British trade resumed.[50] Girvin is also skeptical of the assumption that these early European contacts influenced the subsequent desire to enter the EEC.[51] Girvin argues the overall impact of ERP on the Irish economy was fairly minimal in the longer term, although ERP aid did assist in funding the balance of payments deficit. He concludes that the 1948 Trade Agreement with the UK, which eased access for Irish agricultural exports and many manufactured goods to the UK, while also enabling the Republic of Ireland to retain most of its tariffs, was of much more economic significance than the OEEC and the Marshall Plan.[52]

Ireland did not participate in other major international economic initiatives at this point, including the formation of the International Monetary Fund (IMF) or the General Agreement on Trade and Tariffs (GATT) in 1948. In the absence of a significant steel or coal industry, the formation of the European Coal and Steel Community was also seen as somewhat irrelevant to the Republic of Ireland. When the first inter-party government came to office in 1947, those who expected major changes in direction in economic policy, which might improve the sluggish performance of the economy, were to be disappointed. The Public Capital Programme introduced by the first inter-party government as the main instrument for economic expansion, had limited impact since the main emphasis was on long-term social and infrastructural investment with low output returns in the short term.[53] The end of ERP funding and the balance of payments difficulties experienced during the 1950s temporarily halted the influence of expansionist economic policies. The balance of payments deficit increased from £30 million to £61 million between 1950 and 1951. In order to deal with this, the minority Fianna Fáil government introduced a highly deflationary budget in 1952, while borrowing for capital purposes was suspended.[54] The deflationary policies implemented by Seán MacEntee as Minister for Finance contributed to the defeat of Fianna Fáil, opening the way for the second inter-party government in 1954.

A significant experiment was conducted in monetary policy by the second inter-party government. In February 1955, the Irish Banks Standing Committee was persuaded by the Minister for Finance, Gerard Sweetman, not to implement the British interest rate increase, which was introduced to quell inflationary pressures in the British economy and was deemed inappropriate for Irish conditions.[55] Irish funds were quickly re-invested in Britain to avail of the higher interest rates and imports increased, while Irish banks suffered a drop in their profit margins as Irish companies increased the demand for credit while many bank deposits were also switched to Britain. As a result, the balance of payments current account deficit increased to 6.5 per cent of GNP. Ultimately, the traditional remedial action was taken and Irish interest rates were increased. A deflationary budget in 1956 imposed import levies.[56] Emigration in 1956 rose to the highest levels witnessed throughout the twentieth century. Honohan and Ó Gráda have gone so far as to describe the macroeconomic crisis of 1955–56 as 'the defining event of post-war Irish economic history', whose drastic consequences led to a complete reorientation of economic policy towards export orientated foreign direct investment and the return of Fianna Fáil to power with an overall majority in 1957.[57]

Despite these monetary disasters, there had at least been some important new initiatives in terms of industrial policy, which were to be important in the slow shift to more outward looking policies. In 1947, a customs-free zone was established at Shannon Airport. In the following year the Shannon Free Airport Development Company was established, which constructed advance factories for foreign firms, and provided grants for labour training and machinery.[58] Industries in the Shannon Free Zone were exempt from the Control of Manufacturers Act, and profits on export earnings by companies based there were totally exempt from taxation.[59]

The inter-party government established the Industrial Development Authority (IDA) in 1949 as an autonomous body to promote efficiency within domestic industry. When Fianna Fáil returned to office in 1951, the IDA assumed responsibility for promoting new industrial development.[60] Another indication of a general shift towards more developmental industrial policies that were regionally focused was the Under-developed Areas Act, introduced in 1952, which provided financial supports for firms locating in Connacht-Ulster and the Midlands. An Foras Tionscal, the Underdevelopment Areas Board, was established to administer such aid. This semi-state body cooperated with the IDA in promoting indigenous industries in underdeveloped areas. The Underdeveloped Area Acts were renewed until 1969, when all these industrial grants came under the aegis of the IDA.[61]

In 1953, John A. Costello argued for the removal of restrictions under the Control of Manufacturers Act to attract foreign investment. Two years later as Taoiseach, Costello proposed tax incentives to promote exports.[62] These proposals took time to assume concrete form. Both Fine Gael and Labour sought for more liberal treatment of foreign investors to encourage investment and growth. The second inter party government in 1956 introduced Exports Profits Tax Relief (EPTR) on profits arising from exports for both foreign and domestic industry. This effectively marked the birth of the Republic of Ireland's low corporation tax regime, which was to be centrally important in driving FDI in subsequent decades, though this important policy reform has often been wrongly attributed to the influence of Whitaker, who at the time actually opposed the initiative.[63] Protectionism was still implemented at this time to protect indigenous industry while the state simultaneously promoted the creation of export orientated foreign-owned industries.[64] Recent revisions in the historiography question the central and even heroic role accorded to Lemass and Whitaker as the central drivers of liberalization and the departure from protectionism in the late 1950s. In the more nuanced picture emerging, earlier initiatives of the inter-party governments including the establishment of the IDA, the introduction of EPTR and the formation of the Capital Investment Advisory Committee assume a greater significance in providing the foundation for subsequent economic development. The introduction of EPTR in 1956 in particular heralds the beginning of a new export orientated phase of FDI, and at this point both Whitaker and Lemass were actually opposed to EPTR.[65] This challenges the established traditional view of Lemass and Whitaker as the champions of Irish economic modernisation.

While Lemass has attracted significant attention as the most iconic figure within the Irish economic reformation, recent work has tended to be somewhat less effusive. Bryce Evans' more critical and nuanced revisionist biography for example observes, in relation to Lemass' accession to power, that 'a national coming of age … happened to coincide with his own coming of age'.[66] Fanning praises Lemass' tenure as Taoiseach in relationship to the acceleration of FDI; educational reform (which had revolutionary consequences for subsequent economic development) and increased engagement with the EEC, which only came to fruition after his death. However, Fanning also argues Lemass was fortunate that the economic climate and the buoyancy of international trade, both nationally and internationally, was far better than for any government since independence and he was 'lucky that the emergence of the EEC and of EFTA enabled him to plead the pressures of international reality as a justification for adapting domestic policy to changed circumstances'.[67]

In a wider European context, the debate on trade liberalization in the Republic of Ireland certainly intensified following the formation of the EEC in 1957 and more particularly when seven countries outside the EEC formed the European Free Trade Association (EFTA) in 1959. The Association included Austria, Denmark, Norway, Portugal, Sweden, Switzerland and most significantly the UK, which had major implications for the Republic of Ireland's traditional trading relationship with its large neighbour.[68] The government had to respond rapidly to the new circumstances emerging within Europe, which gave rise to two new trade blocs that fundamentally altered prospective trading relations with the state's premier trading partner, the UK. Although it was decided to remain outside EFTA, the attractions of the EEC were far greater due to its greater emphasis on agricultural subsidies and the relatively higher market prices for agricultural produce than in the UK. Although the British market remained the core focus, there was increasing awareness among politicians, administrators and other vested interest groups (most notably farmers) of the opportunities that were opening up in the European market and the prospects this provided for a new departure in Irish agriculture.

The Department of Finance also began to contribute ideas to policy reform; this was the genesis of T. K. Whitaker's document *Economic Development*, which essentially advocated the reallocation of social expenditure into more productive areas, which would provide sustained employment and more rapid financial returns.[69] While *Economic Development* has been widely heralded as the harbinger of Irish economic revival, it can be more realistically viewed as an additional contribution to the reform process, articulating wider reformist agendas that were already well underway.

Although *Economic Development* provided the basis for the Fianna Fáil government's white paper, *The First Programme for Economic Expansion*, there are many valid reasons to be sceptical about the overriding historical significance traditionally attached to this plan. Leddin and Walsh, for example, argue that none of the growth in GDP in the first half of the 1960s could be attributed to the plan since few of its objectives were ever implemented; the tax burden was not reduced but actually increased; industry, not agriculture acted as the engine of growth. Although the plan placed somewhat greater emphasis on industrial development and exports than previous policy documents and agriculture still took up a much larger section of the plan than other sectors. Moreover, a new phase of growth had already started in 1958–59 before any of the new policies outlined could be effective.[70] National Income growth between 1959 and 1963 was more than double that projected in the plan. Investment in public housing, a sector indentified by Whitaker for expenditure savings, actually increased between 1962 and 1966.[71] Liam Kennedy has argued that a significant rise in state expenditure and investment and the doubling of British growth rates between 1959 and 1963 were more likely factors in accounting for economic growth in these years.[72]

Nonetheless, the widespread perception at the time that the programme had accounted for much of the growth led to the introduction of a successor, *The Second Programme for Economic Expansion*, which was to run from 1964 to 1970. By the latter year it was assumed Ireland would be in the EEC. The targets set by the *Second Programme* were not met and it was abandoned following the Republic of Ireland's second failed attempt to join the EEC in 1967. The *Third Programme for Economic Expansion* quickly suffered a similar fate. Indicative planning of this nature had generally been somewhat discredited by the early 1970s.[73]

Another feature of government economic policy during this period was the establishment of neo-corporatist institutions. This followed the emergence of corporatist institutions in post-war Europe, which promoted co-operation between labour and capital, especially in the sphere of wage determination, while government fiscal policies were implemented to support such wage agreements.[74] In practical terms this took the form of trade union and employer participation in various national institutions concerned with economic policy, such as the Irish National Productivity Committee, the Committee on Industrial Organization and the National Industrial and Economic Council. A national wage agreement process, the National Wage Recommendation was established in 1964, but due to trade union hostility this was abolished in 1966. National wage bargaining resumed in 1969, but the nature of such agreements was based on the national negotiation of a wage norm, to be supplemented by local bargaining.[75]

Other consultative bodies, such as the National Industrial and Economic Council and the National Employer-Labour Conference collapsed due to disputes between employers and trade unionists over income policies. Despite the creation of a corporate superstructure, the Irish industrial relations system in the 1960s was defined, according to Roche, 'by unions' faith in sectional free collective bargaining and most employers' willingness to accommodate such a posture'.[76]

Although Irish agriculture experienced many difficulties in the 1960s, the state made some important advances and interventions in improving marketing in the dairy industry in particular. An Bord Bainne (the Irish Dairy Board) was established in 1961 replacing the old Butter Marketing Committee. The Irish butter quota in the British market increased following the Anglo-Irish-Trade Agreement of 1965 and Bord Bainne took this opportunity to increase butter exports from the co-ops and Dairy-Disposal Company to Britain under the Kerrygold brand.[77]

But as in the rest of Europe, agricultural employment continued its long-term decline, and economic policy from the late 1950s was dominated by the twin objectives of increasing employment and raising living standards.[78] In this regard, industrial development provided far greater prospects to raise living standards. Already in 1956, the introduction of the Industrial Grants Act permitted the IDA to assist industrial undertakings all over the country to a limit of two thirds of the cost, or £50,000. The Control of Manufactures Act was partially repealed in 1958 and finally removed entirely in 1964.[79] These initiatives were part of an emerging emphasis on attracting FDI, which was to become central to the late industrialization of the Republic of Ireland from the 1960s onwards, but native industry continued to be heavily protected. Moreover, subsidies to industry remained relatively small compared to those in agriculture. By 1970–71, the cost to the state of fixed asset grants and EPTR were roughly equal to the annual dairy produce subsidy alone.[80]

However, the role of the IDA was overhauled considerably from the late 1960s. It obtained full autonomy from civil service control in 1969, through the Industrial Development Act, which allowed the IDA (now reformulated as a semi-state agency with wide ranging powers) to control almost every aspect of industrial development policy. This included the promotion of indigenous industry and the attraction of foreign investment, funding company research and development, constructing advance factories and developing industrial estates.[81]

The IDA now began a twin-focus strategy; encouraging notable investments in high productivity, technologically advanced sectors,[82] while also ensuring employment growth through the attraction of companies offering lower-skilled manufacturing employment. There was less emphasis in state investment in industrial enterprises. Exceptions were the establishment of the semi-state company Nítrigin Éireann Teoranta (NET), which produced nitrogen-based fertilizers at Arklow, and expansion of the steel plant in Cork,[83] which was symptomatic of the continuation of the traditional protectionist model by the Department of Industry and Commerce for indigenous industries, in tandem with the encouragement of export orientated foreign investment. The reorganization and enlargement of the IDA in 1969–70 dramatically improved the promotion of employment in industry thereafter.

The IDA also assumed a significant role in regional policy. The Buchanan report (1969) recommended that industrial development be concentrated in the major urban conurbations, together with six regional growth centres and four subsidiary local growth centres. However, fearing the adverse electoral consequences from towns not selected as growth centres, the government abandoned these plans. Instead the IDA assumed responsibility for regional development through the dispersal of industries across the country, a strategy that was implemented from 1972.[84] As this stage, Dublin still accounted for 46 per cent of employment in industry in 1971 and 47 per cent in services. The new policy combined dispersion with greater concentrations earmarked for Cork and the Limerick/Shannon region in particular. Moreover, in the following years IDA policy was beginning to become slightly more selective in terms of the kind of industries targeted for promotion.[85]

State intervention was by no means absent from the services sector either, but it was somewhat less marked than in the industrial sector. In a case study on tourism, Anne O'Brien argues that tourism in particular and services in general were broadly dismissed as a major agent of economic development between the 1920s and the 1980s.[86] Although it is true that much of the services sector was neglected, state support was forthcoming in transportation, notably in aviation, rail and bus services (see services chapter), and in shipping. In 1965, for example, the state took over the British and Irish (B&I) line with a view to improving transportation infrastructure with Great Britain in particular, since the acquired company was tardy about replacing obsolete shipping.[87] This further added to the state's existing investments through Irish Shipping during and after the Second World War. The greater importance attached to earning foreign exchange by the 1950, resulted in increased state interest and investment in promoting and developing tourism in the following decades.[88]

Public employment in the services sector the 1950s and 1960s also increased as a consequence of the general expansion of expenditure by the state on health provision, education and public administration.[89] The reforming zeal which took hold in the 1960s in education was increasingly driven by longer-term economic imperatives. By the mid-1960s about half of children within the state left school at the age of 13, at a time when it was being widely argued that education had made an important contribution to European post-war economic growth, which Ireland had clearly missed out on. Free second level education funded by the state was introduced in 1967, dramatically expanding educational provision thereafter.[90]

Wider European and international influences increasingly permeated state policy initiatives during 1960s. In the preceding decades, the Republic of Ireland had remained somewhat aloof from OEEC efforts to promote free trade between European countries, which led to the establishment of the EEC in 1957.[91] However in the following year the Republic of Ireland joined the IMF and the World Bank, and it became a member of the General Agreement on Tariffs and Trade (GATT) in 1967. Nonetheless, the Republic of Ireland's continued dependence on exports to Britain in this period heavily influenced Irish foreign policy with regard to trade,[92] and the state's increased interest in developing links with Europe in the late 1950s and early 1960s were to a significant degree driven by the growing interest of the UK in EEC entry and the desire to protect the Irish position in its premier market.[93]

But there was also a growing awareness of the high cost of over dependence on the British market and the new opportunities that greater contact with continental Europe offered. In 1959, an application was made to the Common Market Commission in Brussels to establish closer economic relations with the Republic of Ireland. In May 1959, EFTA was formed, with Britain as the principal member. The primary concern for Ireland in these developments was that its preferential access to the British market maybe undermined. Although Ireland did not join EFTA, in 1961, when Britain applied for EEC entry, Ireland made a parallel application.[94]

Some EEC members states expressed doubts about the Republic of Ireland's suitability for membership, given it's over dependence on agriculture, the high level of protection and the low level of industrial development. The Irish government placed great emphasis on the recent economic development of Ireland and the desire of the bulk of the population to be associated with the community. However all these efforts came to nothing as a result of De Gaulle's strong hostility to the prospect of British entry, which finally negated the British and Irish attempts to enter the EEC in January 1963. Yet, Ireland's first failed bid laid important ground work that contributed to the perception among existing members that it was a credible candidate for future entry. The decision to enter the EEC signified the acceptance by Irish policy makers that economic development could not occur in isolation. Maurice Fitzgerald argues the desire to achieve EEC entry facilitated the adoption of more liberal economic policies and eased the acceptance of a more open trading relationship with Great Britain.[95]

Following the failed bid, attempts were made on the Irish side to reopen negotiations with Britain on the issue of Anglo-Irish trade. This resulted in protracted bilateral negotiations for two and half years, in which the British became somewhat more sympathetic to the Irish idea that the two islands could become increasingly liberalized as a staging post to subsequent integration of both into the EEC. These negotiations resulted in the Anglo-Irish Trade Agreement in 1965, which led to the phased reduction of Irish tariffs on British industrial imports over a ten-year period from 1966 and the removal of all British protective duties on Irish imports from July 1966, also securing equality with British producers for Irish agricultural producers selling into the British market.[96] This resulted in a marked improvement in Anglo-Irish relations, with greater emphasis on mutual trading interests. Ireland, the UK and Denmark made a second entry bid in 1967. However, British entry was again vetoed by de Gaulle, who resigned as President of France in 1969, thus removing one of the last major obstacles to Irish and British entry.

The two failed bids bought much needed time for the Irish economy to make some of the initial adjustments to free trade. Irish preparation got underway again at the end of June 1970 when the negotiating process began, and in the following year, these were largely completed.[97] The most important outstanding issues for Ireland were firstly how Ireland was to be gradually phased into the Common Agricultural Policy (CAP), and secondly how long the transition period for dismantling protection for Irish industry would take, and finally what contributions Ireland would make to the community budget. The development of the Common Fisheries Policy on fishing limits and rights for other EEC countries fishing offshore from the Irish coast was the most contentious issue to negotiate from an Irish perspective, as equal access by all community members to the fishing area of all members was an existing principle. Ireland ultimately acquired a 12-mile limit, which protected its off shore fisheries to some degree at least,[98] but in general the subsequent development of the fishing industry was to be hampered by EEC restrictions. In contrast to agriculture, this aspect of membership turned out to be disadvantageous to the Republic of Ireland in the longer term.

It was agreed that there would be a transition period between 1973 and 1977, when Ireland would be phased into the CAP, while tariffs would be removed in stages for industrial goods. Ireland was to pay into the community budget an estimate of its share of community GDP, which was 0.6 per cent. It was anticipated there would be an economic and monetary union within a relatively short period, but of course this was to take decades rather than years. Final negotiations were wrapped up on the 18 January 1972. Ratification of the treaty for the signatory countries was of course subject to their respective national constitutional requirements, which in the Irish case meant a referendum. In May 1972, a referendum took place and 83 per cent voted yes, which demonstrated a significant degree of popular support for the more outward looking economic strategy that membership inevitably entailed.

Entry to the EEC marked a decisive turning point in the economic history of the state in relation to trade, monetary policy and the economic governance of industry and agriculture in particular. Thereafter, there was a significant European dimension to many economic policy issues. The European project was seen more in economic terms than in political terms in the period leading up to entry; the debate on entry was essentially about further economic liberalization, and an acknowledgement of the economic interdependence of the Republic of Ireland with other European states. Entry, it was argued, would lead to the economic modernization of Irish society.[99] Such views were not entirely misplaced.

2 A new frontier

The EEC/EU and economic governance: 1973–2011

It has been argued with some conviction that entry into the EEC in 1973 constituted one of the most decisive breaks in Irish economic history. John O'Brennan in particular has advanced the view that 'For better or for worse, it is undoubtedly the case that the European integration process has had more impact than any other factor (internal or external) on the shape and performance of the Irish economy'.[1] It is clear that entry into the EEC had a marked impact on many aspects of Irish economic governance, most notably with regard to agriculture and competition, and more recently with macro-economic management. The EEC/EU in particular opened up the largest market in the world; today 27 member states constitute a market of 500 million people. This has had major implications for the expansion of foreign direct investment (FDI) in the Irish economy, which by 2005 was the highest in the EU for factories, plant and offices in terms of its equivalence to GDP.[2]

From the outset, another important benefit of community membership was the receipt of financial transfers. Total EEC transfers rose from the equivalent of just over 2 per cent of Gross National Product (GNP) in 1973 to a peak of over 8 per cent in 1991, declining thereafter until by 2008 they accounted for just over 1 per cent. Since entry, the agricultural sector has accounted for the majority of European Union (EU) transfers to Ireland, through the price supports for the Common Agricultural Policy (CAP) with structural funding accounting for the rest.[3] Irish governments successively sought to maximize these transfers from Brussels (see Table 2.1).

EEC entry also had dramatic implications for the development of Irish trade, which expanded in the following decades, as various restrictions on trade were gradually removed (see Chapter 6 for further details). One of the more important pieces of legislation that facilitated this reform was the ratification of the Single European Act in 1986, which came into effect after 1992 and dramatically accelerated the process of market integration. With an extremely low corporation tax rate at this point of merely 10 per cent, the Republic of Ireland benefited significantly in terms of FDI from access to the Single European Market; corporation tax rates were set at 12.5 per cent in 2003 across all sectors, which compared very favourably to a European Union average of about 30 per cent.[4]

The Single Market also resulted in a windfall for the Irish economy in terms of transfers from Brussels. European Structural Funding was reformed and expanded,

Table 2.1 EU transfers to Ireland (£m), 1973–2008

Year	*Total transfers*	*Transfers as % of GNP*	*Structural funds*	*Structural funds as % of GNP*	*CAP price supports*	*Structural funds as a % of all transfers*	*CAP price supports as a % of all transfers*
1973	37.1	2.1	0.0	0.0	37.1	0.0	100.0
1974	67.4	2.1	3.6	0.1	63.8	5.3	94.7
1975	109.1	2.7	6.9	0.2	102.2	6.3	93.7
1976	119.5	2.4	17.5	0.3	102.0	14.6	85.4
1977	272.9	4.5	27.8	0.5	245.1	10.2	89.8
1978	410.2	5.8	44.6	0.6	365.6	10.9	89.1
1979	529.1	6.4	132.6	1.6	396.5	25.1	74.9
1980	560.6	5.7	179.5	1.8	381.1	32.0	68.0
1981	506.8	4.3	202.2	1.7	304.6	39.9	60.1
1982	602.1	4.4	257.8	1.9	344.3	42.8	57.2
1983	727.7	4.8	286.0	1.9	441.7	39.3	60.7
1984	866.7	5.3	222.1	1.4	644.6	25.6	74.4
1985	1,128.7	6.5	292.1	1.7	836.6	25.9	74.1
1986	1,146.6	6.1	262.6	1.4	884.0	22.9	77.1
1987	1,100.3	5.5	360.7	1.8	739.6	32.8	67.2
1988	1,161.6	5.5	323.1	1.5	838.5	27.8	72.2
1989	1,295.3	5.6	331.9	1.4	963.4	24.6	74.4
1990	1,741.0	6.9	454.3	1.8	1,286.7	26.1	73.9
1991	2,201.2	8.3	866.8	3.3	1,334.4	39.4	60.6
1992	1,994.0	7.1	880.4	3.1	1,113.6	44.2	55.8
1993	2,245.3	7.4	963.5	3.2	1,281.6	42.9	57.1
1994	1,841.4	5.6	667.7	2.0	1,173.7	36.3	63.7
1995	2,023.2	5.5	873.0	2.4	1,150.2	43.1	56.9
1996	2,219.5	5.4	855.0	2.1	1,364.5	38.5	61.5
1997	2,506.6	5.4	986.8	2.1	1,519.8	39.4	60.6
1998	2,577.6	4.8	1,077.6	2.0	1,500.0	41.8	58.2
1999	2,109.4	3.5	669.0	1.1	1,440.4	31.7	68.3
2000	2,051.0	2.9	699.8	1.0	1,351.2	34.1	65.9
2001	1,896.6	2.5	632.8	0.8	1,263.8	33.4	66.6
2002	1,982.0	2.4	627.1	0.7	1,354.9	31.6	68.4
2003	2,032.8	2.2	488.0	0.5	1,544.8	24.0	76.0
2004	2,050.6	2.1	561.2	0.6	1,489.4	27.4	72.6
2005	1,873.1	1.7	425.1	0.4	1,448.0	22.7	77.3
2006	1,732.8	1.4	343.9	0.3	1,388.9	19.8	80.2
2007	1,640.6	1.3	214.0	0.2	1,426.6	13.0	87.0
2008	1,623.2	1.3	194.6	0.2	1,428.6	12.0	88.0

Source: D, McAleese, 'Twenty-five years a growing', in R. O' Donnell (ed.), *Europe: The Irish experience*, Dublin, Institute of European Affairs, 2000, p. 96. 1999–2008: *Department of Finance: Budgetary and economics statistics*, Dublin, 2009, Department of Finance.

eventually taking the form of multi-annual programmes. The Delors I programme (which amounted to £3.5 billion) lasted from 1989 to 1993 and Delors II (£4.6 billion) from 1994 to 1999. This increase was justified on the assumption that the Single European Market would widen regional disparities within the European Union and that redistributive measures to help more peripheral countries compete should accompany further integration.[5] Structural funding was used to improve the transport infrastructure, principally roads, but also telecommunications in addition to funding investment in labour force training, while subsidizing private sector investment, marketing and innovation.[6]

The timing of cohesion funding was of vital importance, coming in the wake of the fiscal crisis of the 1980s, since it allowed for investment in infrastructural projects that otherwise would have been unaffordable. In terms of immediate economic effects, structural fund projects stimulated employment in the construction and non-traded services sector during the early 1990s.[7] Barry has estimated that structural funding increased GDP by an extra 2.2 per cent for 1995 and 2.7 per cent for 1999 if a low estimate for supply-side benefits was incorporated. If a high estimate for supply-side effects was incorporated, the increase to GDP growth would have been 2.7 per cent for 1995, 3.5 per cent in 1999, decreasing to 1.4 per cent in 2000 and a mere 0.9 per cent by 2010.[8] According to Laffan and O'Mahony, 'Ireland consistently achieved the highest per capita transfers from the European budget until enlargement to the countries of east central Europe in 2004'. The dramatic convergence of the Irish economy from the mid-1990s with the wealthier European states and accession of 10 new and much poorer member states resulted in Ireland ultimately becoming a net contributor in the budgetary period from 2007 onwards, despite continued support.[9]

Following entry in 1973, the Irish economy became more exposed to trends in both the EEC and the world economy. By 1975, free trade existed between the Republic of Ireland and the United Kingdom and subsequently the markets of the continental European member states were gradually opened up, so that Irish manufacturing ultimately had to compete on equal terms with manufacturers throughout the EEC. This had advantages and disadvantages for the economy. Foreign direct investment in Irish manufacturing increased significantly, but industrial output increased much faster than employment in industry. Job gains in export orientated foreign companies engaged in electronics and chemicals were offset against employment losses suffered by indigenous companies going through the pain of adjustment to international competition with which many could not cope. As a consequence, in the period between 1973 and 1981 job creation only just about outstripped job losses. In 1978 a 10 per cent rate of corporation tax was introduced for manufacturing replacing export profits tax relief. The Republic of Ireland then had the lowest corporation tax rates within the EU, which was a crucial factor in attracting FDI and the consequent expansion of exports during the 1990s.[10]

Diversification of exports following EEC entry in 1973 was also important for the Irish economy since it reduced excessive dependence upon the British market. Much of the expansionary economic effects of non-British trade were due to FDI.

Many US multinationals used the Republic of Ireland as their base for EEC/EU production and distribution. Economic liberalization gathered apace within the EU, between the passing of the Single European Act in 1986 (which sought to complete the internal market and move towards the establishment of a single currency) and the signing of the 1993 Treaty on the European Union. This encouraged both further FDI, and led to an increase in structural funding for peripheral economies to offset the impact of further integration that accompanied this phase of reform, all contributing to the recovery of the economy in the early 1990s, raising public investment.[11]

The Single European Market, enacted in 1992, was of great benefit in terms of increasing market access and trade diversification. Its aim was to integrate the individual national markets of the member states, increasing competition, reducing price discrimination between national markets, reducing transactions costs, increasing productivity and liberalizing the financial and service sectors, while also relaxing border controls.[12] The Irish economy benefited to a greater degree from the dismantling of remaining national barriers to trade, since Irish manufacturing by this date was composed of export orientated firms, to a greater extent than other peripheral EU countries. As a small open economy the Republic of Ireland made disproportionate gains from the formation of the Single Market and the general upturn in demand within the EU market during the 1990s.[13]

Industrial and development policy from 1973 was increasingly dominated by the Industrial Development Authority (IDA), which enjoyed a high degree of institutional independence.[14] In the 1970s, the IDA began to successfully target electronic and chemical firms, which were identified as two areas with significant growth potential in global terms. This decision proved to be exceptionally shrewd and important in the longer term as many new companies and jobs were established in these sectors during the 1970s, but not without considerable costs. By the early 1980s, the IDA absorbed the equivalent of 2 per cent of GNP. The IDA's reliance upon FDI was not without its critics. The Telesis Report, published in 1982, argued that the long-term economic value of FDI based industries was questionable, given their lack of R&D (Research and Development) activity and the high levels of profit repatriation. Telesis recommended that industrial policy should insist that foreign industries establish R&D facilities in addition to the development of linkages with Irish sub-suppliers, while average grant levels to foreign companies should be reduced. To promote indigenous industry, Telesis suggested that grants to indigenous companies should favour export-orientated as opposed to non-traded sectors, while a number of select firms should be actively promoted to attain world-class status.[15] The Telesis report led to some measure of industrial policy reform, though this was less interventionist than the report envisaged. The Company Development Programme of 1984 provided assistance to select indigenous companies and the National Linkage Programme, established in the following year, sought to develop linkages between foreign companies and domestic sub-suppliers.[16]

Despite such criticism the IDA continued to attract FDI and in 1990, at unprecedented costs, it successfully secured major investment by Intel who built a plant near Leixlip, close to Dublin, as their European facility for the production of microchips. While there were already many information technology (IT) companies in the Republic of Ireland at this stage, the demonstration effects of this major investment brought a new wave of IT investment by many of the major companies engaged in information technology(IT) production and services, including companies engaged in the production of integrated circuits, disc drives, software, telesales and servicing. Between 1990 and 1994, the Republic of Ireland consequently attracted 40 per cent of US electronic investment in Europe.[17]

The state played an important role in this new wave of multinational investment. In turn, American companies importing and utilizing cutting edge technologies and R&D had a dramatic impact on increasing Irish industrial productivity in the following years. During the second half of the 1990s, industrial policy placed more emphasis on increasing R&D activities in an attempt to create higher value added in Irish manufacturing. While there has been a major increase in R&D in the pharma sector in particular since the turn of the century, as it came to dominate the Irish industrial sector, these activities according to the research of van Egeraat have been concentrated more at the final stages of the R&D cycle, with the more high level innovative research retained in a few global innovation 'megacentres' outside Ireland.[18]

By the mid-1990s Irish development aid and fiscal policies remained heavily skewed towards manufacturing, in comparison with most European countries, which provides the main explanation for the relatively high share of employment and GDP generated in the industrial sector. Services in general had far less fiscal privileges; at this stage they were mostly taxed at 40 per cent compared to 10 per cent for manufacturing. Service employment had traditionally been viewed in economic thought as non-productive and dependent on the productive elements of the economy. Consequently, the service sector, apart from tourism, received little systematic treatment in the formulation of government economic policy until the 1970s. In policy terms, traded services such as tourism and more recently financial services have been traditionally deemed more worthy of state supports.[19] Service sector exports have grown dramatically in recent decades and by 2004 they accounted for 34 per cent of total Irish exports, largely made up of software, business and financial services.[20]

The state backed greater investment in tourist infrastructure in the 1990s with significant EU supports, and the growth of tourist numbers (a global phenomena) was greatly assisted by the abolition of Aer Lingus' privileged position as the sole domestically-based international air carrier in 1985. Financial services were also given special fiscal privileges and expanded dramatically in the 1990s. While agriculture and industry have traditionally been favoured in terms of state supports and taxation, the EU forced the Republic of Ireland to make the tax system uniform for all businesses in 2003, which led to a general reduction in the taxation of services.[21]

By the early 1970s, the IDA had also assumed responsibility for regional development, with differential rates of grant aid for industries in what were described as 'designated' areas, in order to disperse industrial development more widely across the country.[22] However, the growth of high-technology industries and services concentrated in and around Dublin continued during the 1980s and 1990s. In 2002, the East region, comprising Dublin, Meath, Kildare and Wicklow accounted for 60 per cent of financial and business service employment in the state, despite constituting only 40 per cent of the national workforce. The tendency of financial services to locate in metropolitan areas due to the location of corporate head offices and government offices has reinforced this regional disparity and concentration in Irish service employment.[23]

In the late 1990s, regional policy was revived with the division of the country into two regions; Border, West and Midlands, and South and East. However, this was merely a strategy to secure continued EU structural funding.[24] Earlier attempts to decentralize economic activity were again repeated in the National Spatial Strategy in 2002, which aimed to develop major centres of economic activity outside the Greater Dublin area, to counter the problems of concentrated development there.[25] However, the government decentralization programme, which attempted to relocate large tranches of the civil service outside the Dublin area, proved to be a very costly policy failure, creating major diseconomies and inefficiency in the operative capacity of the civil service.

A significant new departure in Irish economic policy was the use of fiscal policy as a pro-active agent to generate economic growth. In 1972, George Colley, the Minister for Finance, introduced a planned government deficit in an effort to stimulate economic activity. Current budget deficit financing was continued by the Fine Gael/Labour coalition of 1973 to 1977,[26] especially in response to the First Oil Crisis.[27] However, the coalition's policy of managed economic expansion was not as attractive as the reckless bonanza promised by Fianna Fáil, which secured them a landslide electoral victory in 1977. While the party policy was based on a legitimate concern to reduce unemployment, the means to do so were crude and of a short-term nature: namely, the abolition of rates on domestic housing, the abolition of motor tax, reduced income tax and measures to increase employment through the stimulation of the construction sector and the expansion of public sector employment.[28] Martin O'Donoghue became Minister for Economic Planning and Development in 1977, and under his watch there was a sharp increase in foreign borrowing; the current budget deficit increased from 3.6 per cent of GNP in 1977 to 6.1 per cent in 1978. There was no commensurate expansion of capital expenditure, which only increased by 0.3 per cent between 1977 and 1979 (see Table 2.2).

The expansion of government current expenditure initially had impressive results, but stimulating demand without accompanying measures to increase supply, had no lasting beneficial effect on the economy. Instead of stimulating economic expansion, O' Donoghue's plan triggered an inflationary wage–price spiral which made Irish exports uncompetitive, while expanded consumer demand increased imports.[29]

The adverse effect of O' Donoghue's plan was accompanied by turbulent international economic conditions. The second oil crisis in 1979 precipitated an international recession, while interest rates were held at high levels in the US and

Table 2.2 Budgetary stance and government debt, 1976–2007

Year	*Current budget balance as % of GNP*	*Capital budget balance as a % of GNP*	*Total exchequer balance as a % of GNP*	*General government debt as a % of GDP*
1976	–4.4	–6.6	–11.0	–
1977	–3.6	–6.1	–9.7	–
1978	–6.1	–6.3	–12.4	–
1979	–6.8	–6.4	–13.2	–
1980	0.6	–7.4	–13.4	–
1981	–7.3	–8.4	–15.7	–
1982	–7.9	–7.6	–15.5	–
1983	–7.0	–5.8	–12.8	–
1984	–7.0	–5.2	–12.2	–
1985	–8.0	–4.6	–12.6	–
1986	–7.9	–4.2	–12.1	–
1987	–6.2	–3.2	–9.4	–
1988	–1.6	–1.5	–3.1	–
1989	–1.2	–1.0	–2.2	–
1990	–0.6	–1.3	–1.9	94.2
1991	–1.1	–0.8	–1.9	95.6
1992	–1.6	–1.0	–2.6	92.5
1993	–1.2	–1.0	–2.3	95.1
1994	0.0	–2.1	–2.0	89.6
1995	–1.0	–0.7	–1.7	81.1
1996	–0.1	–1.8	–1.1	74.1
1997	1.3	–1.8	–0.5	64.8
1998	3.8	–2.5	1.4	53.9
1999	5.7	–3.7	2.0	48.8
2000	7.8	–4.3	3.6	37.9
2001	4.8	–4.2	0.7	35.6
2002	5.1	–5.0	0.1	32.2
2003	3.7	–4.6	–0.8	31.1
2004	4.5	–4.4	0.0	29.4
2005	4.6	–5.0	–0.4	27.3
2006	6.0	–4.5	1.5	24.7
2007	4.3	–5.3	–1.0	24.8
2008	–2.0	–6.2	–8.2	44.2

Source: *Statistical abstract 1999*, Dublin, CSO. *Statistical yearbook, 2008 and 2009*, Dublin, CSO.

the UK, as both administrations placed price stability above economic expansion as a core policy goal. This combination of endogenous and exogenous factors had an extremely negative impact on the industrial base in Ireland, most notably a host of native industries that were already struggling to deal with increased competition and integration within the EEC. Hopes of devising a coherent policy to guide the economy were handicapped by the unusually turbulent political environment of the early 1980s. Charles Haughey, who succeeded Jack Lynch as Taoiseach in 1979, took no action to remedy the expanding current budget deficit.[30] The period spanning 1981 to 1982 saw three general elections, with a minority Fine Gael–Labour coalition succeeded by a minority Fianna Fáil administration lasting from February 1982 to November 1982, succeeded in turn by a majority Fine Gael–Labour coalition. The current budget deficit as a percentage of GNP increased dramatically between the years 1979 to 1982.[31]

The means by which the current budget deficit was reduced, increased personal taxation and reduced capital expenditure, further depressed economic activity in the following years.[32] Stabilization measures were accompanied by efforts to devise a medium-term economic strategy. The new coalition government established a National Planning Board in 1983, whose membership was drawn from outside the civil service and received advice from economists.[33] The National Planning Board's report informed the Coalition economic strategy, *Building on Reality,* which argued that the aim of economic policy was to improve export competitiveness through the control of wage costs and a reduction in restrictive practices in the economy.[34] However, the aims of *Building on Reality* were contradictory, with deflationary fiscal policy and employment creation simultaneously advocated.[35] The basis for *Building on Reality* was undermined with the Labour party's opposition to further expenditure cuts, which led to the collapse of the coalition in 1987.[36] Throughout this period fiscal contraction was a central feature of all the debates on policy, reflecting the wider emergence of neo-liberal economic thinking, more particularly in the US and in Britain.

While Fianna Fáil returned to power as a minority government after the 1987 election, the most significant aspect of the election was the electoral success of the Progressive Democrats. Founded in 1986 by Des O'Malley, the Progressive Democrats owed their gestation partially to the personality conflicts that riddled Fianna Fáil in the preceding years, but of more significance was its support for neo-liberal economic policies, such as major reductions in personal taxation.[37] The Progressive Democrats temporarily supplanted Labour as the third-largest political party in the 1987 election, which revealed a growing degree of support for neo-liberal economic policies among certain sections of the population. McAleese has argued that this political development was an important step in the reorientation of Irish economic policy in the late 1980s.[38]

Fianna Fáil implemented a policy of public expenditure control, which included reduced public sector pay through a recruitment embargo, deferral of pay awards and reduced investment in public infrastructure.[39] This was made possible through the revived centralized wage bargaining mechanism, which secured trade union acquiescence in a policy of public expenditure control,[40] combined with cross-party support for fiscal retrenchment. Following the 1987 election results, Garret Fitzgerald promised Fine Gael support in the Dáil if Fianna Fáil would reduce public expenditure. Fitzgerald's successor as Fine Gael leader, Alan

Dukes, supported the economic policy of the Fianna Fáil administration, in what was termed the 'Tallaght Strategy.'[41] These measures led to an unprecedented decline in the current budget deficit from 6.2 per cent of GNP in 1987 to 1.6 per cent in the following year. Government capital expenditure was further curtailed, with the capital budget deficit as a percentage of GNP reaching a low of 0.8 per cent in 1991. The major fiscal crisis had therefore been overcome at this stage.

The co-incidence of fiscal contraction and a revival of economic growth led some economists to argue that Ireland experienced an 'Expansionary Fiscal Contraction' whereby government action in reducing public expenditure and taxation had such a favourable effect upon private sector expectations of economic activity that a multiplier effect occurred, further stimulating economic growth.[42] However, it has been argued that the contraction of government expenditure did not have any autonomous effect in stimulating economic growth; rather the deflationary effect of reducing government expenditure was offset by the expansion in trade due to improved wage competitiveness and more favourable international economic conditions.[43]

The rapid improvement of the external environment was centrally important to Irish recovery. Moreover, EU transfers peaked as a share of GDP in the years between 1990 and 1993, which undoubtedly also contributed to the upturn (see Table 2.1). Adherence to the Maastricht criteria for entry to the Single European Currency ensured that a disciplined approach to the public finances continued throughout the 1990s;[44] other helpful European factors included exchange rate stability and low inflation. While the political composition of governments changed between 1989 and 1997, they broadly adhered to social partnership, the Maastricht criteria, the attraction of FDI through low corporation tax and a gradual acceptance of measures to increase competition within the economy. Although the Progressive Democrats were initially skeptical about the social partnership process, the party accepted it as a policy instrument to moderate wage costs when they entered government in 1989.[45] The last challenge by a major political party to this economic consensus was the proposal to increase state borrowing by the Labour Party during the 1992 election. However, these proposals were abandoned during the negotiations with Fianna Fáil to form a coalition government in 1992, with the larger party insisting on adherence to Maastricht fiscal guidelines.[46]

The broad concensus and agreement reached between the major political parties on the parameters of economic policy, especially during the period of the Tallaght Strategy from the late 1980s, is cited by Frances Ruane as a crucial aspect of Irish economic success in the 1990s.[47] Honahan and Walsh have also attributed some significance to the role of macroeconomic policy errors in retarding Irish economic performance prior to the 1980s, while conversely improved fiscal and monetary management from the early 1990s was one of the factors accounting for more rapid growth in the 1990s.[48]

The government fiscal position improved as the expansion of employment increased income tax revenues. The Irish Financial Services Centre (established in 1987) also began to contribute to state revenue. A current budget surplus was finally achieved in 1996 and a current surplus was achieved for the following decade, peaking at 7.8 per cent of GNP in 2000 (see Table 2.2). The current budget surplus of this period was used to revive the state's capital expenditure programme; the capital budget deficit increased from 1.8 per cent of GNP in 1997 to 5.3 per cent by 2007, which along with EU structural funds contributed significantly to the upturn in the construction industry. Current expenditure also increased from 1997, while further reductions in capital and personal taxation occurred; the most notable reduction being a halving of capital gains taxation from 40 per cent to 20 per cent. The Minister for Finance, Charlie McCreevy, justified such taxation cuts as measures that would increase labour force participation. However, in 2001, the EU commission criticized McCreevy's fiscal policy as excessively expansionary, and as Leddin and Walsh noted, 'critics of Mr. McCreevy argue that it would have been better to have used the exceptional period of the late-1990s, to prepare for less favourable times in the future'.[49]

While the fiscal policies of the late 1990s were geared towards stimulating supply rather than demand, as was the case in the 1970s, McCreevy's policies reflected the same willingness as his predecessors in the 1970s to use fiscal policy as a means to generate economic growth.

Capital expenditure fell in nominal terms between 1983 and 1989, while the growth in current expenditure was contained between 1987 and 1989. While continually increasing in nominal terms during the 1990s, current expenditure actually fell as a percentage of GNP as the economy grew (see Table 2.3).

Current expenditure as a percentage of GNP increased from 2004 onwards, funded by the increase in property based tax revenues. An unsustainable expansion in capital taxation revenues occurred due to the bloated property market. Capital taxation as a percentage of all taxation revenue increased from 3.8 per cent to 7.6 per cent between 2001 and 2006. However, this increase in revenue was based on stamp duties levied on unrealistically high property valuations. Furthermore, stamp duty is a tax based on market transactions; tax revenues from this source are highly volatile and dependent on market sentiment.[50] The increase in property related taxation revenues allowed for continued reductions in income tax, which were electorally popular and also facilitated the negotiation of consensual partnership agreements. However, with the collapse of the property market in 2008, government revenue also collapsed, thus heralding the beginning of the fiscal crisis,[51] to which we shall return later in this chapter.

An important aspect of the Irish taxation system has been the willingness of the government to use preferential tax reliefs and taxation rates to stimulate economic activity. This was evident already in the 1950s, with the introduction of preferential taxation rates to encourage industrial exports that favoured foreign direct investment. In 1990, the low rate was extended to all manufacturing companies, including indigenous, and this was harmonized in 2003, so that a rate of 12.5 per cent was extended to all companies in that year.[52]

Reliefs were also extended to a range of development activities to encourage construction, which subsequently generated investment solely for the purpose of minimizing tax liabilities. Pro-cyclical policies were introduced encouraging

Table 2.3 Government expenditure, 1983–2009

Year	*Current expenditure (£m)*	*Capital expenditure (£m)*	*Total expenditure (£m)*	*Current expenditure as % of GNP*	*Capital expenditure as % of GNP*	*Total expenditure as % of GNP*
1983	7,403	1,120	8,523	49.3	7.5	56.8
1984	7,976	1,072	9,048	49.0	6.6	55.6
1985	8,684	1,044	9,728	49.8	6.0	55.7
1986	9,212	1,065	10,277	49.1	5.7	54.7
1987	9,585	967	10,552	47.6	4.8	52.4
1988	9,683	738	10,421	45.7	3.5	49.2
1989	9760	716	10,476	42.0	3.1	45.1
1990	10,404	809	11,213	41.2	3.2	44.4
1991	11,286	863	12,149	42.7	3.3	46.0
1992	12,148	954	13,102	43.3	3.4	46.7
1993	13,014	1,272	14,286	42.9	4.2	47.1
1994	13,710	1,421	15,131	41.8	4.3	46.1
1995	14,621	1,343	15,964	39.8	3.7	43.5
1996	15,357	1,532	16,889	37.6	3.8	41.4
1997	16,958	1,702	18,300	36.2	3.6	39.8
1998	17,590	2,375	19,965	32.6	4.4	36.9
1999	18,988	3,130	22,118	31.3	5.2	36.5
2000	20,408	4,013	24,421	29.0	5.7	34.7
2001	23,569	4,791	28,360	30.5	6.2	36.7
2002	26,013	5,464	31,477	31.0	6.5	37.5
2003	28,582	5,312	33,894	30.8	5.7	36.6
2004	30,812	5,170	35,982	31.0	5.2	36.2
2005	33,943	6,015	39,958	31.4	5.6	37.0
2006	37,415	6,783	44,198	31.2	5.7	36.8
2007	41,373	7,911	49,284	32.6	6.2	38.8
2008	45,146	8,977	54,123	35.2	7.4	44.5
2009	49,166	8,821	57,987	43.4	7.8	51.1

Source: *Department of Finance, Budgetary and Economic Statistics, 2009,* Dublin, Department of Finance.

construction in regions and sectors where there was no demand, furthur contributing to the crippling level of bank debt and a wasteland of ghost estates (unfinished building sites). This malign legacy was a direct consequence of poor governance, inappropriate policies and a lack of regulation in both banking and construction.

Much of the success of the Irish economy between the mid-1990s and 2007 has been attributed to the Irish variant of collective wage formulation, 'Social Partnership', which in its present form dates back to 1987. Collective wage bargaining has been a feature of Irish economic practice since the 1960s, through early corporatist strategies linked to economic planning. The first oil crisis in 1973 and its inflationary effects increased the case for a national wage settlement. The 1975 and 1977 National Wage Agreements, negotiated by the coalition government, were significant as fiscal policy was framed to supplement the awards of the pay agreements. However, O' Donoghue's dash for growth from 1977 increased income growth expectations to unrealistic levels, which acted against the implementation of a successful incomes policy. His initial aim to restrict nominal wage growth to 5 per cent per annum was abandoned in favour of an 8 per cent award in order to gain acceptance of the 1978 National Wage Agreement.[53] This was followed by a 'National Understanding', negotiated in 1979, which attempted to integrate government economic policy and wage formation, as pioneered by the previous Fine Gael–Labour coalition government. The non-pay elements of the 'National Understanding' included the creation by the government of a 'National Enterprise Agency' to create employment. A second 'National Understanding' was negotiated in the following year. However, it was undermined by the inflationary pressures generated by the second oil crisis in 1979. With the fiscal crisis occupying the minds of policymakers, collective wage bargaining was abandoned for a number of years.[54]

Employer organizations were generally opposed to national wage agreements during the early 1980s. A number of factors had militated against the successful operation of national wage agreements during the 1970s. The trade union movement was highly fragmented, while the Irish Congress of Trade Unions (ICTU) had little authority over the behaviour of individual unions. While large unions such as the Irish Transport and General Workers Union (ITGWU) and the Federated Workers Union of Ireland (FWUI) supported national wage agreements, they were opposed by several professional and craft unions such as the Amalgamated Transport and General Workers Union (ATGWU) and the Electrical, Electronic, Telecommunications and Plumbing Union (EETPU). A similar lack of coherence existed on the employers' side. The Confederation of Irish Industries acted as a loose umbrella body for employer organizations, but it had no direct influence over its members and its support for national economic agreements was not always shared by its constituent members.[55]

The Federated Union of Employers acted as the dominant representative body for employers. Yet, according to Hardiman, it did not develop a coherent strategy, instead acting as a resource for individual employers in promoting industrial relations. The diverse nature of industry, which included a spectrum of high and low technology sectors, also militated against a common front among employers. Finally the taxation system militated against the operation of successful national wage agreements. The high incidence of taxation on labour led to a situation where employees, despite high nominal wage awards, experienced little increase in real disposable income as wages entered the higher tax bands. Frustration at the high incidence of taxation upon labour, in comparison to the low burden experienced by farmers and corporations, led to the major tax protest marches of the late 1970s and early 1980s.[56]

The decline of traditional industries and recessionary economic conditions during the 1980s reduced trade union influence in the economy and membership as a percentage of the workforce declined from 56 per cent to 50 per cent between 1980 and 1984. Moreover, trade unionists felt increasingly frustrated by their exclusion from government policy making. Trade union leaders began to revise their priorities. While leading trade unionists during the 1970s were skeptical of the benefits of restricting wage increases as a means of achieving competitiveness and favoured direct state enterprise in the economy and increased public expenditure,[57] their successors in the 1980s placed greater emphasis on employment creation and tax reform.[58]

Accompanying this shift in trade union thinking was the publication of the National Economic and Social Council (NESC) plan, *Strategy for Development*, which provided a macroeconomic framework for collective bargaining and debt reduction simultaneously, and won the support of both employer and trade union representatives.[59] Finally, Fianna Fáil, in opposition, showed a greater determination to secure trade union support for economic policy-making.[60] When they acquired power again in 1987, they commenced negotiations to devise a national wage agreement. The *Programme for National Recovery* granted modest wage increases over a three-year period, while simultaneously reducing taxes and reducing the exchequer borrowing requirements (as a share of GDP). Despite initial employer wariness of national wage agreements, the modest scale of pay awards, negotiated in a context of fiscal retrenchment made them overcome their reservations and support the new process.[61]

A series of successor programmes followed the *Programme for National Recovery*, which included the *Partnership for Economic and Social Progress* (1991) and the *Programme for Competitiveness and Work, Partnership 2000*. The social partnership process was widened to include the participation of voluntary groups,[62] and it was then upheld as the foundation of government economic policy and future economic development. Adherents of social partnership have argued that it has transformed Irish economic life and maintained a middle way between free market capitalism and intrusive state economic interference.[63] Subsequent pay awards negotiated during the mid and late 1990s were modest. Moreover, in the context of high output growth in the economy at large the social partnership process reduced labour's overall share of output.[64] The acceptance of this long-term decline in labour's share of output and the accompanying increase in the profit share in turn led to increased private sector investment. This is seen by Kieran Kennedy as the most notable achievement of the partnership process.[65]

The enforcement of wage moderation is held by several authorities as responsible for improving the competitive position of Irish industrial exports in the late 1980s.[66] Frank Barry argues that the initial wage award had significant benefits; it 'served as a holding action until fiscal expenditure cuts were implemented and/or other exogenous tax receipts came on stream'.[67] The reduction in wage costs had beneficial effects upon export competitiveness and employment, while EU structural funding boosted public investment.[68] However, according to Leddin, higher than expected inflation was the true cause for real wage moderation in the late 1980s, and trade unions in the *Programme for Economic and Social Prosperity* negotiations succeeded in obtaining high wage settlements. This process was repeated during the 1990s: the *Programme for Work and Competiveness* awarded modest wage increases, which gave way to more generous wage settlements under *Partnership 2000.*[69]

By the late 1990s, the rampant economic growth of the 'Celtic Tiger' period undermined the ability of the national wage agreements to moderate wage costs. Inflationary pressures in the economy and the demand for labour increased nominal wages, while public sector workers received an additional wage bonus in the form of the 'benchmarking' process. The wage settlements following *Sustaining Progress Parts One and Two*, made no attempt to reverse the burgeoning wage/price inflationary cycle. Instead, generous nominal wage awards were made. However, with the sudden collapse in economic activity in 2008, the government was unable to make the initial 3.5 per cent pay award previously negotiated, leading to the collapse of the partnership process.[70]

The partnership agreements had provided a context for reductions in personal taxation. Between 1987 and 1997, reduction in taxation accounted for 33 per cent of the increase in post-tax labour income since 1987.[71] The benefit of taxation changes, as calculated by Tansey, indicate that the average tax rate of single earners fell by 9.3 per cent between 1987 and 1997, and by 5.8 per cent for one-income married couples over the same period.[72] Social partnership survived, providing in Teague and Donaghey's words 'a national system of concertation between employers, trade unions and government'. This essentially created flexible institutional complementarities, so that the Republic of Ireland's productive structure could accommodate the kind of advanced organizational demands of information computer technology (ICT) production and services operating in a highly open way, with a reasonable degree of wage moderation and significantly for American FDI, a non-unionised context in which to operate. Unions lost membership but as a trade off gained greater access to government through their stake in the social partnership process. The leadership of seven of the largest 10 trade unions supported social partnership, in the two decades from the late 1980s, which provides testimony to the public support and significant consensus around the social partnership strategy. The unprecedented levels of job creation within the economy in the 1990s further assisted in building support for this approach.[73]

The belated adoption of collective wage bargaining in Ireland, relative to other continental European countries, had unintended beneficial effects. In a wider European context, the combination of trade union militancy in conjunction with strict government regulation and employment transfer laws limited the adoption of information technology-based industries in the 1980s and 1990s, according to Crafts and Toniolo. This, they argue, was one of the determining factors in explaining the poor performance of European labour productivity growth rates relative to the US. In contrast, the Irish social partnership model did not restrain employment displacement due to adoption of ICT and did not stifle private sector investment patterns, and the Irish economy therefore proved more receptive to potential productivity advances in ICT production industries and services. This, they argue, is the main explanation for superior Irish productivity growth and catch up in a wider European context during the 1990s, driven by positive economic policy initiatives that enabled the Republic Ireland to buck the European trend.[74]

Despite the example provided by the UK, Irish policy makers did not consider privatization as an option until the late 1980s, with the entry of the Progressive Democrats into government. The agreed programme for government negotiated in 1989 endorsed privatization with the imprimatur of the social partners.[75] The 1991 Programme for Economic and Social Progress endorsed the sale of government shareholdings in state owned enterprises and joint ventures with private capital.[76] The effects of privatization are further discussed in the investment chapter. Some de-regulatory measures were also passed during the 1980s, such as the 1986 Transport Act, affecting the road haulage sector.[77] Deregulation of service and capital markets has had an important effect on Irish economic growth.[78] In the case of financial markets, the Single European Act led to the Republic of Ireland de-regulating financial markets. Exchange controls were relaxed from 1988, with their eventual abolition by 1993. Credit guidelines were eliminated and the Central Bank discouraged the four major Irish banks from maintaining their collective setting of interest rates. These measures opened up competition in the supply of credit, which in conjunction with macro-economic developments in the 1990s contributed to Irish economic growth.[79] The activities of the World Bank contributed to deregulation in banking from the mid-1990s.[80] All of this increased the flow of credit and investment in the Irish economy; banking was to become one of the most unregulated sectors in the economy as a consequence, with the full support of the government's evolving neo-liberal enterprise model.

Deregulation also had significant implications for the services sector; the de-regulation of airline transport in the mid-1980s and the consequent fall in fares led to an increase in tourist numbers.[81] EU directives stipulated that energy and other utility markets should also be deregulated. For example, telecommunications were deregulated in 1998, while gas and electricity supply were deregulated in 2005.[82] Other competition measures introduced included the repeal of the Groceries Order (2005), which permitted below-cost selling of basic grocery products. However, the OECD argued that major anti-competitive forces still operated in the Irish economy, such as the restriction of private competition in the bus market to selected routes, and the continued control by the ESB of the electrical transmission network.[83]

Monetary policy also experienced major change following EEC entry in 1973. While parity with sterling was maintained until 1979, the advantages of this link had been gradually eroded. The value of sterling declined, while the rate of economic growth in the UK by the 1970s had lagged behind other European countries for many decades. The development of the EEC led to the creation of an alternative monetary grouping of fixed exchange rates, the European Monetary System

(EMS).[84] The aim of the EMS was to create a stable monetary zone to minimize the fluctuations in and between the participating currencies. This was to be achieved through minimizing exchange rate fluctuations between participating currencies within a 2.5 per cent band. In 1978, the Irish punt joined the Exchange Rate Mechanism (ERM), breaking the link with sterling, which, in the words of Ó Gráda, 'was a landmark in Irish economic history, since it brought to an end the monetary union between Ireland and Great Britain that had lasted since 1826'.[85]

Irish authorities anticipated that membership of the EMS would reduce inflation and encourage investment through the elimination of risk. However, the changeover coincided with a period of excessive fiscal expansion from 1977, followed by a painful period of recession and subsequently fiscal adjustment from 1987. Only with the determination of successive governments from that date on to reduce public expenditure, did participation in the ERM bring benefits to the Irish economy, when the interest rate premium between Irish and German bonds fell between 1986 and 1992. However, the Irish economy still faced difficulty as sterling was not part of the ERM, further contributing to rampant Irish inflation in these years as the Irish punt depreciated against sterling. Another effect of ERM membership was the introduction of foreign exchange controls to protect the value of the punt, which according to Murphy limited the amount of foreign capital which could be invested in Ireland. Exchange controls were repealed in 1992.[86] Along with other ERM currencies, the punt was subject to attack by speculators.[87] The Irish punt had been devalued several times against the German mark prior to the devaluation by 10 per cent within the EMS at the beginning of 1993. This significantly improved Ireland's competitive position, particularly in the British market. For the following five years the punt floated within wide ERM bands.[88]

The ERM collapsed in 1993 and was reconstituted with a wider fluctuation band of 15 per cent; the punt effectively became a free floating currency, although the Central Bank stabilized exchange rate with reference to the Deutsche mark and sterling. This resulted in the punt attaining a favourable value relative to other currencies assisting export growth.[89] The Republic of Ireland participated in the successor of the EMS, the European Monetary Union (EMU) from 1999, which brought about the introduction of a single currency, the euro, for participating countries. Thereafter, macro-economic management was centralized and an independent European Central Bank (ECB) was established to coordinate monetary policy throughout the eurozone. In addition to the major political reasons for participating (which dominated Irish considerations of the issue), the entry criteria for the single currency stipulated a low government debt to GDP ratio, which ensured the application of cautious fiscal policies throughout the 1990s. As Ireland was the only English-speaking country committed to participation in the EMU, this contributed to furthur American investment. However, the decision of the UK not to participate again was a complicating factor, exposing the Irish economy to exchange rate fluctuations. The high percentage of international trade conducted with non-eurozone members was another negative factor from an Irish perspective.[90] Participation in the euro also deprived the Republic of Ireland of another important advantage; the positive balance of trade generated by Irish-based multi-national industries increased the exchange rate of the punt and acted as a counter-inflationary influence upon the economy.[91]

Following the locking of the Irish punt to a fixed exchange rate with the still notional euro in 1999 at £1 equal to €1.27, all the euro currencies were fixed, and euro notes and coins were then introduced on 1 January 2002. While participation in the euro assisted the process of financial integration and significantly eased the sourcing of credit by Irish financial institutions through the elimination of exchange rate risk, the Irish economy suffered as relatively low interest rates necessary to stimulate the sluggish European economy also held sway in Ireland where such low rates were inappropriate, stimulating the consumption and construction boom in the following years.[92] The low value of the euro relative to the dollar and sterling increased inflationary pressures in the Irish economy. In conjunction with inherent capacity constraints due to economic growth, inflation increased and the Irish government had little ability to moderate this development

The loss of monetary policy created a less flexible environment for economic management, as it was no longer possible to devalue the currency or adjust interest rates, making it more difficult to respond to outside shocks, or to take 'easy' corrective action to moderate excessive expansion. Nonetheless the government retained control over fiscal policy and regulation and income policy as potential mechanisms through which economic activity could be adjusted.[93] Despite the availability of these instruments, the government in the last decades has favoured progressive deregulation and greater self regulation for certain sectors (such as banking, the drinks industry and financial services for example). Wage adjustment has proved to be a fairly slow and cumbersome instrument to make necessary adjustments, and the government failed to protect Irish competiveness through this mechanism before the crash in 2008, but after the events of that year it has resorted to public sector wage reductions. Membership of EMU also reduced the discretion of the Irish government to use fiscal policy, but it was only from the crisis in 2008 that the government also began to resort to various mechanisms to increase taxation. Although all member states share this policy inflexibility in dealing with external shocks, Smith points out that this has been much more problematic for the Republic of Ireland due to its 'heavy dependence' on the UK and US, so that its cycles are less synchronized with the continental European member states.[94]

Within the financial services sector, the Central Bank held responsibility for the supervision of financial institutions until 2002, although in many instances it proved to be somewhat reticent in policing malpractices, such as the creation of bogus foreign accounts for the purposes of tax evasion and the systematic overcharging of bank customers.[95] In 1999, the McDowell Advisory Group recommended the establishment of an independent financial regulator,[96] which came to pass in 2003. However, the office of the Financial Regulator remained under the aegis of the Central Bank, and had little desire to confront financial institutions.[97] The office of the Financial Regulator adhered to a 'principles-based approach' to financial regulation. In theory this set basic standards of governance and prudence for financial institutions while allowing latitude in the creation of new financial products.[98] But even such a minimal level of supervision did not in reality exist in the Irish case, where effectively the banks were self-regulated and in these circumstances they readily abandoned any reasonable caution.[99] The financial regulator allocated an insufficient number of staff to supervise credit institutions. While inspectors discovered many prudential weaknesses in the governance of Irish financial institutions, they lacked sufficient ability to assess the risk to bank solvency. In addition, the office of the Financial Regulator was unwilling to instigate legal proceedings against financial institutions, having a preference for ineffectual negotiating.[100] Finally, the Central Bank failed to take the simple, but most effective measure, which could have dampened the property boom, by restricting the loan to value ratio of mortgages.[101]

These failures in regulatory policy contributed to the financial and property crash in September 2008, when the government took the decision to comprehensively guarantee the debts of Irish banks to depositors and bondholders in order to buy time, which effectively provided a guarantee to the tune of €440 billion. The banks' problems were down to their dramatic over exposure to the property sector. In the context of these liabilities and the increasingly onerous financial burden to the state of keeping the banks in existence, foreign investors were reluctant to invest in the Republic of Ireland, leading to excessively high Irish government bond yields. Between the bank guarantee in 2008 and the subsequent bailout in November 2010, there was effectively a run on Irish banks with deposits falling from €250 billion to €150 billion. With these funding difficulties, the Irish government was forced to seek financial assistance from the ECB as a lender of last resort, which had reluctantly lent €130 billion to Irish banks by October 2010, which constituted about a quarter of total ECB eurozone stability funding lent to banks. Eager to recoup this and maintain the stability of the eurozone banking system and halt contagion, the ECB (backed by the EU Commission and ECB) forced the state into an unprecedented bailout in November 2010.[102] This effectively converted Irish bank debt into Irish sovereign debt, thus socializing it to the long-term detriment of Irish tax payers, while bondholders were to be paid off in full. British banks had €120 billion tied up in Irish assets, while German banks were owed €99 billion by Irish banks and French banks were owed a further €30 billion. The November 2010 bailout was underwritten by the EU Commission, the ECB and the International Monetary Fund (IMF). In return for continued financial support from this troika, the Republic of Ireland committed itself to what proved to be one of the most expensive bank bailouts since 1970[103], and the ECB and European Commission were determined that the bank bond holders should not take a haircut on all their bad Irish investments; the ECB failed to acknowledge its role in the crisis, taking the view that the Republic of Ireland had to take a hit for the sake of wider European economic interests.[104]

The loss of considerable economic sovereignty in the last decade has significantly narrowed the range of policy instruments available to the Irish government to respond to the current crisis. The flawed architecture of the eurozone for handling monetary issues has resulted in an increasingly inflexible environment for peripheral member states such as Ireland to confront the current economic and financial crisis. But it is clear that the Irish experience has been made far worse by major policy errors by the Irish government in the recent past. Karl Whelan has identified financial regulation and the unsustainable nature of Ireland's fiscal management, combined with the failure of the state to respond to clear signals that the boom times in construction and development were drawing to a close. Since the fundamentals were good in the 1990s, governments were able to reduce public debt and income tax and raise public spending on both infrastructure and public sector employment. The construction boom generated additional revenue, while the increased numbers at work also contributed to offsetting the declining tax rates. However, this ill-conceived balance in revenue hinged on the boom in construction, and when this came to a grinding halt in 2008, total government revenue plummeted from €68 billion in 2007 to €56 billion in 2009,[105] as property transactions severely contracted and unemployment rose, which simultaneously had the effect of decreasing revenue and raising expenditure. By mid-2009, in the wake of the banking crisis, the government reorganized financial regulatory mechanisms, effectively centralizing two regulatory positions into one, under the chairmanship of the Central Bank, with the objective of giving this position more authority and staff.[106]

Regulatory failure in banking, which was an international problem, was however far greater in the Republic of Ireland due to more substantial credit risk concentrations, specifically in property development. The property bubble was based on misplaced faith that property values would rise in perpetuity, justifying the increased exposure of the banks to this sector. In the case of Allied Irish Bank, for example, property-related loans ballooned in the final years of the construction boom from €11 billion in 2003 to €47 billion in 2007. The doomed Anglo-Irish Bank was even more exposed to property development, and much of this debt mountain was also built up in the final years of the boom.[107] A third major policy mistake, in 2008, was the extent of the government guarantee, following negotiations and agreement with the ECB and IMF, which effectively nationalized the repayment of all outstanding Irish bank debts, with no burden sharing with bond holders. Ireland's history of good fortune in relationship to the EEC has therefore been reversed to some degree since the bailout.

Entry to the EEC in 1973 subjected Ireland to a host of extra national influences in terms of economic policy, which on balance have provided far more opportunities and benefits to Irish economic interests in the decades since entry, as Irish living standards rose in absolute and relative terms. The European project enabled Ireland to not only access continental European markets, but deepened its economic links with the US, and recalibrated its economic links with the UK; at several levels London remains just as important in economic and political terms as Boston and Berlin. It has been argued however that Irish support for the European project was always highly conditional, greased until recently by relatively higher transfers from Brussels[108] and assisted by converging living standards with other member states. This ostensibly *communataire* phase has passed into history. Opposition to the EU within Ireland first became more manifest in the rejection of the Nice treaty in June 2001. Since then the Republic of Ireland became a net contributor to the EU budget, as opposed to a net beneficiary.

The crisis since 2008 has opened up an altogether more volatile and stormy chapter in Irish relations with both the EU and the ECB, with the economy on life support entailing the imposition of severe austerity measures hardly helping matters. But even before the Irish government's ill-advised and far too comprehensive bank guarantee in September 2008, the Irish electorate voted in June 2008 against the Lisbon treaty, as they had in the case of Nice. This therefore became the second rejection out of three referendums, in a society that had long been viewed as decidedly pro-European; this had been born out by referendums prior to Nice. Although the Lisbon vote was subsequently reversed in October 2009, these referendums provide an indication that public opinion on further European integration and their economic benefits for the Republic of Ireland have become far more contested and polarized.[109] This greater degree of Irish euro-skepticism in many respects has moved closer to the kind of polarized outlook to be found in much of Europe, not least in Germany, France, Italy and the United Kingdom. Despite such public reservations, from a more long-term economic perspective the benefits of the European connection since entry in 1973 still far outweigh the downsides of membership. Despite the unpopularity of the socialization of Irish bank debt, significant credit provision since the banking crisis in 2008 remains crucial for the prospects of economic recovery.

Part II

3 Nature's bounty

Agriculture and natural resources

Given that agriculture dominated the economy of the Irish Free State, it was hardly surprising that economic development policies initially focused largely on this sector. Raymond Crotty's assertion that 'independence of itself did little to change the fundamentals of the Irish economy'[1] was particularly pertinent with regard to agriculture. The great significance attached to agricultural exports provided the main incentive to retain free trade, in opposition to those revolutionary nationalists who were advocating protectionism. This reflected two important advantages that Irish farmers had in international terms; first, they enjoyed a comparative advantage in livestock farming, which was provided by the conducive nature of the climate. Second, Great Britain conveniently accounted for most of the world market for meat in 1930, accounting for 95 per cent of mutton and lamb entering international trade, 90 per cent of bacon and hams and 70 per cent of beef. Ireland was well situated geographically to service this demand and livestock exports had become the staple trade of southern Ireland during the nineteenth century. According to O'Donovan, five-sixths of Irish livestock output was exported to Britain by 1930 and about 41 per cent of the cattle slaughtered in Britain were of Irish origin. These factors go a long way to explaining why livestock and livestock products accounted for over 73 per cent of the value of Irish agricultural output in 1929–30. Of the 14.3 million acres of land used for agricultural purposes at this point in time, 82.5 per cent was under grass and meadow and a mere 17.5 per cent was under crops.[2]

Dry cattle rearing was another important agricultural sector, dominated by large grazing farmers, popularly termed 'graziers'. Based in the fertile grasslands of north Leinster, east Connaught and north Munster, the graziers purchased calves from dairy farms and small holdings. These calves were subsequently fattened and exported to Britain.[3]

The rapidity with which the new government introduced land purchase legislation in 1923, which aspired to swiftly complete land transfer from the declining landlord class, gives some indication of the significance attached to stemming rampant land agitation. Larger graziers and landlords fell victim to land agitation during the War of Independence and the Civil War. But it was to take many more decades than anticipated to complete the process of land transfer; between 1923 and 1978, 847,000 acres were compulsorily acquired and redistributed, while a further 510,000 acres from estates and large farms were voluntarily sold. As a result, by 1975, 97 per cent of farmers in the state owned their land compared to a European average of just 64 per cent. The amount of land leased remained limited at 7 per cent by the late 1980s. Although many large farmers and former estate owners (who effectively became large farmers) held onto much of their lands during the 1920s, Cumann nGaedheal sought to protect large commercial enterprises (notably those that provided high levels of employment) in addition to stud farms.[4] Nonetheless land reform more than halved the average size of farms within the state between 1900 and 1960. A reduction in size was commonplace across much of Europe in these years. While the average size of farms was almost twice as large in England by 1960 as in the Republic of Ireland, Irish holdings were quite respectable when compared to much of continental Europe, coming in at the same average size in 1960 as France, which was larger on average than Norway, Finland, Denmark, the Netherlands, Belgium, Switzerland, Italy, Greece and West Germany. Thereafter, the average size of farms increased in the Republic of Ireland between 1960 and 2000, but not to the dramatic extent as in England, while average farm size in Denmark, France and former West Germany increased more rapidly than in Ireland.[5] Many small holdings were economically unviable and provided a low standard of living for their occupiers, especially in the former Congested Districts (specific poorer districts located in seven counties along the western seaboard). Even within the remaining 19 counties of the new state, according to Dooley, uneconomic holdings constituted 65 per cent of all holdings.[6] The dichotomy between this group and the smaller number of medium and larger farmers was therefore already well established by the 1920s.

Farmers in general suffered from a number of difficulties in the years after the new state was established. Many had borrowed excessively to purchase land, on the basis of inflated prices when record profits were made during the First World War. Following the collapse in agricultural prices from 1920, many could not service their debts.[7] In addition, a liver fluke epidemic during the winter of 1924–25 was the major factor contributing to the general depletion in cattle numbers from about 4.4 million to 4 million between 1921 and 1931.[8] Moreover, Continental producers during these years regained access to the British market, renewing competition for Irish agricultural exports.

The Commission of Agriculture, formed in 1923, favoured the expansion of dairying and the reduction of commercial tillage farming, making limited state aid available to improve the production and marketing of agricultural produce.[9] The government took a more interventionist approach in the case of sugar beet. Sugar imports were subject to tariffs from 1925, which made both the cultivation of domestic beet, and sugar production in a new factory located at Carlow, more economically attractive.[10] Despite the passing of various acts to improve the quality of dairy produce, eggs and livestock breeding,[11] little progress was made in improving the marketing of agricultural produce. Irish agricultural producers were zealous in safeguarding their independence and were wary of sharing commercial information. For example, because creameries were unwilling to supply details of cheese production to the Department of Agriculture, this stymied official attempts to expand the marketing and production of cheese.[12] For broadly similar reasons, the attempts of the Irish Associated Creameries (established in 1927) to promote the sale of creamery butter on a national basis also failed because of a lack of co-operation between its members.[13] Given the major focus on agriculture, the economic policies of the new state could hardly be deemed a major success, since there was only a very marginal growth of agricultural output in the 1920s. The crash of 1929 and the subsequent decline in international trade altered the entire economic landscape. The following decade, leading up to the outbreak of the Second World War, was to prove particularly perilous for Irish agriculture.

The Great Depression led to a steep fall in agricultural prices, followed from 1933 by the so called 'Economic War' with Britain. On coming to office in 1932, the new Fianna Fáil government withheld land annuities, which were due to the British government under the terms of the Land Acts. The land purchase annuities paid by former tenants (excluding former estate owners who re-purchased) were halved in 1933,[14] but the paid-up portion was retained by the Irish government. The British reacted by putting heavy duties on Irish cattle imported into Britain, both in an effort to re-coup the lost annuities and to demonstrate opposition to De Valera's policies. In retaliation, the Irish government placed heavy duties on British coal, cement, electrical goods, iron and steel manufactures and sugar. Reconciliation only started in 1935 with the Coal–Cattle Pact whereby coal and cattle were exchanged on a pound for pound sterling basis. The Economic War finally came to an end in 1938, when the two governments signed the Anglo-Irish Trade Agreement. In return for a lump sum payment by the Irish Free State of £10 million, the British government agreed to waive all further claims to Irish land annuities, which amounted to £90 million.[15]

The combination of the Economic War and protectionist agricultural policies implemented by Britain had a severely adverse effect on Irish agricultural exports. The Irish Free State's share of live cattle and beef imports into the United Kingdom declined from 27 per cent (1924–31) to 19.7 per cent (1933–39). While Ireland's market share of British agricultural imports recovered from the 1940s, the Economic War caused long-term damage to the exportation of other agricultural produce. Dairy produce imported into the UK from the Irish Free State did not exceed the 1924–31 average of 6.3 per cent UK market share for at least 40 years, while the state never recovered the 10.9 per cent share of UK pig and pig meat imports achieved during 1924–31.[16] In the 1930s and 1940s there was a productivity slow down in agriculture within the state, as trade was depressed by high tariffs, world depression and the Second World War. Even in the short term, the Economic War and the growth of protectionism dramatically reduced the general welfare of farmers. This is reflected in the dramatic fall in 11-month rents (conacre) in the Limerick region, for example, from almost £2 per acre in 1930–32 to just over £1 in 1934–35, which was indicative of plunging farmer expectations in terms of potential future returns.[17]

Fianna Fáil placed particular importance on the issue of land redistribution, given the party's goal of establishing as many families as practicable on the land.

The 1933 Land Act extended the compulsory acquisition powers of the Land Commission and between 1932 and 1937 about 353,000 acres of land were redistributed between 25,082 allotments.[18] Motivated by a sense of social justice, the activities of the Land Commission reduced the size of many larger farms and replaced them with smaller units. Government price supports for agriculture were introduced during the 1930s. Guaranteed prices were paid to farmers for wheat cultivation, with tariffs imposed on imports and the enforcement of a compulsory admixture of domestic grain in all flour produced by millers. In the pig sector, imports were simply prohibited from 1932. From 1935, this sector was subject to government regulation through the Bacon and Pigs Marketing Boards, which set prices and distributed the British export quota among the curing factories. These boards were merged in 1939, which improved both quality and the consistency of market supply.[19]

Butter prices were supported through a system of levying a charge on domestic butter sales, the proceeds being used to subsidize exports. Moreover, in 1936, a Department of Agriculture Butter Marketing Committee was established, which supervised the negotiation of fixed contracts between Irish creameries and British importers, in an attempt to regularize the marketing of creamery butter.[20] Compared to the 1920s, there was a marked upward shift in the share of total state expenditure going to agriculture, from 4.1 per cent in the mid-1920s to 20.4 per cent in the mid-1930s, reflecting the more interventionist approach of the new Fianna Fáil government and the continued significance attached to agriculture, despite the new emphasis on industrial development.

As noted earlier, increased subsidization of wheat cultivation was a central policy of the new government. Increased tillage, it was argued, would lead to self-sufficiency in food production and generate more agricultural employment, while reducing the significance of the livestock sector, thereby lessening economic ties with Britain. However, with wheat and sugar beet being the only crops subsidized, the tillage support policy merely led to the established tillage farmers in Leinster shifting from non-subsidized oat and barley cultivation to subsidized wheat, barley and sugar beet cultivation. As a consequence there was no net gain in the tillage acreage, but costs to the consumer increased.[21]

Neary and Ó Gráda argue that the tillage subsidization policy had the effect of increasing the demand for agricultural labour, and consequently real wages, leading to a transfer of wealth from farmers to agricultural labourers, reducing the on-going decline in agricultural employment.[22] However, there can be little doubt that the cumulative effect of the Great Depression, the Economic War and the advent of full-scale protectionism had a significant detrimental effect upon the overall performance of Irish agriculture, and the anticipated labour gains at a national level proved to be elusive. The value of gross agricultural output fell by 36 per cent between the years 1929 to 1930 and 1934 to 1935, while the value of livestock output fell catastrophically by 55 per cent, only recovering somewhat by the eve of the Second World War (see Table 3.1). Cattle producers thus suffered most from the Economic War. When the crisis reached its peak in 1934, farmers found it difficult to sell cattle at any price, with newspapers reporting dead livestock lying in the fields. The Sligo-Leitrim TD, Patrick Rogers, alleged that poorer farmers in the Ox Mountains in desperation were slaughtering their own cattle and sheep and hawking the meat from door to door. To deal with the collapse in demand, meat meal factories were established to reduce unwanted stock. Free beef schemes were established for welfare recipients, which removed about 1000 cattle a week from stock by 1935, while a meat canning factory was established in Waterford. The pressure to slaughter only subsided by February 1936 when Britain reduced the import duty on imported Irish cattle as part of the Coal–Cattle Pact.[23]

The Economic War starkly revealed the central importance of the cattle trade within Irish agriculture. Livestock and livestock products accounted for the majority share of gross agricultural output, and livestock alone fell dramatically in value in this respect from £33.7 million in 1929–30 to merely £15.1 million.[24] Increased tillage and the payment of subsidies could not remotely compensate for the loss of the states' staple trade. Although some loss was inevitable with the transition to protectionism globally, the damage brought about by the Economic War is evident from the contrasting experience of Denmark in this period, which lost some trade but essentially retained its market share in Britain. Ireland's share of British food imports in contrast more than halved from 4.5 per cent in 1931 to 2.1 per cent in 1937, even leaving aside the cataclysmic decline in the live cattle trade.[25]

With the outbreak of the Second World War, the post-1932 aspiration to achieve national self-sufficiency became a necessity. To secure the major staple of the Irish food supply, namely bread, the Fianna Fáil government imposed compulsory tillage orders from 1940, and these remained in situ until 1948. These orders compelled farmers to dedicate a specified percentage share of their land to crops, increasing from 12.5 per cent at the outset to 37.5 per cent by 1943–44. The orders succeeded in more than doubling domestic cultivation from 5.1 million cwt in 1939, to 11.46 million cwt by 1945. Farmers with less than 10 acres were initially exempt, but the ceiling was reduced to five acres in 1944. This was the most significant intervention by the state in the agricultural sector during the period under review and the extension of corn grown was largely achieved through traditional technologies, in contrast to Northern Ireland where the introduction of tractors made far greater headway. In general, the government and the courts took a robust and coercive approach to any resistance or non-compliance, even among aged farmers, who in many instances had little stomach for the back-breaking task of following the plough.[26]

The shortages during the war years of imported fuel, fertilizers, feedstuffs, agricultural machinery and parts were offset by the increased use of horses and the intensification of labour inputs. Draught horses (and horse dealers) enjoyed something of a renaissance. Since all forms of motorised transport were curtailed by fuel shortages, the expansion of ploughing was largely undertaken by horse. Since the number of animals was limited, dealers enjoyed a brief bonanza. Under Emergency Powers legislation in 1942 (Control of Export), the exportation of usable working horses was prohibited. In place of artificial fertilizers, farmers

Table 3.1 Area planted (000 acres) of selected crops at five-year intervals, 1925–70

	Wheat	*Oats*	*Pasture*	*Potatoes*	*Sugar beet*
1925	22	671	8,411	380	–
1930	27	644	8,081	347	14
1935	163	614	7,925	336	57
1940	305	681	7,616	367	63
1945	662	834	7,130	388	85
1950	366	614	7,826	337	60
1955	358	545	8,008	286	55
1960	366	426	7,578	234	68
1965	182	284	8,270	174	66
1970	234	168	8,263	140	64

Source: *Statistical abstracts of Ireland, 1931–1971*, Dept. of Industry and Commerce and CSO, Dublin, 1931–74.

utilized natural substitutes, such as seaweed and manure, while phosphate deposits in Clare were extensively exploited by Thomas MacDonagh & Son; these evidently became sufficiently important to merit improved lighting at Ennistymon railway station to facilitate round-the-clock-loading.[27] More commonly the natural soil fertility was simply drawn upon and depleted,[28] which constrained production somewhat in the decade after the war.

Crotty suggests that since output was the product 'overwhelmingly' of land and labour, the acute shortages of imported raw materials during the so called 'emergency' had marginal impact, because very limited use had been made of such imports. In his view this indicates the particularly underdeveloped state of Irish agriculture, which could therefore readily adapt to such adverse conditions.[29] But the dramatic rise of the area planted under wheat, oats, potatoes and sugar beet, which collectively rose to peak levels during the war (for the entire period between independence and entry into the European Economic Community (EEC) as a consequence of state directives, is a testament to the state's effective response to war-time shortages.

War-time conditions altered the traditional balance between tillage and livestock, increasing inputs to the former at the expense of the latter. Old pastures were ploughed up and by 1944, crops and turf accounted for a third of total output, compared to only one quarter in 1938–39.[30] The implementation of compulsory tillage reduced the area available for grazing, while the shortage of feedstuffs also curtailed livestock farming. The pig sector was affected by the reduction in imported feedstuffs, and pig numbers fell drastically between 1941 and 1944, with obvious effects on the bacon sector. Sheep stocks also declined. Creamery butter output fell from 766,460 cwt in 1938 to 579,534 cwt by 1944, while butter exportation ceased. While a guaranteed creamery milk price of 6d per gallon was fixed in 1940, dairy farmers claimed it was insufficient to cover their costs. In response, milk prices were increased by the government in 1941, to stave off butter shortages in the towns and cities.[31] War-time food shortages in Britain resulted in increased demand for Irish agricultural produce, but British price controls prevented Irish farmers from benefiting in the way they had during the First World War. During the war (and up to 1953–54) the British Ministry of Food became the sole purchaser of British imports at controlled prices. Nonetheless, the significance of food and agricultural produce for export to the British war economy is evident from concessions made by the British Government to allow exports of extra coal to the Great Southern Railway on the understanding that this would be partially used to facilitate the trade in cattle by rail, and to supply fuel to Guinness, a number of larger creameries and other processed foods plants that were producing commodities such as butter, cheese, chocolate crumb and condensed milk.[32]

The formation of the first inter-party government in 1948 took place at a time when a series of new developments were well underway. Continued food shortages in post-war Britain and Continental Europe had an important influence on Ireland's participation in the European Recovery Programme (ERP), better known as the Marshall Plan. There was also some improvement in Anglo-Irish relations, notably in the economic sphere. The live cattle export trade to Britain expanded with the Anglo-Irish Trade Agreement of 1948, which removed British quotas on livestock imported from Ireland. Butter exports of up to 20,000 tons per annum were permitted, while Britain was willing to import greater quantities of Irish bacon. Of the ERP funding destined for Irish agriculture, a large percentage was used for land reclamation. The scheme, launched in 1949, provided funding to farmers to conduct drainage on their holdings and to assist the reclamation of waste land, in addition to funding fencing. It continued throughout the 1950s, with the domestic exchequer funding the cost after the cessation of ERP funding. By 1957, 617,000 acres had been reclaimed at a cost of £17m. A limestone subsidy was also introduced and the practice of spreading ground limestone on more acid soils helped in the longer term to lift crop yields on acidic soils.[33] However, in the short term the scheme was of limited value to agriculture, only bringing marginal land into cultivation, with little impact on increasing output. A far greater production effect could have been achieved by focusing investment on better quality land. In this respect the social and political agenda of the Irish government to boost employment and help small farmers took precedence over purely economic criteria.

Of greater benefit to the Irish economy was the use of ERP funding to develop rural organizations, such as Macra na Feirme and the Irish Countrywomen's Association. As a result of participation in the ERP and consequently the OEEC, it quickly became apparent that Ireland's statistical data bank in relation to the economy was archaic and needed serious upgrading. As a result, in 1949 the CSO was established,[34] which also improved the collation and distribution of statistics relating to agriculture as part of its much wider remit. The American influence was also important in the creation of a research institute for agricultural and veterinary science, to complement the existing

Table 3.2 Number of livestock ('000) for each decade, 1930–70

	*Dairy cows**	*Other cattle*	*Pigs*	*Sheep*
1930	1,311.1	4,038.3	1,052.2	3,515.1
1940	1,314.1	4,023.0	1,049.1	3,070.6
1950	1,322.3	4,321.6	644.9	2,384.6
1960	1,405.2	4,740.6	951.1	4,314.1
1970	1,909.1	5,956.5	1,192.5	4,082.3

* Includes heifers in calf. Source: *Statistical abstract 1970–71*, Dublin, CSO.

Agricultural Faculty in University College Dublin (UCD) and the Dairy Science Department at University College Cork (UCC). The Agricultural Institute, eventually known as An Foras Talúntas, was established in 1958, with financial support from the USA.[35]

European and British agriculture recovered from war-time disruption during the 1950s and Britain once again became a low-price residual market for Irish agricultural commodities.[36] The fact that the British government generously subsidized its domestic agricultural sector further depressed agricultural prices in the Republic of Ireland, since imports to the UK market from there did not benefit from these subsidies.[37] These circumstances continued until both countries entered the EEC in 1973. Sectors that previously thrived on access to the British market now faced new difficulties. Intensive poultry rearing for example was introduced to Britain by the mid-1950s, which became largely self-sufficient in eggs. Irish eggs, by contrast, were still produced in free-range conditions and were seasonal in supply.

Pig numbers throughout the 1950s remained below their 1931 level (see Table 3.2) and more profitable returns on the home market (still protected by import prohibition) deterred Irish exporters from establishing long-term contracts with British suppliers.[38] Dairying was more influenced by government intervention than market conditions; the cost of subsidizing butter production was a significant drain on the exchequer.[39] However, the increased supply of milk was facilitated by significant investment in the sector. For example, the introduction of rural electrification expanded the use of milking machines,[40] while in 1950 a subsidy was also made available for the provision of piped water to farms, which improved the bacteriological quality of milk. Moreover, cattle breeds with high milk yields, such as Friesians, were introduced into the national herd,[41] gradually in the 1950s and more rapidly in the 1960s (see Table 3.2). Nonetheless, the average size of herds remained very small; farmers supplying milk to creameries as late as 1961 owned on average less than seven cows and outside creamery districts the average size was probably smaller still. Dairying remained the main focus for small farmers in circumstances where most farms remained undercapitalized. This was part of a wider problem in Irish agriculture, in which 40 per cent of all farmers farmed less than 31 acres in 1961.[42] Irish output, per acre and per person, were still relatively low by European standards in the 1950s, and a relatively small marketable surplus was produced on many farms.

State support to agriculture by the early 1960s was even higher than it had been in the mid-1930s, in terms of agriculture's share of total government expenditure. In 1962 and 1963, total state supports amounted to over 21 per cent of the value of net agricultural output. This upward drift in state support since independence was accompanied by very limited increases in agricultural output, and most of this increase was achieved between the early 1950s and 1963, largely (Crotty argues) by the switch from horses to tractors.

Despite the continued dependence on draught animals and human labour in the years immediately after the Second World War, the adoption of tractors was already underway among larger farmers, particularly in the south and east in the more arable orientated farming areas, and among contractors operating threshing sets. The number of tractors in the state (which was merely 804 in 1928) began to rise more rapidly after the war from 5865 in 1947 to 13,567 by 1950. This marked the beginning of a major revolution in Irish farming.[43] Tractors were probably the most critical new engineering development in world agriculture in the first half of the twentieth century. They could be harnessed through three-point linkage and hydraulic lift to an increasing array of functions, including transportation off farm.[44] Horses, which had been used for ploughing, transport and a host of other tasks, were progressively displaced on most farms by tractors in the following decades, more notably in the south and east of the country, with diffusion lagging somewhat in the west, where the small nature of farms and upland terrain made the usage of tractors more difficult. By the 1960s tractors were heavily concentrated on the larger farms, with 44 per cent of them being operated on holdings of upwards of 99 acres (which constituted merely 11 per cent of all holdings). The number of horses deployed in agriculture declined by 45 per cent in the 1950s, and by the end of 1970 the impact of this technological transformation was evident from the fact that the number of tractors then equalled the number of horses used in farming in the state.

Since horse-drawn technologies could not generally be adapted to tractors, this transition entailed the purchase of a whole new range of plant and powered machinery, including ploughs, buck rakes, mowers, manure spreaders, seed drills, harrows, bailers, and forage harvesters. Tractor sales (new and second hand) were buoyant in the 1950s and 1960s. The number and diffusion of tractors continued to expand dramatically in the 1970s, in addition to an increasing array of associated machinery and plant associated with them, while the average power ratings also rose progressively in the 1960s and 1970s.[45] Tractor purchases peaked in 1977–78 following the general rise in farm incomes and bank borrowing together with a new-found confidence in the future of Irish farming, which accompanied the states initial phase of participation in the EEC.[46] In the long term, tractor numbers rose from 29,744 in 1955, to 148,100 by 1985. Combine harvesters were also increasingly used in the 1950s; there were 4254 by 1960, which also reduced labour inputs and time spent on the harvest, but again entailed higher capital inputs.

A positive consequence of farm mechanization was that land previously used for crops and pasture to maintain horses could now be utilized to increase the marketable produce off farm. In 1926, for example, it has been estimated that the 320,000 horses used in Irish agriculture required at least 10 per cent of the land utilized for pasture and crops to be set aside for their maintenance. Moreover, the substantial labour input required for the upkeep of horses was also removed. The post-war years marked an acceleration of this agricultural revolution, which arrived relatively late in southern Ireland, compared to the more developed countries in Western Europe and the UK.[47] However, despite this slow adoption of tractors, Irish farming was quite highly commercialized by European standards. Although to a lesser degree than UK agriculture, where 99 per cent of agricultural output was commercialized in the early 1950s, at 83 per cent, Ireland had a higher degree of commercialization than West Germany, France, Italy, Austria and Norway. Although by the early 1960s, the level of Irish commercialization had risen to 87 per cent of agricultural output, the other Continental European countries noted above had all moved up to a similar level at this stage.[48]

In this period, science played a role in further improving the understanding of plant and animal husbandry, including the growing application of herbicides (from 1950), while fertilizers, pesticides and drug and chemical treatments for animals all increased the intensity of production, more notably after entry to the EEC in 1973; fungicides were also introduced from 1976.[49] Under the auspices of An Foras Talúntas, research activity in Irish agriculture increased. Research on soil activity and fertilizer usage was carried out at Johnstown Castle, Co. Wexford. This was of vital importance, given the depletion in soil fertility that had occurred during the 1940s. Dairy research was carried out at Moorepark, Co. Cork, where developments in grazing management, winter milk production and improvements in monitoring production and profitability were conducted. Research in the beef sector was carried out at Grange, Co. Meath, where developments occurred in grazing and stocking practices, and where improvements were made in cattle breeding.[50] Silage making also increased from the 1960s, which replaced hay, although haymaking survived longer in the western counties where tractors were not as commonly used. Silage making in the Irish Republic increased from 0.3 million tonnes in 1960 to over 20 million by 1990.[51]

Between 1960 and 1980 there was a greater degree of concentration and specialization in Irish farming, and the traditional emphasis on mixed farming receded somewhat, with dairying and beef cattle production increasing from 52 per cent of gross output in 1960 to 70 per cent in 1980. Although arable farming's share of output was declining, it also became increasingly concentrated; by the end of the 1960s, Leinster accounted for 59 per cent of the national arable cropping, with counties Cork, Waterford, Tipperary and Donegal accounting for a further 29 per cent; at this point, land and labour productivity levels were highest on arable land. While total gross agricultural output, which in earlier years had been relatively static, grew by two-thirds between 1960 and 1980, the income gap between large and small farmers widened, with modernization disproportionately benefiting large and medium farmers.[52] While farms over 100 acres accounted for 40 per cent of total tillage acreage in 1960, this rose to 59 per cent by 1987, by which time tillage farming had almost disappeared from small holdings.[53]

By the mid 1970s, it was becoming apparent that medium to larger farmers were accounting for a growing share of farm output and were achieving relatively higher levels of output per acre than smaller farmers, whose competitive position was weakening. The 11 per cent of farmers who farmed more than 100 acres accounted for 39 per cent of output by 1974.[54] Rising incomes in farming facilitated greater capital investment as profits were ploughed back into farms; moreover, the 1970s witnessed a dramatic increase in borrowings by farmers from banks and the Agricultural Credit Corporation, facilitating the further substitution of labour inputs by machinery.[55] Bank loans advanced to farmers increased from 33 million to over 964 million between 1959 and 1979, reflecting the dramatic growth of one source of capital investment. Gross Fixed Capital formation in Irish agriculture during these years rose from less than 11 per cent of gross value added to almost 28 per cent. Of the total investment in farming by the end of this period about 40 per cent was raised through borrowing and the remainder was achieved by ploughing back earnings.[56] Greater capital investment led to the long-term decline of non-family male hired labour, which was relatively more rapid than the decline in family labour employed on Irish farms since the 1920s. Family members by 1979 accounted for almost 88 per cent of the males engaged in farm work, compared to under 71 per cent in 1929, and 74 per cent in 1949. Non-family male paid labourers on farms declined dramatically from over 148,000 in 1929 to a mere 26,000 in 1979.[57]

In addition to the substitution of capital for labour, paid labour was displaced by a greater dependence on family labour, both male and female. If Arensberg and Kimball's ethnographic description of the farmer's wife in Clare in 1932, rising early to revive the fire to put on the kettle, implied that her life revolved around housework, it also incorporated significant manual work including milking, feeding and tending animals and fowl around the farm yard, quite apart from raising children. In comparative European terms, the female share of the agricultural workforce in Ireland was similar to the Netherlands on the eve of the Second World War, which was higher than in the UK and Spain, but slightly less than Denmark and Belgium and far lower than in Germany.[58] By the end of the twentieth century 60 per cent of farm women in the west and 40 per cent in the east undertook manual work on the farm, notably on farms engaged in dairying or market gardening, but with many more commonly working in other occupations off farm. Women also frequently took responsibility for keeping farm accounts,[59] revealing the importance of commercialization.

In the midst of this transition, the question of increasing productivity growth in agriculture began to figure far more prominently in policy terms; this was a core concern in T.K. Whitaker's report, *Economic Development,* published in 1958. The fact that 8 of the 24 chapters in this landmark publication were dedicated to agriculture reveals the significance still attached to the sector among the economic planners of the day. The *Programme for Economic Expansion*, which revised Whitaker's efforts and formally articulated them as state policy, focused more on increasing farm income through achieving higher productivity and output rather than subsidization.[60]

Greater capital investment in productive areas with a potential for increased exports (most notably beef, cattle, sheep and lamb) were central features of Whitaker's strategy. To achieve these aims, the government encouraged the banking sector to extend more credit to farmers.[61] These supply side measures were accompanied by efforts to improve marketing and product quality; the most notable outcome in this respect was the establishment of Bord Bainne in 1961, and a quality-based bonus for creamery milk supplies from 1965.[62] The livestock sector also experienced change. A significant development was the growth of livestock marts, of which there were already 130 licensed by 1967. The calved heifer subsidy, introduced in 1964 (£15 per extra heifer), contributed to increasing livestock based exports. A particularly welcome development was the extension of British deficiency payments to Irish beef exports, which stimulated the development of the indigenous meat processing industry. Over a single year, 1966–67, Irish carcass meat exports increased from 69,000 tons to 205,000 tons, at the expense of fat cattle exports. However, the support of beef prices was a significant burden to the domestic exchequer and Ireland was reliant solely on the British market.[63] While revenue from meat exports was greater than revenue from the home market, for most commodities the heavily protected domestic market remained more important, and by the end of the 1960s, still accounted for half of the gross value of agricultural output.[64]

In the decades after the Second World War, livestock gradually recovered its traditional dominance in Irish agriculture (see Table 3.3). The Anglo-Irish Trade Agreement of 1948 facilitated greater access to the British market for Irish cattle exports, and from this point to entry into the EEC in 1973 livestock accounted for a growing share of the value Irish agricultural output, while tillage experienced a corresponding decline.

Entry to the EEC in 1973 had a profound effect on Irish agriculture, enabling farmers to benefit from far higher EEC prices and price supports as a consequence of the CAP for all member states. The Irish agricultural sector benefited from payments made under the European Agricultural Guidance and Guarantee Fund (FEOGA). This subsidized agricultural production, by subsidizing output and exports and restricting imports; in addition unsold stocks were purchased and placed in intervention. Wheat, barley, sugar beet and milk prices were supported in this manner. At the time of entry sheep production was not in receipt of financial aid, but in 1980 the ewe premium was introduced. The combined effect of the introduction of a ewe premium and the elimination of barriers in the trade of lamb within the EEC, especially the removal of protectionist measures by France against lamb imports, led to a dramatic increase in sheep numbers in the state from 3.29 million (1980) to 6.65 million (1988).[65]

The improved position of farmer incomes, and the increased capital investment in farming had a multiplier effect in the entire economy during the mid 1970s. EEC entry improved the state's terms of trade, increasing trade largely through access to continental European markets, thus reducing dependence on the low priced UK market. The significant expansion in agricultural exports after 1973

Table 3.3 Percentage distribution of gross agricultural output, 1943–70

	Livestock	*Livestock products*	*Crops*
1943	36.7	29.4	33.9
1946	39.2	30.3	30.5
1949	40.7	32.8	26.5
1952	46.8	30.6	22.6
1955	46.5	29.7	23.8
1958	49.1	29.8	21.1
1961	50.9	27.3	21.8
1964	51.1	29.6	19.3
1967	50.8	30.6	18.6
1970	53.5	26.6	19.9

Source: 1943–55, *Agricultural statistics 1934–1956*, Dublin, CSO. 1958, *Statistical abstract 1961*, Dublin, CSO. 1970, *Statistical abstract 1973*, Dublin, CSO.

Note: Livestock products are comprised of milk and milk products, wool and eggs. Livestock figure is inclusive of stock changes.

(including intervention purchases) raised exports to levels approaching 60 per cent of total agricultural output.[66]

Participation in the EEC resulted in a 45 per cent increase in the real prices received by farmers between 1971 and 1978. Entry made a significant contribution to the 23 per cent increase in the volume of GNP, which occurred between 1972 and 1978. From a national perspective, the CAP removed the enormous burden of agricultural support payments from the national exchequer, so that national support to Irish agriculture declined from 65 per cent of total budgetary support in 1973 to 15 per cent by 1989.[67]

After EEC entry, Irish farmers benefited from advantageous 'green pound' devaluations, which also increased the competitiveness of Irish agricultural exports on the British market.[68] Estimates of Total Factor Productivity Growth in the Republic of Ireland compared to the rest of Europe vary greatly, but Irish relative performance appears to improve for estimates dealing with the period from 1973 onwards.[69] Yet the intervention system had an adverse effect upon the food processing industry, as the intervention-based purchase of commodity products hindered the development of a wider range of value added products, especially in the beef and dairying sectors.[70]

However, the benefits of the CAP for farmers gradually diminished. From the late 1970s, the increasing cost of the CAP to the EEC budget and the unpopular intervention system of buying unwanted agricultural produce led to reductions in agricultural price supports. The creation of the EMS in 1979 limited the scope of advantageous 'green pound' devaluations. By 1984, the milk quota and super levy system was introduced across the EEC to curb excess production. Production in excess of 1984 supply by dairy farmers was subsequently penalized in financial terms.[71] The spiralling cost of agricultural price supports and the consequent glut of agricultural produce led to further major reforms in the CAP. The 1992 MacSharry reforms reduced market supports for cereal and beef output, and limited intervention purchases of agricultural commodities, while supply controls were introduced for specific sectors, such as set-aside (non-planting) schemes for tillage and livestock herd restrictions. Farm income supports were gradually 'de-coupled' from production, removing an artificial incentive to increase output, although decoupling diminished the incentive to pursue productivity gains. Partial compensation for the MacSharry reforms was offered in the form of livestock premia, while tillage farmers benefited from area aid, which became increasingly important. Reforms in 1999 further reduced market supports, especially in the dairy sector, while in 2003 it was announced that the link between production and price supports would be formally broken. The livestock premia and arable aid programmes were substituted by a single, fully decoupled payment, based on the subsidy payments received by farmers in 2000 to 2002.[72]

Protection of the environment and the countryside became increasingly important considerations in EU farm policy from the late 1980s especially in the context of increased environmental awareness. The Rural Environment Protection Scheme (REPS) scheme, initiated in 1994, encouraged farmers to adopt environmentally sustainable farming practices. The relative significance of EU supports for Irish agriculture progressively declined as a percentage share of GNP from the early 1990s, as the non-agricultural economy expanded relatively faster. CAP price supports aided the expansion of dairying between 1973 and 1984 at the expense of other types of cattle husbandry, notably in the midlands and south-east.[73] This was related to the expansion of the liquid milk trade and ensured that dairying continued to expand in these regions until the introduction of milk quotas in 1984.[74] The national dairy milk herd has experienced continual decline since 1980 (see Table 3.4). The beef sector has progressively shifted since EEC entry away from live exports, to slaughtering and processing in Ireland largely for export, creating more forward linkages and added value within the Irish economy.[75]

The poultry sector became more market orientated in the last quarter of the twentieth century (see Table 3.4), with the general decline of small scale production in the midlands, east and west, and greater geographical concentration.[76] Between 1970 and 1980, Monaghan and Limerick increased their combined share of the national poultry flock from 24.6 per cent to 46.6 per cent.[77] The pig-rearing sector experienced similar structural change. Between 1960 and 1998, pigmeat production increased at a rate of 1.7 per cent per annum, with a marked acceleration of growth from 1985 to 1998 of 5.8 per cent per annum.[78] The number of pig producers declined from 110,000 in 1970 to 7,000 by 1985, so that a small number of large-scale producers increasingly dominated the sector. By 1997, 365 farms accounted for 90.5 per cent of total pig numbers in the state, making the Irish pigmeat industry the most concentrated in Europe.[79]

Comparisons of productivity of both land and labour with other European countries in 1984 to 1986 indicate that Irish land productivity was under half that

Table 3.4 Livestock and poultry numbers ('000) at five-year intervals, 1975–2009

Year	*Dairy cows*	*Other cattle*	*Sheep*	*Pigs*	*Poultry*
1975	1,379.5	4,834.2	2,653.2	880.2	9,066.8
1980	1,719.3	4,106.2	2,343.6	1,030.8	9,132.7
1985	1,707.3	4,105.7	3,304.0	994.1	8,638.9
1990	1,507.5	4,593.0	5,863.7	1,249.1	10,876.8
1995	1,456.2	4,994.4	5,543.4	1,542.3	12,981.6
2000	1,355.7	4,974.5	5,056.0	1,731.5	13,586.7
2005	1,337.4	4,854.3	4,257.0	1,670.8	–
2009	1,354.8	4,000.5	4,778.0	1,468.2	–

Source: 1975–2005, *Compendium of agricultural statistics 2007*, Dublin, CSO. 2009, *Crops and livestock survey June 2009: Final results*, Dublin, CSO. Note: Dairy cow figure includes heifers-in-calf.

in the EU as a whole. Labour productivity in contrast was superior to that in the EU as a whole. In terms of labour productivity, while the Republic of Ireland was slightly behind the UK and France, it was ahead of West Germany and well ahead of Greece, Italy, Spain, and Portugal.[80] There has been further improvement in the period since, with overall productivity growth in Irish agriculture running at 4.3 per cent per annum between 1995 and 2005, but much of this was achieved through an annual employment decrease in agriculture of 1.7 per cent and a growth in real Gross Added Value of 2.6 per cent.[81] Although per-hour productivity is higher than the EU average, the productivity gap with the US has widened in recent years.[82] The impact of CAP reforms and the removal of direct payment supports for livestock reduced the number of dairy cattle and sheep in the 1990s (see Table 3.4).

By the beginning of the twenty-first century, grassland still accounted for about 90 per cent of Ireland's utilized agricultural land.[83] When compared to the much lower share of the value of gross agricultural output derived from livestock (see Table 3.5) the land extensive nature of this activity becomes apparent, including large tracts of marginal land. Crops, however, have come to account for a more significant share of output in the last decade or more, a development facilitated by increased capital investment. However, wheat is the only major arable crop in which the area planted was increased between 1975 and 2005, with oats, barley, potatoes and sugar beet all witnessing a decline in these years.[84]

Other elements of the primary sector of the economy did not receive the same degree of attention as agriculture from the government of the state. Little progress was made in developing forestry in the early twentieth century and the establishment of the new state did little to change this. By 1926, only 1.4 per cent of the total acreage of the Irish Free State was under forestry.[85] Moreover, the Forestry Service was limited to paying £4 per acre for the purchase of plantation acreage

Table 3.5 Percentage distribution of gross agricultural output (excluding direct payments) at three-year intervals, 1998–2007

Year	*Livestock as % of output*	*Livestock products as % of output*	*Crops as % of output*
1998	46.5	31.5	22.0
2001	44.1	32.3	23.6
2004	42.0	29.1	28.9
2007	43.6	28.9	27.5
2010	42.9	29.8	27.3

Source: 1998 and 2001, *Statistical yearbook of Ireland 2003*, Dublin, CSO. 2004 and 2007, *Statistical yearbook of Ireland 2009*, Dublin, CSO. 2010, *Output, input and income in agriculture 2010: Final estimate*, Dublin, CSO.

at this point, so whatever land was purchased was limited to poor quality soils, diminishing potential timber output. The low level of state forestry planting was also accompanied by very limited activity in the private sector.[86] A private planting grant was introduced in 1928, but this had little effect beyond assisting in the maintenance of a handful of estate woodlands and the small-scale afforestation of poor quality lands. Farmers showed little enthusiasm for placing their land under plantation, given the long time period before a return could be obtained.[87]

No major expansion occurred until the formation of the first inter-party government in 1948, and when funding was made available (initially from the ERP), 159,000 acres of forestry land was acquired by the state between 1950 and 1958. New forestry acreages increased at a more rapid rate than in the inter-war years, taking advantage of new planting techniques and new ploughing and drainage methods that facilitated the mass cultivation of coniferous trees on poor upland soils, especially in the west of Ireland.[88] The pulpwood industries established in the late 1960s processed the first yields from these schemes.[89]

The acreage under forestry rose in the 1960s and 1970s (see Table 3.6) as a consequence of continued state investment. The coalition government in the mid-1980s placed renewed emphasis on forestry development, which in turn led to the formation of a review group that advocated that responsibility for state forestry should be delegated to a new body, which would develop it on a more commercial basis. Consequently, Coillte was established in 1988.[90] This, accompanied by significant support from the EEC, resolved the difficulty of a lack of income for private investors, as compensatory payments were introduced for farmers who put their land under forestry.[91] The resulting investment in private plantations, supplemented by some additional investment in state owned forestry, raised the total acreage to over 1.8 million by 2008, higher than it had been for centuries (see Table 3.7).

The fishing sector is another primary industry that has been surprisingly neglected by the government, in spite of Ireland's obvious maritime potential.[92] While a Ministry for Fisheries was established in 1922, Cumann na nGaedheal

Table 3.6 Acreage of state-owned forestry at three-year intervals, 1927–78

Year	*Acreage*
1927	12,235
1930	21,775
1933	34,134
1936	50,640
1939	72,593
1942	90,212
1945	113,696
1948	116,235
1951	140,722
1954	191,002
1957	236,900
1960	305,829
1963	380,230
1966	450,014
1969	509,837
1972	574,763
1975	635,144
1978	683,251

Source: *Statistical abstract, 1931, 1937, 1944*, Dublin, Department of Industry and Commerce, Statistics Branch. *Statistical abstract, 1949, 1952, 1956, 1961, 1964 1967 1970, 1973, 1976 and 1981*, Dublin, CSO.

did little to promote the sector until 1931, when a semi-state company, The Sea Fisheries Association, was formed, which provided loans for boat and equipment purchase in addition to marketing fish on a cooperative basis.[93] Until the 1950s, the industry was dominated by part-time fishermen operating on a small scale; from then onwards, greater investment, centralization and commercial development took place, and more substantial fishing fleets emerged in the larger ports while fish processing plants were established in Killybegs and Kinsale.[94]

In 1952, a new state organization, An Bord Iascaigh Mhara (BIM), was established, which assisted factory construction and training, in addition to providing financial support for boat and equipment purchase.[95] Fishermen were encouraged to form cooperatives and by 1977, 75.8 per cent of immediate fish sales were by fishermen's cooperatives. Traditionally, fish had been landed at a multitude of small ports, which lacked adequate storage and processing facilities.[96] BIM concentrated investment in improving infrastructure on five major ports; Killybegs, Rossaveal, Castletownbere, Dunmore East and Howth. By 1977, 50 per cent of all sea fish catches were landed in these ports with a superior fishing infrastructure.[97] An indication of some degree of modernization in the industry between the 1920s and the 1980s is apparent from the increase in the number of full-time

Table 3.7 Private and state-owned forestry at three-year intervals, 1981–2008

Year	*Acreage of state-owned forestry*	*Acreage of private forestry*	*Total acreage*	*State owned forestry as % of total*	*Private forestry as % of total*
1981	730,157	241,858	972,015	75.1	24.9
1984	770,426	244,973	1,015,399	75.9	24.1
1987	805,766	259,015	1,064,781	75.7	24.2
1990	842,234	312,391	1,154,625	72.9	27.1
1993	895,627	383,424	1,279,051	70.0	30.0
1996	937,423	495,588	1,433,011	63.4	34.6
1999	948,626	573,257	1,521,883	62.3	37.7
2002	953,667	679,128	1,632,795	58.4	41.6
2005	954,418	747,811	1,702,229	56.1	43.9
2008	982,880	822,171	1,805,051	54.5	45.5

Source: 1981–2005, *Statistical year book 2008*, Dublin, CSO. 2008, *Statistical yearbook 2010*, Dublin, CSO.

fishermen and the corresponding decline in the number of part-time fishermen, but even in 1983 there was still a greater number of part timers, reflecting the seasonal nature of much of the industry.[98]

Nonetheless, a number of factors continued to inhibit the development of the industry. EEC entry in 1973 made Ireland subject to the Common Fisheries Policy, which permitted EEC fishermen to fish in the territorial waters of any member state. While Ireland, along with the UK and Denmark obtained a six-mile fishing zone for domestic fishermen until 1982, it lost exclusive rights to extensive off-shore fishing.[99] Fishing was further restricted by the introduction of national fishing quotas by the EEC in 1980,[100] which have continued to restrict large scale landings of white fish species, such as cod, with concerns about the survival of stocks leading to more stringent conservation measures. Expansion of national fishing fleets was further limited by an EU prohibition on the financial support for fishing vessel modernization and construction, effective from 2004.[101] As recently as 2000, the National Development Plan had provided up to €15.5 million in grant assistance towards the purchase of 36 modern fishing vessels.[102] Yet, the combined effect of EU prohibitions and landing quotas led to the introduction of a decommissioning scheme for older boats in 2005.[103]

The continued reliance on highly seasonal small-scale catches on an inshore basis prevented any major expansion of fish processing during the 1960s and 1970s. While 60 fish processing firms were in operation by 1978, these were of a relatively rudimentary nature.[104] Despite improvements in the quality and range of processed seafood, EU quotas prevented further large-scale development of fishing. Although there was an expansion in the domestic demand for fish during the mid 2000s, restrictions on fish landings reduced supply. In addition to sea fish landings, the controlled cultivation of shellfish and salmon, aquaculture, grew in importance in the 1990s,[105] with aquaculture output (volume) increasing by 200 per cent between 1994 and 2002,[106] revealing the increasing diversification of the marine dimensions to the Irish food industry.

One of the major changes in Irish farming since independence has been the decline in the number of agricultural holdings overall, and an increase in the number of holdings over 120 acres. In 1939, approximately 63 per cent of all holdings were under 30 acres, and this declined to under 48 per cent by 1970. The total number of holdings has declined from 227,900 in 1975 to 132,500 by 2005, with relatively larger levels of decline among smaller holdings. In contrast, holdings over 120 acres increased in this period. By 2005, farms over 72 acres accounted for 38.7 per cent of all holdings, and these farms accounted for the majority share of national agricultural output.[107]

As the number of farms declined, larger and more active commercial farmers have been increasingly taking over smaller and unviable holdings, in many instances from elderly landowners. In addition, it is evident from the National Farm Survey in 2010 that the bigger the farms, the higher the proportion of the land that is rented. On farms over 247 acres, on average a little less than a third of the area farmed was rented and in tillage renting was even more pronounced, approaching a little less than a half of the area farmed.[108]

Although average Irish farm size by 2007 was large in EU comparative terms, the average farm had a relatively low intensity of land use by EU standards. However, there is great diversity in terms of farm size, with small farms being more typical of the west and north-west.[109] Moreover, since the early 1990s, part time farming has increased, as farm households supplemented their income with off farm work; many small farms could only survive by adopting such strategies. The number of farm owners for whom farming was their sole occupation declined from over 73 per cent to under 56 per cent between 1991 and 2000,[110] a development aided by increased off-farm employment opportunities.

Another important development in Irish farming since independence is the major improvement in yields; the amount of barley produced per acre increased from under 20 cwt in the 1920s to over 46 cwt by the 1990s, and the upward trend has continued since. Similar rises were experienced in wheat and oats. Liquid milk yields have also risen dramatically and may have increased further but for the constraint of CAP quotas.[111] Despite these improvements in yields, one of the major problems for Irish farming is that the terms of trade have deteriorated since the Second World War; the cost of inputs have increased from about 24 per cent of agricultural output in 1949 to 54 per cent in 1998. This trend has continued in recent years, with farm input costs between 1995 and 2010 rising faster than output prices.[112]

Crotty argued that a major problem for Irish farming was the considerably higher average age profile of Irish farmers compared to New Zealand, Denmark, England and Wales; these comparisons were drawn from evidence dating from 1951. Crotty believed that the tendency of the older generation to continue farming reduced the 'progressive, energetic and efficient inputs' of younger famers (those under 45) with deleterious consequences for productivity growth.[113] By the mid 1980s, the farm modernization scheme attempted to resolve this problem by introducing 'installation aid' for farmers under 35 who became either the leaseholder or owner of a farm. However, the financial incentives provided by installation aid were insufficient to persuade elderly farmers to retire, many of whom feared that they would lose their pension rights if they availed of it.[114] By 2007, 50.9 per cent of farmers were aged 55 years and over, a similar share as in 1926.[115] If anything, farm mechanization and tractors have probably made age less important than it was in the 1920s and farmers can work and live longer.

More important perhaps was the gap that opened up between small and large farmers. As late as the 1950s, farms between 15 and 30 acres had a higher output per acre than farms between 50 and 100 acres; holdings between 15 and 30 acres were farmed more intensively. The 25,000 farmers working over 100 acres by the mid-1960s were in a better position to increase capital inputs and reaped the rewards of new technologies and mechanization to a greater degree than smaller farmers, who became increasingly marginalized.[116] Crowley in particular has highlighted the increasing division in farming between those who are market orientated food producers using high capital inputs and intensive farming techniques and those who have merely become custodians of the landscape and are primarily using environmentally friendly methods.[117] Farmers have become stratified in economic terms, with a relatively small group of larger farmers utilizing greater capital inputs and new technologies, who account for an increasing share of output, and a much larger group of smaller farmers who have become progressively marginalized, in terms of both production and farm income, with many no longer able to make a living from farming.[118]

The contribution made by agriculture to Irish GDP growth has been extremely modest since the 1960s, accounting for an average of 0.2 per cent of GDP growth between 1962 and 2000. This contribution was a little higher in the 1970s, averaging at 0.3 per cent following entry in the EEC in 1973, and peaking in the 1980s at 0.4 per cent, when growth in other sectors was limited.[119] Boyle estimated that Total Factor Productivity in Irish agriculture increased by an average of 1.94 per cent between 1973 and 1990, which was the second highest growth rate within the EEC, after the UK and Italy.[120] The competitive advantage of Ireland in livestock-based production was reinforced during this period. In 1989, Ireland had both the second lowest cash cost to produce 100 kg of milk solids, and the second lowest percentage of cash cost to milk output, within the EEC. Ireland was the most competitive producer of beef in the EEC, again measured by cash costs as a percentage of output.[121] This favourable comparison graphically illustrates the historical pattern of Irish comparative advantage, which persists in this area, explaining the relatively large land area still used for grassland or rough grazing compared to other parts of Europe. In stark contrast to the 1920s, the great majority of those who live in rural Ireland today are no longer engaged in agriculture or other elements in the primary sector. The share of employment accounted for by agriculture, forestry and fishing industries has decreased continually since the 1920s (see Table 3.8).

Table 3.8 Agriculture and fisheries employment as a percentage of total employment, 1926–2009

Year	*Agriculture and fisheries employment*	*Agricultural employment as a % of all employment*
1926	677.9	51.8
1936	643.9	48.0
1946	597.3	46.0
1951	512.3	40.5
1961	395.1	35.7
1966	347.3	31.1
1971	288.8	25.8
1981	198.5	15.9
1983	189.0	16.8
1986	168.0	15.5
1989	163.0	15.0
1992	155.0	13.6
1995	142.0	11.5
1998	135.0	9.0
2001	120.1	7.1
2004	113.8	6.4
2007	108.5	5.1
2009	97.2	5.0

Source: *Census of population 1926, 1936, 1946, 1951, 1961, 1966, 1971 and 1981*, Dublin, CSO. *Statistical abstract 1982–85, 1986, 1990 and 1997*, Dublin, CSO. *Statistical yearbook 2001, 2007 and 2010*, Dublin, CSO.

This decrease was moderate between 1926 and 1946, accelerating rapidly thereafter as farming became progressively more mechanized. Even for the small minority still engaged in agriculture, farm livelihood strategies entail far more diverse forms of on farm income generation and off farm employment in industry and services; by 2008 off farm income accounted for almost 54 per cent of farm household income from all sources.[122] By 1947, the share of Irish Net Domestic Product accounted for by agriculture was still nearly one-third, but this share has declined dramatically since so that by 2009 it accounted for less than 2 per cent of Net Domestic Product (see Table 9.2).

Although farming has been transformed in several respects, notably with regard to the application of science, technology and capital inputs, there is at least some continuity with the past; dairying and beef remain the central pillars of Irish agriculture, just as they did at the time of independence. Matthews points out that agriculture and forestry still account for 70 per cent of the land area and therefore continues to shape most of the landscape and physical environment of the Irish countryside. It also supplies most of our domestic food (with food processing still being the most important indigenous industry and a major exporter); consequently Matthews argues that agriculture still 'remains the single most substantial contributor to the economic and social viability of rural areas'.[123] Nonetheless, the continuous contraction of the relative significance of agriculture since the 1920s, from a position of dominance over the economic, social and political landscape to its current status as a more marginal contributor to both employment and GNP, and the corresponding emergence of a more urbanized society centred on industry and services, constitutes one of the core transitions in Irish economic and social history since independence, following a pattern already witnessed in the more developed economies of western Europe.

4 Late industrialization

From import substitution to foreign direct investment

One of the major weaknesses of the economy in the 1920s was the limited degree of industrial development that had taken place in the Irish Free State area in the century or more prior to partition. Manufactures (excluding construction) accounted for less than 10 per cent of total employment by 1926, which was quite low by European standards. In contrast to Scotland, Wales and England, coal and iron resources were far less abundant and manufacturing in Ireland had been highly concentrated in the area that became Northern Ireland.[1] Manufacturing employment in the Irish Free State was heavily centred in the food and drink sectors, notably in Dublin, where large concerns such as Guinness and Jacobs Biscuits were well placed to service both the Irish and British markets. Dublin was the centre of activity in the 26 counties for non-traded industries such as construction, railway engineering and utility industries such as gas and electricity. Dublin and its neighbourhood accounted for over half of total industrial output in the new state by the end of the 1920s,[2] making it the only industrial centre of any consequence. This reflected the inherent advantages the capital enjoyed, such as a high population density, local access to services and its status as the major port in Ireland, in addition to acting as the central hub for the railway system. Dublin's cluster of industrial concerns could compete with British industry on equal terms, or alternatively were non-traded and thus sheltered from British competition.

Outside the capital the picture was more geographically diffused, with the food and drink sector also figuring prominently in the ports of Munster; this province accounted for 80 per cent of the labour force in the bacon curing and dairy processing sectors. The leading centre of the textile industry was in Co. Cork. Cork city was the location of the Ford factory, which began tractor production in 1919 and progressed to the production of motor cars in the early 1920s. Creameries were dispersed across dairying districts in particular to exploit the milk supply. A few industrial centres were scattered across the country; untypical examples include the coal mining industry at Castlecomer, a jute factory at Clara that produced bags and sacks, agricultural engineering in Wexford town, a carpet factory in Donegal and ship repairing in Cork harbour.[3] Somewhat more common and numerous were towns or villages that possessed a creamery, a malting plant, a woollen mill, a struggling brewery, distillery or grain mill that had seen better days. Some of these relics of the industrial revolution were still utilizing water-power only.

The economic environment was more difficult for most industrial concerns from 1920 onwards, as recessionary conditions set in throughout north-western Europe during that year.[4] Regime change, labour conflicts, political instability and economic downturn led to some significant industrial casualties. Following the end of the First World War, Kynoch's shut down their explosives plant in Arklow, relocating all its functions to Great Britain.[5] Distillers Company Ltd (DCL), the large UK distilling operation, owned two Irish plants at Dundalk and Phoenix Park, which were shut down following Irish independence, since fiscal autonomy for Ireland meant that spirit exports to Britain became liable for excise duties.[6] British forces targeted large numbers of creameries during the War of Independence. Another sector that experienced difficulties was the woollen sector. Between 1920 and 1921 the output of the top 20 woollen mills in the future Irish Free State fell from 4.9 million square yards to 2.3 million; a number of mills were damaged or destroyed in the political upheavals that occurred between 1918 and 1923.[7]

Nonetheless, an optimist view was held that independence would lead to a more prosperous phase of industrial development. Although full fiscal autonomy granted by the Treaty afforded the opportunity to the new government to utilize tariffs as a potential instrument for reviving and developing native industries, there was significant division among industrialists and the political elite on the merits of protectionism. While the newly established Department of Industry and Commerce was more favourably disposed to protectionist policies than other departments, on most issues it was subordinated to the more powerful Departments of Finance and Agriculture which were opposed to protectionism. However, the evidence gathered by the Fiscal Inquiry Committee shortly after independence revealed that there was a sizable lobby of industrialists (the great majority of witnesses) who favoured protection. Sectors supportive of protection included flour milling, confectionery, clothing, footwear, agricultural machinery, furniture, paper and printing, fertilizer and bottle manufacture. In general, larger, powerful export orientated companies such as Guinness, Jacobs and Fords favoured a continuation of free trade and they were backed by the banking and financial establishment, including the leading figures at the Departments of Finance and Agriculture. This alliance dominated industrial policy in the early days, but their influence diminished somewhat from the mid-1920s.

Despite a general adherence to orthodox free trade policies at the outset, the new Cumann na nGaedheal government cautiously introduced protection in certain industries as public opinion and political opposition to free trade gathered momentum during the 1920s. In the 1924 and 1925 budgets, tariffs were levied on footwear, furniture, confectionery, cocoa preparations, table water, glass bottles, soap and candles, clothing and blankets. From 1926 to 1931, tariffs were introduced on oatmeal, margarine, woollen piece goods, down quilts, butter, harness leather and harness. Although the government's claim that 60 per cent of non-agricultural imports were subjected to tariffs by the end of the 1920s was probably an exaggeration, it does indicate that and tariffs were already becoming a notable feature of the Irish economic landscape.[8]

A growing number of large British industrial companies were operating plants in the Irish Free State, so that by the end of the 1920s they held significant market share in their respective sectors. Wills, for example, had already secured a dominant share of the market for cigarettes in Ireland prior to independence (due largely to the low cost of Woodbine, its cheapest brand). To avoid import duties when the new state was established, Wills opened its first manufacturing plant in Ireland at Marrowbone Lane in Dublin in 1923. Players entered the Irish market in the following year, establishing a factory at Glasnevin. For the same reasons, Gallaher's built a new factory in Dublin in 1929. In the same year, Wills formed an alliance with William Clarke & Sons, who had also just built a new factory on the South Circular Road in Dublin, where Wills relocated their Irish output. Wills went to great lengths to defend their share of the market for cigarettes in the new state.[9] Employment growth in the tobacco industry was one of the early success stories resulting from fiscal autonomy, but much of this expansion was provided by British firms.

In some industries, such shoe making where a tariff of 15 per cent was imposed on imports, there was only limited expansion. Initial success by Irish manufacturers in expanding the sale of heavy boots and agricultural footwear production was not replicated in lighter and more fashionable shoes where British companies absorbed the tariffs and continued to supply the Irish market from British-based factories. British imports of lighter shoes still accounted for 89 per cent of consumption by 1929.[10]

Irish flour milling was contracting in the face of British competition and the government was unsympathetic to demands for tariffs from Irish millers. Ranks, one of the major British millers, was instrumental in implementing flour production quotas in both Britain and Ireland. This fixed prices across the industry, increasing profits for millers. Ranks acquired a significant share of the Irish industry in the early 1930s, through the purchase of large mills in Cork and Limerick.[11] Other sectors of the food industry attracted interest from British firms; in confectionery for example, Crosse and Blackwell, Clarnico, Murray and Rowntree-Mackintosh accounted for over half of Irish output by the end of the 1920s. At the same time, the Lever Brothers combine held a dominant position in the Irish soap industry, while the British Portland Cement Company took over and subsequently closed the only surviving Irish cement works in 1925, continuing to supply its southern Irish customers from British based plants.[12]

The Department of Industry and Commerce estimated that employment in protected industries increased by 5,300 between 1926 and 1929, while employment fell in non-protected industries.[13] The state's official handbook argued in the early 1930s that there had unquestionably been an expansion of employment in protected industries, most notably in industries connected with clothing, but also tobacco, sugar confectionery and furniture. It was noted that 'over a hundred new factories have been opened in these [protected] industries, and many of the old factories had been enlarged and improved.'[14] But some industries experienced additional difficulties as a consequence of policies implemented by Cumann na nGaedheal. The government favoured indirect taxation as a means of raising revenue; in one example beer duties were retained at the war-time level of 100/- a barrel.[15] This led to a decline in sales of the principal breweries including Guinness and Murphy's.[16] Yet such adversity encouraged innovation, uncharacteristic of Irish indigenous industry; Murphy's and Beamish and Crawford placed innovative graphic-based advertisements in the press from 1925. Murphy's newspaper advertisements accompanied their earlier billboard advertisements in sports grounds and their curtain advertisements at cinemas and theatres.[17] In the case of Guinness, it was increased competition in their crucial British export market that prompted the adoption of innovative marketing techniques. In Scotland, Guinness commenced their distinctive advertising campaigns with the 'Guinness is good for you' slogan. English press advertisements commenced in 1929. These measures increased Guinness sales in Britain by 13.8 per cent between 1929 and 1930. However, Guinness Irish sales continued to decline, and the company increasingly focused on maintaining British market share rather than investing any effort in the Irish market where it enjoyed a monopoly in most of country.[18]

Distilling was also badly affected by increased government duties in these years; Locke's in Kilbeggan ceased distilling briefly in the early 1920s, with a more long-term suspension of production between 1924 and 1931. If the new state questioned the moral legitimacy of this industry, ultimately the significant revenue it generated was deemed to be a far more important concern than its future development or survival. High duties and recessionary conditions brought the industry to its knees in the decades after independence.[19] Another important sector that was adversely affected by government policy was the indigenous fertilizer industry. With the decline in the tillage farming, the demand for fertilizers was reduced, while domestic fertilizer producers also suffered increased competition from imports, which accounted for about a quarter of purchases between 1924 and 1931. The principal fertilizer producer in the Free State was W. & H. Goulding, who operated six factories; two in Dublin, and one each in Cork, Waterford, Drogheda and Wicklow, accounting for 41 per cent of fertilizer sales in the state.[20]

Despite a professed commitment to laissez-faire, the government intervened to rationalize the ailing creamery industry, where an excessive number of creameries had been established in areas with plentiful milk supplies. The Dairy Disposal Company (DDC) was established in 1927 to purchase, and ultimately close a number of private-owned creameries. The Condensed Milk Company accounted for 114 of the 180 private concerns and the purchase of this by the DDC was a vital element in the strategy.[21] Sugar beet cultivation and processing was sector that owed its existence to government intervention. In 1926, the Belgian firm of Lippens opened a sugar beet processing plant in Carlow, but despite generous government subsidies, the company was already experiencing difficulties by the early 1930s.[22]

The most significant government intervention in the industrial sector was the establishment of electrical generation and distribution; a large hydro-electrical generating plant was constructed at Ardnacrusha on the Shannon just north of Limerick. In the absence of willing private sector investment in electrical distribution, the government also established the ESB in 1927, which marked the birth of the national grid.[23] The Shannon Scheme allowed for an increase in national energy output from 35 million kilowatt hours in 1924 to 163 million kilowatt hours in 1932.[24] But it was only possible to connect households in urban centres with upwards of 500 persons, in addition to a few villages, farms and households that were adjacent to power lines.[25]

While concessions were made to some industries seeking protection, the position of traditional export-orientated industries and British companies with Irish market share was defended by the desire of the government to maintain trade relations with Britain, which remained the principal market for Irish exports. However, the onset of the Great Depression in 1929 and the resulting reduction in trade made the case for protectionism more compelling. When an increasingly protectionist British government passed the Customs Duties Act in the autumn of 1931, a similar act was subsequently passed by the Irish government; the long era of free trade that had prevailed in the British and Irish markets since the mid-nineteenth century came to an end. Although Cumann na nGaedhael hardly used the powers of this act, Fianna Fáil, who took office in 1932, fully utilized it.

Fianna Fáil's policy of full-scale industrial protectionism to create a larger industrial base and increase employment marked a departure from Cumann na nGaedhael's emphasis on agriculture. Fianna Fáil had some success in expanding industrial production. The Department of Industry and Commerce was elevated to the role of promoting industrial development, acquiring the power to impose tariffs; by 1936 there were 1,900 tariffs in operation in the Free State.[26] Seán Lemass, the new Minister for Industry and Commerce, was far more proactive and directive than his predecessor in promoting industrial development.

If protectionism formed the cornerstone of Fianna Fáil industrial policy, the new government also sought to dilute foreign ownership through the Control of Manufactures Acts passed in 1932 and 1934, which required companies without majority native shareholding to get a license, if criteria stipulated by the Department of Industry and Commerce were adhered to. The potential disadvantage of this policy was that it discouraged foreign investment and could consequently limit the diffusion of improved managerial and technical skills. The government quickly recognized this difficulty, and facilitated and even encouraged foreign investment, particularly in partnerships with native entrepreneurs. Ironically one of the consequences of accelerating protectionism was an increasing presence of British companies in the Irish industrial sector, which dominated flour milling, rubber and cement, while also having a significant presence in footwear, textiles, clothing, tanning, chemicals and confectionery. Large British companies such as Cadbury and Dunlop's built Irish plants because they were made aware that if they failed to do so they would lose their market share in the south of Ireland.

The new industrial programme of Fianna Fáil increased the government's share of economic activity as a number of state-owned companies were set up with varying degrees of success. The government supported the development of turf harvesting by hand to maintain rural employment. From 1933 onwards, 180 cooperative turf societies were established, while the Department of Industry and

Commerce set prices and quality standards for its production.[27] The Turf Development Board (TDB) was established in 1934, a semi-state corporate body organized on the same basis as the ESB. In the same year, a delegation was sent to study turf cultivation in both Russia and Germany, where mechanical methods were used to harvest turf, which was also used for the generation of electricity. In 1935, the TDB purchased the Turran Peat Works. The report of the delegation to Germany and Russia and the purchase of the Turran Peat Works resulted in the TDB changing its mandate from the promotion of hand cultivation to the creation of a mechanized turf harvesting industry. [28] The Irish Sugar Company was established in 1933, acquiring the Carlow Sugar Factory and subsequently building three new ones at Mallow, Thurles and Tuam; by 1938, the state produced 80 per cent of domestic sugar demand, displacing the bulk of sugar imports. A less successful state company was Chemici Teo (which produced industrial alcohol).

Although quotas and licenses were resorted to by the government to impose controls on certain industries and firms, most industrial development was carried out by private companies given favourable tariffs by the Department of Industry and Commerce to reduce foreign competition.[29] Tariffs were granted in any instance where it could be reasonably argued that an Irish manufacturer could eliminate imports. Import substitution generated monopoly profits for Irish industrialists and led to an expansion of industrial employment; this was the major positive consequence of protectionism in the short term.[30] Protectionism led to expansion of the Irish textile, clothing and footwear industries in particular, in addition to flour milling, which had all suffered in the past from strong British competition. These sectors now experienced expansion, frequently with significant British investment and expertise. In the short term, the new policy expanded employment in both industry and services, which were greater than the losses sustained in agriculture. But the limits of import substitution had already been reached by the end of the 1930s. The small scale Irish domestic market became saturated with domestically produced goods. The scope for further industrialization on the basis of domestic demand was therefore limited; exportation was required. In addition, the industrialization drive was largely dependant on imported raw materials and machinery, which undermined the aspiration to achieve self-sufficiency. Moreover, the Anglo Irish Trade Agreement in 1938 improved access to the Irish market for British industrial goods.[31]

Meenan argued that one of the flaws of the protectionist industrial drive was that insufficient emphasis was placed on encouraging industries that sourced inputs from within the Irish economy, especially agricultural inputs.[32] This criticism was not entirely correct; Fianna Fáil insisted for example that footwear factories source local supplies of leather in an effort to revive the tanning industry, although native leather was still more expensive and of poorer quality than imported leather.[33] Between 1936 and 1939, the North Cork Dairy Co-operative established a manufacturing plant for casein (produced from skimmed milk), which eliminated casein imports.[34] The Irish fertilizer industry benefited due to the government-sponsored promotion of tillage and the imposition of tariffs on imported fertilizers.[35]

The creamery system expanded in isolated parts of the south and west, including the Dingle and Beara Peninsulas and Clare under the aegis of the DDC. The operation of travelling creameries (centrifugal separators transported in lorries) made creamery butter production economically viable in such regions.[36] Another significant development in the dairy sector was the beginnings of industrial-scale cheese manufacturing, assisted by the prohibition on cheese imports. The Mitchelstown Co-op obtained the sole license for the manufacture of processed cheese.[37] The Dungarvan Cooperative dramatically expanded throughput and diversified its product range in the 1930s through various acquisitions from the DDC all over Co. Waterford, and in 1936 developed a relationship with the UK-based company Cow and Gate, manufacturing their range of baby foods for the Irish market.[38] The expansion of native sugar production utilizing native beet as the raw material input is another example of industry that does not conform to Meenan's criticism.

One area that was especially affected by the deteriorating trading relationship between the Irish Free State and the United Kingdom was the brewing industry. Guinness became increasingly reliant on the British market, which accounted for 60 per cent of sales in 1933, at a time when demand for Guinness in the Irish Free State was steadily declining. At the outbreak of the Economic War, Guinness was fortunate that British duties were not imposed on Irish beer. However, a threat from the British Secretary of State for the Dominions in October 1932, that the British government would impose the special duty on Irish beer imports unless Guinness built a brewery in England, led to the construction of Park Royal in London. This led to a loss of 500 jobs at St. James' Gate. Surprisingly, Seán Lemass' reaction to Guinness' partial relocation, evident at his meeting with the managing director of Guinness, was muted.[39] The Economic War also had an adverse effect on the Ford plant in Cork, which ceased tractor manufacturing in 1932. This plant employed around 7,000 workers at the end of the 1920s,[40] briefly making it a larger employer than any of the large multinationals in Ireland today, but this facility was one of the casualties of the transition to protectionism. In 1932, it shifted production in the Cork plant from tractor manufacturing to car assembly for the domestic market, which employed far fewer workers. Generally, little progress was made in the establishment of capital good industries in these years.[41] One exception was the creation of a steel-producing factory at Haulbowline, Co. Cork, which commenced production in 1939.[42]

The industrial sector was more adversely affected by war-time disruption than agriculture. Ireland's dependence on Britain for industrial equipment and spare parts, raw materials, coal and petroleum became all too apparent, and industrial output experienced a significant decline during the war.[43] The volume of industrial production by 1942 was 25 per cent below what it had been in 1939. War induced shortages had a severe effect upon many industries, with a number of companies closing down and overall industrial productivity declining dramatically. In construction, for example, the number of houses completed annually declined from 12,300 in 1939 to 1,300 by 1945–46.[44] The footwear industry suffered from a shortage of imported inputs, such as polish, cardboard boxes and spare parts for machinery. Between 1939 and 1943, output in the footwear sector fell by 20 per cent.[45] The effective suspension of private motoring, due to fuel shortages, brought many cognate industries to a standstill. Production at the Ford Plant ceased for a four-year period.[46] Dunlop's, in contrast, resourcefully utilized salvaged rubber that provided them with sufficient raw material to at least manufacture bicycle tyres, which were in short supply and in big demand as other forms of transportation were curtailed.[47] Output at the Haulbowline Steel Plant was severely limited to 2,000 tons between 1939 and 1941 until the plant was placed in receivership.[48] New machinery and parts for many industries simply became impossible to acquire from Britain.

Some industries prospered during the war, as their products were in high demand in Britain or were then in demand in Ireland due to shortfalls in British supplies. In an attempt to make up the shortfall in coal supplies, for example, a number of Irish coal mines were expanded or reopened, including Arigna in Leitrim, Castlecomer in Kilkenny, Rossmore in Laois and the Slieveardagh mines in Tipperary. Although Irish coal mining output expanded during the war years, with all operational mines working at full capacity, coal output constituted a mere 4,000 tons a week, roughly the equivalent of the consumption of the Great Southern Railway alone. Certain commodities were especially sought after in the UK, notably Guinness and jute yarn from Goodbody's factory in Clara. Other Irish-produced industrial commodities exported to the UK included cheese, chocolate crumb, malt, cement, rubber, agricultural machinery, animal feeds, talc, glycerine, binder twine and cordage. Despite the contracting supply of British coal, it is apparent that the relevant British authorities desired that certain Irish creameries and food producing companies engaged in large export consignments to Britain should retain a full allocation of coal.[49] Dungarvan Co-op, through its association with Cow and Gate, was able to develop milk powder exports to the UK from 1941. Denny's and Clover Meats in Waterford city were able to service British and US army contracts, while Clover developed the Erinox Cube, which could be used during the war as convenient substitutes for both oxo cubes and tea, but these Waterford examples were exceptions as by and large the trade and industry of the port was severely restricted and unemployment prevailed.[50]

Since supplies of coal and other fuel for domestic and industrial purposes were drastically curtailed, turf began to assume greater importance in the fuel supply, especially for domestic purposes.[51] Peat briquette production commenced at the Lullymore factory in Co. Kildare in 1941 as part of the drive to substitute turf for imported coal. Output increased from 11,500 tons in 1941 to 17,900 tons by 1944. Briquettes were used as an additional fuel source by the railways and other priority industries, such as baking and distilling, during the war.[52] However, the bulk of the increased war-time supply was largely hand cut by large teams of young men, including soldiers. By 1942, the government had 26,000 people out on the bogs cutting turf. Great ricks of turf were built up along the roads in the Phoenix Park to supply Dublin; but since all this extra effort was insufficient to meet demand, by 1943 turf had to be rationed to half a ton a month per household. The

Table 4.1 Distribution of employment in transportable goods sectors, 1929–47

Sector	*1926*	*1929*	*1931*	*1938*	*1941*	*1944*	*1947*
Food, drink and tobacco	27,495	27,716	28,007	31,673	31,022	30,831	34,634
Timber	2,776	2,601	2,283	3,610	3,596	4,172	4,016
Metals an engineering	3,804	6,889	4,661	11,526	8,872	8,141	13,353
Clothing and textiles	9,807	11,669	12,165	27,964	29,666	27,321	34,665
Printing and publishing	5,739	5,977	6,399	9,315	8,477	8,408	10,724
Chemicals and fertilisers	1,102	1,711	1,613	3,551	3,165	3,006	4,027
Mining and quarrying	1,233	1,470	1,655	2,455	2,031	3,484	3,402
Total	67,620	72,622	72,084	99,740	95,936	95,133	117,538

Source: *Census of industrial production 1926–29, 1931, 1938–44, 1945–47*, Dublin, Dept of Industry and Commerce, Statistics Branch.

more intensive exploitation of turf during the war years clearly influenced the subsequent development of the modern mechanized turf industry.[53]

The share of industrial output accounting for clothing and textiles increased, as a consequence of the shift to protectionist policies from 1932.[54] The employment gains from the growth in textiles and clothing were significant in the 1930s and immediately after the Second World War, so that by 1947, textiles and clothing employed as many people as the food and drink sector. There had also been a modest expansion in employment in the food and drink sector, which also benefited from protectionist measures (see Table 4.1).

By the mid-1950s, T. K. Whitaker, who drew attention to the very low level of investment and capital formation in the industrial sector, nonetheless conceded that some progress had been made 'in the processing and canning of beef, ham and other vegetables'.[55] However, it should be noted that employment gains registered by the Census of Industrial Production exaggerate gains due to the expanding coverage of the census since independence. Fitzgerald has revealed far more modest employment growth rates in industry between 1926 and 1957 from the Population Census figures.[56] The performance of the industrial sector overall between 1949 and 1958 remained relatively dismal, with the volume of industrial output expanding by a mere 23 per cent in these years, compared a figure of 73 per cent achieved by all OEEC countries.[57]

The drive for greater self sufficiency in the inter-war years, and the need for greater energy security, which became starkly apparent during the Second World War, provided incentives to further develop hydro-electric generating capacity on the Liffey at Leixlip and at Poulaphouca, Co. Wicklow. These were brought into operation between 1944 and 1947; the Erne station came into operation in 1950 and Iniscarra in Co. Cork in 1957.[58] In 1946, the TDB was succeeded by Bord na Móna, which commenced the mechanized harvesting of turf, chiefly in the midlands. Turf was used to supply a new range of power generating stations, constructed during the 1950s and 1960s.[59] In terms of contribution to industrial activity, the share of net industrial output accounted for by turf processing averaged between 2 and 3 per cent between the 1950s and 1970s. The turf sector accounted for a similar percentage of industrial employment. While the harvesting of turf provided a valuable source of energy and contributed to expanding industrial employment in the midlands and west of Ireland where industrial employment was scarce, limited supplies prevented dynamic growth in this sector and provided further evidence of the scant contribution of natural resources to Irish economic development. Moreover, the ESB were particularly unhappy at paying artificially high prices for turf supplies. This became contentious in the 1960s, when the price of oil fell relative to turf. The dramatic expansion of demand in the 1960s could not be met by hydro or turf, and with increased oil supplies globally and reduced costs, oil fired stations became a far more economic and reliable solution to expanding supply.[60]

The growing importance of oil in the expanding demand for energy (notably as a consequence of increased car ownership), was apparent in the decision taken in June 1957 to establish the Irish Refining Company Ltd at Whitegate, Co. Cork, undertaken by a consortium of major international oil companies. This important project, which got underway at the cusp of a major shift in industrial development policy, was in many ways symptomatic of the changing attitudes to direct foreign investment. This investment was the largest sum yet invested in the state in a single private enterprise. In contrast to future foreign investment (which was export orientated), the extensive capital investment in this refinery (with a capacity of 2 million tonnes) was to service expanding domestic demand for petroleum products.[61] Cheap imported oil made the economics of generating from peat look increasingly anachronistic, particularly for the ESB who had to absorb the extra costs and logistical problems with this source of native energy.

By 1974, only 26 per cent of electricity generated in the state was derived from peat; 10 per cent of electricity generated still came from hydro, and oil at this point accounted for 64 per cent of the total, reflecting a dramatic shift in generating capacity and increasing dependence on this source of imported fuel.[62] Fortunately, another indigenous energy source appeared during the 1970s when natural gas was discovered in the Kinsale gasfield.[63] This was utilized for electricity generation; gas-fired generating stations were constructed at Marina and Aghada in the late 1970s, thus again increasing generation from indigenous fuel, and reducing the cost of imports,[64] assisting both the balance of trade and balance of payments.

In general the scope for protectionist measures to expand industrial employment had reached its limits by the Second World War and industrial employment actually contracted between 1946 and 1951. Protected industries were unable to take advantage of the gradual re-opening of export markets in the aftermath of the

Second World War. However, some favourable developments took place in food processing. Meat processing began to develop as favourable price trends led to the export of chilled meat to the US. However, the large-scale development of the slaughter industry was hindered by British agricultural policy. The subsidy paid by the British government on cattle fattened on British farms, led many Irish farmers to export live cattle to Britain rather than slaughter them in Ireland.[65] The terms of the Anglo-Irish Trade Agreement of 1948 discriminated against meat exports.[66] Following the Second World War, milk and sugar supplies in the UK were limited and a number of chocolate manufacturers there sought to make up the shortfall by sourcing inputs in Ireland. The creamery in Rathmore, Co. Kerry, for example, co-operated with Cadbury's to establish a large-scale chocolate crumb processing facility that commenced production in 1948; chocolate crumb production increased from 4,100 tons in 1948, to 14,350 tons by 1956. The Rathmore factory utilized milk supplies from a wide radius, while sugar beet from Mallow was also an important input.[67]

Another example of a joint venture within the sector was the formation of the Miloko co-operative society in 1951, which also produced chocolate crumb to supply Terrys, Shuttleworths, Mackintosh and Rowntree. Based in Carrick-on-Suir, the Miloko Society was a joint venture between 38 co-operative societies in the south-east and British investors, and production continued until 1974.[68] Cheese production also expanded. The context for changes in the dairying sector was the financial burden of subsidizing butter exportation. In 1958, the government decided that only two-thirds of butter subsidies would be funded by the exchequer; the remaining one-third would be funded by the dairy industry. Cheese production increased 11-fold between 1958 and 1967, while grading was introduced for cheese exports in 1966.[69] Other forms of diversification included skim milk powder and milk replacement feeds for calves.[70]

Through An Bord Bainne, the state had already become actively involved in marketing butter, launching the highly successful Kerrygold butter brand in 1962, which became an exemplar in marketing strategy. Exports to the UK were greatly assisted by the increase in the Irish butter quota in the British market as a consequence of the Anglo-Irish Trade Agreement in 1965; they were 10 times greater in 1972 than they had been in 1960. However, with entry into the EEC, An Bord Bainne was reconstituted as a co-operative since it effectively had a marketing monopoly for butter exports. It now sought to improve its distributing capabilities through acquisitions and distribution agreements in Britain, Europe and further afield.[71] National milk output rose from 480 million gallons in 1960 to 740 million gallons in 1973, partly as a consequence of government supports. The 1960s also witnessed the beginnings of rationalization within the creamery sector. Creamery units, numbering 192 in 1966, had been reduced to just 46 by 1978. Six major co-operatives emerged from this wave of amalgamations; Waterford, Mitchelstown, Ballyclough, Golden Vale, Avonmore and Kerry.[72] The Kerry group had its origins in the North Kerry Co-operative Creameries, which built a casein factory at Listowel. This plant came into production in the summer 1972; the capital was put up by both state organizations and private interests, and much of the product was exported to the US. Subsequently, Kerry Co-operative Creameries Ltd took over the local assets of the DDC thus amalgamating and rationalizing the dairy industry in Kerry. This transformation of agriculture and food processing in Kerry and the consequent increase in the demand for milk in the 1970s[73] was symptomatic of the general transition underway in Irish agriculture and food processing in these years.

New departures were already apparent in other areas in the food and drink industry in the 1960s, assisted to some extent by the general rise in living standards. The distilling industry had become over dependent on the home market. Several factors militated against the recovery of the export trade from the 1920s, which limited the industry's potential development; these included restrictions on exports by the state, which was more concerned by the industry's revenue generating potential. Amalgamation took place in 1966 when all three of the surviving distillers (Cork Distilleries Company, John Jameson & Son, and John Power & Sons) formed the United Distillers of Ireland, which later became Irish Distillers Group, and thereafter more emphasis was placed on advertising and marketing and sales improved somewhat. An entirely new distilling plant was built in Midleton, Co. Cork and the older plants were shut down, thus centralizing production in an area where the principal raw materials had traditionally been excellent for distilling purposes.[74]

Mining experienced moderate development in the post-war era. War-time shortages had stimulated production, with the state backed excavation of pyrites at Avoca, Co. Wicklow. This was accompanied by the mining of lead and zinc in locations such as Glendalough in Co. Wicklow Silvermines in Co. Tipperary and Abbeytown in Co. Sligo. Post-war developments in geological survey methods revealed mineral deposits in many locations and the industry was further stimulated by a range of income and corporation tax incentives introduced from 1956. This led to the excavation of minerals such as lead, zinc, copper and silver from a range of mines. Consequently, the contribution made by mining and quarrying to net industrial output increased substantially in both absolute and percentage terms, with an especially sharp increase during the late 1960s and early 1970s. However, employment growth in this sector did not match the growth of net output. Mining activity peaked in the 1970s; tax relief on mining profits was abolished by the coalition government in 1973, while fluctuations in world prices and the exhaustion of many deposits prevented the sector from making a more sustained contribution to Irish industrial development thereafter.[75]

The increased use of fertilizers in the post-war period assisted the expansion of sales. Goulding's remained the largest company, accounting for more than 50 per cent of Irish fertilizer sales in 1972. At this stage, the original firm of W. & H.M. Goulding was the holding company for an unwieldy range of firms. Goulding Chemicals continued to invest in phosphate-based chemicals, despite the general shift in demand from phosphate to nitrogen-based fertilizers. The semi-state company Ńitrigin Éireann Teo (NET), which operated a nitrogen-based fertilizer plant in Arklow from 1965, was more responsive to this new trend.[76] This was one of the last of the major wave of state industrial initiatives, which had been such a characteristic feature of the economy since the 1930s; the continued investment in the Irish Steel plant in Cork provides another example of continued protectionist influences, despite the advent of more open trading policies from the late 1950s.[77]

The decreased reliance on domestic demand by Irish industry was not achieved instantaneously. As late as 1970, about 73 per cent of manufacturing output was sold on the home market and much of it still remained protected by tariffs. Despite a range of regional policies instigated to disperse industrial employment, about 46 per cent of industrial jobs were still concentrated in the Dublin region by the 1970s.[78] Decades of protectionism had not therefore altered this geographical concentration of manufacturing in and around Dublin since the first quarter of the twentieth century. The greater population density of the Dublin region still dictated the concentration of industry in the region. Average plant size in Ireland had increased fairly marginally during the protectionist era and was low by European standards in the late 1950s; but establishment size increased more rapidly during the 1960s as industrial policy became more export orientated and the Control of Manufactures Acts were eased and then abolished.[79]

Foreign capital dominated new investment in export-orientated industries in particular in the 1960s, but this did not always lead directly to optimal forms of development. In mining for example, where capital investment was predominantly from North American companies, most of the minerals were merely exported with little or no processing. This generated few benefits to the Irish economy other than mining employment, and frequently these investments had damaging environmental consequences. Even in manufacturing, where foreign enterprises were engaged in metals, engineering, food and drink, clothing, pharma and chemicals, it was noted that the jobs provided tended to be largely unskilled and there were few inter-industry linkages. Skilled managers were generally brought in. On the positive side, foreign investment accounted for the bulk of new jobs between 1958 and 1971, reducing emigration. They paid higher wages than indigenous industries and diversified economic activity away from the traditional dependence on agriculture, while also improving Irish trade performance.[80]

Growth in manufacturing employment surged from less than 2 per cent in the 1950s to 20 per cent in the 1960s. But by 1973, foreign firms still only accounted for 22 per cent of manufacturing employment; 43 per cent of this was in British plants and 27 per cent in American.[81] British firms, who had maintained a strong presence in the Irish economy during the protectionist era, continued to be significant employers in the 1960s. They were accompanied by the establishment of a number of German firms, including Liebherr Cranes, located in Killarney, and the leading pencil manufacturer, Faber-Castell in Fermoy. A number of firms from the US also began to invest in Ireland; General Electric established subsidiaries in Shannon and Dundalk. Pfizers made their initial investment in Ringaskiddy in 1969.[82] This period of industrial growth witnessed the expansion of the existing industrial base due to trade liberalization in the 1960s and increased foreign investment, and the introduction of a number of advanced new industrial processes, in chemicals, metals and engineering.

Table 4.2 Value of transportable goods net output (£m) for three-year intervals, 1951–72

Sector	*1951*	*1954*	*1957*	*1960*	*1963*	*1966*	*1969*	*1972*
Food	27.3	35.6	37.7	45.4	60.7	78.6	111.2	174.4
Timber and furniture	2.2	3.9	3.5	3.9	5.9	7.4	10.6	15.5
Metals and engineering	5.9	10.7	12.8	18.8	29.0	43.2	69.0	94.9
Clothing and textiles	14.2	17.7	18.8	25.5	34.5	42.8	65.0	85.8
Printing and publishing	6.8	8.1	9.5	9.1	15.4	19.4	28.8	45.6
Chemicals and fertilisers	2.2	3.5	4.2	5.8	9.0	15.0	28.6	40.5
Mining and quarrying	1.6	2.4	2.6	3.4	4.4	9.6	21.4	28.0
Turf	–	2.0	3.1	3.1	4.5	5.1	9.4	10.8

Source: *Statistical abstract 1954, 1957, 1961, 1963, 1965, 1970–71 and 1975*, Dublin, CSO.

The significant growth in output of the food sector and in clothing and textiles indicates that traditional industries also experienced growth in the 1960s and that rising living standards increased demand. Moreover, access to the British market improved in the 1960s, with 59 per cent of manufactured exports for the period 1959 to 1970 destined for the UK market. While UK companies contributed only about 29 per cent of foreign investment in industrial enterprises, they still accounted for 44 per cent of all new industrial projects, and it seems probable that food, textiles and clothing figured strongly here. Food processing was the only industry where the linkages between old established and new industries were strong.[83] This probably reflects Ireland's continued comparative advantage in this area and it was still the largest sector in 1972, even though some of the new industries had experienced more rapid growth from a very low base in the 1950s. The native industrial sector experienced an Indian summer in the 1960s as the expansion of consumer demand stimulated growth. Older sectors, such as clothing, footwear and textiles and food processing, experienced growth. Net industrial output and industrial employment experienced substantial growth in the 1960s.

In terms of output and employment, the food and drink sector, together with textiles remained the most important sectors throughout the 1950s and 1960s, reflecting the continued importance of domestic demand (see Table 4.2 and 4.3). However, metals and engineering experienced more dramatic growth. Employment and manufacturing output continued to increase in Ireland following EEC entry, which resulted in significant inward investment by firms wishing to gain access to the European market. This led to low-productivity traditional industries gradually giving way towards high-productivity modern industries.[84] By 1981, foreign firms

Table 4.3 Distribution of employment in transportable goods sectors at three-year intervals, 1951–72

Sector	*1951*	*1954*	*1957*	*1960*	*1963*	*1966*	*1969*	*1972*
Food	42,038	35,630	37,671	44,694	49,022	49,683	53,156	52,510
Timber and furniture	8,776	7,478	7,395	6,839	7,668	7,716	7,972	8100
Metals and engineering	12,022	10,653	12,800	24,101	30,237	33,152	37,760	41,390
Clothing and textiles	39,457	41,287	18,752	44,048	46,763	46,656	52,770	46,880
Printing and publishing	12,343	8,091	9,451	10,743	14,908	14,522	15,990	16,650
Chemicals and fertilisers	4,369	3,493	4,188	5,361	5,837	6,727	7,775	8,540
Mining and quarrying	3,444	3,866	4,086	4,084	4,420	4,959	5,870	6145
Turf	–	4,404	4,656	5,168	5,113	5,150	4,731	4500

Source: *Statistical abstract 1954, 1957, 1961, 1963, 1965, 1970–71 and 1975*, Dublin, CSO.

accounted for 35 per cent of manufacturing employment and US firms at this point accounted for 42 per cent of foreign sector employment; Ireland became attractive to American firms in this period as a location within the EEC, which was English speaking, broadly pro-American with strong links there culturally, combined with political stability.[85] To these attractions could be added low taxes for foreign corporations, a relatively light regulatory environment and a relatively generous array of grants and additional incentives provided by the IDA.

Irish industry was also characterized by a high level of employment creation *and* employment loss more comparable to the US than other EU member states. Between 1972 and 2006, when disaggregated by nationality, UK-owned firms experienced a net employment decline, indigenous industry showed little net employment creation, while US firms exhibited the highest gross job creation figures and the highest net employment change.[86] Another notable feature of Irish industrial development in this period was the increased export orientation of industrial output; industrial exports as a percentage of industrial output increased from 10 per cent in 1965 to 70 per cent by 1995. This development was encouraged by the gradual adoption of free trade and activist trade promotion policies by the government, which led to the evolution of a highly dualistic industrial structure composed of efficient-export orientated firms co-existing with less efficient firms servicing the domestic market.[87]

EEC entry in 1973 and the final removal of tariffs by 1978 created major problems for non-food based traditional sectors. Imports, which competed with domestic industrial produce, steadily increased during the 1960s and 1970s, with the once dominant textiles, clothing and furniture sectors being particularly adversely affected.[88] The recession of the 1980s delivered a fatal blow to a number of long standing industries in Ireland, both native and foreign. Prominent victims included Dunlop's and the iconic Ford plant in Cork City.[89] Traditional firms that survived lagged in performance behind the high and medium technology sectors. Despite the revival in Irish indigenous industry after 1987, clothing, textiles and tobacco did not expand.[90] Productivity growth rates in textiles and clothing were below the industrial average for the period 1995 to 2003. Prominent casualties included the Fruit of the Loom plant in Buncrana, which closed in 2006.[91] Another example of a sector adversely affected by the adoption of free trade was footwear. The demand for Irish produced footwear collapsed, leading to the closure of a number of footwear plants.[92]

Some sectors of traditional industry survived the transition to free trade; glass and cement were largely immune to import penetration due to the bulk nature of their output. A number of indigenous firms prospered such as Smurfit and Cement Roadstone, who expanded their operations internationally. However, this did not stimulate manufacturing in Ireland to any extent.[93] The food and drink sector remained important, though some older firms collapsed, such as Ranks mills and Lunhams (who processed pig meat) in Cork. These firms, according to Brunt, suffered from increased competition and poor product development activity.[94] The brewing sector benefited in part from foreign capital and expertise; Murphy's in Cork was purchased by Heineken in 1983. Heineken invested substantially in the Lady's Well Brewery and commenced sustained exportation.[95]

Food processing benefited from EEC assistance. The Department of Agriculture and the IDA co-ordinated grant applications from this sector, with meat processing and cold storage in particular taking advantage of this, while the creamery sectors share was utilized to assist further amalgamation.[96] The dairy industry faced particular difficulties with the introduction of milk quotas in 1984, but the resulting milk supply shock led Kerry and Avonmore to devise a new corporate strategy, based on diversification out of milk, and entry into the consumer food market and internationalization, which ultimately provided far greater opportunities. This commenced for Kerry in 1986 when the Kerry Group ceased to be a co-op and was launched as a publicly owned multinational company; this flotation raising about £7.5 million in capital. The company diversified and began to compete more effectively in the world market. Kerry's transformation from a dairy co-operative engaged in commodity processing to an international food conglomerate was one of the major indigenous success stories of that era.[97]

The Waterford Co-op expanded its activities by introducing yoghurt to the Irish market in 1974, in co-operation with French interests, while Avonmore concentrated on liquid milk production. In 1997, these two groups amalgamated into Glanbia, which subsequently became one of the largest diary processing enterprises globally. By 1990 the five largest co-ops, who then accounted for three-quarters of total turnover, had pursued expansion through diversification in Ireland and acquisition abroad, notably in the food ingredient sector in the UK, US and Europe. As a consequence of Kerry Group acquisitions for example, only 26 per cent of its turnover was generated in Ireland by 1998, and less than 10 per cent came from dairy products.[98] Moreover, by 1990, four of the six largest co-ops had followed Kerry's initial example and gone public, adopting a plc structure, while the other two (Ballyclough and Mitchelstown) amalgamated into Dairygold. In many respects this spate of corporate reorganization, diversification and greater internationalization was the response to limitations imposed by the implementation of the milk production quotas by the EEC in 1984. Kerry made the transition from operating in a low margin zone making food commodities at the bottom of the food pyramid, to operating a host of ingredient companies operating closer to the top in terms of value added. Through the acquisition of Beatreme in the US in particular, Kerry became the premier supplier of speciality food ingredients in that market. This was followed up by a series of acquisitions of food companies in the UK, which enabled it to build a significant trade with the major multiples there and subsequently in Europe. By 1999 less than 17 per cent of the Kerry Groups operating profits were generated in Ireland.[99]

In contrast to the declining role of agriculture as a source of economic growth, food processing remained vitally important as a dynamic element within the economy. Indigenous firms accounted for 75 per cent of total employment in the food manufacturing sector in 2001, compared to 49 per cent for the economy as a whole, while also contributing 55 per cent of total Irish indigenous exports. The food, drink and tobacco sector still generated 6.4 per cent of GDP by 2004.[100] One of the major advantages of the food, drink and tobacco sector (at least that part of it with production facilities in Ireland) is that the great majority of materials purchased for production are produced in Ireland, in contrast to the pattern in most other areas of manufacturing so the backward linkages into the Irish economy have been greater.[101] In 2009, food and drink remained Ireland's most important indigenous industry, accounting for 6 per cent of GNP and 8 per cent of employment and the sector accounts for about half of indigenous manufacturing employment and 64 per cent of the manufactured exports of indigenous companies.[102]

Despite some successes in food processing, the most spectacular growth in the industrial sector during the Celtic Tiger years took place in the foreign sector (largely American) where total employment increased by over one third between 1993 and 2000. By 2000, foreign firms accounted for about 49 per cent of total manufacturing employment.[103] American investment in two industries dominated this phase of rapid growth: electronics/computers and chemicals/pharmaceuticals. The electronics sector expanded rapidly following Irish entry into the EEC. It was one of the industries targeted by the IDA for selective development. The early wave of electronics-based manufacturing was composed of large plants (predominantly foreign owned), producing components for electronic devices, which did not locate research and development facilities in Ireland and had few linkages with local suppliers.[104] A host of foreign firms arrived, who sought to use Ireland as a low cost location within the EEC following Irish entry, since labour costs and taxation were relatively low, and a host of other incentives were provided by the IDA to attract companies engaged in minicomputers, computer peripherals and subassemblies. But indigenous industrial development within the sector and research and development were extremely limited, and the majority of jobs provided by the early 1980s were in 'routine semiskilled assembly work', despite its hi-tech reputation.[105]

The initial wave of computer hardware investment was based on mini-computer production. But the development of the personal computer (PC) rendered this sector obsolete and all six mini-computer production plants closed. However, the IDA succeeded in attracting PC manufacturers, beginning with Apple in 1980. The growth of computer hardware manufacturing was accompanied by the establishment of firms such as Alps and Mitsumi, producing computer components. Computer manufacturing firms that invested in Ireland from the late 1980s, carried out greater research and development functions. When Intel built its European head quarters near Leixlip in 1989, which subsequently included a microprocessor wafer plant, a motherboard assembly and PC plant, a host of other computer companies followed suit. The more advanced nature of the new wave of electronic firms was reflected in their demand for more highly-skilled workers. Moreover, Irish companies emerged to supply inputs to these plants, such as technical support, sales, packaging and manuals. The significant growth and increasing importance of electronics and computers in this period was evident from the fact that the employment share of electrical and optical equipment in total manufacturing employment rose from less than 17 per cent to over 27 per cent between 1991 and 2000, while its share of gross industrial output rose from less than 19 per cent to almost 34 per cent. Ireland became a major centre of computer hardware production by the late 1990s, accounting for roughly a third of all European PC production.[106] Growth in Irish manufacturing was highly concentrated in multinational companies and within three specific sectors; chemicals, computers and electrical engineering, which collectively accounted for 40 per cent of Irish GDP growth in the 1990s, and even more than this towards the end of the decade.[107]

It has been argued that the high concentration of information technology-based industries in Ireland was a critical factor in explaining the recent boom. Crafts and Toniolo, for example, argue that the relatively low contribution of information technology industries to European economic activity led to lower labour productivity growth rates than the US. Ireland, they argue, was a European exception in this respect because of its greater ability to attract FDI engaged in Information and Computer Technology (ICT) production (largely for export), due to policies that were liberal and empathetic to FDI (including in particular low taxation and light regulation), enabling the Republic of Ireland to increase productivity growth to a greater degree than other European economies. This explains much of the catching up Ireland achieved in the 1990s.[108] Crafts argues that the expansion of information technology-based industries accounted for much of the 2.24 per cent total factor productivity contribution to the 2.99 per cent labour productivity growth rate experienced by the Irish economy per annum between 1990 and 2003.[109] Transfer pricing probably exaggerated the picture here somewhat.[110]

Moreover, by the mid-1990s, computer component manufacturers were locating away from Ireland to lower wage economies. By 2002, microcomputer companies were sourcing the great bulk of their components outside Ireland, notably in the

Far East.[111] The IDA took cognisance of this and ceased to attract further investment from computer component manufacturers. The computer hardware sector lost one-third of its employees between 2000 and 2004. Peak employment was also reached in the microcomputer assembly sector by 1998, declining thereafter as companies began to relocate to lower wage economies in central and eastern Europe, while component manufacture increasingly shifted to the Far East.

Electronics developed more intensive links with local input producers than other multinational companies in the 1990s. Even indigenous-owned electronic companies had higher export intensity (62.3 per cent) than all indigenous-owned industry (37.3 per cent), which was an indication of its competitiveness for much of the 1990s. But this changed rapidly; before the end of the decade many began to source a growing share of their components from low wage countries in eastern Europe or Asia, and many foreign electronic companies began to move out of Ireland. Employment in the electrical and electronic industry fell rapidly from about 50,000 jobs in 2001 to 31,900 by 2003.[112] Electronics, which had become the most important sector in terms of employment during the boom years, and remained so even up to 2007, experienced further contraction in that year, with major redundancies at the Dell plant in Limerick. Dell was one of the few computer hardware companies still engaged in mass production in Ireland.

Employment in software, research and development and cognate services such as supply chain management held up better, even expanding until to 2007; International Business Machines (IBM), for example, still employed over 3,700 people in its Irish division in Dublin. The historical emphasis on manufacturing for IBM globally had shifted to services at this point.[113] Ireland also had success in expanding the production of medical instruments and devices in the 1990s, which was less subject to economies of scale and quality was of greater consequence.[114] But these kinds of high-end industries were not as employment intensive as electronics, in which Ireland steadily lost ground to lower wage economies. Although many of the major firms engaged in computer hardware production ceased manufacturing activities in Ireland, with about one-third of jobs being lost in this sector between 2000 and 2004, a number of them expanded their investment in higher-end service activities, contributing to the rise in service sector exports. By 1998, Ireland already accounted for 30.7 per cent of the EU trade in computer and information services. The blurring of industry and service activity has increased in the last decade, disguising the successful emergence of multi-national and indigenous information technology services including software, Research and Development (R&D) and support services, partially accounting for the decline in industrial employment and the corresponding rise in relative importance of service employment and exports.[115]

Since 1956, when taxation on exports was removed, the far less labour-intensive pharmaceuticals sector has achieved a more consistent growth pattern than the ICT sector, notably following EEC entry in 1973 when access to the European market became an important attraction, combined with a range of other inducements made by the IDA who selected fine chemicals at this point as one of its special targets for development. The industry includes two major strands; one producing the major ingredients and the other blending these into drug products. The IDA's success in attracting Pfizer to invest in Ringaskiddy acted as the catalyst for other pharmaceutical firms to invest in Irish plants. Between 1975 and 1986, 10 drug substance companies, who produce the active components in drugs, located in Ireland, six of them in the Cork harbour area. The concentration of drug substance firms in this region (encouraged by the IDA) was partially due to the presence of adequate water supplies for production and waste disposal. However, from the mid-1980s onwards, new drug substance plants were more dispersed in location, many locating in Dublin, as the IDA relaxed its regional dispersal policy. Firms that produce finished drugs have not been as concentrated in terms of location, with major new centres emerging in Dublin, Mayo and Waterford.[116] From the 1960s until the 1990s, the drug substance plants imported inputs and were engaged in bulk manufacture with limited research and development activity.[117]

From the 1990s onwards, research and development activity for new drug products has increased in Ireland, more particularly in recent years, facilitated by the increased supply of scientific graduates and the introduction of tax credits for research and development (R&D), and the selective decentralization of some R&D functions by drug companies. However, little success has been achieved in attracting core research activities, notably the location of discovery laboratories where drug products are created, to Ireland, despite recent investment in scientific research and co-operation between Irish universities and international pharmaceutical companies. Multinational companies have further concentrated their most important R&D functions in core research centres, which are located in their home countries. Ireland does not host such research centres despite government aspirations to attract such facilities.[118]

The chemicals, chemical products and man-made fibres sector expanded significantly during the 1990s. The importance of pharmaceuticals to Irish exportation is indicated by the comparative advantage enjoyed by organic chemicals, pharmaceuticals and cosmetic exports.[119] The pharmaceutical sector is dominated by foreign ownership; only 7 per cent of total employment in pharmaceutical employment is generated by Irish-owned firms.[120] Pharmaceuticals continued to grow after 2001, when manufacturing employment in general was contracting, with relatively high labour costs in Ireland not being as important a negative factor as in electronics, but low corporation tax remained centrally important. Wyeth Medica in Newbridge, Co. Kildare consolidated the activities of 13 formulation plants throughout Europe (which were closed down) into this single plant as part of its restructuring. Pharma is now by far the most important industry in terms of net output, but not in terms of employment. However, it is superior to electronics in terms of added value, skill intensity or in terms of wage levels per employee. By 2005 it accounted for 5 per cent of total manufacturing employment, by far the highest in Europe, although the decline of other manufactures in the preceding years explains part of this impressive score. By 2006, Ireland's share of world pharmaceutical exports had grown to 6 per cent, leaving few doubts about its significance. Most of the profits generated in the pharma sector are repatriated from Ireland and again transfer pricing probably exaggerates its performance in terms of gross value added per person (with Ireland being double the EU 15 average in 2001),[121] but higher levels of FDI per head probably accounts for part of this divergence. Nonetheless, it seems likely that chemicals and pharmaceuticals will remain the principal industrial sector in the future, having accounted for 52.8 per cent of gross added value in the transportable goods sector in 2010, which reveals the increasingly concentrated nature of Irish industrial output in one sector.[122]

Although the history of the construction sector is inadequately covered in the historiography, it became a centrally important element in the spectacular growth of the economy during the Celtic Tiger period (notably its second phase roughly between 2000 and 2007) and its even more spectacular collapse in recent years. Construction expanded from the mid-1950s to the late 1970s as state expenditure on roads and school buildings increased. In the private sector factories and shopping centres were built, in addition to private residences (see Table 4.4). The contraction in house building in the 1980s, along with the decline in other branches of civil engineering, led to a marked decline in employment in the sector from 110,000 in 1980 to 70,000 by 1989.

EU structural funding and state funding for infrastructure contributed to a revival in the construction sectors during the 1990s. Urban renewal programmes assisted investment in urban housing, while consumer demand led to the construction of a number of new shopping centres. FDI led to the construction of major factories such as Intel at Leixlip and Wyeth Biopharma campus at Grange castle. Investment in roads continued, and residential housing construction expanded (see Table 4.4), encouraged by cheap and easy credit and a host of tax incentives to developers.[123] This unprecedented rise continued during the Celtic Tiger years, peaking in 2006. Although it remained high in the following year, housing completions declined dramatically and continually from 2008.

The unprecedented growth of the economy in the 1990s contributed to the major expansion of the construction sector, which experienced the highest rate of Gross Added Value (GVA) growth of any sector between 1995 and 2005. Sexton estimates that GVA growth in the construction sector was of the magnitude of 8.1 per cent per annum between 1995 and 2005, while employment growth ran at 9.9 per cent per annum.[124] A rise in living standards from the early 1990s and by the beginning of the twenty-first century and easy access to cheap credit witnessed the dramatic rise in approved loans from the equivalent of €1.7 billion in 1996 to €13.9 billion by 2007. Ireland entered the EMU in 2001 with its economy booming, and national interest rates were reduced to ECB rates, further accelerating construction demand.[125] Taxation policies in relation to property development had long favoured developers from the 1986 Urban Renewal Act. This provided stimulation to property investment and development from the early 1990s onwards through tax incentives and rates rebates for commercial and residential developments; this (section 23) was subsequently confined to designated areas from 1992. A host of similar concessions were subsequently advanced in relation to car parks, holiday homes in certain seaside resorts, hotels in which substantial amounts of the capital costs could be written off against income tax, and student accommodation (section 50), all of which brought a host of new investors into

Table 4.4 Total number of dwellings completed in Republic of Ireland, 1970–2010

Year	*Dwellings*
1970	13,887
1971	15,380
1972	21,572
1973	24,660
1974	26,256
1975	26,892
1976	24,000
1977	24,548
1978	25,444
1979	26,544
1980	27,785
1981	28,917
1982	26,798
1983	26,138
1984	24,944
1985	23,948
1986	22,680
1987	18,450
1988	15,654
1989	18,068
1990	19,539
1991	19,652
1992	22,464
1993	21,391
1994	26,863
1995	30,575
1996	33,725
1997	38,842
1998	42,349
1999	46,512
2000	49,812
2001	52,602
2002	57,695
2003	68,819
2004	76,954
2005	80,957
2006	93,419
2007	78,027
2008	51,724
2009	26,420
2010	14,602

Source: Department of Environment, Community and Local Government Housing Statistics, available from http://www.environ.ie/en/Publications/statisticsandregularPublications/housingstatistics/FileDownload,15293,en.xls (accessed 1 June 2012).

property development. Huge profits were made on land banks in Dublin with about half the value of houses in the middle of the boom often being accounted for by land costs; these inflated values were passed onto the high mortgages paid by purchasers, contributing to the high rental and living costs, which diminished the competitiveness of the economy in international terms.

Commercial development was even more lucrative. Much of the vast proceeds of these investments were subsequently invested in Britain, but also in Europe, the US and elsewhere. By 2005, Ireland had even overtaken the US as the largest foreign investor in UK commercial property. At home, by 1998 the demand for construction workers was still rising and, at 150,000 persons, employment in the industry was about double the figure in 1995. This rose further on the new wave of construction after the turn of the century to 280,000 persons by 2007, 30 per cent of whom were immigrants, providing further demand for accommodation and a virtuous circle for developers and landlords. The government failed to remove the tax incentives that contributed to the construction sector over heating.[126]

There was a gross imbalance relative to the rest of Europe in the scale and focus of Irish construction, with over 50 per cent of construction activity by 2007–08 in new residential dwellings. The share of gross national incomes at factor costs accounted for by the construction sector increased from 7.5 per cent in 2002 to 14.9 per cent by 2007.[127] In 2006, annual personnel costs in the Irish construction sector averaged at €49,300 per employee, the second highest figure in the EU in excess of the EU 27 average of €27,900 per employee.[128] By 2007, the Irish construction sector employed 270,000 persons, which accounted for over 47 per cent of those employed in the industrial sector as a whole, excluding those employed indirectly.[129] The annual value of the industry in 2007 at the peak of the housing bubble was €38.5 billion, or 21 per cent of GNP, at a time when the construction sector in many economies would have amounted to something in the region of 5 per cent of GNP.[130] This reveals how dependent the economy had become on construction.

The continued contraction of construction since 2007 has contributed significantly to the general contraction of the entire economy (with a fall in GDP of 11.3 per cent in 2009 alone). Housing completions, which stood at 14,602 by 2010, were at a level not experienced since Ireland entered the EEC.[131] Now there are numerous ghost estates in Ireland with many vacant or partially completed dwellings.[132] The expansion of the construction sector was not based on new demand but on inappropriate tax incentives. This has left a host of empty dwellings in places where there is no demand, many of which will never be occupied. These empty ghost estates provide a stark testament to the monumental misallocation of resources within the economy due to lack of adequate regulation and appropriate governance during the boom years.

Industrial employment and output in the state expanded in the two periods following major changes in policy; in the first phase over a brief period following the adoption of full scale protectionism from 1932, and then second in a more sustained fashion from the late 1950s, when a more outward-looking policy was adopted to boost export orientated industries. While the role of foreign capital in the improved performance of the Irish industrial sector from the 1960s onwards is widely recognized, the significance of British industrial companies from the protectionist era down to Irish entry into the EEC remains under-researched to date; more specificaly, the way in which the experience gained by the state in dealing with foreign companies on a case by case basis (which is more feasible in a small economy) may have had an influence on the evolution of development policies subsequently under more open conditions, which were to be extremely successful in underwriting much of the Republic's late industrialization from the 1960s onwards.

Industry's contribution to the economy broadly increased in the post-war era. Excluding construction, industry's share of gross value added at basic prices by 1997 was 33.1 per cent of total gross value added, which was extremely high by European standards; Ireland in this respect recorded the highest share in Europe (just marginally ahead of the Czech Republic and Norway). Subsequently, the relative significance of the manufacturing industry declined. By 2006, Ireland's share of GVA in industry had fallen significantly to 25 per cent so that by this stage it was falling closer into line with the general pattern in the rest of Europe.[133] Industrial production had become highly concentrated; Keating's estimates imply that the 34 largest multinational companies accounted for 16.4 per cent of Irish GDP in 1998. However, when GNP is used instead, this figure is dramatically reduced to 5.7 per cent, revealing the extent to which repatriated profits of these large companies significantly reduces their direct effects on the economy.[134]

The share of total employment accounted for by industry declined from 2001, as key areas in Irish manufacturing (electronics and computer hardware) became uncompetitive and multinationals relocated their production activities to low wage economies. This was more than offset temporarily by the growth of employment in construction. The sharp fall between 2007 and 2009 indicates the effect of the recent recession on industrial employment, most notably the dramatic exodus from the construction industry (see Table 9.1).

Slevin estimates that industry contributed to nearly half of GDP growth between 1962 and 2000, accounting for slightly over half in the second half of the 1990s when GDP growth rates were running at over 9 per cent.[135] While productivity growth in manufacturing was apparently high, O' Leary's sectoral productivity estimates indicate that high productivity gains were heavily concentrated within sectors dominated by multi-national companies, such as chemicals, and the extent of such gains were exaggerated by transfer pricing.[136] Sexton's disaggregation of manufacturing into 'traditional' and 'modern' sectors estimates that productivity in modern manufacturing increased by 9.4 per cent per annum between 1995 to 2005, while productivity in 'traditional' manufacturing increased by 4.3 per cent.[137] Although by 2006, employment in the foreign owned sector (153,510) was only marginally higher than indigenous firms (151,610), the yawning gap between them is apparent in their respective output values; the value for Irish firms stood at under 10 billion while the foreign sector was over 50 billion accounting for almost 84 per cent of total output.[138]

During the 1990s the Republic of Ireland attracted a disproportionately high share of FDI per capita within the EU, due to tax concessions and the proactive approach of the IDA in attracting individual investment projects. This is one of the reasons that the share of GDP accounted for by industry by 2003 was quite high by European standards. Ireland was one of the only European countries where manufacturing employment continued to expand in the 1990s.[139] By 2003 this expansion had stalled, and industries' share of GDP in Ireland has been contracting ever since. The tide was going out on electronics and computer hardware. The continued rapid expansion of construction and construction employment up until 2007 (based largely on borrowed money) offset the loss of jobs in manufacturing, in the short term at least. By 2006, employment in the bloated construction sector (then building houses and offices, which remain empty and derelict) had ballooned to a level that almost equalled employment in manufacturing industry. This kind of lopsided development was simply not sustainable in the longer term, and when this bubble finally burst in 2008, it dramatically accelerated the general decline of industrial employment thereafter and the general contraction of the economy as a whole. The increasing blurring between industry and services, notably among manufacturing companies engaged in internationalized manufacturing services, also accounts for part of the decline in manufacturing employment in the last decade, and a corresponding rise in the share of services in total employment in the economy.

5 From good haircuts to bad bankers

The services sector in the Irish economy

Services constitute all forms of economic activity that are not concerned with the production of physical output. Although this diverse range of activities accounted for just over a third of total employment in the economy in the 1920s, being much more important in this regard than industry, agricultural employment was still far more significant than service employment at that point. The services share has consistently expanded since then, with the exception of the 1950s, while conversely agricultural employment has experienced decline; by the 1980s services accounted for just over 51 per cent of total employment. By 2009, with over 74 per cent of the occupied workforce in services (see Table 9.1), the great bulk of employment in the Republic of Ireland economy was now in services, thus broadly following the historical pattern in most of western Europe, if at a somewhat slower pace. This chapter provides a historical survey of this highly eclectic range of economic activity on a sectoral basis, as opposed to the more chronological treatment followed in Chapters 3 and 4. This approach has been taken in order to capture both the wide spectrum of activity across the services sector as a whole and the central importance that services have assumed in the economy since independence, which has not always been fully recognized or appreciated by policy makers, economists and economic historians, who until recently have tended to attach far greater significance to industry and agriculture.

By independence, many core aspects of the services sector were reasonably well developed in European terms, including the transport and communications system, retailing and banking. In occupational terms, the two most important sources of employment in services were to be found in domestic service and retailing, followed someway behind by public administration and clerical work, hotel catering and bar work, and education and health (see Table 5.1).

As a consequence of regime change and British military withdrawal, a large source of expenditure transferred from the British exchequer was lost to the economy and this was reflected in the state of many of the old garrison towns that languished once British military expenditure ceased. Although this was offset in the short term by significant expenditure by the new state on the national army during the civil war, thereafter the size of the army was reduced to a level more affordable and appropriate for a peacetime democracy. Both the First World War and the political turmoil associated with the period 1919–23 had a particularly

Table 5.1 Distribution of service employment (by occupational sub-sector), 1926–66

Occupational group	*1926*	*1936*	*1946*	*1951*	*1961*	*1966*
Transport	45,973	46,831	40,230	49,254	41,713	45,553
Communications	18,900	22,212	18,949	23,391	14,954	12,924
Warehousing	6,935	9,853	10,716	15,956	20,111	22,293
Clerical staff	30,007	37,629	43,720	53,244	63,998	75,188
Sales and retail staff	87,985	88,111	81,277	92,568	88,882	91,833
Business and commercial	5,311	6,279	6,720	5,637	5,533	6,202
Scientific and technical	1,288	1,192	2,132	2,611	4,035	8,665
Health	11,383	12,768	16,961	18,779	21,317	22,857
Education	16,950	17,228	15,476	15,969	18,287	20,439
Legal	1,356	1,759	1,849	1,909	1,863	1,848
Hotel, bars and catering	24,999	25,035	26,749	26,025	32,765	38,308
Domestic service	93,738	92,959	84,811	64,563	38,376	31,740
Personal service	7,342	10,041	10,681	8,951	9,918	10,976
Sports, creative and entertainment	4,882	4,636	5,359	5,894	5,994	6,275
Public administration	37,333	30,840	42,867	31,502	30,943	31,756
Total	440,564	491,589	510,317	513,957	443,918	470,058

Source: *Census of population 1926, 1936 and 1946, Vol. II, occupations*, Dublin, Dept. of Industry and Commerce, Statistics Branch. *Census of population 1951, Vol. III Part 1, occupations; 1961, Vol. III, occupations; 1966, Vol. IV, occupations; 1971, Vol. IV, occupations; 1981 and 1986, Vol. VII, occupations,* Dublin, CSO.

disruptive effect on the transport network, and as a consequence, upon the economy. These years constituted a watershed in the history of Irish railways. The imposition of government wartime control from 1916 was not lifted until 15 August 1921, by which time the railways were facing a new set of challenges. Short-term problems included rising labour costs and strike action. In the long term, the rail network faced increased competition from road transport due to the widening use of the more flexible combustion engine; in the short term the rapidly rising cost of labour since the beginning of the First World War in a relatively labour intensive industry also posed major problems. These issues were compounded following the outbreak of civil war when the railways and road system became major targets for republican forces. By November 1922, one-third of the system of the largest rail company in the state, the Great Southern and Western

Railway, had been rendered inoperative by such attacks. The government had to give much attention to defending and maintaining the railways. The railways never received compensation for this loss of traffic, which further contributed to undermining the commercial viability of the railway network. Due to the significance of rail transport to the wider economy the government passed an act in 1924 to merge the existing 26 railway companies into a single company, Great Southern Railways (GSR). In 1932, the Minister for Industry and Commerce obtained the power to close uneconomic branch lines, while in 1933 the Railways Act reduced the value of capital in GSR and allowed for the further rationalization of branch lines.[1]

Despite these interventions the railways struggled to deal with the rapid proliferation of road traffic. Licensed road vehicles increased from 25,000 in 1925 to 49,000 in 1931. In the 1930s railway freight declined as road transport continued its relentless expansion, so by 1938 rail receipts reached their lowest level since 1922.[2] The Second World War witnessed a revival of rail freight services as petrol supplies were severely curtailed, despite the severe difficulties in acquiring British coal, the staple source of fuel for the railways.[3] In 1944, legislation was passed that merged the GSR and Dublin United Tramway Company into Coras Iompair Éireann (CIE). The new company inherited 2,000 miles of railway and a multitude of associated properties, including the Royal Canal; 500 locomotives, 800 carriages and 2,500 wagons; about 600 buses and 500 road vehicles; 300 horses and about 40 trams. It assumed responsibility for about 80 per cent of the state's transport services and over 21,000 employees, which made it the largest employer in the state. The poor condition of the rolling stock was made starkly evident by the Milne Report, which revealed that in 1948 only 9 per cent of locomotives were less than 20 years old, while the average age was 51 years. In the following years the system was converted to diesel and much of the obsolete rolling stock was scrapped. However, the company (which had been nationalized in 1950) was unable to operate without annual losses covered by the state. The Beddy Report (1957) acknowledged that in comparison with other continental European countries, Irish railways faced additional obstacles, excluding competition from road traffic. The Irish rail network for example did not enjoy the benefits of international through traffic, while demand for passenger services was reduced due to low and declining population density. Moreover, potential income from mineral traffic and industry were relatively more limited. The Beddy Report recommended a reduction in the network of 1,000 miles and the closure of 150 stations. Rationalization got underway in 1958, leading to a host of unpopular closures, while from 1964 the state accepted that the principle of subsidization was essential for the survival of the system.[4]

Rail freight began to increase again gradually from a low point in the mid-1950s until the recession of the early 1980s (see Table 5.2). Dublin suburban commuter traffic increased from the 1970s, justifying the subsequent investment in electrified train transport. This was embodied in the DART system, which opened in 1984. New inter city services with track upgrades were also undertaken, which led to subsequent increases in traffic. But leaving commuting aside,

Table 5.2 Railway lines and railway freight traffic at three-year intervals, 1945–2008

Year	*Railway line length (Km)*	*Freight traffic (million tons/Km)*
1948	3,927	409
1951	3,927	370
1954	3,642	309
1957	3,574	338
1960	2,911	332
1963	2,353	340
1966	2,342	412
1969	2,145	505
1972	2,190	564
1975	2,007	561
1978	1,894	620
1981	1,876	678
1984	1,872	600
1987	1,872	563
1990	1,872	588
1993	1,872	574
1996	1,872	569
1999	n/a	526
2002	n/a	426
2005	n/a	303
2008	n/a	103

Source: 1948–1975, B. R. Mitchell, *European historical statistics*, London, Macmillan, 1982, p. 614, 624. 1978–2008, *Statistical abstract 1981, 1987, 1989, 1993, 1997 and 2010*, Dublin, CSO.

by the mid-1980s cars had come to account for roughly 85 per cent of inland passenger transport; buses accounted for 12 per cent and rail a mere 4 per cent, while mainline rail then carried only 11 per cent of goods traffic. This trend was evident in the fact that the bulk of CIE's employees worked on buses, not trains, and the two functions were split in 1987 when CIE was restructured and split into Iarnrod Éireann and Bus Éireann.[5] Unsurprisingly, capital investment in transport has since concentrated on improving the road system; however, some expansion of the rail system occurred under the National Development Plan, with the introduction of the Light Rail Network (LUAS) to Dublin and additional investment in mainline routes.[6]

If rail has declined in significance since independence, the aviation industry in contrast has become an increasingly more important aspect of the service economy, which had important ramifications for other aspects of economic activity such as tourism and trade. With the establishment of a national airline, Aer Lingus in 1936 on the initiative of Seán Lemass, followed by the establishment of the airport authority, Aer Rianta in 1937, air services were initially confined to routes between Baldonnel military aerodrome and Great Britain. Dublin Airport was opened at its current site at Collinstown in 1940, which had also been a former British military airbase. The new iconic building that emerged on this rural site (designed by Desmond Fitzgerald, the brother of the Taoiseach-to-be) was one of few really fine pieces of modern architecture in the state during the 1940s and it stood as a great beacon to modernity in subsequent decades.[7] The site of the airport proliferated in scale through a sprawl of new facilities and buildings, not always with the same architectural elan as the first, although Terminal 2 has all the brash flare of the last days of Celtic Tiger. Dublin Airport now handles 60,000 passengers a day rising to 80,000 at peak periods and has long been a core hub within the service economy.

The distance limitations of the first generation of trans-Atlantic aircraft initially gave Ireland a strategic advantage on the European side of the Atlantic. In 1935, the British, Irish and Canadian governments agreed to establish an air base at Rineanna, Co. Clare, and a flying boat service was established at Foynes, Co. Limerick.[8] The danger to shipping during the Second World War opened up new opportunities there. Cross channel services were also in demand during the war and Aer Lingus made improvements to the airport infrastructure at Dublin, Shannon and Foynes. At Shannon after the war flight freedom rights were offered to Britain and other countries, which expanded business there dramatically,[9] including the opening of the world's first duty free airport shop by 1947.[10] Traffic volumes for passengers and freight increased in the following decades and a number of new routes were opened up, notably trans-Atlantic services from 1958. New European routes were also opened.

The fleet was extended and other airports commenced operations from the 1960s; Cork Airport was established in 1961, which was serviced by both Aer Lingus and various charter companies and it experienced rapid growth, with the number of passengers using the airport increasing from 77,649 in 1962 to 160,443 by 1966, exceeding all expectations.[11] Knock International Airport, situated in County Mayo, opened in 1985. Other regional airports were established at Sligo, Castlebar, Galway, Farranfore (Co. Kerry) and Waterford. The economic impact of airports was significant, in terms of direct service employment and sales on-site, and by attracting tourists into the catchment area.[12]

The cargo traffic handled by Aer Lingus rose steadily during the 1960s, reaching an all time peak (in terms of short tons) in 1973–74, for the period between establishment and 2001. The two major oil crises in 1973–74 and 1978–79 halted expansion in the aviation sector and created major financial problems for Aer Lingus. This coincided with the Troubles in Northern Ireland and major industrial relations disputes, although the adverse effect of these difficulties was offset to some extent by Aer Lingus' investments in a range of ancillary activities such as aircraft maintenance and hotels.[13] By the late 1970s, other Irish airline companies began to emerge. Both Aer Arann and Avair were established, opening up some new domestic routes. Aer Lingus' monopoly on external flights from Ireland ceased in 1983 when Avair was granted a licence to operate routes from Ireland to regional airports in the UK, but Aer Lingus crushed Avvair by cutting fares and competing on domestic flights.[14]

A more formidable challenger to Aer Lingus emerged in the form of Ryanair, founded by Tony Ryan in 1985, who justified the launching of a second major airline carrier in the anticipation that the future de-regulation in European aviation would follow the pattern of internal deregulation within the US industry in the late 1970s. With a European Court of Justice ruling that price-fixing by airlines was contrary to the Treaty of Rome, and a greater willingness within the Department of Transport to embrace de-regulation, Ryanair was granted a license to act as a competitor to Aer Lingus in the Ireland–UK flight market. It started out with a staff of 57 in the first year, taking 5000 passengers, rising to 85,000 in the second year when it commenced operations between Dublin and London, expanding subsequently to other UK routes. Aer Lingus responded by cutting fares and increasing the number of flights. Predatory pricing by Aer Lingus posed a threat to Ryanair's survival, but Ryanair's position was secured in 1989, when the government endorsed a formal two-airline company policy, ending the favoured position of Aer Lingus.[15]

Competition had an adverse effect on Aer Lingus' profitability. To survive, non-core businesses were sold off to reduce debt, and it returned to profitability in the second half of the 1990s with rising passenger numbers. However, Aer Lingus was confronted with a new set of challenges after 2000, not least the problems of the global downturn in aviation following the terrorist attacks on the World Trade Centre in New York in September 2001, in addition to operating within a more competitive environment on many of its routes. Ryanair, operating from small, under-utilized airports, adopted a low fare model and expanded its operations in Continental Europe. By 1994, with a relatively small staff of 500 people, Ryanair annual passenger numbers had risen to 1.5 million, and the business had become highly profitable, with the airline carrying the largest numbers on the London–Dublin route. Ryanair benefited from European airline deregulation in 1997, when new routes were opened. By the turn of the century, Ryanair had become the second largest carrier airline in the UK and the largest low fare airline in Europe with a staff of 1400 with 45 routes to 11 countries and seven million passengers. The company was one of the great service sector success stories of recent decades and it contributed to the development of the Irish economy by reducing the cost of air travel in general, boosting the tourist industry in particular.[16]

The state sold off a large part of its interest in Aer Lingus when it underwent a public flotation in 2006. But the government remained one of the two largest shareholders, the other being Ryanair. In 2009 Aer Lingus became a private listed company employing 3,500 staff; in that year it handled 10 million passengers, including almost 40 per cent of all passengers entering Irish airports.[17]

The potential contribution by tourism to economic growth was recognized at a relatively early stage. The new state retained much of the profile and character of the tourist industry prior to independence. British visitors dominated, but there were also Americans, usually of Irish extraction, despite the greater distance and costs involved for them in reaching Ireland. A private body, the Irish Tourist Association, was formed in 1924, to represent the various organisations and interests groups within the industry at a national level. The association engaged in promotion activity, yet it received no central government support. The only source of public funding for tourism was an optional increase in the local authority rate, introduced by the Local Government Act of 1925. The promotional activities of the Irish Tourist Association did little to address the problem of insufficient accommodation and lack of modern hotel management methods in the sector.[18] Assistance at national level was not provided until 1939, when the Irish Tourist Board assumed responsibility for promoting and funding hotels and seaside resorts. Prior to the 1950s, visitors typically visited Dublin, Cork, Galway or Killarney, a few sites of historical significance such as Clonmacnoise, Glendalough or seaside resorts,[19] such as Salthill, Lahinch, Youghal or Bray.

The Second World War disrupted the regular tourist trade, but US military based in Northern Ireland, in addition to artists, musicians, refugees and conscientious objectors along with some wealthy British tourists barred temporarily from their familiar continental haunts such as Cannes and Monte Carlo, brought some business to Emergency Dublin, which could accommodate them more commodiously than war torn Europe and Britain. A new updated tourist guide, *Ireland of the Welcomes*, came out in 1943 to explain the mysteries and attractions of rural Ireland to such visitors. If these 'immigrant flyboys' lampooned by Flann O'Brien[20] were hardly the basis for long-term tourist development, the post-war era attracted a far greater volume of a more familiar kind of tourist, considerably boosting the industry, since foreign exchange restrictions in Britain and continued food shortages, combined with post-war recovery in Continental Europe all provided greater incentives for British tourists to visit Ireland. Income from tourism rose dramatically in the years up to 1948, far exceeding pre-war levels, so that it then became an important source of foreign exchange. Nonetheless, official attitudes to the assistance and development of the industry remained ambiguous.[21]

With the continental tourist industry re-established by 1950, the influx of British tourists diminished somewhat. Despite this setback, the potential for tourism to earn foreign exchange was at least increasingly appreciated in governing circles, at a time when it was badly needed. Net tourist receipts rose from a mere £5 million in 1943 to £18 million in 1946, peaking at £33 million in 1948, then falling back somewhat to £25 million in 1950 and net receipts were still at this level in 1952.[22]

A number of surveys on the sector were prepared in the years after the Second World including those by the European Economic Co-operation Agency, by a US-based Tourism Survey Group and by members of the Irish Hotels Federation. All were in favour of increased state aid for tourism, the construction of new hotels, improved sanitation and hygienic standards and a concentration of promotional efforts in the south and west. Partly in response, a new state promotional body, Bord Fáilte was formed in 1952, subsequently bringing together the various organisations under a single statutory body.[23] Tourism was identified as a potential source of employment expansion in the *First Programme for Economic Expansion*. State investment occurred in hotels; from 1958, grants in payment of 20 per cent towards the construction of new bedrooms in hotels were introduced and two years later grants were introduced to upgrade existing hotels. By 1963, 20 per cent grants were introduced towards the payment of staff accommodation and guest entertainment facilities,[24] and the General Tourist Development Fund began to widen its brief from merely signposting and fishing prior to 1965, to promoting equestrian, entertainment and golf facilities,[25] reflecting a growing demand for these kinds of leisure activities during the 1960s, not just from tourists.

Tourism expanded dramatically in the 1960s, contributing 5.3 per cent to GNP and making a significant contribution as an 'invisible' to the balance of trade. Tourist numbers from Britain, the US and Continental Europe all increased, at least until the outbreak of the Troubles in Northern Ireland at the end of the decade. The 1960s witnessed a growth in private investment in tourist-focused projects such as the rebuilding of Bunratty and other castles, or the restoration of Kilmainham Jail. The state, constrained by low budgets, nonetheless invested in a few traditional popular locations from 1952 onwards such as the ancient monastic site at Glendalough in Co. Wicklow, for example.[26] Rising living standards and the growing use of cars in the 1960s also increased the importance of domestic tourism.

Over 90 per cent of foreign visitors to the state in the 1960s were from the UK and the US, falling by the early 1980s to 75 per cent, with the balance largely made up of a growing number of Continental European visitors.[27] While the Republic of Ireland in this period remained a cheaper (though damper) alternative to the continent for many UK visitors, there was clearly also a strong ethnic dimension, with many UK and US visitors having Irish origins. Between the 1960s and the 1980s Ireland lost some of its share of the UK market as European tourism became more competitive, while the outbreak of the Troubles in Northern Ireland made Ireland a less desirable location. Receipts declined by 33 per cent between 1968 and 1972.[28]

While tourist numbers by 1977 matched the 1970 figure, they remained static between 1980 and 1984. The Irish tourist sector was adversely affected by growing competition from Mediterranean package holidays and uncompetitive cost structures arising from high inflation relative to other European countries,[29] while at this point the shorter and cooler nature of the Irish summer was a disadvantage, which increased the restricted seasonal nature of the Irish industry. The quality of hotels also declined during the 1970s; the number of high-rated hotels (A and B) fell from 50 per cent of total hotel stock in 1972 to 42 per cent in 1977. The grant system of the 1960s proved to be over generous, with too much money distributed to too many hotels, leading to over-capacity.[30] The rising cost of air travel as a consequence of the two oil crises in 1973–74 and 1978–79 furthur raised costs.

However, the sector revived from the mid-1980s. Anne O'Brien has argued that greater synergies developed between the public and private sectors, which had a more optimal impact on growth as the state began to place more priority on tourism as a potential area for development and job creation. There was a dramatic increase in public and private investment, combined with EU funding between 1989 and 1993. Tourism went on to experience spectacular growth throughout the Celtic Tiger years, tripling its capacity between 1987 and 2007. In the latter year the number of visitors rose to a peak of 7.7 million and the tourism industry employed 322,000 people, having played a central role in job creation during the boom, providing employment for foreign migrants and becoming one of the largest domestic industries.[31]

The phenomenal growth of tourism was partly due to the deregulation of air transport in 1987–88, which reduced costs and improved access. Capital investment, the peace process in Northern Ireland and the development of more negative attitudes to sun holidays helped subsequent development. By 1995, tourism accounted for half of service exports.[32] Tourist-dependant employment increased from 52,300 or 4.8 per cent of total employment in 1985 to 95,100 or 7.7 per cent of total employment in 1995. The share of GNP accounted for by tourism increased from 3.6 per cent to 4.8 per cent between 1987 and 1995.[33]

The expansion of tourism stimulated developments in the hotel and catering sector. After a protracted decline in capacity from the mid 1970s until the early 1990s, they increased again during the 1990s until the mid 2000s; standards also increased, with the number of four-star hotels increasing by 41 per cent between 2001 and 2005.[34] The expansion in the number of large-scale hotels and the number of bedrooms within hotels, stimulated by tax incentives, led ultimately to oversupply.[35] The total number of hotel beds, which had risen from under 15,000 in 1958 to just over 24,000 in 1994, began to rocket up during the Celtic Tiger period to almost 46,000 in 2006 and over 60,000 in 2009, leaving a malign legacy of over capacity in the sector at large.[36]

The beneficial impact of tourism on the Irish balance of trade diminished somewhat as Irish citizens began to discover the joys of foreign holidaying in the 1960s, when sun holidays began to eclipse religious pilgrimages to Lourdes and other religious destinations. This trend became far more marked with the rise in disposable income and employment during Celtic Tiger; Catherine Kelly noted that by 2003 foreign expenditure by Irish overseas visitors actually exceeded revenues from tourists visiting Ireland.[37] Outbound trips by Irish tourists increased by 64 per cent between 2000 and 2005. This in turn was offset by an expansion in domestic tourism by Irish citizens. Domestic tourist expenditure by Irish citizens was estimated to have increased by 39 per cent in constant terms between 2000 and 2005.[38]

Tourist earnings (see Table 5.3) had made a considerable positive contribution to Irish GNP during the 1950s and 1960s. However, the net positive balance of tourist earnings declined during the 1970s, and would never again achieve the share of national income that was attained in the previous decades, although the net balance did increase slightly as a share of national income during the early 1990s. The expenditure by Irish tourists abroad grew at a faster rate throughout the second half of the 1990s and in the first decade of the new millennium, leading to a negative balance of tourist earnings by 2004.

During the inter-war years the largest category of paid employment in the services sector at large was in domestic service, with females dominating this form

Table 5.3 Earnings from foreign tourists and expenditure by overseas Irish tourists at three–year intervals, 1953–2007 and 2009

Year	*Earnings from visitors to Ireland (£m)*	*Expenditure by Irish visitors abroad (£m)*	*Net balance (£m)*	*Net balance as % of GNP*
1953	28.4	10.9	17.5	3.3
1956	33.4	12.7	20.7	3.7
1959	37.8	13.0	24.8	3.9
1962	45.6	19.2	26.4	3.4
1965	67.7	28.2	39.5	3.9
1968	75.7	36.3	39.4	3.0
1971	79.0	42.8	36.2	1.8
1974	102.3	72.8	29.5	0.9
1977	184.6	135.6	49.0	0.8
1980	303.8	318.5	–10.2	–0.1
1983	521.0	363.0	158.0	1.1
1986	649.0	511.0	138.0	0.7
1989	991.0	698.0	293.0	1.3
1992	1,229.0	797.0	432.0	1.5
1995	1,679.0	1,267.0	412.0	1.1
1998	2,280.0	1,701.0	579.0	1.1
2001	3,088.0	2,528.0	560.0	0.7
2004	3,201.0	3,291.0	–90.0	–0.1
2007	3,860.0	4,853.0	–993.0	–0.8
2009	3,879.0	6,148.0	–2,270.0	–1.7

Source: *Statistical abstract 1956, 1965, 1971 and 1981*, Dublin, CSO. *Tourism and travel quarterly, 2nd Q, 1989, 1st Q, 1992, 1st Q, 1997, 1st Q 2003, 1st Q 2007, 2nd Q 2009, 4th Q, 2009*, Dublin, CSO.

of service (see Table 5.1). Servants in the 1920s, who had also long dominated Irish female emigration,[39] were the offspring of smaller farmers and estate workers, the poor and unskilled or those raised in institutions. There was a significant decline in this form of employment during the Second World War, and in the six years after the war it was eclipsed as the premier employment category by the growing number employed in sales and retail, which was indicative of the increased commercialization of the economy in this period and the growing emphasis on increased household consumption. A growth of unpaid houseworkers working in their own homes from over 550,000 in 1926 to over 601,000 in 1961 (or almost 49 per cent rising to 60 per cent of the total adult female population) gives some indication of the move away from hired help between the 1920s and the 1960s, during a period when the population was declining. This transition was facilitated to some extent by an emerging range of labour saving devices and technologies such as washing machines and cookers, combined with running water and electricity, as a growing share of households undertook their own housework. Domestic service became increasingly less desirable compared to other available employment or the options of marriage or emigration, despite increased wages.[40] Domestic service employment went into free fall between 1951 and 1966 when the number of positions occupied more than halved (see Table 5.1), with many presumably emigrating.

Employment in general clerical occupations increased significantly in both absolute and percentage terms from 1926 to 1971, as clerical and management functions expanded within the economy, notably within the Greater Dublin region, where there was an agglomeration of a diverse range of public and private office workers. Despite a continued growth in absolute terms from 1971 to 2006, clerical employment as a percentage of service employment has decreased from 1991.

Employment growth has been evident in the general expansion of non-commercial services since independence, particularly in health and education, which expanded their relative employment shares particularly since the 1960s as more resources were invested in these areas, notably by the state. Since the 1980s, those engaged in clerical work remained the largest single sub-group occupied in services (see Table 5.4), in that decade eclipsing the dominant position that sales and retailing had held since the 1950s; retailing remained, however, the second most important sub group in occupational terms.

At the beginning of the twentieth century most retail stores in Ireland were small family-owned concerns. In many rural areas, unspecialized general stores serviced the locality, often combining a public house and grocery. Goods were sold on an over-the-counter service, with credit-based purchasing and supplies delivered from wholesalers on a piecemeal basis, with the commercial agents of the wholesalers taking orders from individual shopkeepers. Retailing in Dublin, and to a lesser extent Cork, exhibited a different structure, with more specialized shops. At the pinnacle were the department stores, such as Arnotts, Brown Thomas, Clerys and Switzers in Dublin and Roches in Cork. The department stores expanded their influence beyond the cities by attracting loyal customers from rural areas. For example, Clery's refunded train fares for customers outside Dublin, stimulating demand for luxury goods beyond the urban middle classes.[41]

Chain stores emerged after independence; Denis Guiney established his chain of Dublin-based clothing shops in 1921, characterized by aggressive marketing and discount sales.[42] Chain stores also emerged outside the Greater Dublin area. In 1920, the brothers P. and J. Ryan opened a grocery shop in Charleville and two years later opened a second store in Mallow, which formed the basis of one of the earliest multiple retailing groups in the Irish Free State. By 1930, P. & J. Ryan Ltd comprised 22 shops, based in North Cork, Limerick City and County with outliers in Cork City, Listowel and Tipperary Town. The shops were supplied from a centralized complex comprising a bacon factory, bakery and confectionary located outside Charleville. However, this pioneering group collapsed in the

Table 5.4 Distribution of service employment (by occupational sub-sector), 1971–2006

Occupational group	*1971*	*1981*	*1986*	*1991*	*1996*	*2002*	*2006*
Transport	48,223	53,392	51,539	52,748	62,106	71,240	78,164
Communications	13,752	15,634	13,169	11,967	6,266	6,823	7,426
Warehousing	22,492	22,687	22,880	22,279	20,856	24,381	29,329
Clerical staff	86,199	112,554	120,428	139,373	141,504	156,068	182,200
Sales and retail staff	90,763	108,169	115,662	132,257	132,722	152,550	177,287
Business and commercial	11,008	24,717	30,381	32,016	41,855	64,760	83,192
Scientific and technical	12,241	20,702	15,489	21,437	35,319	52,796	58,978
Computer programmers	–	–	–	–	19,598	37,770	45,588
Health	26,368	27,305	44,576	48,986	68,076	78,732	93,065
Education	26,237	42,478	50,376	56,156	61,709	70,458	80,898
Child care	–	–	–	–	20,223	35,712	60,565
Legal	1,963	3,557	4,460	5,317	6,717	9,352	12,244
Hotels, bars and catering	29,443	32,839	49,317	58,473	79,080	85,410	104,569
Domestic service	28,884	27,714	28,938	30,317	32,471	33,394	42,108
Social workers	831	3,690	5,079	5,910	7,081	12,083	17,694
Security	4,553	9,101	11,124	11,848	8,713	10,168	14,116
Personal services	9,900	10,876	13,973	14,760	18,446	19,378	27,052
Sports, creative and entertainment	4,659	6,472	7,558	11,101	17,069	22,188	26,272
Public administration	29,442	56,487	58,550	41,178	61,629	71,168	77,839
Total	495,580	643,815	684,246	767,009	931,543	1157224	1332131

Source: *Census of population 1971, Vol. IV, occupations; 1981 and 1986, Vol. VII, occupations; 1986, Vol. VII, occupations; 1991 and 2002, Vol. VI, occupations; 2006, Vol. VIII, occupations*, Dublin, CSO.

1950s with the death of the Ryan brothers.[43] Findlater's of Dublin in contrast, exemplified the old school grocery business. The company was one of the largest distributors of food in the state on the eve of the Second World War, serving each customer individually and taking in large stocks in bulk of food, whiskey and wines, also bottling and brewing, advancing credit and delivering orders to customers, all at huge costs; by the 1950s, the profit margins of this essentially Victorian model of business were slim and debts were mounting.[44]

Table 5.5 Percentage distribution of service employment (by occupational sub-sector), 1926–2006

Occupational group	*1926*	*1936*	*1946*	*1951*	*1961*	*1966*	*1971*	*1981*	*1986*	*1991*	*1996*	*2002*	*2006*
Transport	10.4	9.5	7.9	9.6	9.4	9.7	9.7	8.3	7.5	6.9	6.7	6.2	5.9
Communications	4.3	4.5	3.7	4.6	3.4	2.7	2.8	2.4	1.9	1.6	0.7	0.6	0.6
Warehousing	4.3	4.5	3.7	4.6	4.5	4.7	4.5	3.5	3.3	2.9	2.2	2.1	2.2
Clerical staff	6.8	7.7	8.6	10.4	14.4	16.0	17.4	17.4	17.6	18.2	15.2	13.5	13.7
Sales and retail staff	20.0	17.9	15.9	18.0	20.0	19.5	18.3	16.8	16.9	17.2	13.2	13.2	13.3
Business and commercial	1.2	1.3	1.3	1.1	1.2	1.3	2.2	3.8	4.4	4.2	4.5	5.6	6.2
Scientific and technical	0.3	0.2	0.4	0.5	0.9	1.8	2.5	3.2	2.3	2.8	3.8	4.6	4.4
Computer programmers	–	–	–	–	–	–	–	–	–	–	2.1	3.3	3.4
Health	2.6	2.6	3.3	3.7	4.8	4.9	5.3	4.2	6.5	6.4	7.3	6.8	7.0
Education	3.8	3.5	3.0	3.1	4.1	4.3	5.3	6.6	7.4	7.3	6.6	6.1	6.1
Child care												3.1	4.5
Social workers							0.2	0.6	0.7	0.8	0.8	1.0	1.3
Legal	0.3	0.4	0.4	0.4	0.4	0.4	0.4	0.6	0.7	0.7	0.7	0.8	0.9
Hotel and catering	5.7	5.1	5.2	5.1	7.4	8.1	5.9	5.1	7.2	7.6	8.5	7.3	7.8
Domestic service	21.3	18.9	16.6	12.6	8.6	6.8	5.8	4.3	4.2	4.0	3.5	2.9	3.2
Personal services	1.7	2.0	2.1	1.7	2.2	2.3	2.0	1.7	2.0	1.9	2.0	1.7	2.0
Security	–	–	–	–	–	–	0.9	1.4	1.6	1.5	0.9	0.8	1.1
Sports and entertainment	1.1	0.9	1.1	1.1	1.4	1.3	0.9	1.0	1.1	1.4	1.8	1.9	2.0
Public administration	8.5	6.3	8.4	6.1	7.0	6.7	5.9	8.8	8.6	5.3	6.6	6.1	5.8

Source: Calculated from *Census of population 1926, 1936 and 1946, Vol. II, occupations; 1951, Vol. III Part 1, occupations; 1961, Vol. III, occupations; 1966 and 1971, Vol. IV, occupations; 1981 and 1986, Vol. VII, occupations; 1986, Vol. VII, occupations; 1991 and 2002, Vol. VI, occupations; 2006, Vol. VIII, occupations.*

By the 1950s, the traditional grocery system was forced to compete with emerging new forms of retailing. The first self-service retailer opened in Dublin in 1950, which was accompanied by changes in distribution systems. In 1956, the Retail Grocers, Drapers and Allied Trades Association established a wholesale business, the Merchants National Co-operative. However, the traditional wholesaling sector was responsive to this challenge. Jack Musgrave, chairman of the long-established Cork wholesale firm, Musgrave Bros, investigated the possibility of introducing the group-trading system to Ireland, whereby retailers sourced their inventories exclusively from a single wholesaler on a cash-and-carry basis, following emerging practices in England and the Netherlands.[45] Other independent traders also continued to consolidate and re-organize themselves. A number of group traders emerged such as Spar, backed by the Munster United Merchants and the Dublin-based Amalgamated Wholesalers, and Mace, formed by the Cork Wholesalers, Punch and the Dundalk-based firm of Hazletts. The pioneers of group trading, Musgrave, continued their reorganization having introduced group trading in 1960 with 150 shops participating, collectively sharing more modern store layouts and branding characteristics. Musgrave also formed partnerships with other wholesaling firms, such as Nilands of Galway, thus expanding their geographical reach.[46] The growth of voluntary trading groups during the 1960s and 1970s is illustrated in Table 5.9.

Musgrave continued to modernize and rationalize the retail and distribution sectors with the expansion of the Cash and Carry system. Large warehouses were constructed in Cork, Limerick and two in Dublin. In the 1990s, Musgrave expanded beyond the Republic of Ireland, through the purchase of the Spanish Group retailer Dialsur and the UK convenience store chain Budgens in 2000.[47] Some major Irish supermarket chains also emerged during the 1960s; Dunne's Stores, initially based in Cork, expanded on a nationwide basis. The SuperQuinn chain first appeared in Dundalk (1960) while Quinnsworth began operations with a store in Longford in 1966. The growth of supermarkets' share of food and drink sales (see Table 5.6) marked something of a revolution in retailing, changing the consumer landscape dramatically, reflecting the emergence of a more centralized, motorized convenience culture, which reduced the time spent shopping. This new model entailed self service and the rapid sale of stock so that large amounts of capital were not tied up in stock. In the face of such competition old style groceries increasingly shut down, including Findlater's in Dublin in 1968.[48]

By 1998, multiple supermarket chains accounted for 56 per cent of grocery sales nationally and 81 per cent in Dublin.[49] Market conditions became more intense after 2000, with the abolition of the groceries order and the entry of the Central European discount chains, Aldi and Lidl to the Irish market. Another aspect of Irish retailing since the late 1980s has been the entry of British retail chain stores, such as Tesco, Marks & Spencer, Boots and Debenhams.[50] There was some government intervention in retailing; Irish supermarket groups engaged in considerable price competition during the 1980s, which led to the introduction of the Groceries Order in 1987 prohibiting the below-cost sale of non-food

Table 5.6 Number, total sales and percentage of food/drink sales accounted for by supermarkets, 1966–87

Year	*No. of supermarkets*	*Sales (£000)*	*As % of total food and drink sales*
1966	41	12,315	6.8
1977	250	244,521	23.2
1987	433	1,412,961	40.8

Source: *Census of distribution 1966 and 1977*, Dublin, CSO. *Statistical abstract 1995*, Dublin, CSO.

commodities and forcing wholesalers to sell at uniform prices to retailers. The order remained in force until 2006. Another significant interventionist measure was the Retailing Planning Guide. This directive to local authorities imposed a maximum limit to the permitted floor space of retail outlets, which was designed to prevent the emergence of 'superstores' on the outskirts of towns and to protect small shopkeepers. However, the directive was recently relaxed in the case of non-food retail establishments, contributing to the arrival in Dublin of the large Swedish retail store IKEA. Regarding the structure of Irish retailing, the major change has been the absolute decline in the number of trading establishments, with an especially marked decline between 1971 and 1988 (see Table 5.7), as smaller grocery shops closed due to competition with supermarkets.

In contrast, sectors engaged in the motor trade experienced an expansion in the number of establishments. Garages and filling stations increased continuously as a percentage of retail establishments, as did vehicle sale establishments, while those selling bicycles contracted in the decades from the mid-1950s. The relentless advance of the motor car continued as new small, low priced models such as the Volkswagen, Ford Anglia and Mini opened up motoring to growing numbers from the end of the 1950s. Urban landscapes and public buildings increasingly had to accommodate car access and parking spaces, as the growing volumes of traffic invaded urban landscapes. By 1961 there was one vehicle for every nine people and 25,000 cars were driven into Dublin on working days. Car registrations more than doubled during the 1960s and the mileage travelled increased. In rural areas dirt tracks were surfaced, easing access for local and long-distance traffic, facilitating greater freedom of movement and altering lifestyles in terms of the greater access it provided to work. In terms of leisure, they provided greater access to dance halls, show band venues, the seaside and sporting contests, to name but a few. It also had implications for widening marriage fields, changing sexual practices and extra marital affairs. The staggering growth of car usage from under 10,000 in 1923 to almost 1.9 million by 2007 has been closely connected to rising living standards, making Ireland one of the most car dependent societies in Europe. Its growing usage constituted a core shift in Irish economic and social history, which remains curiously under studied.[51] A host of new services developed to

Table 5.7 Number of retail establishments, 1951–88

Sub–sector	*1951*	*1956–59*	*1966*	*1971*	*1977*	*1988*
Grocery	11,040	13,111	10,811	9,642	7,305	5,429
Grocery and public house	3,768	3,742	3,077	2,346	1,362	916
Public house and off–licence	5,810	6,204	5,876	6,456	6,839	6,450
Tobacco, sweets and newspapers	4,408	4,480	2,739	2,581	2,404	1,609
Country general shop	1,058	448	215	87	105	76
Other food	2,889	3,015	2,800	2,633	2,649	2,971
Footwear	482	483	428	454	512	411
Menswear	222	214	–	480	517	356
Womenswear	353	348	–	807	1,129	971
Drapery	2,451	2,603	–	1,220	840	908
Fuel	183	207	203	187	138	135
Jewellery	250	285	268	319	240	370
Chemists	1,043	1,322	1,232	1,093	1,089	984
Stationery	281	312	167	198	240	328
Hardware	820	824	669	766	777	756
Radio and electrical	376	441	631	759	581	532
Furniture and carpets	231	250	301	395	500	555
Motor vehicle sales	–	229	–	504	680	695
Cycles	–	510	261	202	166	204
Garages	–	–	–	687	1,769	1,727
Filling stations	–	–	–	1,006	1,068	963
Department stores	–	–	–	15	12	11
Total	37,628	40,913	35,011	33,850	32,332	29,337

Source: 1951, *Census of distribution 1951*, Dublin, CSO. 1956, *Census of distribution 1956 and 1959*, Dublin, CSO. 1966, *Census of distribution, 1966, final report: Retail trade*, Dublin, CSO. 1971, *Census of distribution 1971, summary results for retail and wholesale trade*, Dublin, CSO. 1977, *Census of distribution, 1977 Vol. II, detailed results for retail establishments*, Dublin, CSO. 1988, *Census of services 1988, Vol. I, retail and wholesale trade*, Dublin, CSO.

service motor cars from garages to filling stations/shops; garage forecourt shopping now constitutes one of the fastest growing areas of the grocery sector, reflecting growing car usage and convenience.[52]

Some entirely new services emerged in the 1960s, most notably television, established by the state, with control nonetheless being heavily contested by the agendas of management and producers, commercial advertisers with church and other vested interests all seeking a slice of the action and an inevitable conflict between the desire to protect traditional values against the strong Anglo-American influences that much of the imported material broadcast entailed.[53] The rapidly expanding audience was evident in the rise in the number of television licenses in the state from 127,000 in 1962 to 565,000 by 1975.[54] The expansion of this new medium was a central feature of the new consumer revolution, with commercial advertising acquiring a strong stake. Its dramatic political influence in extending the public sphere and more cultural nationalist mission in language revival, sport and culture was matched by the impact it had in promulgating a new kind of consumer materialism in which mainstream Anglo-American values prevailed, collectively resonating an increasingly more hybrid public culture.

It is evident from a breakdown of the distribution of sales by type of retail outlet that the period between 1951 and 1988 witnessed a long-term decline in the percentage of sales accounted for by the traditional public house/grocery and country general stores (see Table 5.8). Nonetheless the grocery sub-sector increased its percentage of sales, with the expansion of supermarkets contributing to this development. Between 1956 and 1966 a significant increase occurred in the percentage of sales accounted for by department and chain stores. The percentage of sales accounted for by radio and electrical goods and furniture and carpets also increased between 1956 and 1966, reflecting the growth in demand for such consumer goods as incomes rose and rural electrification facilitated a wider consumer revolution.

Increased disposable income, favourable demographic trends given the increase in the number of consumers and changing consumer tastes, with increased demand for a greater range of goods and services led to impressive growth in distribution during the 1990s and most of the following decade,[55] with a marked increase in the percentage of retail sales accounted for by the motor trade.[56] However, the difficulties in increasing productivity growth in services identified by Cogan in the 1970s continued in the distribution sector during the 1990s and 2000s, in comparison to the impressive productivity growth experienced in the US distribution sector.[57]

Other non-tradable services illustrated how government regulation hindered the development of these sectors. The OECD had commented, 'the pub market is another good example that illustrates how entry restrictions can be a clumsy way of pursuing social policy objectives and can have unintended consequences that make consumers worse off'.[58] The provision of pub licences was subject to the potential licensee purchasing a second licence from a closed pub in an effort to hold the total number of licences constant. While this provision was sensible in the context of provincial Ireland, it limited the number of new pubs within urban areas, and created an incentive towards the formation of scaled up super pubs. The restriction on licences contributed to Irish alcoholic drink prices being 80 per cent higher than the EU average by 2006, providing additional unwelcome affects in raising prices.[59]

Financial services were another element within the services sector that became relatively more important in the Irish economy in the last decades of the twentieth century. Developments in information technology during the 1980s, in conjunction

Table 5.8 Percentage distribution of retail sales by sub-sector, 1951/54–1987

Sub–sector	*1951–54*	*1956*	*1966*	*1971*	*1977*	*1987*
Grocery and provisions	18.1	22.0	22.2	21.4	21.3	29.4
Public house and grocery	9.1	8.8	5.9	4.3	2.4	1.7
Public house/off licences	6.6	7.0	9.1	11.1	10.9	10.4
Country general store	8.9	6.2	1.7	1.0	0.9	0.6
Specialist food	7.5	7.5	7.3	6.3	5.8	5.9
Tobacco, sweets and newspapers	3.8	4.0	3.0	2.8	2.8	3.1
Drapery	10.5	9.6	4.4	7.4	5.5	1.2
Boots and shoes	1.7	2.7	1.6	1.3	1.3	1.2
Personal clothing	4.0	2.7	4.4	3.9	3.3	3.4
Garages/filling stations	9.4	4.2	3.3	6.3	6.2	7.9
Motor vehicles	–	6.4	12.8	11.6	17.5	13.0
Cycles	0.6	0.4	0.2	0.3	0.3	0.2
Chemists	2.0	2.3	2.6	2.0	2.6	2.9
Hardware	4.0	3.5	2.5	3.6	3.0	2.7
Radio–electrical goods	1.2	1.0	2.0	2.3	1.8	2.4
Jewellery	0.8	0.8	0.8	0.8	0.7	0.6
Books and stationery	0.8	1.0	0.8	0.9	0.8	1.1
Furniture and carpets	1.1	1.0	1.7	1.8	1.5	1.4
Solid fuel	4.0	3.2	2.7	1.5	0.5	0.5
Leather, sport and fancy goods	0.5	0.4	1.5	1.1	0.6	0.7
Departmental/variety chain stores	5.4	5.3	9.5	8.3	10.3	9.7

Source: *Census of distribution 1951–54, 1956, 1966, 1971 and 1987*, Dublin, CSO. *Statistical abstract 1995*, Dublin, CSO.

with deregulation of financial markets, led to greater flexibility on the part of financial firms and banks to relocate elements of their activities to Ireland since rents and wages were then cheaper in Ireland than in the larger metropolitan centres.[60] From 1987, the International Financial Services Centre (IFSC) was developed on the Custom House Dock and a licensing system was implemented to ensure that only *bona fide* financial firms would participate in the centre. The preferential 10 per cent corporation tax rate associated with manufacturing firms was extended to the centre to allow it to compete with existing financial centres such as Luxembourg and the Channel Islands. The preferential tax rate was applied until 2003, when the universal 12.5 per cent corporation tax rate was introduced.[61] By 1990, 600 were employed in firms affiliated to the centre. In addition to preferential taxation rates, a number of European financial firms were attracted to the IFSC due to the relative absence of regulation compared to the traditional continental European centres such as Luxembourg and Switzerland. Financial de-regulation, which was introduced by the European Union in the wake of the Single Market, facilitated the location of European financial firms to the IFSC.[62] During the course of the 1990s a number of large US financial institutions such as Merrill Lynch and Citibank also located there.[63]

By 2005, employment in the IFSC had risen dramatically to over 20,000 accounting for 40 per cent of total financial services employment in the Republic of Ireland.[64] The financial services sector was dominated by foreign firms in 2006 when 80 per cent of all financial firms in Dublin were of non-Irish origin. Of these, 42 per cent were engaged in fund and asset administration ('back office' functions). A further 37 per cent were banking firms and 21 per cent were insurance firms.[65] The advantages offered by affiliation to the IFSC were no longer tied to locating in the Customs Dock area, facilitating the expansion of financial services firms outside Dublin.[66]

Insurance firms also located to the IFSC; by 2003, 10 of the world's 20-largest insurance firms had located there, attracted by low corporation tax rates and Ireland's participation in the euro and its unique status as the only English-speaking, common law based country participating in the eurozone.[67] By 2006, Ireland had established itself as the largest centre for the cross-border life insurance sector in Europe and as one of the largest centres globally for the re-insurance sector.[68] The IFSC also attracted firms that provided debt products and debt securitization. By 2006, Ireland was the sixth-largest debt market in the world and was the second-largest centre for debt securitization activity.[69] After 2000, the IFSC diversified its activities from mutual fund administration towards the administration of hedge funds.[70] All of this created further employment in related legal and accounting services.

Another sector of recent origin is the 'business offshore process sector', which incorporates call centres. Call centres were promoted by the IDA from 1992, who marketed Ireland as an attractive location with the lure of competitive telephone rates in comparison with other European countries. This was in addition to the standard range of grant and tax incentives. US firms dominated, accounting for 70 per cent of call centre investment.[71] By 2002, between 12,000 and 19,000 were employed in call centres. At 3.6 per cent, Ireland had the highest percentage of the workforce employed in call centres globally.[72] Despite the employment generated, this sector has been criticized for the poor wages, low skill level and repetitive nature of work, the lack of linkages with the local economy and the potential ease with which call centres can relocate given their low level of fixed investment.[73]

The software sector is the only example of a sector established through foreign direct investment that generated an indigenous counterpart. The establishment of the Irish software sector followed the example of other sectors, with leading international software firms locating in Ireland as a centre for their European operations, such as Lotus in 1984 and Microsoft in 1985.[74] The development of computer software and other related computer service by multinational companies gathered pace after 2001, as many firms that previously produced computer hardware in Ireland now provided computer services and software development.[75] Although exports and sales were dominated by larger multinationals, there were also opportunities for indigenous firms and indigenous employment in this sector expanded.[76] Specific measures to promote the sector had been in existence since the 1970s, with the promotion of software companies under the early IDA Services Industries Programme and the extension of export profits tax relief to software exports.[77] Another advantage of the software sector was that it is not capital intensive. Fixed capital expenditure is limited to office premises and computers. The provision of working capital was of more importance, given the need to finance product development and marketing. In the case of Ireland, state bodies assisted in providing the required aid.[78] While the growth of the software sector was heralded by Ó Riain as a crucial element in the growth performance of the Irish economy, representing a shift towards high value-added activities, a more sombre assessment of the indigenous software sector's performance is made by O' Hearn, who points out that the volume of their sales remains small in comparison to the multinational companies located in Ireland and many of the successful companies were subsequently purchased by foreign interests.[79]

Since the late 1970s the economic importance of the entertainment industry, notably the music and audiovisual industries, has increased. During the 1960s, an Irish music *industry* emerged. Although showbands provided significant employment for musicians, many Irish popular musicians had to leave Ireland to develop their careers, partly due to the lack of radio airtime, the absence of high quality recording studios and the absence of a developed commercial infrastructure. Irish musicians who experienced success abroad, such as Thin Lizzy, Rory Gallagher and Van Morrison, were followed by the Boomtown Rats. Horslips, in contrast, retained an Irish-based operation, which helped to stimulate an Irish-based industry. Traditional Irish music also had a popular renaissance in the 1960s and 1970s, attaining an international audience with the emergence of groups such as the Dubliners, the Clancy Brothers, the Chieftains and subsequently Planxty. By the late 1970s, the necessary infrastructure for the development of an Irish industry emerged, with the opening of Windmill Lane Studio in Dublin, the launching of the official popular music radio station 2FM and the presence of pirate radio stations, and the launching of the periodical *Hot Press.* The international success of U2 further stimulated the Irish industry, attracting attention to Irish bands and on a practical level, providing both employment and experience for Irish sound engineers and stage crews. Export sales by indigenous Irish record companies increased from €616,000 in 1990 to €12 million by 1995.[80]

The Irish industry was assisted by the use of English, which gave it some advantages in the exportation of music relative to non-Anglophone European countries. Government measures such as the tax exemption on artists' earnings, introduced in 1969, allowed recording artists to remain in Ireland, while the Business Expansion Scheme (BES) of 1984 provided tax relief for investments in recording studios and, by the late 1990s, for investment in the production, marketing and promotion of audio-visual recordings. Despite the growth of a domestic Irish recording industry, many Irish record companies remained on a small-scale and could not offer the necessary management and legal support services offered by the major international recording companies.[81]

The film industry is another element of the entertainment sector that experienced considerable growth since the 1980s. As in the case of the music industry, the 1984 BES allowed for tax relief for investment in the sector. Three years later, a specific tax relief was introduced for film productions if at least 75 per cent of the production work was carried out in Ireland. The relief was originally confined to corporate investors and was subsequently extended to private individuals by 1993. These tax concessions attracted US film companies to locate productions in the Republic of Ireland, with consequent benefits to employment and the balance of payments.[82] In contrast the development of the indigenous film sector remained relatively sluggish.[83]

Increased attention has been devoted to the tradability of services on an international basis. Tourism to the Irish economy provides the most significant historical example. However, developments in information technology together with the deregulation and privatization of communication utilities, and the expansion in general international trade have led to the increased tradability of services in recent decades.[84] This was assisted by the extension of the low corporate tax regime to the business and financial services sector, a process that saw the rate of corporate taxation decline from 40 per cent in 1994 to 12.5 per cent by 2003. In comparing the performance of service exports in the absence of this corporate tax reduction, Fitzgerald and Conefrey estimated that service exports in 2005 would have been 85 per cent lower.[85] Service exports during the early 1990s were dominated by tourism and travel, which experienced a declining share of service exports from 1995 onwards. While 'other services' were not disaggregated during the 1990s, their share of service exports increased steadily from 1994, probably reflecting the expansion of computer software exports.[86]

Financial services were another growing net exporter of services, assisted by the activities of the IFSC, which accounted 24 per cent of total service exports in 1998 to a peak of over 34 per cent in 2004, falling back thereafter to around 28.5 by 2010. Although the IFSC imports a significant share of total service imports (16 per cent in 2010, for example) it has consistently been a net exporter of services.[87] Leasing and insurance have increased their net share of service exports since 2000, the latter having been a net importer as recently as 2001.

While service exports were concentrated in a small number of discrete sectors, the principal source of service imports were associated with general costs incurred in operating in a modern market economy. A significant growth occurred in 'Royalties and Licence' service imports during the 1990s, and this category still dominates service imports, consistent with the intense importation of intellectual property by multinationals from their parent companies in the US. This reflects payments to operate shop franchises and the use of computer software.

Table 5.9 Percentage distribution of service exports by sub–sector, 1999–2010

Year	*Transport*	*Tourism and travel*	*Insurance*	*Financial services*	*Computer services*	*Leasing*	*Others*
1999	9.7	18.1	7.0	11.6	35.1	–	18.5
2000	8.0	15.7	6.7	12.3	32.5	–	24.6
2001	6.7	13.0	6.9	11.3	37.0	5.4	18.7
2002	6.3	11.7	9.7	11.6	35.0	5.9	19.8
2003	5.3	10.2	13.8	9.8	37.8	4.9	18.2
2004	5.0	9.1	13.0	9.9	38.8	5.3	18.9
2005	4.6	8.3	14.8	10.1	32.6	7.1	22.5
2006	4.3	7.7	14.8	11.0	30.0	7.9	24.3
2007	3.9	6.7	13.3	10.5	32.9	7.9	24.8
2008	3.7	6.6	12.3	10.2	34.8	7.3	25.1
2009	4.3	5.3	11.4	8.6	36.4	8.6	25.4
2010	4.7	4.2	10.7	8.2	38.4	8.4	25.4

Source: *Balance of international payments, final quarter and year ending 1999, 2001, 2002, 2004, 2006 and* 2008, Dublin, CSO. *Statistical yearbook 2010*, Dublin, CSO.

Table 5.10 Percentage distribution of service imports by sub-sector, 1999–2010

Year	*Tourism and travel*	*Royalties and licenses*	*Trade services*	*Other business services*	*Others*
1999	9.4	26.7	19.2	23.1	21.6
2000	9.1	27.4	17.4	24.4	21.7
2001	8.3	25.2	19.7	28.0	18.8
2002	9.1	25.1	22.5	22.7	20.6
2003	9.1	30.9	22.9	19.5	17.6
2004	8.9	30.5	22.2	20.6	17.8
2005	8.7	27.8	14.0	28.9	20.6
2006	8.7	27.8	14.0	28.1	21.4
2007	9.3	25.2	15.8	25.5	24.2
2008	9.9	27.7	16.3	25.1	21.0
2009	8.4	33.4	12.7	26.9	18.6
2010	7.1	35.2	13.3	26.8	17.6

Source: *Balance of international payments , fourth quarter and year ending 1999, 2001, 2002, 2004, 2006 and 2008*, Dublin, CSO. *Statistical yearbook 2010*, Dublin, CSO.

Royalty and licence payments are also a feature of manufacturing activity and reflect the dominance of FDI in the advanced sectors of the Irish economy.

These payments contributed to the net services trade deficit recorded in the late 1990s. At 12 per cent of GDP, the Irish services trade deficit was the highest for

Table 5.11 Contribution of services to Net Domestic Product at three-year intervals, 1947–2007 and 2009

Year	*Services as a % of Net Domestic Product*
1947	46.5
1953	40.9
1956	44.0
1959	44.2
1962	45.5
1965	47.1
1968	47.1
1971	48.8
1974	51.7
1977	51.9
1980	57.4
1983	56.8
1986	58.0
1989	56.3
1992	59.7
1995	55.4
1998	54.0
2001	53.9
2004	59.8
2007	62.0
2009	64.9

Source: Calculated from *National income and expenditure 1938 and 1944–49*, Dublin, Department of Industry and Commerce, Statistics Branch. *National income and expenditure 1960, 1969–70, 1975, 1982, 1991, 2004, 2007 and 2009*, Dublin, CSO.

any industrialized country. However, after 2000, the services trade deficit declined. In addition to increased service exports, many multi-national companies located in Ireland were able to provide management and other trade services internally rather than importing such services from their international headquarters. This has weakened the close historical relationship between merchandise exports and service imports.[88]

'Trade services' in Table 5.10 constitute commissions earned by agents engaged in external trade, while 'other business services' refers to a whole multitude of activities such as inter-affiliate management fees, a sector with particular relevance to Ireland given the strength of FDI, public relations, advertising and marketing.[89] Regarding the destination of service imports and exports, the US is the largest exporter of services to Ireland.[90] Service exports in contrast were concentrated towards the European Union by location, and in terms of sector were dominated by computer services, which accounted for almost a third of all service exports in 2007.[91]

Service employment accounts for a larger share of total employment in the economy (see Table 9.1) than the service share of GDP (see Table 5.11). Absolute growth in service employment is significant as productivity in the service sector is difficult to increase.

O' Leary's estimates that productivity growth in the service sector averaged at 2.2 per cent per annum between 1960 and 1979, falling to 1.1 per cent per annum for the years 1979 to 1993 and falling again to 0.3 per cent per annum for the period 1993 to 1999.[92] The growth in service employment in these years was far more impressive. The services share of total employment in the Irish economy has continued to rise, accounting for 74.1 per cent by 2009 (Table 9.1) so that the shift to services in the Republic of Ireland has broadly followed the wider European pattern, though in terms of timing this shift has occurred more slowly. This increasing dependence on service employment will reduce the potential for productivity growth across the economy in the coming decades. Since roughly three-quarters of the population now works in services, and service sector exports have become increasingly important to economic performance, it seems likely that economic policy will increasingly focus on improving productivity and developing new capacity in the service exports in particular. International experience suggests that it is highly likely that the service share of total employment in the economy of the Republic of Ireland will further increase in the years to come.[93]

Part III

6 International trade and Irish economic development

Due to the small size of the domestic market, Ireland has, since the eighteenth century, been more dependant on international trade as a source of growth than most European economies. Lloyd George's last-minute offer of full fiscal autonomy during the Treaty negotiations in December 1921 (which was accepted and came into effect from 1 April 1923) was certainly the most significant economic aspect of the negotiations, as it gave the newly-formed Irish Free State the ability to impose tariffs and regulate trade. The traditional trade to Britain in agricultural products continued to dominate Irish trade throughout the 1920s and access to the British market for these commodities remained a core issue in the political relationship between the two islands for decades. Irish trade dependence on the British market remained a dominant feature of the economy until long after the Republic of Ireland entered the EEC in 1973. Eventually EU membership changed the fundamentals of Irish trade and opened up an altogether more diverse range of trading opportunities.

Due to the continued dominance of export-orientated agricultural and food processing sectors, Cumann na nGaedheal adhered more to the traditional free trade policy, following the recommendations of the 1923 Fiscal Inquiry Committee. Yet, the Department of Industry and Commerce argued in favour of selective protectionism from 1924 onwards and its efforts led to the imposition of tariffs on certain sectors.[1] Ernest Blythe, Minister for Finance, imposed a series of experimental tariffs in the 1924 budget, most notably on boots and shoes, while the 1925 budget imposed tariffs on clothing and furniture. A Tariff Commission was established in 1926 to consider the merits of imposing protection on a sector by sector basis, with the deliberate objective of removing this contentious issue from cabinet discussion since Cumann na nGaedheal was divided on the matter.[2]

Between 1926 and 1930, the Tariff Commission published eight reports, advocating the imposition of tariffs on margarine, rosary beads, down quilts and a selection of woollen products, but rejecting tariffs for fish barrels, motor bodies, flour and paper products. In addition to the published reports, applications for tariffs on cooked foods, animal feeds and maize, among other items were rejected.[3] The Department of Finance succeeded in gaining control of the Tariff Commission, with J. J. MacElligott securing the position of chairman. Since he was a committed supporter of orthodox economic policies, this ruled out the introduction of large-scale protectionist measures.[4] Nonetheless, as the 1920s drew to a close, the traditional policy of free trade increasingly came under pressure, both nationally and internationally. The Great Depression resulted in many governments worldwide, including the UK, adopting protectionist policies. By the early 1930s, with falling agricultural prices, Cumann na nGaedheal had introduced tariffs on agricultural imports. The general fear was that surplus world agricultural production would be 'dumped' on the Irish market. Tariffs on butter, bacon and oats were imposed by a revitalized Tariff Commission,[5] while legislation for a general import levy was also introduced. By 1931, there were 59 categories of goods subject to duty, so protectionism had at this stage become more important for certain sectors of the economy than it had been in 1922.[6]

When it came to power in 1932, Fianna Fáil implemented protectionist measures in a far more proactive manner. The average tariff level rose from 9 per cent in 1931 to 45 per cent in 1936, and by 1937 almost 2,000 commodities were subject to some form of import control.[7] Ireland therefore made a radical transition to an intensive form of protectionism, which further curtailed trade with Britain, already reduced by the impact of the economic war, international recession and the advent of protectionism in Britain itself. The shift to protectionism provided an economic adjunct to the desire for greater political and cultural autonomy from all things British. To that end, prohibitive tariffs were placed on consumer imports and on cereal imports with the objective of increasing self sufficiency.

During the 1930s an attempt was made to create greater diversity in the origin and destination of Irish trade in order to reduce the dominant UK share of both. However, the worldwide glut of agricultural produce and the introduction of protectionist measures by countries to safeguard their own agricultural sectors prevented any major diversification of Irish exports. Germany briefly became a minor exception. Despite attempts by the Nazi regime to increase agricultural production during the 1930s, it remained a net importer of food. After a series of protracted negotiations in the mid 1930s, Ireland obtained an increase in its cattle export quota to Germany. As a consequence Germany became the second largest importer of Irish agricultural produce. In return, German engineering firms supplied government contracts for capital goods, including wiring, electrical and telegraphic equipment.[8] However, this mutually beneficial trading relationship ended with the outbreak of the Second World War.

Since independence, the Irish-owned merchant shipping fleet was relatively small. Reorganization and amalgamation of smaller companies engaged in Irish trade into larger British combines such as Coast Lines Ltd meant that cross channel passenger traffic and much of Anglo-Irish trade was handled by British shipping companies.[9] British companies also handled most deep-sea bulk cargoes destined for Ireland such as timber, wheat, fertilizer and maize. Ships registered in the state were generally engaged in Anglo-Irish trade and included colliers, passenger, cargo and livestock vessels. But a number of Irish registered ships switched to the British register at the outset of the Second World War, including all the B&I ships and seven new oil tankers. The state was therefore highly dependent on space on British registered merchant shipping, and an adverse effect of Irish neutrality was that this was significantly reduced. Many British shipping lines that had been operating to Ireland withdrew their Irish services after the outbreak of war in 1939.

Although protectionism was relaxed to some degree during the war to facilitate trade in difficult circumstances, the disruption to commercial shipping led to severe shortages of imported raw materials for both agriculture and industry in the early years of the war, in addition to shortages of wheat and tea. The onerous task of supplying, distributing and allocating raw materials, fuel and foodstuffs within the Irish economy was entrusted to the newly formed Department of Supplies, of which Seán Lemass became the Minister. Lemass established the Irish Shipping Company in March 1941, to boost the capacity of the Irish mercantile marine, so that vital overseas commodities could still be imported. With extensive state backing and the involvement of some of the major Irish shipping companies, the Limerick Steamship Co. Ltd., the Wexford Steamship Co. Ltd., and the Saorstat and Continental Steamship Co. Ltd., along with Grain Importers (Éire) Ltd, the company had the necessary expertise to keep open supply lines to secure the food and other essential commodities. Under emergency powers, all cargo space utilized on Irish or allied shipping was allocated by the Department of Supplies. Fifteen ships were acquired by Irish Shipping with great difficulty; a number of these were old and in poor condition.[10]

The most important commodities carried during the war years were 712,000 tons of wheat, which helped augment the increased production of native wheat (see Chapter 3) and underpinned the primary staple of Irish diet; bread. Another vital commodity carried was 178,000 tons of coal in addition to 63,000 tons of phosphates; less vital perhaps was 24,000 tons of tobacco (presumably securing a precious space allocation due to its revenue generating capacity). During the course of most of the war, Lisbon in Portugal became the major transhipment centre for cargoes destined for Ireland that could no longer be shipped directly. This was one of the more dangerous routes undertaken. 135 lives were lost in service to the Irish mercantile marine during the war years. The state continued to be almost entirely dependent on the vessels of Irish Shipping until the end of June 1946.[11] The desperate shortage of shipping in the war years was such that even some old Arklow schooners got a new lease of life, with 11, employing 55 seamen, still operating out of the port in 1949.[12]

The geographical distribution of Irish trade during the interwar and war years is shown in Table 6.1. Ireland relied heavily on the UK market throughout the period, despite the Economic War. Between 1934 and 1937 a slight increase in the percentage of exports destined for Europe occurred, but this trade collapsed with the outbreak of war. The figures relating to imports need to be interpreted with caution. The sharp fall in imports from Britain in 1937 arose from a change in the way in which trade data were returned. Up until 1936 the origin or destination referred to the port from which or to which the goods had been shipped. Since some of Ireland's imports simply passed through British ports and hence were credited to the UK, from 1937 origins and destinations refer to the places in which the goods were produced or consumed.[13] Hence the true figures for imports from Britain before 1937 were a good deal lower (see Table 6.1).

Table 6.1 Geographic distribution exports and imports (value) by percentage, 1925–45

Year	*Imports from UK*	*Exports to UK*	*Imports from Europe*	*Exports to Europe*	*Imports from USA*	*Exports to USA*	*Imports from rest of world*	*Exports to rest of world*
1925	81.1	97.2	6.5	1.3	5.0	0.7	7.4	0.9
1926	75.6	96.7	11.0	1.5	8.1	0.7	5.3	1.1
1927	77.4	95.8	7.8	2.1	7.7	1.0	7.2	1.1
1928	78.0	96.2	8.6	1.9	6.4	0.7	7.1	1.2
1929	78.1	92.3	7.9	3.9	7.8	2.1	6.3	1.8
1930	80.6	91.3	8.3	4.3	6.8	2.6	4.3	1.8
1931	80.8	96.6	8.9	1.8	4.1	1.1	6.2	0.6
1932	76.7	96.2	10.2	2.2	3.1	0.4	10.0	1.1
1933	69.9	94.0	16.3	3.5	2.9	0.8	10.8	1.7
1934	66.7	93.4	18.8	4.1	4.8	0.7	9.7	1.8
1935	72.4	91.7	14.3	5.6	3.9	0.9	9.5	1.8
1936	70.8	91.5	14.7	5.8	4.6	1.2	9.9	2.1
1937	50.0	90.9	17.8	6.2	6.6	1.0	26.1	1.9
1938	50.5	92.6	17.3	5.6	11.4	0.5	20.9	1.3
1939	55.7	93.6	15.0	4.0	8.3	1.1	21.1	1.3
1940	53.1	96.0	6.6	1.2	8.8	1.5	31.5	1.3
1941	71.5	97.1	4.0	0.0	7.8	2.2	16.7	0.7
1942	57.3	98.8	6.0	0.0	8.8	1.1	27.9	0.1
1943	50.6	98.9	10.4	0.1	13.5	1.0	25.6	0.1
1944	47.1	98.8	4.8	0.1	10.4	1.0	37.7	0.1
1945	47.6	97.8	7.2	1.0	9.9	1.0	35.4	0.2

Source: 1925–31, *Trade and shipping statistics 1931*, Dublin, Dept. of Industry and Commerce Statistics Branch. 1932–38, *Trade and shipping statistics 1938*, Dublin, Dept. of Industry and Commerce Statistics Branch. 1939–44, *Trade and shipping statistics 1943–44*, Dublin, Dept of Industry and Commerce Statistics Branch. 1945, *Trade and shipping statistics 1945*, Dublin, Dept. of Industry and Commerce Statistics Branch.

Irish exports between independence and the end of the war were dominated by agricultural commodities. Live animals consistently remained the largest single export; in 1931, at their peak, live animals accounted for over half the value of Irish exports. The composition of Irish exports did not alter significantly between 1925 and 1945, the only major disruption being the fall in the percentage share accounted for by live animals between 1933 and 1934, due to the Economic War.[14] The value and share of manufactures in Irish trade was exceedingly low throughout this period, and composed mainly of processed foods and drinks. Ireland had a strong and competitive tradition in food processing, distilling and brewing. Textiles were the only other manufacture of any consistent consequence in the export trade. Vehicle exports from Ford's plant in Cork expanded briefly in the late 1920s, but this trade ceased following the opening of Ford's Dagenham plant near London in 1931 and the Cork plant reverted to producing merely for the Irish market.[15]

Changes in trade policy and world events had a more significant effect on the composition of imports. The imposition of tariffs on imported grain and measures to promote domestic tillage further reduced the percentage of imports accounted for by cereals and foodstuffs after 1932. With the industrialization drive by Fianna Fáil, the percentage of imports accounted for by raw materials, capital goods and semi-manufactured goods increased. Protectionism succeeded in reducing the share of imports accounted for by apparel and other consumer goods as import substitution got underway. But World War II led to a decline in imports of industrial inputs and raw materials, which had an adverse effect on Irish industrial output.[16]

The post-war era witnessed some major changes in the nature of shipping. Irish Shipping replaced older ships with larger vessels more suitable for deep-sea bulk cargoes. From 1947, large liberty ships from the US arrived under the Marshall Plan and the ports of Dublin and Cork required investment in improvements to accommodate larger ocean going vessels. The 1946 Harbour Act preceded the expansion of facilities in the major ports; by the 1960s, specialized zones began to be put in place in Dublin, for example, for ro-ro operations (handled by B&I from 1965), containerization and bulk cargoes, especially oil. In 1965 the state took over the B&I, which was operating 27 ships on seven routes, with a view to improving and upgrading transportation between Ireland and Great Britain. In order to increase containerization suitable vessels were brought into operation from 1968 and 28 acres were reclaimed in Dublin Port for a new container terminal that was operational by 1972, by which time containerized services to and from Great Britain and the continent were experiencing rapid expansion. The throughput of Dublin port increased from 2.94 million tonnes in 1949 to the peak years of 7.94 million tonnes in 1979 and almost as much in 1980.[17]

In the post-war era the port of Cork also witnessed significant improvements. The growing demand for oil had to be accommodated with oil jetties and special storage facilities. In May 1959 a new oil refinery was brought into production at Whitegate by several international oil companies, who had invested £10.5 million so that crude oil could be received, stored, refined and products despatched. The ports of Waterford, Limerick, Drogheda, Galway and even New Ross carried out some improvements in the post-war era, but many smaller ports such as Dungarvan and Kinsale began to lose significance.[18] The old port of Wexford for example languished due to a problematic sand bar, but further south Rosslare's trade became more important. Rosslare harbour was already handling containerized traffic in the 1950s (which Dublin dockers would not yet handle) and facilities were upgraded. In 1964 it opened the first drive-on drive-off car ferry service in the state. By the end of the 1960s more modern multi-purpose ships handling passengers, cars and roll-on roll-off freight and trade on the Rosslare-Fishgaurd route rose steadily in the early 1970s, with more sporadic services to France opening from 1968.[19]

After the war, the US emerged as a significant supplier to Ireland, mostly to supply rising consumer demand that had been suppressed during the war years.[20] The increase in imported consumption goods, in conjunction with the sluggish export performance of agricultural and industrial goods caused a deterioration in the balance of payments, which placed constraints on Irish economic growth during the 1950s. This problem gave greater urgency to improving export earnings. A Dollar Exports Advisory Committee was established in 1950. The Industrial Development Authority (IDA), which had been established in 1949, began to recognize the need for increased exports and especially for industrial exports.[21] Both bodies argued for the formation of a state funded export corporation.[22] Córas Tráchtála (the Irish Export Board) was established in 1952 to assist in an advisory capacity in the marketing of exports, with a special focus on the North American market.

Although the manufacturing sector in the Republic of Ireland was among the most highly protected in Europe between 1932 and the mid-1960s,[23] trade policy was liberalized on a gradual basis from the mid-1950s onwards. The Export Profits Tax Relief Scheme launched in 1956 (and extended in the following years) was to be vital in attracting export-orientated companies to invest in Ireland. In 1958 foreign owned companies who exported their output were made exempt from the Control of Manufacturers Acts,[24] which were subsequently repealed entirely in 1964. Thus in less than a decade, policy shifted from constraining foreign direct investment to actively encouraging it through zero corporate profits on manufactured exports, along with investment grants for such companies. (This level of taxation was retained until 1980, when a 10 per cent flat rate was imposed on all manufacturing.)[25] Unilateral tariff cuts of 10 per cent were made on imports in 1963 and 1964.[26]

The emergence of various new trade blocs, most notably the EEC in 1957, made Ireland's adherence to protectionism increasingly untenable. With the establishment in 1960 of the European Free Trade Association (EFTA), of which Great Britain was the largest member, Ireland's trade in agricultural exports to Britain came under increasing pressure. Competition from New Zealand butter also intensified in these years. The failure of the first attempt by both Britain and Ireland to gain entry into the EEC was utilized on the Irish side as a pretext to seek further liberalization of Anglo-Irish trade as an interim step before both eventually entered the EEC. This strategy ultimately worked and improved relations resulted in the Anglo-Irish Free Trade Area Agreement of 1965, which allowed free access to the UK for Irish manufactured goods from 1966. Quotas on Irish agricultural imports to Britain were increased, while Irish tariffs on British imports were to be reduced progressively by 10 per cent per annum. Nonetheless, in 1966, cattle on the hoof and beef still remained the largest agricultural exports, collectively accounting for over half the value of agricultural exports.[27]

Although the declared objective to switch from protectionism to a more open trading environment was clearly articulated by the state from 1958, trade with the UK was only gradually liberalized in the 1960s and most European trade was only opened up in the years following EEC entry in 1973. But even before the 1960s, the composition of exports reveals the gradual emergence of a significant

Table 6.2 Geographic distribution of exports and imports (value) by percentage, 1946–63

Year	*Imports from UK*	*Exports to UK*	*Imports from Europe*	*Exports to Europe*	*Imports to USA*	*Exports from USA*	*Imports from rest of world*	*Exports to rest of world*
1946	52.2	92.3	12.2	5.2	11.9	1.5	23.8	1.0
1947	41.5	88.6	16.4	9.8	22.9	0.7	19.9	0.9
1948	53.9	87.3	11.9	10.7	8.4	0.8	25.9	1.2
1949	57.3	90.0	14.2	8.3	14.2	0.6	14.3	1.1
1950	52.9	86.7	16.3	10.0	13.0	1.9	17.9	1.5
1951	46.6	84.0	20.2	9.8	12.0	4.0	21.3	2.2
1952	50.8	86.1	19.6	9.0	10.7	3.2	18.9	1.8
1953	50.7	90.6	21.8	5.3	9.0	2.1	18.5	2.1
1954	55.7	88.6	20.4	7.3	6.8	1.9	17.1	2.2
1955	48.2	87.2	20.6	8.0	8.6	2.7	22.6	2.1
1956	57.3	80.6	20.5	13.8	7.5	3.0	14.8	2.6
1957	56.8	79.7	20.6	17.1	6.0	3.2	16.7	0.0
1958	56.5	76.8	20.8	15.0	7.1	5.7	15.6	2.5
1959	51.8	73.8	21.9	15.2	6.6	7.5	19.8	3.4
1960	49.6	73.5	25.2	15.3	8.3	7.3	17.0	3.6
1961	50.8	74.4	24.1	15.1	7.6	7.2	17.5	3.5
1962	50.0	73.3	26.2	14.4	7.6	8.1	16.3	4.5
1963	50.9	72.4	21.6	9.6	6.0	8.9	21.5	9.1

Source: *Trade and shipping statistics 1951, 1956, 1962 and 1965*, Dublin, CSO.

non-agricultural component. After considerable fluctuations during the late 1940s and early 1950s, the percentage share of exports accounted for by live animals declined between 1957 and 1960. The composition of non-agricultural exports experienced a gradual shift towards higher-value manufactured products.[28] Between the end of the Second World War and the early 1960s, the UK remained the largest single source of imports (see Table 6.2). However, imports from other European countries continued to increase their share while those from the USA declined from a high plateau during the early 1950s. The UK also remained the leading destination for Irish exports, but its share began a more long-term decline in these years from over 92 per cent of all exports in 1946 to under 73 per cent by 1963.

Non-agricultural exports continually increased their share of all merchandise exports in the 1960s and by 1973 their share exceeded that of agricultural exports. The share of exports accounted for by live animals decreased sharply, which was a welcome development, as it reduced the dependence of the economy upon exports that were subject to marked seasonal fluctuations.[29] This shift in the composition of exports and the general increase in trade were both accompanied by major structural changes at the principal ports. Between 1956 and 1971 there was a marked increase in productivity in air and sea transport, which was much higher than average for the services sector and reflected increased volumes handled. At the ports containerization and a greater degree of mechanical handling got underway, though Cogan concluded in the late 1970s that port mechanization still warranted significant investment.[30]

Growth in exports accelerated in the 1960s, especially following the Anglo-Irish Trade Agreement in 1965. The volume of total exports, which had expanded by an average of 4.5 per cent per annum between 1949 and 1961 (which was low by European standards), grew by 6.9 per cent per annum between 1961 and 1973 and by 8.1 per cent per annum between 1973 and 1984. Exports came to play a more significant role in increasing GDP growth in the 1960s and 1970s than in the preceding decades. The value of total exports as a proportion of GDP rose from 32 per cent in 1960 to about 60 per cent in 1984.

One of the more striking developments in Irish trade between the 1960s and the 1970s was the growing significance of industrial exports as a share of total merchandize exports, rising from 45 per cent of the total in 1960, to 69 per cent by 1979. These figures reveal the extent to which the late industrialization of the Irish Republic was largely an export driven phenomena. Since the introduction of Exports Profits Tax Relief in 1956, the presence of multinational companies in the Republic began to have a progressively greater influence in altering the nature and destination of Irish exports. By 1974, foreign firms accounted for a third of total Irish exports, contributing significantly to diversifying and increasing merchandize exports. They also contributed to dramatically reducing the significance of the UK as a destination for Irish exports from over 71 per cent of the total in 1964 to under 34 per cent by 1990 (see Table 6.4). More outward looking trade policies and increased FDI resulted in a positive shift in Ireland's revealed comparative advantage; between 1954 and 1971 Ireland enjoyed a revealed comparative advantage in terms of labour costs in manufacturing, which proved attractive to export orientated multi-nationals engaged in the production of labour intensive products. In the 1970s, Ireland's revealed comparative advantage shifted towards newer industries requiring higher skilled inputs that were more capital intensive, which had a positive impact in raising average income levels, increasing both industrial output and industrial exports.[31]

The increasing significance of trade in this period is evident from the fact that real exports as a proportion of GNP rose from under 29 per cent in 1960 to over 70 per cent by 1989. Real imports increased from 33 per cent of GNP in 1960 to 65 per cent in 1989. Much of this stellar increase was a consequence of the growing significance of multinationals in Irish economic activity; they imported many of their inputs, so there was a high imported-input content, contributing to the general rise in imports. They also developed trade links with their own affiliates in the mother country and elsewhere so that intra firm trade became more common,[32] which of course facilitated an increase in transfer pricing that progressively makes the trade data more difficult to interpret in this period.

Table 6.3 Selected industrial commodities as a percentage of all exports, 1974–89

Year	*Chemicals*	*Office and data equipment*	*Other machinery*	*Clothing and footwear*	*Textiles*	*Metal ores and mining products*
1974	9.1	–	10.9	5.0	7.7	4.3
1975	7.9	–	11.7	4.2	5.7	3.1
1976	9.5	–	14.4	3.9	6.7	2.2
1977	9.7	4.9	8.0	2.5	6.4	2.1
1978	11.9	4.5	8.0	3.4	6.2	1.9
1979	13.0	5.3	10.8	3.4	5.7	2.7
1980	12.7	6.3	10.0	3.0	5.3	2.5
1981	13.4	9.8	12.2	2.7	5.5	1.8
1982	14.2	10.9	11.0	2.6	4.5	2.0
1983	13.9	13.8	9.8	2.4	3.9	2.4
1984	13.9	17.3	9.8	2.4	3.9	3.8
1985	14.4	18.7	9.9	2.1	3.1	3.1
1986	13.3	19.7	9.9	2.3	3.2	2.2
1987	12.2	20.9	9.7	2.1	2.9	2.1
1988	13.1	18.4	11.7	1.9	2.8	2.4
1989	14.3	19.9	10.8	1.8	2.4	2.7

Source: *Statistical abstract 1974–75, 1976, 1978, 1981, 1982–85, 1988 and 1990*, Dublin, CSO.

Regarding the composition of exports, the decline of live animal exports as a share of total exports continued unabated between 1974 and 1989, as industrial goods increasingly dominated merchandize exports, but processed foods remained an important element despite its relative declining share. The textiles, clothing and footwear sector experienced reversals following entry into the EEC in 1973 as domestic producers increasingly fell victim to the intensification of competition within the common market. Metal ores and mining products also suffered a decline in their share of the value of exports, which never recovered.

In contrast, the share of exports accounted for by chemicals and office data equipment registered increases across this period, reflecting the growing importance of multinational investment in chemicals and pharmaceuticals and the electronics sector, which had been earmarked for fast track development by the IDA in the early 1970s (see Table 6.3). This focus on FDI in specific export orientated sectors was absolutely crucial to subsequent trade growth and the development of the economy at large.

EEC entry further reduced the dependence on the British market. Ireland benefited from this, as the new trading partners were more dynamic economies than Britain. Doyle argues that between 1960 and 1993, increased exportation to the

British market was a *result* of increased Irish output, whereas increased exportation to the US and EU countries had a multiplier effect, or was a *cause* of increased Irish output.[33] Prior to entry, four-fifths of Irish agricultural exports went to the UK, yielding relatively poor prices; by 1976–18 this had already been reduced to 56 per cent of agricultural exports, with the EEC other than the UK taking one third at that point.[34] Moreover, a host of American multinationals invested in the Republic of Ireland, using the country as the base for EEC/EU production and distribution. The Single European Market, enacted in 1992, was also of great benefit to Irish trade diversification. The Irish economy was not alone in benefiting from the dismantling of remaining national barriers to trade, thereby reducing transactions costs, but the structure of Irish manufacturing was composed of firms orientated towards exportation, above the average of other peripheral EU countries. The Single Market also had the effect of increasing the import demand within the core EU countries and Ireland benefited from this during the 1990s.[35] Due to the export orientation of the Irish economy, it therefore made disproportionate gains from the formation of the Single Market.[36]

In addition to the general economic benefits of the Single Market, such as liberalization of financial markets and reduced transaction costs, its creation was an important factor in encouraging a new wave of American investment to the Republic of Ireland, with many companies locating their European base there. Irish industry, being composed of high-technology firms, responded favourably to the Single Market, as opposed to traditional heavy manufacturing and textiles firms, which reacted unfavourably. Due to the favourable composition of Irish manufacturing and the general openness of the economy, Ireland benefited more from the Single Market than many wealthier EU countries.[37]

The growth in exports, both in absolute terms and relative to GNP, was dramatic by any standards during the 1990s. Information technology and pharmaceutical exports expanded during this period, while imports grew at a more modest rate. From the mid-1980s through the so called 'Celtic Tiger' era the Irish economy developed a significant surplus in the balance of trade. Much of this export growth was highly concentrated; Keating estimated that by 1999, 33 per cent of the total export of goods and services were accounted for by the 10 largest foreign owned firms in Ireland.[38] In certain sectors this concentration was extreme. Although the media by the turn of the century began to proclaim triumphantly that the Republic of Ireland was the second largest software exporter in the world after the US, surpassing India and Israel, in reality much of this was concentrated in multinationals, which accounted for 87 per cent of software sales and 92 per cent of exports. Of software exports from the state in 1995, Microsoft alone was reputed to have accounted for about 40 per cent of the total.[39]

O'Leary argues that from the beginning of the Celtic Tiger to 2002, exports were the main driver of growth, with the share of GDP rising from around 30 per cent in the late 1980s to 87 per cent by 2002. There is certainly strong empirical support for this contention in the longer term (1960–2008), which suggests that exposure to export markets was the key factor explaining productivity growth, with the hothouse performance of multinationals in the export base figuring as a major explanatory factor here.[40]

To handle the dramatically increased volume of trade in the 1990s, further improvements had to be made at the ports. At Cork for example, the fastest growing container port in the 1990s, investments were made in higher productivity cargo handling equipment at Tivoli, while dock rationalization in the 1980s at the ferry port at Ringaskiddy made this operation far more cost effective. The oil refinery and its handling facilities at Whitegate were also upgraded in the 1990s.[41]

The destination for Irish exports has changed dramatically since entry to the EEC. During the 1970s, exports to the EEC (excluding the UK) increased significantly, from 18.2 per cent of all exports in 1974 to 30.2 per cent by 1978. Although the UK still remained the premier destination of Irish exports, its share continued its long-term decline (see Table 6.4).

The growth of trade links with the US, more especially since the mid-1990s through the international trade in services and FDI, made the Irish economy especially vulnerable to adverse economic conditions in the US. An IMF study has revealed that adverse shocks to US GDP growth had a substantial adverse effect upon Irish GDP growth following a time lag of a year and three-quarters, in comparison to the brief effect that shocks to eurozone and UK GDP growth have upon Irish growth.[42] Outside the UK, US and continental European markets, the Irish export share destined for other parts of the world has not markedly improved, with the fairly minor exception of China and Hong Kong (see Table 6.5).

While the creation of the European Single Market facilitated the growth of international trade in Ireland, the introduction of the euro did not have the same impact. In contrast to the buoyant economic growth experienced by continental European countries relative to the Anglo-American world in the early 1990s, economic growth in the eurozone was relatively sluggish from 2000, compared to the UK and the US, which limited the growth of Irish exports to the Continent. Between 1999 and 2004, non-pharmaceutical Irish exports to the eurozone actually fell by 6.4 per cent.[43] Lawless notes that the EU-15 share of Irish exports differed little from its share in the early 1980s. Language and cultural differences, in addition to sluggish economic growth in continental markets, militated against any further growth of exports there.[44]

The changing composition of mercantile exports between 1990 and 2010 (see Table 6.6) reveal a continuation of the long-term decline in the relative significance of agricultural product exports, but this decline halted around 2000. Manufacturing increased its share of merchandize exports until the following peak years (2001–02) when they accounted for almost 93 per cent of merchandize exports, declining slightly since then.

In a wider European context, Crafts and Toniolo in particular have highlighted the unique significance of the Irish ICT production sector, largely for export, as the key aspect of Irish productivity performance in the boom years.[45] The growing export share of office and data equipment during the 1990s reflects the growing importance of ICT production in trade, but this was not sustained after the turn of

Table 6.4 Geographic distribution of exports (value) by percentage, 1964–94

Year	*UK*	*EEC*	*USA*	*World (rest)*
1964	71.4	11.5	4.5	12.5
1965	69.7	12.9	4.0	13.4
1966	69.3	10.9	7.0	12.8
1967	72.1	9.8	9.1	9.0
1968	65.4	9.1	13.5	12.0
1969	62.0	10.3	14.1	13.6
1970	62.7	10.8	12.9	13.6
1971	66.0	8.7	11.1	14.2
1972	60.8	15.7	9.4	14.1
1973	54.7	21.3	9.9	14.1
1974	55.9	18.2	9.6	16.3
1975	54.0	25.0	6.3	14.7
1976	48.7	27.1	7.5	16.7
1977	47.0	29.2	6.2	17.6
1978	47.2	30.2	6.2	16.4
1980	43.2	35.8	5.3	15.7
1981	40.2	34.2	6.4	19.2
1982	38.8	35.7	7.1	18.4
1983	36.9	36.0	8.1	19.0
1984	34.4	38.0	9.7	17.9
1985	33.0	38.9	9.8	18.3
1986	34.2	40.8	8.7	16.4
1987	34.2	42.4	7.8	15.6
1988	35.4	41.6	7.7	15.3
1989	33.5	43.7	7.9	14.9
1990	33.7	44.1	8.2	14.0
1991	32.0	45.3	8.7	14.1
1992	31.5	45.5	8.2	14.8
1993	28.4	42.1	9.0	20.5
1994	28.1	44.6	8.4	18.9

Source: *Statistical abstract 1965 1966, 1967, 1970–71, 1972–73, 1974-75, 1976, 1978, 1981, 1982–85, 1988, 1990, 1993 and 1996.*

Note: EEC figures pre-1972 are inclusive of Denmark for comparative purposes. EEC figures post-1978 comprise the EU15 as of 1992.

the century and its share actually fell from 2000 onwards, reflecting the withdrawal of a number of computer hardware firms from Ireland thereafter (see Table 6.7). A falling trend was also evident in exports of other machinery. The growth of such

Table 6.5 Geographic distribution of Irish exports (value) by percentage, 1995–2010

Year	*UK*	*EU 14*	*USA*	*China/ Hong Kong*	*Japan*	*Malaysia/ Singapore*	*Switzerland*	*World (rest)*
1995	25.5	47.2	8.2	0.5	2.9	1.4	1.8	12.5
1996	24.6	43.8	9.3	0.6	2.8	1.7	1.8	15.4
1997	24.6	43.0	11.3	0.6	3.2	1.5	1.7	14.1
1998	22.5	45.6	13.5	0.6	2.6	1.2	2.0	12.0
1999	21.9	43.0	15.4	0.7	2.9	2.0	2.4	11.7
2000	22.5	39.8	17.0	0.9	3.7	1.5	2.4	12.2
2001	24.0	37.9	17.0	1.1	3.5	1.9	2.9	11.7
2002	24.0	40.0	17.6	1.1	2.8	1.6	3.3	9.6
2003	18.1	44.5	20.6	1.6	2.6	1.6	3.2	7.8
2004	18.0	43.9	19.6	1.7	2.8	1.6	3.3	9.1
2005	17.7	45.6	17.8	1.7	2.6	1.5	3.7	9.4
2006	17.9	43.9	18.6	1.7	2.3	1.8	2.9	10.9
2007	18.7	42.8	17.8	2.2	1.9	1.4	3.7	11.5
2008	18.4	41.8	19.3	2.7	2.0	1.9	3.0	10.9
2009	16.2	42.9	21.1	2.9	2.1	1.6	2.9	10.3
2010	15.4	40.0	23.2	2.8	2.0	1.4	4.0	11.2

Source: 1995–2001, *Statistical yearbook 2002*, Dublin, CSO. 2002–2007, *Statistical yearbook 2008*, Dublin, CSO. 2008–2009, *Statistical yearbook 2010*, Dublin, CSO. 2010, *External trade Dec 2010*, Dublin, CSO.

Note: Figure for world (rest) includes the EU accession countries.

exports during the 1990s, especially those from indigenous firms, was cited by O' Malley as a sign of vigour within Irish manufacturing.[46] However, this was not sustained after 2002. Irish exports became increasingly reliant on the chemical sector, with a notable expansion of medical and pharmaceutical-based products contributing to the growing share of industrial output accounted for by chemicals and scientific or medical instruments and equipment. Chemicals by 2010 had risen to account for almost 60 per cent of total exports, revealing a somewhat less diverse composition of mercantile exports than in the 1990s (see Table 6.7) and an over reliance on a fairly narrow group of commodities. The fact that some of the major drugs produced in the Republic of Ireland are coming off patent poses a threat to exports in this sector.[47]

Although less attention is generally given to imports, they also played an important role in Irish economic development. Much of Irish industry has been dependant upon imported raw materials and inputs. The relative share of imports destined for Irish consumption has changed little over the period between 1952 and 2007 (see Table 6.8). There was a more marked surge in producer capital good imports during the 1960s, reflecting the expansion of medium-scale manufacturing in the Republic

Table 6.6 Percentage composition of mercantile exports (value) by broad commodity groups, 1990–2010

Year	*Agricultural products*	*Drink and tobacco*	*Non-agricultural exports*
1990	19.9	2.3	77.8
1991	20.2	2.4	77.4
1992	22.1	2.3	75.6
1993	19.9	2.2	77.9
1994	18.6	2.0	79.4
1995	17.4	1.7	80.9
1996	13.6	1.7	84.7
1997	10.3	1.6	88.1
1998	8.6	1.3	90.1
1999	8.2	1.2	90.6
2000	7.1	1.1	91.8
2001	6.3	1.1	92.6
2002	6.2	1.1	92.7
2003	7.0	1.3	91.7
2004	7.2	1.2	91.6
2005	7.4	1.3	91.3
2006	8.1	1.6	90.3
2007	8.5	1.6	89.9
2008	8.2	1.4	90.4
2009	7.5	1.3	91.2
2010	7.8	1.3	90.9

Source: 1995–1999, *Statistical yearbook 2001*, Dublin, CSO. 2000–2008, *Statistical yearbook 2008*, Dublin, CSO. 2009, *Statistical yearbook 2010*, Dublin, CSO. 2010, figures from CSO.

of Ireland during that decade. The growth of FDI also accounted for the growth in non-consumer imports. In parallel with the dominance of a small number of foreign firms of exports, the 10 dominant exporting firms identified by Keating accounted for 27 per cent of all imports in 1999, reflecting the huge significance in imports for further production among this small group of firms.[48]

Table 6.8 reveals that inputs for further production have long accounted for the majority of imports by value, but this share has begun to decline since the peak levels achieved in mid-1990s. This continued contraction since the turn of the century gives some indication of 'the ending of a protracted period of foreign firms building from scratch or adding to new manufacturing production capacity in Ireland'.[49] While producer capital goods at least consistently maintained their share between 2001 and 2007, the importation of consumption goods in these years increased from 21.7 per cent to 27.2 per cent. These changes in the composition of

Table 6.7 Selected industrial commodities as a percentage of all exports (value), 1990–2010

Year	*Chemicals*	*Office and data equipment*	*Other machinery*	*Clothing and footwear*	*Textiles*	*Mining products*	*Scientific apparatus*
1990	15.9	19.3	12.0	2.0	2.4	2.3	2.8
1991	17.6	16.5	12.9	2.2	2.4	2.1	3.0
1992	19.2	15.6	11.3	2.2	2.0	4.0	2.8
1993	19.3	18.4	10.6	1.8	2.3	3.3	2.4
1994	20.8	17.7	12.3	1.7	2.1	1.5	2.1
1995	18.9	21.0	13.5	1.3	1.3	1.3	1.9
1996	22.1	21.4	13.6	1.2	1.2	1.1	2.5
1997	25.3	22.9	14.9	0.9	1.0	1.2	2.5
1998	31.7	22.6	14.8	0.8	0.8	1.0	2.4
1999	31.6	22.6	16.5	0.6	0.6	0.8	2.1
2000	32.6	23.4	17.2	0.5	0.6	1.0	2.0
2001	34.8	22.7	17.9	0.4	0.5	0.9	2.0
2002	41.7	18.5	16.9	0.4	0.4	0.8	2.2
2003	43.6	18.1	10.6	0.4	0.4	0.8	4.0
2004	44.4	15.9	11.3	0.4	0.4	1.1	4.5
2005	46.6	16.1	9.4	0.3	0.3	1.4	3.1
2006	45.7	16.2	10.5	0.3	0.2	1.8	2.7
2007	48.3	14.1	10.3	0.2	0.2	1.9	2.4
2008	51.2	10.8	10.4	0.2	0.2	1.9	3.2
2009	56.6	8.0	8.5	0.2	0.2	1.3	3.5
2010	59.4	3.7	9.3	0.5	0.2	2.3	8.6

Source: 1995–99, *Statistical yearbook 2001*, Dublin, CSO. 2000–2008, *Statistical yearbook 2008*, Dublin, CSO. 2009, *Statistical yearbook 2010*, Dublin, CSO. 2010, figures from CSO.

imports reveals some underlying structural shifts in the economy at large during the second phase of the Celtic Tiger, with less emphasis on manufacturing production after the turn of the century and greater emphasis on consumption.

Although its share has declined, the UK has remained the premier supplier of Irish imports, still accounting for over 32 per cent in 2010. Barry and Bradley argue that the UK has been better able to retain a significant share of the Irish import trade due to the traditional cultural links between Ireland and Britain.[50] Certainly British retail giants such as Tesco, Marks & Spencer and a host of high street brands increased their presence in Ireland as incomes rose from the early 1990s. This helped to slow down, but not halt, the declining percentage share of UK imports into the Republic of Ireland (see Tables

Table 6.8 Percentage distribution of imports (value) by usage at three-year intervals, 1952–2007

Year	*Producer capital goods*	*Consumption goods*	*Inputs for further production*
1952	11.2	24.6	61.2
1954	11.7	24.5	60.5
1957	10.9	22.6	61.9
1960	10.7	20.5	64.1
1963	15.4	21.2	58.9
1966	15.5	22.6	58.8
1969	19.0	22.9	56.4
1971	17.7	22.8	56.7
1974	13.9	23.6	62.4
1977	14.4	21.9	63.6
1980	13.8	25.4	60.5
1983	12.7	25.5	61.6
1986	13.8	27.0	58.5
1989	16.1	25.9	57.3
1992	13.1	28.1	58.2
1995	10.0	20.4	63.5
1998	13.0	20.8	61.1
2001	13.1	21.7	61.5
2004	13.0	25.8	57.0
2007	13.4	27.2	55.0

Source: *Statistical abstract 1953, 1956, 1958, 1961, 1962, 1965, 1966, 1971–72, 1976, 1981, 1984, 1988, 1993, 1996 and 1999*, Dublin, CSO. *Statistical yearbook 2002, 2005, 2008*, Dublin, CSO.

6.9 and 6.10), with the result that the UK now remains far more important to the Republic of Ireland as a source of imports, than as an export destination. For exports, in contrast, the UK has become relatively less important and plays a far less significant role in Irish economic performance; even as late as 1972 for example, the UK accounted for the majority of Irish exports (see Table 6.9) and this was one factor explaining the Republic of Ireland's dependence on the UK market.

The most dramatic change in the composition of Irish imports since the beginning of the twenty-first century has been the recent emergence of China/Hong Kong as a significant source of imports, notably between 2001 and 2007, reflecting its importance in the importation of consumer goods. The EU share (excluding the UK) has also increased since the mid-1990s (see Table 6.10).

Table 6.9 Geographic distribution of merchandize imports (value) by percentage, 1967–94

Year	*UK*	*EEC*	*USA*	*World (rest)*
1964	50.4	15.4	7.7	26.5
1965	50.6	15.2	8.0	26.2
1966	51.8	13.5	9.3	25.4
1967	50.2	15.4	8.1	26.3
1968	49.9	16.4	7.4	26.3
1969	51.3	15.8	8.9	24.0
1970	52.1	17.0	7.2	23.7
1971	49.5	17.3	8.7	24.5
1972	51.0	18.2	7.5	23.3
1973	50.7	20.9	6.9	21.5
1974	46.6	21.7	6.5	25.2
1975	48.9	20.4	7.2	23.5
1976	49.2	20.1	8.5	22.2
1977	48.2	19.9	8.9	23.0
1978	49.4	20.8	8.4	21.4
1980	50.8	24.2	8.8	16.2
1981	49.7	25.4	11.7	13.2
1982	48.0	25.9	12.9	13.2
1983	45.3	24.7	14.7	15.3
1984	42.8	24.7	16.4	16.1
1985	42.7	24.2	17.0	16.1
1986	41.6	28.5	15.8	14.1
1987	41.7	26.7	17.0	14.6
1988	42.1	26.9	15.9	15.1
1989	40.9	27.3	16.1	15.7
1990	42.2	27.2	14.6	16.0
1991	41.4	26.8	15.0	16.8
1992	42.5	26.7	14.2	16.6
1993	35.9	22.7	17.0	24.4
1994	36.5	22.1	18.3	23.1

Source: *Statistical abstracts 1965, 1966, 1967,1970–71, 1972–73, 1974–75, 1976, 1978, 1981, 1982–85, 1988, 1990, 1993 and 1996*, Dublin, CSO.

To assess the impact of trade on the Irish economy since independence it is necessary to take account of the balance between mercantile imports and exports (the balance of trade) and the balance of payments, which takes account of non merchandize imports and exports, in addition to other international transactions

Table 6.10 Geographic distribution of merchandize imports (value) by percentage, 1995–2010

Year	*UK*	*EU (rest)*	*USA*	*China/Hong Kong*	*World (rest)*
1995	35.4	21.5	17.6	1.8	23.8
1996	34.8	22.0	15.4	1.7	26.2
1997	39.9	21.6	15.0	1.8	21.8
1998	41.0	20.4	16.0	2.2	20.4
1999	33.0	22.0	16.7	2.5	25.8
2000	31.5	23.5	16.4	2.8	25.8
2001	35.4	23.7	15.2	2.8	22.9
2002	36.2	24.5	15.3	3.6	20.5
2003	30.7	26.3	15.5	5.4	22.1
2004	31.4	31.3	13.7	6.4	17.2
2005	31.8	26.5	13.9	7.4	20.5
2006	31.9	28.3	11.2	7.8	20.8
2007	32.2	29.1	11.3	8.3	19.1
2008	33.3	30.1	11.7	7.4	17.5
2009	30.3	27.0	17.5	6.4	18.8
2010	32.1	25.8	14.1	6.1	21.9

Source: 1995–2009, *Statistical yearbook 2010*, Dublin, CSO. 2011, *External trade Dec 2010*, Dublin, CSO.

(see Appendix, Table 4). Ireland consistently experienced a negative balance of mercantile trade between 1925 and 1941, despite the best efforts of Cumann na nGaedheal to promote agricultural exports in the 1920s, and the imposition of protectionist policies by Fianna Fáil in the 1930s. The negative balance of trade between 1925 and 1941 was funded in part by non-tangible international payments, such as emigrant's remittances and income from foreign savings and investments held by Irish citizens. Ireland was also able to draw on reserves built up by the exceptional balance of trade export surplus of almost £77 million between 1914 and 1921.[51] The balance of payments deficit in the 1930s was consequently lower than the balance of trade deficit. Wartime conditions resulted in a substantial balance of trade surplus being built up again between 1941 and 1943, though this time it was due largely to the fall in imports.

As normal conditions returned after the war the expansion of imports in the late 1940s increased the balance of payments deficit substantially,[52] reaching the equivalent value of 18 per cent of national income by 1951. While exports as a share of national income increased gradually between 1948 and 1952, this was not sufficient to match the huge increase in imports, notably in 1951 when a crisis emerged in the balance of trade.[53] In order to reduce the trade deficit, the government responded with drastic deflationary budgets, which contributed to the stagnation of the economy in the 1950s. A balance of trade deficit continued to be a problem throughout the 1960s, but the greater expansion of output reduced its share in GNP.

The first and second oil crises had an impact on the balance of payments during the 1970s, increasing the deficit in 1974 and in 1979, while the expansionary fiscal policy of the Fianna Fáil government in the late 1970s further contributed to increasing the deficit. Despite adverse economic conditions in the 1980s, the expansion of exports reduced the balance of payments deficit and in 1987 a surplus was recorded (see Appendix, Table 4). One of the benefits of increased FDI in the decades after the 1950s was that multinational companies helped improve the volume and competiveness of Irish exports, also thereby reducing the deficit that had traditionally prevailed in the balance of trade. However, since a significant portion of the earnings from manufactured exports was repatriated (two-fifths according to an estimate in 1987), this element had an increasingly adverse affect on the balance of payments.[54] Conversely, the growth of tourism since the 1950s had helped improve the balance of payments. By the end of the 1970s it had become Ireland's third largest export,[55] though the invisible net income derived from tourism was returned in the balance of payments.

The balance of payments was in surplus for most of the 1990s, although this accounted for a lower share of national income than the balance of trade surplus. After 2001, a balance of payments deficit recurred, as export growth stalled, imports increased, and with the Irish increasingly travelling abroad, tourism was no longer a surplus item in the balance of payments. Paradoxically, the decline of the economy in the late 2000s has led to an improvement in the balance of payments as imports declined and as the balance of trade improved (see Appendix, Table 4).

An important change in the profile of Irish trade impacting on the balance of payments during the last decades of the twentieth century has been the increasingly dynamic role of invisible exports. Being non-tangible in nature, the trade in services is reflected in the balance of payments rather than the balance of trade. Due to the strength of the tourist sector for example, Ireland was a net exporter of services from the 1950s until the 1990s. The nature of service exports changed from the 1990s, as advances in information technology led to many financial services becoming tradable in international terms.[56]

Service exports grew dramatically between 1990 and 2010, despite the downturn in manufacturing in the latter years of this period. Foreign firms accounted for the bulk of growth in service exports. Since the turn of the century, a number of information technology companies that had been engaged in manufacturing in Ireland (such as IBM, Hewlett Packard, Microsoft and Dell) began to shift their Irish focus away from manufacturing towards service functions, such as R&D, technical support and software development. The contraction of employment in manufacturing was, however, only partly compensated by an increase in service activity employment. By 2003, the Republic of Ireland accounted for over one third of the EU trade in computer and information services, an activity largely clustered in the greater Dublin region.[57]

Table 6.11 Service imports and exports (£m) at three-year intervals, 1953–2010

Year	*Service exports*	*Service imports*	*Balance*
1953	31.7	12.0	19.7
1956	36.9	14.0	22.9
1959	41.8	14.3	27.5
1962	55.1	19.6	35.5
1965	82.1	28.9	53.2
1968	122.0	55.3	66.7
1971	142.5	64.9	77.6
1974	210.1	106.6	103.5
1977	392.8	294.3	98.5
1980	634.2	553.8	80.4
1983	939.0	830.0	109.0
1986	1,167.0	1,114.0	53.0
1989	1,632.0	1,574.0	58.0
1992	2,233.0	2,699.0	–466.0
1995	2,913.0	5,659.0	–2,746.0
1998	8,859.0	15,943.0	–7,084.0
2001	18,754.0	32,439.0	–13,685.0
2004	29,854.0	37,032.0	–7,178.0
2007	51,693.0	53,952.0	–2,259.0
2010	57,733.9	64,443.3	–6,709.4

Source: *Statistical abstract 1958, 1962, 1966, 1971, 1976, 1982–85*, Dublin, CSO. *Balance of international payments, final quarter and year ending 1999, 2001, 2002, 2004, 2006, 2008 and 2010*, Dublin, CSO.

After major growth between 2001 and 2004, service exports as a percentage of all exports have grown at a more modest rate. While the growth of financial service exports has provided considerable employment, much of this activity is reliant upon service imports (see services chapter). Therefore, the financial service export sector is of an entrepôt nature. Moreover, many of the IT services traded are intra firm transactions. Significantly, the imports of internationally traded services have consistently exceeded exports since the early 1990s (see Table 6.11), so the net impact on the economy in terms of the balance of payments should not be exaggerated.

The magnitude of international trade can be illustrated with reference to the percentage of national income accounted for by exports and imports combined. Despite increased trade liberalization, international trade grew modestly as a percentage of Irish GNP between the 1950s and beginning of the 1970s. More significant growth occurred in international trade following EEC entry in 1973, as

Table 6.12 International trade as a percentage of GNP at five-year intervals, 1950–2010

Year	*Imports and exports as a % of GNP*
1950	89.9
1955	77.0
1960	75.0
1965	78.1
1970	82.8
1975	97.6
1980	128.3
1985	151.1
1990	159.7
1995	188.9
2000	212.7
2005	277.8
2010	351.9

Source: 1950–80, *Statistical abstracts 1952, 1958, 1962, 1966, 1971–72, 1976 and 1982–85*, Dublin, CSO. 1985–2005, *Balance of international payments, quarter four and year ending 1990, 1995, 2001, 2006 and 2010*, Dublin, CSO.

increased FDI by multinationals became significant. A growing share of economic activity in the Republic of Ireland, more particularly in the industrial sector but also in agriculture and to a lesser extent in services, has become connected with trade. In short, the Irish economy has become increasingly open (see Table 6.12).

In the last decade or so the Irish share in world merchandize exports has fallen as certain sorts of manufacturing have been relocated to low wage economies in China and eastern Europe. During this period Ireland's share of global service exports has increased, as it has supplied computer, business, insurance and financial services, largely to the EU. Newman estimates that by 2009 about one third of total sales in the Irish service sector were exported.[58]

The profile of Irish trade has altered dramatically since independence. Livestock, processed food stuffs and drink accounted for the bulk of Irish exports during the 1920s and they continued to be centrally important in the following decades (see Appendix, Tables 5–8). Moreover, Irish exports in the inter-war years were largely concentrated on a single destination, the UK (see Table 6.1). The combination of internationally depressed economic conditions from 1929, the Economic War with Britain and the advent of full-blooded protectionism from 1932 hurt Ireland's economic growth prospects. The disruption caused by the Second World War, and Ireland's relatively slow retreat from protectionism were probably major factors accounting for the poor performance of the Irish economy between the 1930s and the 1960s compared to most of continental Europe. Dependence on Britain, one of the other relatively poor performers, did little to help the cause of the Republic of Ireland in these years. Ó Gráda concludes that Irish economic history has provided little or no support for the policy of import substituting industrialization (ISI) and that 'of all the reasons given for the Irish economy's poor performance before the 1960s, the failure of ISI to deliver the goods is perhaps the single most plausible one'.[59] Conversely, he argues that the shift in policy during the 1960s away from discouraging imports through tariffs to one of encouraging exports through grants and tax reliefs proved to be an altogether more successful strategy in helping the Republic of Ireland to begin to close the gap in the following decades with the rest of Europe, more notably in the 1990s, by which time its comparative advantage had shifted decidedly in favour of high tech industries and, to a lesser extent, services.[60]

Since the late 1990s the trade in services has become increasingly more important, with Dublin in particular becoming an entrepôt for this activity. However, although Ireland was among the European economies with a relatively higher level of trade in services, it should be noted that it was ultimately a net importer, and these were paid for by the surplus achieved in the balance of trade in merchandize. In 2008, Ireland had the highest goods trade surplus as a share of GDP in the EU.[61] This apparently positive indicator of Irish trade performance in an increasingly bleak economic landscape is partially explained by the decline in both consumer imports, with the downturn in purchasing power of consumers combined with a decline in manufacturing inputs, which have long constituted a large component of imports, as the Republic of Ireland lost its comparative advantage in some sorts of manufacturing to lower wage economies.

Perhaps the most striking feature of Irish trade since EEC entry in 1973 is that the Republic of Ireland has become one of the most trade dependent and open economies in Europe. Increased trade has been vital in enabling the Republic to close the gap with the rest of Europe in terms of living standards. Irish trade performance has held up better than other aspects of the economic activity since the downturn of 2008, but this has been insufficient to avert the continuous contraction of GNP between 2008 and 2010.

While the Republic of Ireland has clearly benefited from trade liberalization since the 1960s, increasing participation in the international economy has increased the risk of destabilizing macro-economic shocks in global downturns in international trade. Although luckily since the economic crash pharma exports have held up very well in recent years, the high concentration of total exports in this sector is a cause for concern. This lack of diversification and sectoral specialization in both industrial production and exports has increased the vulnerability of the Irish economy in the last decade. It should be noted that this problem is a feature shared by many small economies globally[62] and new policy initiatives are urgently required to increase trade diversification.

7 Investment and credit in Irish economic development

Investment and credit creation are important elements in economic development, both in terms of the areas private sector investment is directed towards and the role played by government in prioritizing specific areas for public investment. Productive investment is crucial in a developing economy and modern economic growth theory places emphasis on the phenomenon of convergence: the tendency of low-income economies to grow faster than wealthier economies, due to higher investment, which in turn was encouraged by the relatively higher rate of return on capital in poorer economies. This chapter broadly considers how many of these issues impacted on economic development in independent Ireland since 1922.

State investment provided an important stimulus to various sectors in the economy from the 1920s. Despite its general adherence to conservative fiscal and economic policies, Cumann na nGaedheal pioneered state-sponsored investment in electricity generation and distribution. The government also lent directly to the private sector. In the case of industry, Guaranteed Trade Loans were introduced in 1923, which extended state-guaranteed credit for funding private sector fixed capital investment. However, the loans were used more often to fund working capital expenditure.

From 1932, the new Fianna Fáil government increased public investment in general and the liabilities of the Irish government rose markedly from under £32 million to over £61 million in 1939.[1] While a significant share of this was tied up in land transfers, investment in state companies and housing provided some badly needed stimulus; many notorious slum areas in Cork and Dublin were cleared and new suburbs were built.[2] The number of houses constructed under state-aided schemes increased from a total of 27,427 between the years 1924 and 1933, to 80,173 between the years 1933 and 1939.[3]

Regarding the private sector, in 1933 Fianna Fáil removed the prohibition of the use of Guaranteed Trade Loans for working capital purposes, while taxation concessions and protectionism policies also increased private investment in the industrial sector in the 1930s. Following the precedent set by Cumann na nGaedheal with the establishment of the Agricultural Credit Corporation (ACC), Fianna Fáil established the Industrial Credit Corporation (ICC) in 1933,[4] to provide credit for industry. The formation of the ICC was suggested by the chairman of the ACC, who argued that Irish industrial investment was inhibited by competition from British share issues and the inadequate nature of the Dublin Stock Exchange. The extension of the Guaranteed Trade Loans scheme and the formation of the ICC contributed to industrial development in this period. A thousand new joint stock companies were registered between 1932 and 1938.[5] The ICC was active in its early years, underwriting issues by large companies such as Ranks, the Irish Sugar Company and Irish Cement. But it suffered from inadequate funding, which prevented further large-scale capitalization of the Irish industrial sector.[6]

The focus of state investment changed with the introduction of the Public Capital Programme following the Second World War, which led to a greater concentration on basic social and economic infrastructural investment. Between 1947 and 1951 government capital spending increased fourfold. Exchequer funding for turf development, tourism and telecommunications were expanded in the 1946–47 budget. These innovations provided the background for the formal adoption of capital budgeting by the first inter-party government, which came to power in 1948.[7] The inter-party government continued with the capital investment projects planned by the outgoing Fianna Fáil administration. Investment in social infrastructure such as housing was augmented, reflecting the priorities of Clann na Poblachta and the Labour Party. Expenditure on the State Capital Programme increased from £7.93 million in 1947–48, to £32.73 million by 1951–52. The percentage of expenditure accounted for specifically by housing increased from 11.5 per cent to 38.7 per cent over the same period.[8] One immediate effect of the new emphasis on social and economic infrastructural investment was the commencement of the rural electrification scheme. Between 1947 and 1956, 163,000 households in rural areas were connected. By 1957 rural electrification accounted for 10 per cent of national capital expenditure.[9]

Government borrowing for capital expenditure became far more significant in the 1960s and 1970s in expanding economic activity and employment. External borrowing was increasingly undertaken to fund capital expenditure, which was facilitated by the high credit rating enjoyed by the government. Ó Gráda and O' Rourke argue that an excessively high percentage of gross fixed capital formation was accounted for by the public sector during the 1970s.[10] State companies accounted for 8 per cent of total employment by 1980, and many of the 24 state companies were among the top 20 companies in Ireland in terms of turnover. However, following the massive borrowing that the government undertook in the late 1970s and early 1980s, the national debt mounted dramatically to unsustainable levels well in excess of £24 billion by the end of 1986; the equivalent of 148 per cent of the value of annual Gross National Product (GNP).[11] The 1982–87 coalition government began the difficult task of restoring order to the public finances. It succeeded in reducing inflation from 17 per cent to less than four per cent, and it reduced government borrowing considerably. Fiscal and monetary policy entered a highly constrictive phase as the government grappled with the debt problem at a time of rising unemployment.

Some important state investments were made in this period including a comprehensive digitalization of the telecommunications system, so that by the mid-1990s Ireland had a relatively sophisticated telecommunications network by European standards.[12] However, neo-liberal economic policies, which had been implemented in both the US and the UK, began to have an influence on Irish government thinking (see Chapter 2). From 1982 onwards, the coalition government began to consider the privatization of state companies, partly as an attempt to reduce government expenditure, while attempts were made to promote efficiencies within the state-owned sector. Between 1984 and 2002, four state companies were shut down; Irish Shipping (1984), Ceimici Teo (1986), Fóir Teo (1990) and Irish Fertiliser Industries (2002). In the same period, 10 state companies were privatized. Irish privatization receipts amounted to £8.13 billon over the period 1990 to 2001, the eight highest out of 29 surveyed OECD countries.[13]

The state's investments in food and sugar, which performed badly in the 1980s, were partially privatized as Greencore in 1990. Irish Steel was sold at a net loss to a private concern in the mid-1990s to eliminate another loss-making company from the state balance sheet. The flotation of a 75 per cent stake in the airline, Aer Lingus, was undertaken in 2006 to fulfil the urgent need for capital investment considerably diluting the state's stake in aviation.[14] The most notable privatization was of Telecom Eireann, later Eircom, which has not been a success in terms of transforming telecommunication's infrastructure. The company has built up huge debts and reduced employment. While the publicity surrounding privatization aimed at creating mass share ownership, following the iconic British privatizations of the 1980s, shares subsequently fell in value.[15]

By 2004, there remained only 10 companies in state hands; Aer Lingus, Aer Rianta, Bord Gáis Éireann (BGE), Bord na Mona, CIE, Coillte, the ESB, An Post, RTE and the Voluntary Health Insurance (VHI) in addition to eight commercial port companies. The declining position of state-owned companies is evident from the contraction of their share of total employment in the economy from 8 percent in 1980 to a mere 2.5 percent by 2004.[16] Therefore government influence on investment in the Irish economy became more indirect and policy became more focused on influencing the rising tide of private sector investment in the economy from the early 1990s through the IDA.

When the state was first established, Ireland was not lacking in private sector financial institutions, with eight joint-stock banks in operation: the Bank of Ireland, Munster & Leinster, Provincial, National, Royal Bank of Ireland, Hibernian, Northern Bank and the Ulster Bank.[17] However, the potential benefits of competition were limited by the existence of the Irish Banks Standing Committee, formed in 1920, which fixed overdraft and deposit rates for virtually the entire sector.[18] The existence of the committee limited bank restructuring; a limited rationalization occurred in 1939 with the closure of 25 branches, while complaints were aired that overdraft rates were excessively high and that too much of Irish savings were used to purchase monetary assets in the London financial markets rather than to fund investment in Ireland.[19]

The utilization of Irish savings to purchase British financial assets followed the traditional pattern established long before independence. The policy of holding Irish interest rates one per cent above British rates encouraged the retention of savings in Ireland. It was argued that Irish banks were excessively cautious in extending long-term credit for domestic investment. Such complaints were dismissed by the 1938 Commission on Banking, which argued that adequate credit was extended to Irish business, and that the pre-dominance of agricultural loans, secured only by personal securities on the part of farmers, introduced an extra risk factor for Irish banking.[20] Evidence in the early 1950s from a survey of 83 Irish manufacturing firms revealed that they actually utilized bank loans to a significantly greater degree than British firms. Despite this situation, the great bulk of investment (75 per cent) by the major Irish banks, the Bank of Ireland and Allied Irish Bank, was still centred on London at the end of the 1960s,[21] revealing the perceived lack of investment opportunities in Ireland and the wider range of investment prospects and superior returns on offer in the larger market, which had been a traditional magnate for Irish capital investment.

The banking system experienced considerable rationalization during the late 1950s and 1960s. The Bank of Ireland purchased the Hibernian Bank in 1958, followed by its purchase of the National Bank in 1966. The expansion of the Bank of Ireland led to co-operation between the remaining clearing banks, the Munster and Leinster, the Provincial and Royal Bank of Ireland. These three subsequently formed Allied Irish Banks as a collective holding company in 1966. Over the following six years they eventually amalgamated under the Allied Irish Banks banner.[22] In effect, this created a duopoly, which limited competition in the banking sector until the 1990s.[23] Eventually a challenger emerged; Anglo-Irish Bank. Established in 1964, Anglo Irish expanded through its merger with several smaller banks in the 1980s. Sean Fitzpatrick, who became chief executive of Anglo in 1980, developed a reputation for supplying credit to medium-sized businesses and to individual professionals and business people, whose needs were not met by either the major retail banks or by specialized merchant banks.[24]

An additional source of credit provision emerged with the establishment of credit unions, based on savings held by co-operative societies, but these agricultural credit societies largely collapsed after independence.[25] Co-operative financial institutions experienced a revival in the late 1950s,[26] with the number of credit unions expanding rapidly from 20 in 1962 to 400 by 1971. However, the rate of formation slackened in the 1970s.[27]

The provision of agricultural credit was expanded, in theory at least, with the formation of the ACC in 1927, but the interest rates charged were higher than market rates, making this new source of credit prohibitive for most farmers.[28] It has been argued that farmers were financially conservative and averse to utilizing credit, and there was a degree of social stigma attached to being in debt; indeed during the 1930s farmers were major net creditors to the banking system.[29] Advances to farmers from the banks and the ACC were still limited to £33 million at the beginning of the 1960s. However, the banking sector became a more significant source of capital for farming in the following decades, particularly after

EEC entry in 1973, so that advances had risen dramatically to £964 million by 1979. In general there was a significant rise in the share of gross value added in agriculture, which was invested or reinvested in the sector. Of all total investment in agriculture (including land purchase) from all sources, between 1976 and 1979, 60 per cent came from earnings.[30]

Despite the best efforts of the government to increase capital investment in the economy, the share of Irish GNP given over to capital formation in 1938 at 10 per cent was low in comparison with the 15 per cent average achieved for all countries in that year that subsequently became part of the OEEC.[31] The war had a severely adverse effect on investment activity, with a steep decline in the percentage of national income accounted for by gross domestic investment, which slumped to 2.5 per cent by 1944. But in the immediate post-war period, the gross domestic investment share of national income increased significantly to over 19 per cent in 1947, up from merely 9 per cent in 1938, with a combination of post-war recovery and government investment in infrastructure, declining thereafter to under 14 per cent by 1949.[32] Capital available for private sector investment remained somewhat scarce, as the banking industry continued to use deposits to purchase external assets, while the Control of Manufactures Acts restricted the potential amount of foreign capital that could be invested in the state.[33]

While the relatively low rate of growth of GNP in the late 1940s and 1950s, a comparatively lower propensity to save and the impact of emigration have all been identified as a contributory factors in limiting capital formation (which was relatively low by European standards), the priorities of government capital expenditure plans were also cited as a reason why capital formation was low. T. K. Whitaker argued that too much was spent on social expenditure such as hospitals and social housing and investment in domestic electricity and turf production, rather than on more productive aspects of the economy that could yield higher returns. He pointed out that annual capital investment in the entire industrial sector (excluding depreciation) was merely £7–8 million or less in the mid-1950s, which severely limited the growth of productive capacity within the economy.[34] Direct net investment was just under the equivalent of two per cent of GDP in 1962 and it had fallen to 0.6 per cent by 1971,[35] by which time FDI had become a more important source of investment.

FDI by non-national companies had been a feature of the Irish economic landscape from the 1920s. Ironically, the introduction of protectionist measures in the mid 1920s, and especially from 1932 onwards, instigated a new phase of investment by British companies who wished to retain or extend their share of the Irish market. The Control of Manufactures Acts, while in theory a measure to restrict non-national investment in Ireland, was in practice amended to facilitate British investment in certain sectors (see Chapter 4). From the 1950s, the focus of policy changed to maximize FDI.

The major policy instrument that encouraged this was preferential corporation taxation for exporting companies, which was introduced in 1956. Restrictions on foreign investment were removed and the Control of Manufacturers Acts were partially repealed from 1958 and abolished shortly afterwards, so that profits earned by foreign companies based in Ireland could be repatriated freely thereafter.[36] In global terms, the Republic of Ireland attracted a relatively small share of FDI between 1970 and 1980, but the inflows were growing dramatically in absolute terms and they were significantly more important than net domestic investment. This global share increased very dramatically during the 1990s, even increasing thereafter, transforming the performance of the entire economy relative to the rest of Europe (see Table 7.1).

The IDA concentrated its promotional efforts on the chemical and IT sectors; its proactive promotional activities and the low rate of corporation tax were both critically important in enabling the Republic of Ireland to reap disproportionate benefits in global terms from the wave of FDI that occurred in the 1990s. FDI inflows into both manufacturing and services were a major contributor to the boom in the 1990s and beyond. FDI inward stock per head was many times the EU average. By 2006, the Republic of Ireland still accounted for 10 per cent of USA manufacturing sector FDI stock in Europe.[37]

During the late 1980s and the early 1990s, major developments occurred in IT, with the US as the pioneer. In the context of low inflation internationally, and low interest rates, profitability and investment rates in such companies were high and these sectors looked to the EU to expand their growth prospects.[38] Low corporation tax was especially important, rather than low wages, as high-technology sectors had a low ratio of wages to profits.[39] The nature of IT products, which have a high added value compared to bulk, was of benefit to Ireland. Transport costs of IT products were negligible, which eliminated the disadvantages of the Republic of Ireland's peripheral location. The use of English has been cited as a reason why US multi-nationals have located in Ireland, yet according to Murphy, Ireland's true attraction to such multi-nationals was due to it being the only English speaking European Union member that fully supported European economic integration, while the UK was opposed to European Monetary Union (EMU) entry.[40]

The Republic of Ireland's earlier expertise in attracting multi-nationals led to what Krugman describes as 'cascade' effects, as firms located in the Republic of Ireland on the basis of favourable treatment received from fellow firms already located in Ireland.[41] These effects led to a major increase in US FDI in the Republic of Ireland. Crafts estimated that inward US FDI stock per capita increased from $1241.2 in 1986 to $2212.5 by 1995, reaching $141,134.3 by 2003. By 2007, the US FDI stock per capita in Ireland was treble the UK figure and nine times greater than the European Union figure.[42] The Irish share of Global FDI inflows increased from 0.3 per cent in 1990 to 1.9 per cent in 2000 (see Table 7.1). US multinationals based in the Republic of Ireland earned profits five times greater than elsewhere in the world in the 1990s, which was up from two and half times higher in the 1970s. Transfer pricing and easy profit repatriation explain part of this picture, which goes a long way to explaining the dramatic increase in American investment, also driven by the expansion of the American economy in this period and expanding opportunities offered by the large and relatively wealthy EU market. The US share of fixed industrial investment in the Republic of Ireland therefore rose dramatically from

Table 7.1 Global Foreign Direct Investment inflows ($m) to selected countries and regions, 1970–2009

Region	*1970*	*1980*	*1990*	*2000*	*2009*
Ireland	32 (0.5%)	286 (0.5%)	622 (0.3%)	26,447 (1.9%)	24,971 (2.2%)
EU15 (rest)	5,094 (39.4%)	20,872 (38.0%)	95,764 (45.9%)	48,506 (46.5%)	308,961 (27.7%)
Central and Eastern Europe	–	10 (–)	807 (0.4%)	22,519 (1.6%)	19,644 (1.8%)
USA	1,260 (9.7%)	16,918 (30.8%)	48,422 (23.2%)	314,007 (22.5%)	265,957 (23.9%)
China	–	57 (0.1%)	3,487 (1.7%)	40,715 (2.9%)	95,000 (8.5%)
Asia (rest)	853 (6.7%)	485 (0.9%)	19,134 (9.2%)	108,014 (7.8%)	206,367 (18.5%)
Africa	928 (7.1%)	392 (0.7%)	2,429 (1.2%)	8,489 (0.6%)	58,565 (5.3%)
Central and South America	1,611 (12.5%)	7,538 (13.7%)	9,862 (4.7%)	95,767 (6.9%)	116,555 (10.5%)
World	12,926	54,923	208,501	1,392,957	1,114,189

Source: United Nations Conference on Trade and Development, Foreign Direct Investment Database, available from http://unctadstat.unctad.org/TableViewer/tableview.aspx?ReportId=88 (accessed 1 June 2012).

Note: Central/Eastern Europe includes Bulgaria, Czech Republic, Estonia, Hungary, Latvia, Lithuania, Poland, Romania, Slovakia and Slovenia. Ireland constitutes 26 counties only.

under 33 per cent of the total to almost 66 per cent, with output and investment in US manufacturing heavily focused in computers, electronic engineering and pharmaceuticals, with these sectors (excluding software and telesales) collectively accounting for 40 per cent of Irish GDP growth.[43]

Table 7.1 also illustrates that the rate at which FDI inflows to the Irish economy slowed from 2000, but Ireland more than retained its global share reflecting the international decline between 2000 and 2009. Ruane and Görg argued that the Irish economy experienced a major 'one-off' increase in FDI in the early to mid-1990s due to the creation of the Single European Market.[44] The composition of direct investment in Ireland also altered. Service-based FDI accounted for 66 per cent of the USA direct investment stock by 2000, while in 1994 manufacturing had made up over half of the total stock.[45] However, much of the service-based FDI was of more limited value to the Irish economy. Foreign owned companies based in the IFSC conducted capital movements into treasury, fund management and other financial subsidiaries, which in turn were used to purchase overseas assets.

While Ireland still attracts new FDI projects in the pharmaceutical and healthcare sectors in particular, the role of manufacturing-based FDI has diminished in the Irish economy as a whole. The relocation of many computer hardware companies to central and eastern Europe, and the attraction by these countries of new FDI projects, led to a decline in new FDI manufacturing projects in Ireland, while disinvestment of €1.6 billion was recorded in new FDI projects between 2001 and 2002.[46] FDI in the manufacturing sector was increasingly used to upgrade and maintain existing plants rather than to create new capacity, while FDI-based firms increasingly retained profits made in Ireland to fund investments in Irish plants.[47] While the retention of profits made in Ireland was welcome, it signified how the flow of new manufacturing FDI declined after 2000. There was also a marked switch out of IT production into services within some of the large IT multinationals.

Another effect of the economic boom in the Republic of Ireland was the growth of direct investment abroad by Irish companies. Individual Irish firms across a range of sectors had amassed substantial foreign investments, such as the Kerry Group, Smurfit and Musgrave, for example, but overall this kind of direct investment had little impact on Irish economic development. By 1997, the stock of Irish outward FDI accounted for 7.9 per cent of GDP, lower than any EU member country, except Austria, Greece and Portugal. The low stock of Irish FDI was attributed to the presence of few Irish firms in sectors characterized by FDI flows, the relatively recent industrialization experienced by the Republic of Ireland[48] and the cautious investment decisions made by Irish financial institutions. However, Irish companies' investments abroad increased from €5 billion in 2000 to €16 billion by 2007, was concentrated in four major sectors; financial services, construction and property, food, drink and agri-business and print, paper and publishing. Companies investing extensively abroad included Kerry Group (food) operating in 22 countries, CRH (mineral products) in 26 and Jefferson Smurfit (paper and packaging) in 31.[49]

Initially the majority of Irish outward FDI was concentrated in the US and the UK; 84 per cent of Irish outward direct investment between 1998 and 2000 was

Table 7.2 Financial account balances (£m), 1998–2010

Year	*Direct investment balance*	*Portfolio investment balance*	*Other investment balance*
1998	3481.9	6666.1	5,944.1
1999	8944.1	–11,292.9	–766.9
2000	18,076.4	–4218.9	–7,115.7
2001	4914.2	– 19809.4	14,991.3
2002	15,310.2	–29,904.7	15,167.7
2003	12,023.6	–31,478.0	16,981.9
2004	–18,185.0	11,249.6	9,000.0
2005	–29,127.6	41,494.5	–13,909.4
2006	–13,097.6	6405.5	10,380.0
2007	5648.0	–2055.1	7,309.5
2008	–13,722.0	–17,315.8	45,363.8
2009	375.0	14,772.0	–17,820.0
2010	6437.8	74,568.5	–70,077.2

Source: *Balance of international payments, final quarter and year ending 2000, 2002, 2004, 2006 2008, and 2010*, Dublin, CSO. *Balance of international payments second quarter 2010*, Dublin, CSO.

destined for non-eurozone countries.[50] However, in the decade following the establishment of the euro, Irish companies began to acquire more assets within the eurozone.[51] The introduction of the euro, low interest rates and liberalization of capital markets facilitated further expansion of Irish direct investment abroad.[52]

Irish portfolio investment also grew during this period, in tandem with economic growth. The outflow of funds from Ireland to purchase financial assets abroad is a long-established feature of the Irish economy, but the magnitude of the net portfolio investment outflow diminished from 2003 onwards with the growth of portfolio investment in Ireland. In addition to the purchase of stocks and shares, a new feature of Irish portfolio investment abroad was the purchase of commercial and residential property abroad.[53] According to Cooper, €3 billion was invested by Irish citizens in foreign commercial property by 2004. The final category of investment, 'other', refers to financial derivatives, options and long-term trade credits,[54] and was chiefly concerned with financial services activity.

Due to increased FDI and increased domestic saving in the Irish economy during the 1960s and early 1970s, investment, as measured through the percentage of GDP accounted for by Gross Domestic Physical Capital Formation,

Table 7.3 Gross Domestic Physical Capital Formation as a percentage of GNP for three-year intervals, 1953–2009

Year	*Gross Domestic Physical Capital Formation as % of GNP*
1953	16.4
1956	12.7
1959	16.8
1962	18.1
1965	22.1
1968	20.2
1971	21.5
1974	26.6
1977	25.4
1980	27.6
1983	18.1
1986	20.1
1989	20.7
1992	18.4
1995	20.6
1998	27.1
2001	28.0
2004	29.0
2007	31.0
2009	17.1

Source: *Statistical abstract 1953*, Dublin, CSO. *National income and expenditure 1958, 1969–70, 1975, 1979, 2002, 2007, 2009*, Dublin, CSO. Historical National Income and Expenditure CSO, available from www.cso.ie.

increased. High levels of private saving continued during the rest of the 1970s, despite inflationary pressures and real negative interest rates. However, this was offset by government debt creation. Gross Domestic Physical Capital Formation as a percentage of GDP fell between 1972 and 1978. After an increase in the late 1970s, Gross Domestic Physical Capital Formation as a percentage declined sharply between 1981 and 1987 (see Table 7.3). The supply of domestic capital for productive purposes fell during the 1980s, although savings as a percentage of GDP actually increased during the same period.[55] With increasing unemployment, real incomes and savings fell. High interest rates made investment prohibitive for the private sector and funds were shifted from physical to financial assets. Private capital inflows to the Irish economy virtually ceased.[56] Nugent, who measured Irish company profitability through both the ration of gross operating surplus as a percentage of GDP (rate of profit per unit of output) and the ratio of net operating surplus per unit of net fixed capital stock (profitability of capital), found that both measures declined during the 1970s. A particular difficulty was the increase in real labour costs per employee of 3.9 per cent between 1974 and 1978, while the real rate of return on capital grew by only 1.7 per cent, limiting the rate of return on capital investment. Despite troubled international economic conditions, company profitability increased after 1981. Nugent observed that this recovery in profitability was mostly due to the activities of multi-national companies and transfer pricing, while indigenous Irish companies did not recover their pre-1979 profitability levels.[57]

Prior to the 1980s, most Irish manufacturing firms were financed through bank borrowings and government grants. With the recovery of company profitability in the 1980s, share capital and reserves increased as a percentage of total capital from 59 per cent to 65 per cent between 1976 and 1989. Borrowing as a percentage of total capital fell from 32 per cent to 25 per cent over the same period.[58] The economic environment for productive investment changed during the 1980s. The initial drive to implement a greater degree of fiscal rectitude by Fianna Fáil from 1987 onwards, accompanied by the beneficial effects of the 1986 devaluation and benign international economic conditions, increased company profitability.[59] Adherence to the Maastricht criteria and the general political consensus, based on the acceptance of fiscal stability, encouraged greater private capital inflows to the Irish economy thereafter.[60] The process of financial de-regulation eased the ability of financial institutions to extend credit.[61] Participation in the EMU reduced interest rates, facilitating further investment.[62]

Savings actually fell as a percentage of GNP during the 1990s. The inverse relationship between savings and investment that was observed during the 1980s calls into question the applicability of classical economic theory to Irish economic circumstances. Economic theory argues that a positive relationship exists between the level of savings and the level of investment. Yet the trend of savings and investment in Ireland suggested that a negative relationship existed, and that investment was positively related to domestic consumption.[63] Another explanation for the divergence between the level of savings and investment in the Irish economy is a more practical one; that Irish financial institutions did not utilize available savings to fund domestic investment. While the growth of industrial employment led to the growth of savings in absolute terms, such increased savings were increasingly used by pension funds during the 1980s and 1990s to purchase foreign assets. By 1995, 39.4 per cent of Irish pension funds were held in foreign assets while only 27 per cent were held in Irish equities.[64] In contrast, many small businesses and new firms in Ireland had difficulty raising capital from financial institutions during the 1980s and early 1990s. Irish banks charged prohibitive personal overdraft rates when lending to small businesses.

Alternative sources of capital acquisition such as the Irish Stock Exchange were seldom utilized as a means of raising equity. Irish companies continued to rely on bank borrowings. Over the 12-year period 1972 to 1984, only £233 million was raised in the Irish Stock Exchange, compared to £1.04 billion raised by companies through corporate sector borrowings. Of companies who issued rights on the stock exchange, only 2.7 per cent were composed of share issues for new manufacturing companies, the remainder being accounted for by established companies such as the major banks, Cement-Roadstone Holdings, Smurfit and Waterford Glass.[65] As recently as 2007, an IMF report concluded that capital market development was at a low level in Ireland, with particular reference to the relatively low utilization of the stock market.[66]

Some of these constraints were reduced during the 1990s, chiefly through easier access to credit, which expanded on a global basis.[67] Investment capital was sourced by domestic financial institutions from abroad. A combination of exchange control liberalization and the EMU facilitated Irish financial institutions in accessing foreign credit.[68] As Honohan observed in the early 2000s, 'the economy has relied heavily on external providers of finance to supplement what locally controlled intermediaries cannot do'.[69] In the period 1987 to 1993, investment increased by 2.4 per cent per annum and then accelerated to 15.32 per cent per annum for the Celtic Tiger years between 1994 and 2000.[70] A noteworthy example of financial deregulation was the Building Society Act (1989), which allowed building societies to access capital on wholesale fund markets rather than be completely dependant on customer deposit accounts for funding. This facilitated the subsequent expansion of the Irish Nationwide Building Society.[71]

Growth was experienced by leasing companies, which also eased constraints on investment. Credit extended to leasing companies increased by 700 per cent, from £600 million to £4.7 billion, between 1994 and 1998. Leasing companies were especially important to economic growth as they leased assets to productive sectors such as manufacturing and distribution.[72] Of further significance were the three sectors that experienced the highest private sector credit growth; construction, hotels and restaurants and financial and other business experienced high employment growth during this period.[73] The increase in the share of output accounted for by profits provided another source for investment by individual companies.[74]

Policy changes also eased constraints on investment for small businesses. The Seed and Venture Capital Measures, which operated between 1994 and 1999, provided assistance in the acquisition of capital by new firms, while the Access to Finance Scheme provided government funding for loans taken out by small firms from the major Irish banks.[75] Deregulation of financial institutions further facilitated the provision of investment finance. Finally, the traditional aversion to risk in the Irish financial sector abated during this period. This was in part due to the effect of competition in the banking sector. The Royal Bank of Scotland, which entered the Irish market in 1999, systematically undercut the mortgage lending rates of the existing banks from 2001.[76]

With low interest rates and financial deregulation, Irish financial institutions enjoyed a surplus of funds available for credit creation. Given the sensitivity of Irish investment patterns to expected demand in the economy, rather than savings, the favourable expectations of economic growth encouraged the extension of credit. This was reflected in the major growth of personal credit extended by financial institutions, and the decline of the ratio of deposits to credit. Anglo-Irish Bank was the first financial institution that allowed loans to exceed deposits;

Table 7.4 Percentage composition of Gross Domestic Fixed Capital Formation for four-year averages, 1953–2010

Year	*Dwellings*	*Roads*	*Buildings*	*Transport equipment*	*Agricultural machinery*	*Other machinery*	*Software*
1953–1956	18.7	5.7	37.3	12.3	5.2	20.9	–
1957–1960	14.1	5.6	36.1	17.6	5.5	21.2	–
1961–1964	15.9	5.2	34.1	13.6	5.0	26.4	–
1965–1968	20.2	3.7	33.9	12.8	4.4	25.2	–
1969–1972	19.3	2.4	31.8	14.4	4.5	27.6	–
1973–1977	23.6	2.0	27.7	12.0	4.7	30.0	–
1978–1982	21.7	2.3	28.6	13.0	4.0	30.4	–
1983–1987	24.6	4.1	23.2	13.1	2.5	32.4	–
1988–1992	24.2	4.3	24.5	17.1	2.3	27.6	–
1993–1997	29.6	4.8	21.7	16.1	2.1	21.7	0.7
1998–2002	33.8	4.7	22.4	13.4	1.0	17.7	1.3
2003–2005	47.5	5.1	16.8	9.4	0.8	16.0	1.1
2006–2009	41.0	5.6	22.5	11.9	3.2	8.9	1.9
2010	24.6	7.7	24.3	21.2	0.8	11.7	5.0

Source: *National income and expenditure, 1960,1969, 1975, 1982, 1986, 1989, 1997, 2004, 2006, 2009 and 2010*, Dublin, CSO.

between the years 1994 and 1999, Anglo-Irish deposits increased from €1 billion to €4.4 billion, while its loan book increased from €1 billion to €5.7 billion.[77] This however was positively cautious, compared with what was to follow. Before euro entry, Irish bank lending broadly remained linked to the level of deposits. After entry, that link was entirely broken and bank lending began to far exceed deposit levels, throwing caution to the wind. The state foolishly allowed banks to maintain the lowest bank capitalization ratio in Europe.[78] This excessive latitude and lack of regulation by the state in the preceding decade witnessed the birth of an unsustainable casino economy, which became all too apparent in the complete meltdown of the banking sector in 2008.

Taking a longer-term perspective over many decades, the composition of investment reflected the structural changes that occurred in the Irish economy. Looking at the period from 1953 to 1972, the share of gross domestic fixed capital investment accounted for by other machinery increased significantly, with the majority of this increase occurring between the sub-periods 1957–60 and 1961–64, reflecting the growing significance of industry and the relative decline of agriculture (see Table 7.4).

During the 1970s and 1980s, the dominance of industrial development is reflected in the high share of gross domestic physical capital formation accounted for by other equipment and other buildings. Transport equipment increased its share of investment over the period 1973 to 1997, with an especially sharp increase between the 1983–87 and 1988–92 periods. Agricultural machineries' share of investment between the periods 1978–82 and 1983–87 continued its decline, while the emergence of the software sector is indicated in its increase in the share of Gross Domestic Physical Capital Formation in 1993–97 and 1998–2002, and again in 2006–09 and 2010. Yet, the most significant trend was the increase in the percentage of Gross Domestic Physical Capital Formation accounted for by dwellings, especially between the time periods 1998–2002 and 2003–05 (see Table 7.4). This reflected the general shift in investment priorities between the first and second phases of the Celtic Tiger. The collapse in the construction sector is indicated in the collapse of its share of Gross Domestic Physical Capital Formation between the period 2006–09 and 2010.

Rossa White has argued that the private sector made poor investment decisions, between 2000 and 2008, with excessive investment in property, especially retail property, which is underutilized in periods of recession, while no significant growth occurred in the investment share accounted for by software and the communications network. In contrast, public sector investment in roads, energy and water supply had a more beneficial effect in increasing productivity than private sector investment.[79] White's argument has particular force with reference to the domestic property sector.[80] Significant investment occurred in residential dwellings after 2000. The construction sector share of overall credit advances increased from 3.3 per cent in 2001 to 6.9 per cent by 2007 (see Table 7.5).

Increased housing prices were a common phenomenon in the industrialized world during the late 1990s and 2000s, due to expansionary monetary policies and house zoning policies by local authorities. Yet the increase in Ireland was the highest, in both real and nominal terms, for the period 1995 to 2005 within the OECD. This increase peaked in 2007. Fundamental economic and demographic factors, such as increased disposable income, low interest rates, the expansion of the young house-forming cohort within the population and immigration, were cited by many authorities as the cause of the property boom.[81] However, the dual effects of inappropriate policy and investment incentives and an irrational speculative mentality were ignored as major causal factors. Incentives in the tax system, which stimulated the housing market beyond the demand for accommodation, included the abolition of residential property tax in 1997; the reduction of capital gains tax in the late 1990s from 40 per cent to 20 per cent, which stimulated the demand for second homes; tax relief on the construction and refurbishment of apartments and tax relief on the construction of student accommodation.[82] The Upper Shannon Rural Renewal Scheme, for example, introduced tax reliefs on the construction and refurbishment of residential and commercial properties in Counties Sligo, Leitrim, Cavan, Longford and Roscommon, leading to a dramatic over expansion of residential property in these counties.[83] Other policies that stimulated the excessive demand for housing included mortgage tax relief and land zoning practices by local authorities, which created an artificial scarcity of building land.[84]

The effect of this collage of inappropriate policies (seemingly to stimulate construction at any cost) was to create a vast stock of vacant houses, frequently in

Table 7.5 Percentage distribution of private sector credit, 1991–2009

Year	*Total credit advanced (£m)*	*Personal credit as % of all credit*	*Manufacturing credit as % of all credit*	*Construction credit as % of all credit*
1991	13,760.3	30.3	12.5	3.1
1992	14,159.4	30.6	12.4	2.6
1993	14,948.9	30.3	10.5	2.2
1994	16,506.9	29.7	8.9	2.1
1995	19,168.0	29.1	8.0	2.3
1996	33,166.0	43.0	6.6	2.0
1997	42,326.0	40.8	5.8	1.7
1998	52,361.0	39.3	6.2	2.7
1999	72,292.0	35.9	5.3	2.6
2000	87,144.0	35.5	5.2	3.3
2001	101,636.0	35.3	4.4	3.3
2002	111,966.0	39.7	3.5	3.2
2003	125,954.0	42.8	2.8	3.9
2004	156,716.0	45.7	2.8	4.8
2005	203,194.0	44.7	2.3	5.4
2006	249,343.0	42.3	2.2	6.6
2007	295,694.0	39.6	2.2	6.9
2008	309,989.0	35.2	2.3	5.6
2009	290,046.0	35.3	1.9	4.1

Source: *Statistical abstract 1992, 1994 and 2001*, Dublin, CSO. *Statistical yearbook 2007 and 2010*, Dublin, CSO.

places where there was absolutely no demand, resulting in a massive waste of resources, landscape damage and other problems with partial occupation of such unfinished developments. Fitzgerald has observed that a significant element of this increase in the housing stock was due to the expansion of vacant dwellings, which accounted for 19.3 per cent of the total increase in the number of dwellings between 1996 and 2002, and this increase was more pronounced in Atlantic seaboard counties, where vacant dwellings, located in scenic areas, accounted for 35.5 per cent of the total increase of dwellings. Fitzgerald observes that much of this vacant housing was held for investment purposes.[85] Vacant housing created an excess demand for basic infrastructure and was in conflict with the 'desire for balanced regional development, making it unnecessarily expensive for individuals to live and for businesses to operate in regional locations'.[86] Kitchin and his co-authors argue that inadequate planning practices by local authorities were as significant a factor in the creation of the unsustainable property boom as government monetary and fiscal policies. Local authorities permitted the construction of surplus residential estates and commercial developments in the expectation of income accruing from development levies and the assumption that property development would generate local economic expansion of its own accord.[87]

Taxation policies and uncoordinated local authority planning processes led to the creation of property empires based on artificially created incentives rather than the inherent demand for residential and commercial property.[88] Investment in property also enjoyed a social prestige within the Irish population beyond any intrinsic economic value. Lee, and more recently Coleman, suggested that the historic influence of the famine and the land war created a societal craving for property acquisition.[89] In practical terms, Kitchin and his co-authors observed that the 'strong cultural imperative to own one's home ... has undoubtedly contributed to new purchasers over-extending their credit in order to step onto the housing ladder'.[90] The urgency among first time buyers to acquire mortgages encouraged the financial institutions to offer ever more generous mortgages.[91]

Further evidence for the speculative contribution to the housing price increase is provided by Morgan Kelly, who observed that the ratio of rent to income remained stable from 2000, which indicated that increased housing demand was not due to demand for residences and instead was founded on excessive speculative gains.[92]

The OECD economists, Rae and Van der Nood, estimated that up to 20 per cent of the Irish housing price increase during the property boom was due to purely speculative factors, with the expansion of credit and incentives in the taxation system encouraging such speculative housing demand.[93] Kearns and Woods estimated that residential mortgages as a percentage of all property related loans, at 64 per cent in 2006, were at an all-time low; the remaining 36 per cent of loans were extended to the construction sector. This was further evidence that the expansion of the property sector had outrun residential demand.[94] Finally, prices for existing houses increased more rapidly than those for new housing between 2000 and 2008, which indicates a demand for property for its own sake rather than reflecting a demand for new accommodation.

By 2007 the perversely large share of construction in the Irish economy was evident from the fact that it employed double the European norm.[95] The housing market peaked in the Dublin region in that year and for the rest of the country in 2008, declining rapidly thereafter.[96] It has been argued by Rae and van den Noord in 2006 that the booming housing market combined with the tax treatment of housing might have been impacting on the economy's productive potential by diverting a large amount of investment into residential construction.[97] In turn, the increase in land prices encouraged the further extension of credit, which the banks were able to fund through foreign borrowings, as described earlier. As McWilliams observed:

> the more money they lend, the safer it looks in terms of the ratios they use to assess secure lending. So it becomes a self-reinforcing dynamic where the more money they lend the more they feel they should lend.[98]

Table 7.6 House price indices for March of each year, 1996–2008, 1996=100

Year	*National housing prices*	*Non-Dublin housing*	*Dublin housing*	*New houses*	*Existing houses*
1996	100.0	100.0	100.0	100.0	100.0
1997	112.8	109.7	120.0	110.0	114.4
1998	130.4	122.0	151.1	130.2	132.0
1999	167.0	152.6	201.3	162.7	170.1
2000	199.9	185.2	233.8	188.9	209.5
2001	238.1	218.9	287.3	226.9	247.2
2002	245.8	229.0	287.5	233.3	254.4
2003	281.4	257.4	338.1	255.6	297.0
2004	315.5	292.2	381.2	288.8	334.6
2005	341.5	311.1	412.5	315.4	359.8
2006	382.7	349.1	466.3	353.1	397.5
2007	411.2	372.2	520.7	377.9	425.7
2008	374.5	394.6	473.6	356.1	383.4

Source: *ESRI/ Permanent tsb monthly housing price index, Sept 2009.* http:www.esri.ie/irisheconomy/permanent.tsbesri.house.p/ (NB this index is no longer published).

In addition, the demand among first time buyers to acquire mortgages, observed by Kelly, encouraged financial institutions to offer higher mortgages, which in turn increased property prices; this increased the value of mortgages, creating a dangerous financial spiral dependant upon the expectations among buyers of continually rising prices.[99] This concentration in property lending left the banks vulnerable to any declines in the property market. Five banks had 80 per cent of all property related loans concentrated in the residential mortgage sector.[100] At this stage 60 per cent of all bank lending was property related, and this dramatic over exposure to one sector was the fatal weakness of both the banking system[101] and the economy of the Republic of Ireland.

The rapid growth in bank balance sheets was another signal of the unsustainable nature of the boom. A simple rule-of-thumb cited by Honohan is that unsustainable growth is indicated by an annual growth rate in excess of 20 per cent in a bank's balance sheet. Between the period 1998 and 2007, Anglo-Irish Bank exceeded the 20 per cent per annum balance sheet growth rate; its average annual growth rate was 36 per cent for this period. The Irish Nationwide Building Society also exceeded the 20 per cent rate for six years during the relevant period, while the other major banks experienced balance sheet growth in excess of 20 per cent for at least one of these years.[102]

Yet this behaviour was uncharacteristic of Irish financial institutions; as we have noted above, these institutions had historically generally been quite cautious in extending credit.[103] Honohan posed the question; 'How could traditionally conservative banks –some of them with a 200-year history – have been so careless as to leave themselves exposed in such a conspicuous and obvious property bubble?'[104] Clearly many bankers were fooled in classic bubble fashion by inflated property values, which had experienced a long-term upward rise. Economic factors, such as excessive demand fuelled by optimism about the strength of the Irish economy, and a ready supply of credit at low interest rates from foreign banks, stimulated lending to the residential property market.[105]

The Irish credit market experienced a race to the bottom, with Anglo-Irish Bank being the first to engage in reckless lending to developers from the late 1990s onwards. Anglo Irish implemented inadequate and hasty risk appraisal procedures and concentrated its activities to an excessive extend in funding the property sector.[106] The Irish Nationwide Building Society also engaged in unsustainable high risk funding of the property sector. By 2007, specialist site financing accounted for 52 per cent of the building society's commercial loans.[107] In the case of Anglo-Irish Bank, the 20 highest debtors, the majority of whom were engaged in property development, accounted for 18.5 per cent of Anglo-Irish's total loan book.[108] The fortunes of both these institutions were dangerously linked to the interests of a very small group of developers, dramatically raising the level of financial risk.[109]

The traditional banks followed in their wake and funded the property market, motivated by the hope of benefiting from the expanding property boom, driven by fear of losing market share to Anglo-Irish Bank and of a foreign take-over if balance sheet growth lagged behind other Irish financial institutions. Allied Irish Bank in particular participated in the property bubble. By September 2008, 47 per cent of the bank's commercial and property loan portfolio was accounted for by property development finance, while existing guidelines regarding the extension of credit to the property sector were relaxed. In the case of the Bank of Ireland, by September 2008, 34.5 per cent of its loan book was accounted for by property development finance.[110] Ironically, as the traditional banks were expanding their activities in the property sector, David Drumm, Sean Fitzpatrick's successor as Chief Executive of Anglo-Irish Bank, attempted to limit the bank's exposure to the property sector by implementing a ban on credit to new property-based clients. However nothing was done to restrict credit to existing property-based debtors.[111] As outlined previously, weaknesses in the financial regulatory system led to a failure in curbing imprudent lending, especially the failure to limit the expansion of mortgage lending.

Eventually, these reckless lending policies led to the banking crisis of 2008. The financial acceleration model, described by Kelly, began a downward spiral in 2007, as buyers became unwilling to accumulate new debt, thus lowering land prices. The difficulty of falling land prices was gravely compounded by the global collapse in asset prices and the withdrawal of credit following the collapse of the US sub-prime mortgage market in September 2008.[112] Irish banks could not access the foreign credit they were dependent upon. Irish financial institutions had not invested in the notorious securitized financial products that triggered the global financial crash. To prevent a run on the banks and

Table 7.7 Value of loans transferred to NAMA by institution, September 2010

Firm	*Nominal loans (€ billion)*	*Realised loans (€ billion)*	*Nominal loans (by institution) as % of total*	*Realised loans (by institution) as % of total*
Anglo-Irish Bank	34.0	21.1	47.0	50.5
Allied Irish Bank	19.6	10.7	27.1	25.6
Bank of Ireland	9.3	3.9	12.9	9.3
Irish Nationwide Building Society	8.5	5.5	11.8	13.2
Educational Building Society	0.8	0.5	1.1	1.2
Other	0.1	0.1	1.2	0.2
Total	72.3	41.8		

Source: *Misjudging risk: Causes of the systemic banking crisis in Ireland*, Dublin, Department of Finance, 2011, p. 33.

building societies, the government introduced a deposit guarantee on 28 September 2008, which included deposits, long-term bonds and subordinated debt. This was the result of consultation between the Taoiseach, the Minister for Finance and leading executives of the AIB and the Bank of Ireland; both banks feared that the pending collapse of Anglo-Irish Bank would bring down the entire Irish financial system. The scope of the guarantee in protecting liabilities other than bank deposits has been criticized by the current governor of the Central Bank, Patrick Honohan.[113] Nyberg has criticized the haste in which the government issued the guarantee, arguing that the banks withheld the extent of losses due to the collapse of property prices. As a consequence, the government perceived (incorrectly) that the banking crisis was due to restricted liquidity.[114] While the guarantee secured the deposit base of the banks, it did not resolve the fundamental problem: the collapse in the value of property-based assets held by the banks and the increase in liabilities due to mortgage defaults. This was followed by the acquisition of preference shares in the three major banks. The much discredited Anglo-Irish Bank was finally nationalized in January 2009 at huge costs to the state.[115]

The major initiative by the government to confront the crisis was the formation of the National Asset Management Agency (NAMA), which purchased impaired property loans from the banks at a discount. Yet, as Kelly demonstrated, the creation of NAMA did not resolve the difficulty of the banks' mortgage liabilities.[116] Loans purchased by NAMA and the discount applied illustrates both the costs of the property collapse and the level of 'wasted investment' that had occurred in the Irish economy, and especially the debt that was generated by Anglo-Irish Bank.

The crushing liabilities faced by the banks undermined the Republic of Ireland's international economic credibility, which, it was perceived, posed a threat of contagion to the precarious financial position of the entire eurozone. This was a deciding factor in the decision to force the Irish government to seek financial assistance from a troika composed of the ECB, the European Commission and the IMF in November 2010.[117] This opened a new chapter in Irish economic history in which austerity and debt repayment figured far more prominently, witnessing a marked decline in bank lending and public capital investment programmes.

8 A European outlier?

Demography and the labour force

A crucial factor influencing the development of any economy is the size and capability of the labour force. Demography therefore has a number of important implications for economic performance. In turn the cyclical nature of economic activity influences demographic behavior, with implications for the size of the population, the domestic market and the potential size of the labour force in future years. Moreover, the capability of the labour force is influenced by the level of educational attainment of the population and any improvements in this sphere tend to improve economic performance.

Although the region that became the Republic of Ireland is generally considered to have had a somewhat distinctive demographic history in European terms, notably with regard to the general decline of population since the Great Famine of the 1840s, population decline was also a feature of some other European regions during this period. However, Ireland deviated from the European norm in several respects, experiencing for example relatively higher levels of net emigration. Citizens of the new state were also far more reticent to marry than other Europeans, with the number of marriages per 1,000 of the population being only half that of other Catholic countries such as Spain and Belgium, for example. The age of marriage in the 1920s was also relatively higher; the average age of bridegrooms was six years over those in England, though the gap closed somewhat in the next half century. Compared to the rest of Europe the relative rate of marriage in the state declined further in the first half of the twentieth century. However, the low marriage rate was offset to some degree by high martial fertility. Consequently Irish demography was characterized by both exceptionally high fertility levels within marriage and an exceptionally high level of celibacy.[1]

In one other respect Ireland was different to the rest of the Western world; in the first third of the twentieth century, women had shorter lives than men, which was probably due to a combination of their 'systematically disadvantaged position' in Irish society and maternal mortality.[2] However, between the 1940s and the 1990s Irish females regained their advantage in terms of life expectancy relative to men by an average of 5.5 years by the end of the period.[3] This is symptomatic of a gradual movement closer to European norms over the past half century, but this was by no means linear, and even down to the present day Ireland remains an outlier in demographic terms. Although the Republic of Ireland was not markedly

Table 8.1 Birth rates, death rates and natural increase (per 000) for inter-censal periods, 1926–2011

Census period	*Birth rate*	*Death rate*	*Natural increase (birth rate-death rate)*
1926–1936	58	42	16
1936–1946	60	43	17
1946–1951	66	40	26
1951–1956	63	36	27
1956–1961	61	34	26
1961–1966	63	33	29
1966–1971	63	33	30
1971–1979	69	33	35
1979–1981	73	33	40
1981–1986	67	33	34
1986–1991	56	32	24
1991–1996	50	31	18
1996–2002	54	31	23
2002–2006	61	28	33
2007–2011	73	28	45

Source: *Statistical abstract 2009. Census 2011, preliminary results.*

out of line with European population growth in the years between 1950 and 2000, differences existed both in the timing and the extent of the demographic and economic factors underpinning this growth.[4] The major demographic issues and other factors impacting on the size and quality of the labour force since independence will be considered in this chapter.

While there was initially a brief surge in European births after the Second World War, in the decades after the war, birth rates fell. Irish rates in contrast remained consistently high,[5] peaking in the 1970s and early 1980s. Birth rates in the Republic of Ireland began falling from the mid-1980s, with some demographers concluding that Ireland was now finally converging with European norms,[6] but they began to rise again from the mid-1990s reaching a new peak in 2007–11 (see Table 8.1). So the Republic of Ireland continues to retain some elements of its traditional demographic regime, as well as displaying some degree of convergence with European norms. The results of the 2011 census indicate that natural increase between 2007 and 2011 was higher than at any time since independence and well over double what it was in the inter-war years (see Table 8.1). Moreover, emigration has resumed since 2008, following a brief period of net immigration, with many younger people departing again following an all too familiar historical pattern.

Relatively high marital fertility has been identified as an important factor contributing to Irish economic underdevelopment in the inter-war years and beyond.

Ireland only very partially participated in the European fertility transition during the first half of the twentieth century. High marital fertility rates were not uncommon among traditional agricultural-based economies, where it was common to maximize the size of one's family so that offspring could provide care and maintenance in old age. In advanced economies, in contrast, family size was typically smaller, as children required a greater endowment of human capital to earn an adequate standard of living. Ó Gráda has argued that Irish marital fertility remained too high for a developing economy, leading to large families that could not obtain an adequate education. The decline in Irish marital fertility from the 1960s has been attributed to urbanization, increased employment opportunities for women and the declining role of Catholic religious influence, notably in the use of artificial contraception,[7] or abortion as an option. The role of structural change is vital here, as the growth in the industrial and service sectors allowed for the greater participation of women in the workforce, contributing to the decline in fertility, and the emergence of smaller families.

Bloom and Canning argue that legal restrictions on the availability of contraceptives between 1922 and 1979 contributed to high Irish marital fertility rates relative to other European countries. The sale of contraceptives was liberalized in successive stages between 1979 and 1985. Bloom and Canning argue that with the consequent fall in marital fertility, the birth rate fell from 63 per thousand in 1966–71 to 50 per thousand in 1991–96, in conjunction with the expansion of the working age cohort of the population, contributing to the more dramatic economic growth of the Celtic Tiger period.[8]

Brendan Walsh argues that birth rates were also affected by economic conditions; for example, the depressed economic conditions of the 1980s contributed to the decline in the birth rate for the period 1981 to 1986, while an increase occurred in 2002 to 2006. However, it should be noted that the downturn since 2008 has not prevented a further increase between 2007 and 2011, to the highest levels yet witnessed since independence.[9] The marked changes in the pattern of migration away from the traditional emphasis on net emigration to net immigration during the periods preceding 1979–81 and 2007–11, provides part of the explanation for the relatively higher birth rates returned in these years. This was because economic conditions during the Celtic Tiger swelled the ranks of the more fertile female cohorts in the population, retaining more Irish-born women in these cohorts (which had been particularly prone to emigration historically), in addition to attracting more foreign-born women and returned migrants. But it seems unlikely that changing migration patterns alone provide all the explanations and the fact that high birth rates also defied the onset of more recessionary conditions after 2007 imply that other non-economic issues were at play. It is possible, for example, that residual positive cultural attitudes towards having children may be a factor, since the state has certainly not been more child friendly in terms of childcare support than in other European societies; if anything it is less so. As yet, the causes of the current high levels of fertility and natural increase in the Republic of Ireland have yet to be firmly established.

Kennedy has charted a gradual decline in average family size in the Republic of Ireland between the 1950s and the 1980s. Earlier and more frequent marriage occurred from the 1960s and contributed to a recovery in the birth rate. This baby boom started in the 1950s and peaked in 1964, probably for similar economic reasons to those increasing fertility in much of the Western world at this time. But Irish fertility was very high by European standards and this was sustained in the 1970s, rising to a new peak in 1980, with births and birth rates collapsing during the 1980s after this peak. Kennedy argues that the improvements in the performance of the economy in the 1960s and 1970s and conversely the downturn in the 1980s provide a likely economic explanation for these trends. The latter decade was also marked by a surge in non-marital fertility, with a general reduction in the stigma attached to births out of wedlock. Conversely, there was also a greater willingness to utilize various forms of birth control in the 1980s. Although these trends can be taken to indicate some belated convergence to European norms, it should be noted that by the end of the 1980s, the Republic of Ireland still had somewhat higher birth rates and a higher natural increase in population than the EU average. However, marriage rates were still slightly lower and fertility rates still slightly higher, so some traditional demographic patterns persisted, despite greater convergence with European patterns in the 1970s and 1980s.[10]

In the 1990s the Irish total fertility rate stabilized at the upper end of the European fertility spectrum, despite the lack of state supports, high and rising costs for childcare and the general expansion of female labour force participation. Fahey has argued that these trends can be accounted for by residual Catholic pronatalist views within the general population. The number of births actually increased by 14 per cent between 1994 and 2000, but this was due more to the expansion of the number of women of child bearing age than increased fertility at a given age. The Irish fertility levels, while high in European terms, are comparable to those in other Western societies, such as New Zealand and the US. Recent work indicates that Ireland remains at the top of the EU 27 fertility league. Moreover, it has been recently suggested that if anything, official fertility estimates for Ireland are currently too low.[11] All of this is consistent with the particularly high birth rates registered in Table 8.1 for 2007–11, which are comparable to those in the previous peak of 1979–81, but since death rates have declined in the interim, natural increase has consequently risen to record levels for any period since independence.

Children born in the late 1960s and early 1970s benefited from greater educational attainment relative to the generations that preceded them. By the early 1990s, much of the population cohort born in the expansion of the late 1960s and early 1970s were now entering the labour force,[12] fortuitously in conjunction with the emergence of large waves of FDI. Bloom and Canning argue that a ‘bulge’ in the working age cohorts of the population relative to other age groups will be of benefit to the economy only if appropriate labour force measures exist that can enhance the productivity of new labour force entrants. This was indeed the case for the labour force entrants in the Republic of Ireland of the 1990s, as was the case in the eastern Asian economies.[13]

Table 8.2 Population summary, 1911–2011

Census period	*Population*	*Births registered*	*Deaths registered*	*Natural increase*	*Change in population*	*Estimated net migration*
1911	3,139,688					
1926	2,971,992	–	–	–	–	–
1936	2,968,420	583,502	420,323	163,179	–3,572	–166,751
1946	2.955,107	602,095	428,297	173,798	–13,313	–187,111
1951	2,960,593	329,270	201,295	127,975	5,486	–122,489
1956	2,898,264	312,517	178,083	134,434	–62,329	–196,763
1961	2,818,341	302,816	170,736	132,080	–79,923	–212,003
1966	2,884,002	312,709	166,443	146,266	65,661	–80,605
1971	2,978,248	312,796	164,644	148,152	94,246	–53,906
1979	3,368,217	548,413	267,378	281,035	389,969	108,934
1981	3,443,405	146,224	65,991	80,223	75,188	–5,045
1986	3,540,643	333,457	164,336	169,121	97,238	–71,883
1991	3,525,719	277,546	158,300	119,246	–14,924	–134,170
1996	3,626,087	249,455	157,300	92,066	100,368	8,302
2002	3,917,203	324,147	186,912	137,235	291,116	153,881
2006	4,239,848	245,156	113,842	131,314	322,645	191,331
2011	4,581,269	–	–	222,771	341,421	118,650

Source: 1926–2006, *Census of population 2006*, Dublin, CSO. 2011, *Census 2011, preliminary results*, Dublin, CSO.

Note: Births, deaths, natural increase, changes in population and net emigration returned above relate to the preceding inter–censal period.

The death trends since independence have been far less volatile, registering a fairly consistent decline, with the most substantial decrease occurring in the inter-censal periods of 1936 to 1946 and 1961 to 1966. This is consistent with improvements in living standards and public health provision, combined with measures such as rural electrification improving water supply and sanitation. In general, during the period between independence and the 1970s, natural increase was roughly offset by net emigration, with the result that the population remained exceedingly static during these years (see Table 8.2).

The rise in population from the beginning of the 1970s was very gradual, stalling in the second half of the 1980s. In the early 1990s slow growth resumed, accelerating during the Celtic Tiger years, more notably after the turn of the century during the second phase. Despite the severe economic crash from 2008, the population has continued to rise dramatically between 2006 and 2011 (see Table 8.2).

The incidence of emigration was still among the highest in Europe in the 1920s,[14] and it continued to play an important role in Irish demographic history. The negative effects of emigration on the economy at this time include its reductionist impact on the domestic market, thereby reducing potential demand and investment. Relatively low population density by European standards also raised the relative cost of service provision and resulted in a less diversified economy.

Emigration also had the effect of reducing the more reproductive age groups, further lowering the crude birth rate. It also increased the dependency ratio, incurring costs on Irish society by raising substantial numbers who departed just at the point when they might enter the work force. On the positive side, it raised Irish wages through the relationship established with the US and British labour markets, also reducing the supply of underemployed and low-wage workers. For example, it removed labourers and small farmers from the Irish countryside, which increased productivity and average incomes in Irish agriculture and averted even sharper rises in unemployment during major recessions such as the 1950s, 1980s[15] and in the period since 2008. Net migration has been the most volatile influence on Irish demographic history,[16] and remains so to the present day.

Emigration has also had an important influence on the ethno-religious profile of the state. During and after the War of Independence and Civil War a substantial share of the minority Protestant population departed from the Irish Free State area due to regime change, economic instability, land reform, British withdrawal and in some cases intimidation. Protestants continued to leave in relatively greater numbers until the end of the Second World War, thus increasing the predominantly Catholic profile of the population. Moreover, in the decade from the beginning of the First World War, the UK eclipsed the US as the premier destination for Irish migrants.[17]

The historical pattern of economic emigration had been re-established by the mid-1920s, with the counties of the west, south-west and north-west registering higher rates of emigration. Emigrants tended to be young and single and the magnitude of emigration was influenced by labour market conditions in the US and the UK, especially in urban areas. The US remained the principal destination of Irish emigrants during the 1920s. However, the Great Depression reduced the demand for labour in the US and its attractiveness as a destination declined thereafter. From the mid-1930s onwards the United Kingdom became the premier destination for Irish emigrants.[18] About 80 per cent of Irish emigrants went to Britain between the 1920s and 1980s, with the highest annual gross outflow since independence recorded as late as 1989 (70,000). However, emigration in the 1940s and 1950s was more sustained, with much larger net outflows (see Table 8.3). Although the gross outflow declined dramatically in the 1990s, Britain still remained the principal destination in 2000, declining sharply thereafter, as greater numbers were destined for continental Europe and the rest of the world.[19]

The inter-war years witnessed a general increase in the traditional connection with Britain as a major migrant destination; this accelerated dramatically during the Second World War, as diminishing employment opportunities within the Irish economy were offset by a major increase in the demand for labour in the United Kingdom where the war economy opened up new opportunities for a new generation of largely younger migrants. Travel permit data from the 1940s reveals that the skills threshold of emigrants to Britain was relatively low; 73 per cent of the male emigrants were in agriculture or unskilled occupations and 57 per cent of females were in domestic service. By 1951 the number of Irish in Britain had risen rapidly to almost 700,000.

This transnational migratory flow also had a direct impact on GDP, with remittances from abroad in the mid-1920s valued at 3.4 per cent of GDP and this figure was estimated to have risen again to 3.2 per cent at the beginning of the 1960s following the exodus in the 1950s, declining somewhat thereafter.[20] The munificence of these migrants has seldom been adequately recognized by later generations, more particularly those who ended their days in straightened circumstances in Britain.

Returning migrants with new skills also made an important contribution to the expansion of the Irish economy from the 1960s. Many nurses, for example, received training in Britain and later returned to work in Ireland, notably from the early 1970s.[21] Other emigrants to Britain returned with a diverse range of skills across a multiplicity of occupations, not least in construction among male migrants. Another benefit to the Irish economy of emigration historically was (and is) that a substantial share of tourists were Irish-born; 51 per cent in the case of British and 14 per cent in the case of North America in 1991, while two-thirds of the North American remainder had an Irish ethnic connection. It has been estimated that ethnic tourism in that year may have accounted for 1.5 per cent of GDP.[22]

Recessionary conditions during the 1980s increased the incentive to emigrate; Tansey estimated that a total of 160,000 people left the country between 1985 and 1990. Up to 66 per cent of this figure was composed of people aged between 15 and 24 years.[23] They were mostly single; female emigrants on average left at a slightly younger age, following a familiar historical pattern.[24] But this outflow was somewhat different than in the 1950s because there was an over-representation of professional and managerial occupations, and an under-representation of those in agriculture. The typical emigrant by the late 1980s was from an urban background and had some post-primary education.[25] But the volume of emigration in the 1980s taken as a whole was far lower than in the 1950s, even though both decades were well ahead of any other decade since independence (see Table 8.3).

During the Celtic Tiger period, unprecedented levels of net immigration diversified the ethno-religious composition of the population to a degree not witnessed for centuries, going back to the plantations. Although the Republic of Ireland experienced net immigration from 1996, the all too familiar historical pattern of net emigration quickly began to assert itself again from 2009 onwards.

If emigration remains a persistent feature of the Ireland's demographic regime, unemployment and underemployment have also been another problematic aspect of the Irish economic landscape. Although the unemployment rate had been relatively low during the 1970s, an increase was recorded between 1974 and 1976, as a consequence of the oil crisis.[26] After a fall in the late 1970s, unemployment rose during the 1980s and early 1990s, so that by January 1993 it surpassed 300,000 persons or roughly 21 per cent of the labour force, topping the EU unemployment league. Kieran Kennedy, in a contemporary pamphlet on the subject, argued this had long been the most serious social and economic problem in the state. He observed that employment in the economy was 10 per cent lower at the beginning of the 1990s than it had been in the 1920s, and no other country in the Western world had experienced a similar pattern of employment contraction.[27] Liam

Table 8.3 Estimated annual net migration rates, 1926–2011

Census period	*Net migration (000s)*
1926–1936	–17
1936–1946	–19
1946–1951	–24
1951–1961	–81
1961–1971	–27
1971–1981	11
1981–1986	–14
1986–1991	–27
1991–1996	2
1996–2002	26
2002–2006	48
2007–2011	24

Source: *Census 2006, principal demographic results. Census 2011, preliminary results.*

Kennedy noted that the Republic of Ireland had become a high wage economy with a high rate of unemployment; GNP per person in work was then close to the European norm, but GNP per inhabitant in contrast was running at only 60 per cent of the EU norm.[28] This high unemployment rate only began to recede significantly from the mid-1990s due the voracious demand for labour during the first phase of Celtic Tiger, which reduced unemployment levels to approximately 4 per cent by the turn of the century, with unemployment stabilizing at this level throughout the second phase of the Celtic Tiger period (see Table 8.4).

Unemployment increased again sharply from 2008, with notable rises in construction and property-related sectors and in the hotel and restaurant sectors. The 2010 Live Register figure showed an annual total of 431,505, which was significantly higher than the peak of the early 1990s.[29] The dramatic reduction of unemployment during Celtic Tiger now looks increasingly like an aberration, in a long history of relatively high unemployment and under employment in the Republic of Ireland relative to the EU 15 average from the 1960s through to the mid-1990s.[30]

The occupied workforce still remains much higher in absolute terms than in the early 1990s, despite the impact of the crash. The size of the labour force since independence has also been influenced by female labour force participation rates, which actually declined between 1926 and 1971. Female participation in the industrial workforce increased between the mid-1920s and the mid-1930s as women found employment in the expanding textile and clothing industries, which expanded as a consequence of the more advanced protectionist regime introduced from 1932. In 1936, female workers in the textiles sector accounted for 75.6 per cent of all female workers in industry.[31] However, the protracted decline in the textile sector witnessed a collapse in female employment. Participation rates by

Table 8.4 Unemployment rate (percentage of labour force not gainfully employed), 1985–2011

Year	*Unemployment (000)*	*Unemployment rate (%)*
1985	219.6	16.7
1986	225.5	17.1
1987	226.0	16.9
1988	217.0	16.3
1989	196.8	15.1
1990	172.4	12.9
1991	198.5	14.7
1992	206.6	15.1
1993	220.1	15.7
1994	211.0	14.7
1995	177.4	12.2
1996	179.0	11.9
1997	159.0	10.3
1998	126.4	7.8
1999	96.9	5.8
2000	74.5	4.3
2001	65.1	3.6
2002	77.0	4.2
2003	82.1	4.4
2004	84.2	4.4
2005	85.6	4.3
2006	91.4	4.3
2007	103.1	4.7
2008	126.7	5.7
2009	264.6	12.0
2010	293.6	13.6
2011	304.5	14.3

Source: 1985–2008, *Statistical yearbook 2009*. 2009, *Statistical yearbook 2010*. 2010–011, http://www.cso.ie/en/statistics/labourmarket/principalstatistics (accessed 1 June 2012).

women in agriculture also experienced a long-term decline between 1926 until 1981, although a moderate recovery has occurred since then.

In 1971, female labour force participation, at one in four of the total labour force, was low by European standards. This climbed to slightly less than one in three by 1991, as service sector employment increased in the economy.[32] This trend accelerated further during the 1990s and again for the first half of the following decade,

Table 8.5 Female labour force participation rate (percentage of total female population in the labour force), 1926–2009

Year	*Female participation rate*
1926	30.5
1936	32.8
1946	31.0
1951	30.6
1961	28.6
1966	28.3
1971	27.3
1981	29.7
1986	32.2
1991	35.9
1996	40.7
2002	46.5
2006	53.1
2009	54.0

Source: 1926–2006, *Census of population 1926–2006, occupations.* 2009, *Statistical yearbook 2010.*

stabilizing thereafter. In the years between 1970 and 1990 average family size also began to fall, as did the birth rate, perhaps reflecting the growing share of the female population at work. The rate of increase in female participation between the years 1990 and 2004 was the third-highest among OECD member countries. A major increase was observed in the participation rate of younger women in the labour force in particular, increasing from 30 per cent in 1975 to 76 per cent by 2004.[33] Another factor that influenced the upward trend in female labour force participation was the greater tendency of married women to enter, re-enter or remain in the labour force. The percentage of married women aged 35 to 44 who participated in the labour force increased from 19.5 per cent in 1986 to 52.1 per cent in 1996 and increased again to 67.3 per cent in 2010.[34]

Increased rates of female labour force participation became a defining feature of economic development since the 1970s, and this growth was heavily concentrated in the services sector in the 1990s, which had traditionally employed a far higher share of females than industry and agriculture (see Table 8.6). Females dominated employment in domestic service, accounting for 97 per cent of employment in this sub-sector in 1926.[35] However, the decline of domestic service employment actually contributed to the decline in female participation rates in the service sector between 1966 and 1971. This was offset to some degree, in 1973, by the removal of discriminatory measures against married women taking up employment in other services, such as national school teachers and public servants, and the removal of similar prohibitions in sectors such as banking.[36]

Table 8.6 Percentage female share of employment in different sectors, 1926–2009

Year	*Agriculture*	*Industry*	*Services*
1926	18.0	17.5	42.1
1936	16.4	18.6	45.1
1946	13.6	18.8	44.4
1951	12.9	20.1	40.8
1961	10.5	17.0	44.7
1966	9.4	15.4	44.2
1971	8.6	14.4	42.5
1981	6.2	12.6	42.9
1986	6.7	16.6	40.3
1991	9.4	17.6	41.7
1996	9.2	15.7	48.6
2002	7.5	19.0	51.1
2006	9.4	15.3	53.1
2009	10.2	17.9	55.4

Source: *Census of population 1926–2006, occupations. Statistical yearbook of Ireland, 2010.*

Despite such measures, the female employment share in services actually declined between the 1960s and the mid-1980s. There was a marked growth in the female share of service employment during the 1990s and after the turn of the century it began to exceed the male share (see Table 8.6).

Despite this increase, it is worth noting that the female participation rate in the Republic of Ireland was still slightly below the OECD average in 2004. A number of factors still limited the full participation of women in the workforce. Participation rates of older women in the labour force were still low (at only 33 per cent) reflecting low educational attainment as well as negative traditional societal attitudes towards employment of married and older women.[37]

Historically, the combination of high martial fertility and the emigration of many young people of working age, gave rise to a high level of economically non-active citizens including children and retired persons. The dependency ratio increased dramatically following the Second World War, as a result of high emigration, and it remained persistently high until a decline got underway in the 1980s. Much of the contraction in the gainfully employed share of the population in the intervening years was down to the mechanization of farming, which was not sufficiently offset by new job creation in industry and services.

The increase in the size of the working population led to a further decrease in the dependency ratio between 1991 and 2006, despite the fact the there was a growing amount of immigration into Ireland in these years, which provided significant additional recruits to the labour force. Kieran Kennedy attributed much significance to this dramatic expansion from the early 1990s and the reduction in

Table 8.7 Dependency ratios 1926–2009

Census year	*Population cohort aged 65< as % of working age population*	*Population cohort aged <15 as % of working age population*	*Total dependency ratio (column 2 + column 3)*
1926	14.8	47.3	62.1
1936	15.5	44.1	59.6
1946	17.3	45.3	72.6
1951	17.7	47.8	75.5
1961	19.4	54.0	75.4
1971	19.2	54.2	73.4
1981	18.2	51.4	69.6
1986	18.0	48.1	66.1
1991	18.5	43.1	61.6
1996	17.6	36.5	54.1
2002	16.4	31.2	47.6
2006	16.1	29.7	45.8
2009	16.3	31.0	47.3

Source: 1926–2006, calculated from *Census 2006, principal demographic results*. 2009, *Statistical yearbook 2010*.

the dependency ratio in facilitating growth and escaping one of the major constraints on development.[38] This can be demonstrated with reference to the percentage of the entire population that was gainfully employed. After a modest rise between 1926 and 1936, the percentage of the population employed fell between 1946 to 1981. However, from 1986 to 2006, the percentage of the population employed increased between every inter-censual period, breaking with the decline or stasis witnessed in earlier decades. In addition to this marked rise in employment from the beginning of the 1990s down to 2006, the average annual hours worked by persons employed was relatively high compared to economies at a comparable level of development.[39] The dramatic impact of the recession can be seen in the rapid decline in the gainfully employed percentage of the population after 2006, which reversed the most dramatic phase of employment expansion in the history of the state going back to the end of the 1980s (see Table 8.8).

Net employment creation increased during the 1990s, due to the expansion of the industrial and services sectors. The demand for labour increased to such an extent that migrant labour was required to meet it. With economic recovery in the early 1990s about half of immigrants were Irish-born returnees, many of whom had left during the 1980s. Return migration accounted for between 23 per cent and 55 per cent of immigration in the decade after 1996. While there are a multiplicity of factors why people returned (including retirement, kinship and locality factors) improved employment prospects in this period accounted for many;

Table 8.8 Number and percentage of population (14 years and over 1926–66, 15 years and over 1971–2009) employed, 1926–2009

Year	*Nos. in gainful occupation*	*As % of total population*
1926	1,304,920	43.9
1936	1,339,088	45.1
1946	1,298,367	43.9
1951	1,272,038	43.0
1961	1,108,108	39.3
1966	1,118,204	38.8
1971	1,119,531	37.6
1981	1.250,923	36.3
1986	1,286,545	36.3
1991	1,348,855	38.3
1996	1,506,372	41.5
2002	1,779,786	45.4
2006	2,080,126	49.1
2009	1,938,500	43.5

Source: 1926–36, *Census of population 1926–2006*. 2009, *Statistical yearbook of Ireland, 2010.*

Jones found that in the 1990s return migration was high in counties with a significant presence of multinational companies or other forms of employment growth, such as teaching, medicine, government, transportation, construction and tourism.[40]

The number of persons born outside the state remained extremely low between the 1920s and the early 1960s, accounting for less than four per cent of the total population. The great majority of these came from Great Britain and Northern Ireland. It still remained under seven per cent until after 1991, climbing to over 10 per cent by 2002 and increasingly rapidly thereafter to almost 15 per cent of the total population by 2006, or 613,000 persons.[41] From the mid-1990s a larger number of immigrants from continental Europe and the rest of the world began to enter the Republic,[42] diversifying the workforce and increasing labour force participation in the economy as a whole, which is typical of immigrant communities historically. This dramatically altered the social and economic landscape. Immigrants, according to one estimate, accounted for something in the order of three per cent of GDP growth per annum between 1993 and 2003.[43] If this estimate is correct, immigration was a vital and understated factor underpinning growth during the Celtic Tiger years.

The majority of migrants came to Ireland to work, filling many of the new jobs in the rapidly expanding economy, with migrants accounting for one in six jobs by 2008. Although they worked across the occupational spectrum, more were employed at the lower levels, clustering in areas where labour shortages began to emerge in agriculture, food, catering, domestic service, care, health security, cleaning, construction, factory work and in the black economy in jobs in which they were generally paid less than the native population; moreover, much of this expanding labour force was not subject to traditional labour regulation norms. Many were hired through a growing myriad of employment agencies and sub contractors. Following the accession of 10 new EU member states largely in eastern Europe in May 2004, the government sought to draw more upon them to supply cheap labour, while simultaneously reducing permits servicing that demand from the rest of the world. Other immigrants higher up the occupational ladder helped to reduce acute bottlenecks in information technology, health and other sectors where there was a demand for specialist skills in short supply.[44] Migrants from Poland, Lithuania and Latvia dominated the flow of migrants from the accession countries from 2004. The participation of non-European migrants in the Irish work force continued to be regulated by a work permit system.[45] Loyal argues that rather than competing with Irish workers, immigrants have complemented the indigenous workforce in areas where there were skill shortages and in areas where the native workforce was unwilling to work for the wages paid. This growing reservoir of cheaper labour, he argues, contributed to increasing the share of non-agricultural incomes going to profits, rents and self-employed earnings, while reducing the share going to wages, pensions and social security.[46]

The economic effects of migration were of great benefit to the Irish economy. Between 1993 and 2003, 81.5 per cent of migrants were between 20 to 44 years of age, compared to 44.2 per cent of the native population, thereby enhancing the share of the population who were of working age (and also increasing fertility levels). By 2006, the labour force participation rate of non-nationals was 75.7 per cent compared to 60.9 per cent for the Irish population as a whole. Non-nationals fulfilled the increased demand for labour from the services sector in particular, accounting for 49 per cent of the 280,600 increase in employment recorded between 2002 and 2006. [47] The timing of migration was fortuitous, as labour shortages threatened continued economic growth. Immigration allowed employees to source additional workers from abroad.[48] Hotels and restaurants had the highest percentage of non-national employees, accounting for 31.9 per cent of total employment. The business and health sectors also employed a significant number, with work permits specifically offered for foreign medical staff due to a lack of Irish graduates in these areas.[49]

Barrett, Bergin and Duffy estimate that the educational attainment of migrants who arrived in Ireland between 1993 and 2003 was higher than that of the native population, with 40.2 per cent of emigrants having attained a third-level degree, compared to 16.7 per cent for Irish citizens. This is confirmed by a more recent study for 2009–11 that indicates that Irish nationals are less likely to have third-level qualifications than those born outside the state, with about 32 per cent of nationals at this stage having acquired a third-level qualification compared to over 50 per cent for British and other EU citizens born outside the state.[50] This indicates the importance of immigration in increasing human capital within the economy, and also the general improvement in educational attainment in the indigenous population since the 1990s.

However, not all immigrants obtained employment in Ireland that corresponded with their educational status. Barrett, Bergin and Duffy argue that this 'immigrant occupation gap' was the result of non-English speaking immigrants experiencing difficulty in locating employment worthy of their educational status, and is reflected by the occupational under-representation of immigrants in higher managerial and administration roles despite their higher educational profile. By 2002, immigrants accounted for only 10.5 per cent of higher managerial and administrative roles, compared to 17.7 per cent for Irish workers.[51] While it is reasonable to assume that this differential would decrease once immigrants accustomed themselves over time to Irish social and economic conditions, recent research by Barrett reveals that the immigrant-native wage differential for workers with high education levels persists over time. He argues that 'the wage disadvantage for euro immigrants is not about discrimination of low-skilled and vulnerable immigrants but about the failure of more skilled immigrants to fully capture returns to human capital'.[52] Despite the leakage of skills through this 'immigrant occupation gap', the influx of highly-skilled immigrants increased labour supply in advanced occupations, moderating wage growth and increasing output, while lower-skilled immigration fulfilled labour demand in many areas. The ESRI have estimated that immigration increased GNP growth rates between 2.8 per cent to 3.0 per cent for the period 1993 to 2003.[53]

Immigration peaked at unprecedented levels between 2005 and 2008, declining thereafter as the economic environment deteriorated. Concern was expressed that migration outflows could result 'in a loss of the skills that are critical for future economic growth'.[54] These concerns came to pass in 2009: the reduction in inward migration and the increase in outward emigration, with many workers from the accession countries leaving Ireland, led to a return to the historical pattern of net outward migration for the first time since 1995. CSO estimates indicate that less than one-third of all emigrants in 2009 were Irish, rising to less than half in 2010,[55] with most being in younger adult age cohorts following the traditional age profile.

From a historical perspective, the level of educational attainment of the Irish labour force has been of great significance for economic development. While basic literacy levels were high for the early years of the Irish Free State,[56] access to second-level education remained limited. Moreover, there was a noticeable deficiency in vocational education. The provision of wide-scale vocational education in Germanic countries is cited by Mjøset as a principal factor in their economic development.[57] A vocational education school system was established in the Irish Free State in 1930, with a further significant expansion in the early 1950s during the tenure of Seán Moylan as Minister for Education.[58] However, the vocational system was handicapped by funding difficulties and clerical disapproval of its secular ethos. The vocational aspect of the system was also diluted in favour of cultural subjects.[59] The half-hearted introduction of vocational education in Ireland reduced the economic prospects of the country during the 1950s,

Table 8.9 Annual migration rates, 1987–2010

Year	*Immigration (000)*	*Emigration (000)*	*Net migration (Immigration–emigration)*
1987	17.2	40.2	–23.0
1988	19.2	61.1	–41.9
1989	26.7	70.6	–43.9
1990	33.3	56.3	–22.9
1991	33.3	35.3	–2.0
1992	40.7	33.4	7.4
1993	34.7	35.1	–0.4
1994	30.1	34.8	–4.7
1995	31.2	33.1	–1.9
1996	39.2	31.2	8.0
1997	44.5	25.3	19.2
1998	46.0	28.6	17.4
1999	48.9	31.5	17.3
2000	52.6	26.6	26.0
2001	59.0	26.2	32.8
2002	66.9	25.6	41.3
2003	60.0	29.3	30.7
2004	58.5	26.5	32.0
2005	84.6	29.4	55.1
2006	107.8	36.0	71.8
2007	109.5	42.2	67.3
2008	83.8	45.3	38.5
2009	57.3	65.1	–7.8
2010	34.5	65.2	–30.7

Source: 1987–2009, *Population and migration estimates*, CSO, April 2009. 2010, http://www.cso.ie/px/pxeirestat (NB. Web link no longer active).

as continental European countries, with long-established vocational educational systems, were better able to exploit the technological and managerial innovations originating from the US in the 1950s.[60]

Between independence and the 1950s, the curriculum of secondary schools did not reflect any concern for socio-economic development. Humanities-based subjects, such as Greek, Latin and religious knowledge were taught at the expense of science, modern languages and social subjects. French was the only modern European language taught to any appreciable degree, and it was, according to Garvin, 'looked upon less as a cultural or business asset and more as a social decoration for young middle class ladies and gentlemen'.[61] In the 1950s, an early

Table 8.10 Persons in secondary and tertiary-level education, 1965–2009

Year	*Second level*	*Second level growth 1965–66 = 100*	*Third level*	*Third level growth 1965–66 = 100*
1965–66	142,983	100.0	20,698	100.0
1970–71	197,142	137.9	24,496	118.4
1975–76	270,956	189.5	33,148	160.2
1980–81	300,601	210.2	41,928	202.6
1985–86	338,207	236.5	55,088	266.2
1990–91	345,941	241.9	69,988	338.1
1995–96	373,665	261.3	102,662	515.1
2000–01	349,274	244.3	126,300	610.2
2005–06	335,134	234.4	145,287	701.9
2008–09	344,893	241.2	152,686	737.7

Source: *Statistical yearbook of Ireland 2007*, p. 115. *Statistical yearbook of Ireland, 2010*, p. 100.

opportunity for educational reform presented itself with the formation of the Council of Education. This body rejected the need for any significant reform of the education curriculum and actually opposed the expansion of second-level educational attainment.[62]

Yet, by the 1960s, the expansion of educational attainment became an important government priority. In 1961, the provision of scholarships to secondary school students was extended and in 1964, state capital grants to secondary schools were introduced. The culmination of this policy was the introduction of free secondary education in 1966. The context for this bold measure was the OECD sponsored report, *Investment in Education*, published in 1965, which proposed the introduction of a merit-based education system to encourage the talents of the population, and for increased investment in education to promote economic growth.[63] This was accompanied by an expansion of comprehensive and badly needed vocational schooling.[64] The number of students attending secondary-level education doubled between 1965–66 and 1980–81: the growth of numbers slowed down in the 1990s, and actually declined after 2000. In contrast the rate of growth of those attending third-level education has continually expanded, with an especially high increase over the period 1980–81 to 2005–06. The abolition of university fees in 1995 was introduced with a view to further expanding third-level attendance.

The structure of third-level education was radically altered in the late 1960s and early 1970s. In addition to the traditional universities, a new third-level institution, the National Institute of Higher Education, was established in Limerick in 1972 to encourage the development of technological skills. As it was under direct government control, it was, according to Frank Barry, 'able to respond more rapidly to changing technological and manpower needs'. A second National Institute of Higher Education was established in Dublin in 1980.

Of particular importance was the establishment of five Regional Technical Colleges (RTCs) in 1969. Initially, they provided trade certificate courses and professional qualifications. Later sub-degree third-level courses were introduced, mostly in disciplines such as engineering, construction, business studies and applied sciences. The introduction of a third-level system offering more qualifications with a practical vocational orientation towards industrial and business disciplines fulfilled a vital need in the Irish economy, which had long been lacking. The European Social Fund allocation was in part directed towards assistance for students attending RTCs. By 1986, 90 per cent of students engaged in full-time RTC courses were in receipt of such funding.[65]

The traditional universities also played a central role in the expansion of technological skills within the economy. At the behest of the IDA-sponsored Manpower Consultative Committee, which reported in 1978, extra undergraduate places were created in engineering and computer science courses. Within the universities, the share of science, computing and IT graduates increased from 11.7 per cent in 1971 to 19.5 per cent by 2003. A breakdown of third-level attendance shows that the number of students attending Institutes of Technology (formerly RTCs) or comparable vocational institutions increased from 5 per cent of all third level students in 1965–66, to 26 per cent by 1980–81, increasing further to 37 per cent by 1997–98.[66]

The combination of an increase in the working age population in the late 1980s and early 1990s, in conjunction with the increased tertiary educational attainment in science, engineering and computer science was fortuitous. It further enhanced Ireland's attractiveness as a location for high-technology multi-national industries and coincided with the expansion of high-technology FDI in the early 1990s.[67] It seems that foreign companies were better able to exploit the improved educational attainment of the workforce than indigenous companies.

Improved educational attainment, termed 'human capital' in economic growth accounting theory, can improve economic growth in a number of ways. Hamilton cites how workers of high educational attainment are more likely to receive specialized training, increasing their value to employers and reducing the probability of unemployment. Also, workers of high educational attainment are more likely to travel in search for work, which also reduces the prospect of unemployment.[68] In addition, third-level graduates are more likely to have acquired a higher degree of skills and exposure to ICT applications than those without third-level qualifications.

The quantitative effects of increased educational attainment on economic growth can be ascertained in a number of ways. Fitzgerald estimates that the 'Human Capital Index', the rate at which retiring workers of low educational attainment are replaced by workers of higher educational attainment, increased from 0.3 per cent in the 1960s to 0.45 per cent in the 1970s, 0.65 per cent in the 1990s and finally peaking at 0.8 per cent for 2000–05. This increase in the educational attainment of the Irish workforce, due to the provision of free secondary education and the even more dramatic expansion of the third-level sector, progressively helped increase Irish productivity. By 2011, the Republic of Ireland was ranked joint first in the EU in terms of university attainment among the age cohort from 25 to 34, 48 per cent of whom had attained third-level qualifications, compared to an EU average of 33 per cent.[69] Bergin and Kearney argue that increased educational attainment can lead to increased productivity per worker, as workers have an advanced ability to utilize technology.[70] This may have been particularly true with regard to ICT production industries; Crafts and Toniolo argue that Ireland developed a specialist niche in ICT production, achieved through the attraction of selected multinational ICT firms. This concentration enabled Ireland to reap the benefits of ICT related productivity gains more effectively than most other European countries, and the same probably holds for ICT services that have become increasingly important in the last decade or more.[71]

Fitzgerald argues that the Celtic Tiger period broadly reflected the peaking of growth in the human capital index. Ireland experienced the same phenomenon witnessed in other western European countries some decades earlier, when universal secondary education, introduced in countries such as Britain, Germany, Sweden and the Netherlands in the 1940s and 1950s, had a similar effect on economic growth rates.[72] Alternative measurements by Hamilton show that the increase in the number of high productivity workers, possessed of high educational attainment, contributed 97 per cent of the increase in Hamilton's labour quality index. This index in turn accounted for 1 per cent of GDP growth per capita between 1995 and 2003.[73]

The rate of young people who completed secondary education has stabilized since the early 1990s. Of those who left school before completing the Leaving Certificate, 40 per cent were from unemployed backgrounds. Another difficulty in eliminating the problem of early school leaving was, ironically, the expanding economy during the Celtic Tiger period. The boom in the construction sector resulted in young people leaving school early,[74] or not participating in third-level education. This issue manifested itself with the decline in construction-related employment; between the first quarterly periods for 2007 and 2009 the unemployment rate increased from 7.3 per cent to 15. 8 per cent among those with a maximum educational attainment of lower-secondary level, compared to an increased of 2.4 per cent to 5.4 per cent for those with third-level educational attainment. In the case of young workers, the unemployment rate stood at 25.6 per cent for the 15 to 19 year old cohort and 17.8 per cent for the 20 to 24 year old cohort. These figures suggest that 'unemployment and educational attainment are closely linked'.[75]

Despite relatively high and rising levels of participation at tertiary level, it seems that at the lower end of the income spectrum there are serious grounds for concern around Ireland's relatively poor performance in terms of literacy. During the high watermark of the Celtic Tiger between 1994 and 1998 the performance of the Irish-born population in literacy tests was relatively poor in comparison to other countries at a similar level of economic development globally, with over a quarter of the native population, 26 per cent, merely commanding the most rudimentary levels of literacy. This evidence, taken in conjunction with the improved throughput of third-level students, reveals the stark disparity in educational access and the divided and grossly unequal nature of Irish society in terms of educational indicators. Conversely, the foreign-born population in Ireland in this period had a far lower share of its students at this lowest educational level, at less than 10 per cent, and a far greater number at the highest level than the native population. Moreover, the foreign-born component of the Irish population appears to have been more accomplished in terms of its command of literacy than the foreign-born component of all other countries measured.[76] This provides some evidence of the relatively high level of immigrant human capital entering the Irish economy during this intensive growth phase compared to other societies. More recent measures suggest that in the final phase of the Celtic Tiger, the level of educational attainment of immigrants and the indigenous population has become somewhat more similar,[77] with the improved educational attainment within the indigenous population contributing to this.

Much concern has been voiced at the decline of Irish performance in the international OECD rankings between 2000 and 2009. In the latter year, the OECD PISA survey revealed that Irish ratings for reading and science were slightly above the OECD average while the rating for maths was below the OECD average.[78] These measures fail to take account of other aspects of human capital development, notably research and development and its application to economic activity. Historically speaking, this activity was not a significant feature of Irish economic development, given the significance of low value-added food processing and a protected domestic market for the manufacturing sector. Technological advancement that did occur was generally dependant upon the transfer of technological knowledge from multinational companies.[79] While the efforts of An Foras Talúntas and later Teagasc promoted scientific research and the application of such research in agricultural production,[80] this was somewhat atypical and such efforts were not replicated in the wider economy. R&D expenditure increased as a percentage of GDP between 1991 and 1997, but lagged behind most comparable economies, and it was heavily concentrated within multi-national firms, which accounted for 72.1 per cent of private sector R&D activity in the Republic of Ireland. Moreover, the sectional distribution of this was highly skewed, with 72.6 per cent concentrated in the software/computer, electrical/electrical engineering and pharmaceutical sectors, compared to 42.8 per cent in these sectors for the EU 25 countries taken as a whole.

As early as 1996, efforts were made to expand R&D within the economy, with the establishment of the Irish Council for Science, Technology and Innovation. This was followed by the Irish Research Council for Science, Engineering and Technology, established in 2000–01, and the Irish Research Council for the Humanities and Social Sciences, both of which funded postgraduate and postdoctoral research at an individual level, while the Programme for Research in Third-Level Institutions funded research at an institutional level. The Science Foundation Ireland was established to develop bio-technological and niche information technology sectors.[81] However, despite these initiatives, R&D as a share of GDP was actually lower in 2007 than it was in 1995. In the latter year Irish expenditure remained low by European standards (see Table 8.11).

However, after the turn of the century there was an increase in R&D expenditure in the third level sector,[82] although in recent years many of the state programmes

Table 8.11 Research and development expenditure as a percentage of GDP in Ireland and selected countries at four-year intervals, 1991–2008

Country	*1991*	*1995*	*1999*	*2003*	*2007*	*2008*
Ireland	0.9	1.4	1.2	1.2	1.3	1.5
UK	2.1	2.0	2.0	1.8	1.8	–
France	2.4	2.3	2.2	2.2	2.1	–
Germany	2.5	2.3	2.4	2.5	2.5	–
Sweden	2.8	3.5	3.6	4.0	3.6	–
Finland	2.0	2.3	3.2	3.4	3.5	3.5
USA	2.7	2.5	2.7	2.7	2.7	–
Japan	3.0	3.0	3.0	3.2	3.4	–
Euro Area	–	1.8	1.8	1.9	1.9	–

Source: 1991–99, *Eurostat yearbook, 2002*. 2003, *Eurostat yearbook, 2008*. 2007 and 2008, *Eurostat yearbook, 2010*.

have had their funding cut back. While business expenditure on R&D increased from 38 per cent of the EU average in 1988 to 87 per cent by 1995,[83] this progress was not matched in subsequent years: the percentage of manufacturing plants that introduced either process or product innovations increased from an average of 62.8 per cent for the years 1991 to 1993, to 67.9 per cent for 2005, a low increase considering the dramatic expansion of the economy.[84] Private sector R&D activity has been encouraged through tax credits.[85]

Improvements in work practice and education, in addition to capital investment, tend to increase output per worker, or labour productivity. The 1950s are commonly referred to as the 'golden age' of European economic growth, as western European countries experienced high rates of labour productivity growth. Eichengreen has estimated that during the 1950s output per worker in the EEC increased by 4.71 per cent; in Scandinavian countries it grew by 3.55 per cent and in Mediterranean countries by 3.57 per cent. The growth rate of output per worker in Ireland was only 2.77 per cent over the same period. Ireland's relatively poor performance in terms of output growth per worker has been explained by Eichengreen in terms of low growth rates in human capital per worker and physical capital per worker, which he attributes to low educational attainment and the dominance of small-scale industrial concerns.[86]

Using Crafts' and Toniolo's estimates, Ireland's average labour productivity growth figure of 4.21 per cent for the 1960s appears somewhat more impressive, easily surpassing UK growth rates, while it was also higher than the Scandinavian countries. Given that Ireland started from a lower per capita income base, labour productivity growth should have been higher. The Mediterranean countries, who were of a similar income base and economic structure to Ireland, recorded higher labour productivity growth and higher contributions from the three sub-categories: capital-deepening, the ratio of investment per worker; human capital deepening, the increasing educational attainment of the workforce and Total Factor Productivity

(TFP), which consists of labour productivity increases due to greater efficiency and technological usage in the economy. In the case of Spain and Portugal, Barry argues that corporatist wage bargaining structures in these countries moderated the growth of wages to national income, in comparison with Ireland.[87] Crafts places considerable emphasis on the slow growth rate of Irish TFP in the 1960s that averaged 2.2 per cent per annum, relative to Mediterranean countries that averaged at 3.0 per cent, which he attributed to the survival of Irish protectionist policies.[88] However, TFP made the largest contribution to Irish productivity growth in this period. Capital deepening, which averaged at 1.8 per cent per annum, also contributed a large share to labour productivity, reflecting the growing significance of more capital intensive multinationals in the Irish economy.

Another characteristic of the Irish labour market is the lack of employment protection, relative to continental European countries. The presence of high job creation and redundancy rates as a percentage of the workforce, according to Lawless and Murphy, has been facilitated by the relative lack of legislative intervention relating to employment protection and redundancy. While not as unregulated as the US and the UK, Irish employment protection, as measured by Crafts and Toniolo, was low compared to other European countries, and such low rates have been maintained over time.[89] Brendan Walsh argues that while the Irish social welfare system was not as generous as in continental European countries, it did contain some disincentives towards assuming gainful employment. Some reforms of the social welfare system took place in the 1990s, with the most important reform introduced by 1998; the payment of unemployment benefit now conditional on making applications for vacancies and/or training. These measures contributed to the reduction of unemployment benefit as a percentage of net income, from an average 50 per cent during the period 1980 to 1987 to 35 per cent in 1999, the largest fall in the OECD.[90]

The sources of labour productivity growth have changed over time. As measured by Crafts and Toniolo, labour productivity growth for the period 1970 to 1990 were to a large extent due to the increase in the labour to capital ratio; the effect of increased educational attainment is reflected in the increase in the contribution of human capital deepening to Irish productivity growth, while the rate of productivity growth due to capital deepening and TFP was high.[91] Ireland's superior labour productivity growth rate for the period 1990 to 2003 is due to the contribution of TFP, rather than an increase of the capital/labour ratio, or the increase in educational achievement, which is surprising given the emphasis placed on human capital by Irish economists. This implies that the contribution to productivity from highly educated workers entering the workforce was exhausted more rapidly than is generally believed and that the nature of employment growth over the 1990s did not require advanced educational skills. The skewed occupational profile of immigrants concentrated more in low skilled sectors would tend to confirm this conclusion. The growth in Irish TFP is more unusual as it was highly dependant upon IT. In the first half of the 1990s, the ICT contribution to TFP growth of 39.5 per cent, was comparable to the US figure of 41.0 per cent. Yet, in the second half of the same decade, Irish TFP growth was solely dependant on the ICT contribution, which was of such magnitude that it masked a *decline* in the TFP contribution from other sources. The over-reliance on ICT-based productivity gains indicates that the Irish growth performance of the 1990s may have been due to a one-off gain, which would be dissipated over time.[92]

Demographic factors and the educational attainment of the Irish labour force played an important role in determining the trajectory of Irish economic growth, both for good and for ill. Brendan Walsh concluded that the rate of population growth in Ireland since 1922 is unusually volatile, due to the interaction of natural increase and net migration trends.[93] Until the 1960s, Ireland experienced a high birth rate, which was regulated by a relatively late age of marriage. However, in the absence of major expansion of non-agricultural labour, this led to emigration. The departure of young people of working age had a further adverse effect upon the dependency ratio, reducing the size of the labour force. Furthermore, limited access to secondary and tertiary education reduced the potential human capital of the labour force.

Government policy during the 1960s, both in promoting industrial development and expanding educational attainment, enhanced the contribution of the labour force, both in qualitative and quantitative terms. Also, the expansion of service employment and changing social views encouraged women to participate in the work force, especially from the 1980s onwards. While persistently high birth rates during the 1960s and 1970s relative to the rest of Europe maintained a high dependency ratio, this would be eliminated by the 1990s as the children resulting from this population boom would enter the work force. The economic growth of the 1990s was facilitated by the expansion of a suitably trained domestic labour force, the increased participation of women in the work force, the growing use of immigrant workers and the more successful application of ICT than other European countries, which increased productivity. While much has been made of native skills and education an important conclusion emerging from this survey is the significance of both increased female labour force participation and the role of immigrants in relieving labour shortages, both in the lower reaches of the occupational spectrum, but also reducing bottlenecks for skilled workers and professionals in various sectors. This combination of factors facilitated an unprecedented and dramatic expansion of the labour force, a reduction of the dependency ratio, and an improvement in the quality of the labour force, coinciding with an increase in capital investment, transfers from Brussels in addition to more credit in the economy at large. All these factors collectively contributed to a marked improvement in Irish economic performance in the following decades. However, many of the beneficial demographic factors discussed in this chapter, which contributed to improved Irish economic performance in recent decades, are finite in nature, with limitations on the rate of increase of female participation rates and future limitations on human capital index growth, as the pool of retiring workers with low educational standards dissipates.

Although the share of the younger population acquiring third-level qualifications is markedly higher than the EU average, in addition to those finishing secondary education, the relatively poor performance of a significant share of the population with regard to literacy is a major cause for concern as Ireland has fallen down the OECD rankings between 2000 and 2009, revealing the highly unequal achievements of the educational system[94] and its two tier nature, which point to the deepening of social inequalities during the period covering Celtic Tiger. Moreover, the highly educated younger cohorts in the population (by European standards) are precisely those cohorts most affected by both emigration and unemployment. These two factors reduce the capacity of Irish society to utilize its significant human capital to good effect and provides one of the greatest policy challenges in the immediate future.

Conclusion

The most striking feature of the economic history of independent Ireland has been the general rise in living standards since the 1920s, which Johnson and Kennedy have referred to as 'the primary fact of modern Irish economic development'.[1] Recent estimates of GDP per capita for independent Ireland measured in fixed prices suggest that per capita income was almost 11 times higher in the Republic of Ireland in 2008 than at the birth of the state in 1922 (see Appendix, Table 1). The scale of national income growth over this period broadly followed the wider European pattern, but was distinctive in terms of both timing and the specific growth sectors.

This rise in living standards was by no means linear, with periods of stagnation and even decline. Growth was exceptionally slow during the first three decades of independence: by 1959, GDP per capita was merely one and a half times higher than in 1922. The Republic of Ireland at this point still had a relatively low share of the workforce engaged in industry and a high share in agriculture in European comparative terms. This and the inhibiting impact of protectionism on trade, the sub-optimal size of the home market, an extremely narrow export focus (see Appendix, Tables 5 and 6) with the great bulk of exports still based on agriculture by the end of the 1950s were all features that were collectively unhelpful in improving the performance of the economy. The global shift towards protectionism was generally not beneficial to small micro-economies like the Republic.

The rate of national income growth increased from the 1960s, but even as late as 1987 Irish per capita income was still less than four times the 1922 level. Much of the rise in living standards and the most intense phase of catching up with the rest of Europe took place in the years after 1987 (see Appendix, Table 1), when Irish growth was spectacular, coinciding with the most dramatic phase of employment creation and capital investment in the history of the state.

The best way to assess Irish performance since independence is to compare it to the rest of Europe. Irish living standards (32 counties) had been catching up with Britain between the mid-nineteenth century and the 1920s. But in the inter-war years this process of convergence with Britain ceased in the Irish Free State.[2] UK growth rates were slightly higher than those in the Irish Free State in the inter-war years (1926–38), while between 1938–50 and 1950–60 the growth rates of both countries were roughly equal. Irish performance was therefore quite poor relative to the UK between 1922 and 1960. Moreover, since the main trading partner of the state, the UK, experienced sluggish growth rates in comparison to the rest of Europe, this contributed in some measure to a fairly dismal performance in a wider European context.[3] Brian Girvin's use of UN data implies that much of the stellar decline in the performance of the Republic of Ireland against the more developed European economies took place specifically during the 1950s.[4]

Conversely, the performance of the Republic of Ireland improved during the 1960s, when per capita income growth rates exceeded those of both Britain and Northern Ireland, beginning the slow process of convergence with the UK.[5] Trade liberalization between the UK and the Republic of Ireland contributed in some measure here along with the first wave of FDI.

From a wider European perspective, Irish performance during the period between the 1950s and 1980s was generally compared unfavourably with Western European average growth rates. Ó Gráda and O'Rourke, for example, attributed this lacklustre performance to the small size of the economy, the continued importance of agriculture, poor investment decisions, rent seeking, sluggish employment generation and proximity to the slow-growing UK economy as factors contributing to the lack of convergence with the EU countries up to 1988.[6] If the historiography was broadly pessimistic on Irish performance up to the mid-1990s, as the Celtic Tiger gathered momentum, more buoyant assessments began to emerge, including that of Johnson and Kennedy, though they noted the 'uneven distribution of the gains from growth' during the 1990s.[7]

Crafts (utilizing Maddison's data) also took a more bullish view of Irish performance through ranking the growth performance of 16 European countries in the periods between 1950 and 1973 and between 1973 and 1992 using GDP per capita. For the earlier period, Europe's 'golden age' of economic growth, the Republic of Ireland ranked joint twelfth (along with the wealthier economies of Switzerland, Sweden and Denmark), with an annual average growth rate of 3.1 per cent, during a period when most of Western Europe was experiencing more dramatic growth. Conversely, for the years 1973 to 1992, when European economic growth was generally more sluggish, Ireland then ranked joint third with Austria, at an annual average growth rate of 2.2 per cent. This assessment provides support for our contention that EEC entry was the most critical turning point in the economic history of the state. Growth rates between 1973 and 1992 marked the beginning of Irish convergence with continental Europe.[8]

Maddison's most recent estimates provide the best long-term European comparative overview of the entire period since Irish independence. They imply that per capita income in the Irish Free State rose far more slowly than for Western Europe as a whole (29 countries) between 1922 and 1938, and this gap further widened during the 1950s and 1960s. Conversely, in the period between 1970 and 2001, the Republic of Ireland converged with the rest of Western Europe. Much of this progress was made during the 1990s, with Ireland actually overtaking the European GDP per capita average during the last years of the twentieth century.[9] Crafts and Toniolo's survey of European growth rates suggests that the Republic of Ireland, which was firmly at the bottom of the European growth league

Table 9.1 Sectional distribution of employment (percentage shares), 1926–2009

Year	*Agriculture share of total employment*	*Industry share of total employment*	*Service share of total employment*
1926	51.8	14.5	33.7
1936	48.0	15.4	36.6
1946	46.0	14.7	39.3
1951	40.5	19.1	40.4
1961	35.7	24.2	40.1
1966	31.1	26.9	42.0
1971	25.8	29.9	44.3
1981	15.9	32.6	51.5
1983	16.8	29.4	53.8
1986	15.5	28.8	55.7
1989	15.0	28.0	57.0
1992	13.6	27.8	58.6
1995	11.5	27.9	60.6
1998	9.0	28.7	62.3
2001	7.1	28.9	64.0
2004	6.4	27.6	66.0
2007	5.1	26.9	68.0
2009	5.0	20.9	74.1

Source: *Census of population 1926–1981, occupations. Statistical abstract 1990 and 1996. Statistical yearbook 2001, 2007, 2009.*

between 1950 and 1973, thereafter exhibited the best growth performance in Europe between 1973 and 2005.[10]

Employment figures provide the most reliable indicator of structural change in the Irish economy (see Table 9.1). In the 1920s the majority of the occupied population worked in agriculture. Following the international trend, this has steadily contracted down to the present day, so that the primary sector now provides relatively limited employment and an even smaller share of net domestic product (see Tables 9.1 and 9.2). But the contribution of agriculture today remains far more important than these figures imply. Agricultural land still dominates the landscape of the country, so its management still has an undue influence on the environment; this also has implications for sectors such as tourism. Moreover, agriculture provides the raw materials for one of the state's other significant indigenous industries: food processing. It is worth noting that productivity in the Republic of Ireland in the food and drink sector (in 2000) was higher than the EU average while a higher share of the Irish manufacturing workforce was employed in the food and drink sector than the EU average.[11]

Table 9.2 Composition of net domestic product (NDP) at current factor prices, 1947–2009

Year	*Agriculture as % of NDP*	*Industry as % of NDP*	*Services as % of NDP*
1947	32.3	21.2	46.5
1953	31.1	27.3	40.9
1956	27.8	29.7	44.0
1959	27.0	28.7	44.2
1962	23.8	31.4	45.5
1965	21.6	32.0	47.1
1968	19.7	34.8	47.1
1971	16.4	36.1	48.8
1974	15.9	39.0	51.7
1977	17.7	38.1	51.9
1980	10.3	40.9	57.4
1983	11.3	40.6	56.8
1986	9.0	38.4	58.0
1989	10.5	39.5	56.3
1992	9.0	37.2	59.7
1995	7.3	37.7	55.4
1998	4.6	42.5	54.0
2001	3.2	42.7	53.9
2004	2.5	37.7	59.8
2007	2.3	35.8	62.9
2009	1.7	33.4	64.9

Source: 1947–2009, *Tables of National Income and Expenditure, 1944–49. National Income and Expenditure 1960, 1969, 1975, 1982, 1989, 2004, 2008 and 2009.*

The share of industrial employment in the state remained relatively small in European comparative terms until well after the Second World War, although it expanded thereafter up to a peak in 1981. Following some contraction thereafter, industrial employment assumed a fairly steady share of total employment in the economy between the mid-1980s and 2004 (see Table 9.1). Industries' share of total net domestic product in contrast grew more erratically, reaching an initial peak in 1980, contracting until the mid-1990s and then climbing to an all time peak in 2001 before declining thereafter (see Table 9.2).

In the 1990s, industrial employment grew at a high annual rate in the Republic of Ireland, at a time when it was stagnating or declining elsewhere in Europe. This was the period when convergence with the rest of Europe was most rapid and industrial productivity growth was centrally important to this; but rapid employment growth in services was also a distinctive and important feature of the

Irish story during the 1990s (see Table 9.1). The Irish share of employment in services now makes it predominantly a service economy in employment terms, following the wider European pattern. But the shift towards this position in the Republic of Ireland has been a fairly recent development, which has become far more marked since the new millennium.

While non-gross residential investment in the state as a share of GDP was not markedly higher than in the rest of Europe between 1960 and 1999 (and it was actually lower than in Austria, Finland, Belgium, France, Netherlands, Spain and Germany),[12] the Republic of Ireland did attract significant non-residential investment from US multinationals (whose presence was well over three times the EU 15 average in terms of their contribution to host country GDP), with relatively high outlays on R&D expenditure and high value added per head.[13] The industrial and policy chapters have identified the considerable achievements of the state in attracting manufacturing-based FDI from the 1960s. In particular, the decision to concentrate many decisions relating to industrial development in the hands of the IDA in the late 1960s, who in turn decided to focus from the early 1970s specifically on attracting FDI in the chemical and electronics sector, was absolutely critical for the subsequent development of the manufacturing sector, on which so much of the Republic of Ireland's improved export performance was based, more notably after the Single European Act (which came into effect after 1992).[14]

The attraction of FDI had a positive influence on Irish productivity. Output per hour in the Republic of Ireland is estimated to have been almost eight times higher in 1996 than it had been in 1950. While output per hour was still behind Germany, France and the US in 1996, it was already ahead of the UK, Spain and Japan.[15] This progress continued between 1995 and 2005, when the rate of growth of real GDP per hour worked was over double that in Belgium, France and Germany, and almost double the US rate.[16] Crafts and Toniolo have argued that the spectacular growth in Irish total factor productivity and labour productivity between 1990 and 2003, were due to its relatively stronger capacity to utilize ICT.[17]

But Irish productivity gains also occurred in sectors other than the ICT industries. About 56 per cent of the Republic of Ireland's manufacturing workforce in 2000 worked in sectors in which gross value added per person was markedly higher than the EU average. About half of these worked outside ICT intensive sectors including chemicals, food, beverages and tobacco, so even for manufacturing alone, a more broadly-based explanation of success is required.[18]

The growing share of national income going to profits has also been relatively higher in the Republic of Ireland; the wage share of the Irish economy dropped from as high as 80.2 per cent in 1974 to 70.7 per cent in 1986, falling to 67.1 per cent in 1993 (which was already lower than in the UK and EU). By 2001 it had fallen as low as 54.2 per cent at a time when the EU average was 67.2 per cent.[19] While transfer pricing partially distorts the Irish share, there is no doubt about the rising share of profits in economic activity and this made Ireland attractive for multinational investors, since they could enjoy the benefits of relatively lower corporate taxes, access to the EU market and relatively easy profit repatriation simultaneously. The growing attractiveness of the Republic of Ireland in all these respects is evident from the rise in inward FDI flows from the equivalent of 2.2 per cent of Ireland's GDP in 1990 to 49.2 per cent in 2000.[20]

Increased investment in the economy during the 1990s improved employment creation in industry and services. The Republic of Ireland still had a relatively large agricultural sector, which employed 15 per cent of the labour force in 1989, compared to the more developed European economies such as Germany and France for which the corresponding figure was four and seven per cent respectively.[21] This contributed to rapid catch up with Europe during the 1990s. Kennedy has attributed great significance to the dramatic employment expansion achieved in the economy between 1993 and 2000, and the corresponding contraction of unemployment that had dogged potential development historically.[22] The historical mould had been broken and favourable demographic trends contributed to the spectacular Irish growth performance of the 1990s, when the percentage of working-age people in the total population expanded; moreover, the voracious demand for labour created sufficient employment during the 1990s to turn the migration tide from net emigration at the beginning of the decade to net immigration.

Much has been made of human capital and the capability of the Irish workforce in recent years. Curiously, in terms of the average years of schooling of the labour force, the small Irish increase between 1950 and 1998 has been less than in Germany, the UK, Sweden or the Netherlands, for example.[23] The expansion of access to third-level education has been more impressive in the Republic of Ireland, particularly among younger age cohorts; by 2010, 33 per cent of 25 to 34 year olds in Europe had third-level qualifications compared to 48 per cent in Ireland. But much of this Irish rise was a relatively recent phenomena, as in 2000 attainment levels among this cohort was still only 30 per cent.[24]

Widening access to third-level education was the most impressive feature of Irish educational reform, with a tenfold increase in the number of students entering higher education between the mid-1960s and 2010.[25] This had an important influence on the quality of the labour force. Increased educational attainment may, for example, have increased exposure to a wider range of ICTs, which have been identified as a particularly important source of economic development during the Celtic Tiger.[26] Net immigration to Ireland also contributed to economic growth between 1991 and 2007. There is clear evidence that the immigrant population has a higher level of education attainment than the indigenous population; 32 per cent of Irish nationals aged 15 to 64 had attained third-level qualifications in 2011; the corresponding proportion for UK nationals resident in Ireland was 43 per cent, while for other EU 15 nationals it was 59 per cent.[27] Although this higher score for immigrants is partly a consequence of the fact that they are concentrated more in the younger adult cohorts, it indicates the extent to which immigration appears to have considerably increased the available human capital within the occupied workforce since the mid-1990s, and this effect appears to have been more beneficial to the Republic of Ireland than to other countries.

In the half-century following independence, a high level of dependence on the UK continued within the economic domain. Independent Ireland recognisably suffered from many of the handicaps of other small micro-states, conveniently summarized from the now dated theoretical literature for the period between 1960 and the early 1990s by Armstrong and Read as

> a small and undiversified natural resource base; output and export concentration, with increased risks arising from poorly diversified export markets; problems associated with having a small domestic market, often below the minimum efficient scale of output, which raises costs (particularly of non-tradeables) and reduces competition; and additional problems, often associated with micro-states of being either islands or land-locked.[28]

Although Armstrong and Read proceed to challenge all these assumptions empirically with data from the last decades, they still have some salience for the earlier phases of the state's economic history.

The chapter on trade in this volume has revealed the persistent extent of Irish trade dependence on the UK prior to EEC entry. The movement of labour from Ireland to Britain also remained high, particularly between the Second World War and the mid-1960s, by which time the Irish-born population in Britain numbered almost one million (about three-quarters of whom came from the Republic).[29] The Irish pound had an equal exchange value to sterling (as it had since 1826), while the Irish banks held large holdings of British securities and sterling balances, since Irish savings were used to purchase UK based external assets.[30] The chapter surveying industrial development in this volume reveals that even much of the limited achievements of import substitution in the private sector were due to British companies, expertise and capital investment. In all these respects, the regional economy model promulgated by Barry is particularly appropriate for the period between 1922 and 1973. Barry argues that Ireland's close integration with the British market led to outflows of labour and capital to Britain, which stymied the development of non-agricultural economic sectors in Ireland.[31]

An implication of the 'regional economy' model is that state intervention in the economy is required to promote the development of the non-agricultural sector. While the Irish government never subscribed to a complete policy of laissez faire, the economic policies implemented by Cumann na nGaedheal were cautious, concentrating on improving the quality of livestock exports and introducing a limited form of protectionism for consumer good sectors. State intervention expanded during Fianna Fáil's long tenure between 1932 and 1948, when industrialization through import substitution got underway and state investment in industrial production and public utilities created a more mixed economy. These interventions were bolstered by war-time emergency measures when the state took control of the movement, storage and sale of goods. The state's influence on economic activity rose further in the post-war era, when the ratio of public expenditure to GNP rose from an average of under 29 per cent in 1947–49 to over 56 per cent in 1975–77, with growth being more marked in the 1960s and 1970s.[32] Some highly important state initiatives were undertaken in the realm of public infrastructure between the 1920s and the 1960s, which were to be critically important for subsequent economic development. Industrialization and the consumer revolution could never have got underway effectively in the 1960s in the absence of a national electricity grid in the preceding decades.[33] The surfacing of roads was also absolutely vital to the subsequent emergence of a modern economy.

The decades after 1956 marked a major policy transition from import substitution to an emphasis on developing exports and the attraction of FDI. Trade policy was liberalized, initially with the UK in the 1960s, followed by entry into the EEC in 1973. This contributed to improving the performance of the Irish economy in a wider European context, assisted by growing FDI and the receipt of EEC funding. However, these long-term benefits were offset to some degree by inappropriate fiscal policies implemented from 1973 onwards, as successive Irish governments attempted to expand the economy through borrowing to offset the negative effects of successive oil crises. Such inappropriate policies assume particular importance in the delayed convergence perspective adopted by Honohan and Walsh. The response to the recession and the debt crisis in the 1980s led to significant improvements in fiscal and monetary management by the 1990s, which was combined with greater co-operation in relation-social partnership and wage restraint from 1987, facilitating the re-emergence of long-term convergence assisted by a more positive external environment in the 1990s.[34]

During the 1980s, international neo-liberal political thinking began to influence the orientation of economic policy and direct state intervention declined. Public service employment actually contracted in the 1980s and a new phase of rationalization, closure, privatization and deregulation got underway. While the beneficial impact of EEC market access, CAP and EU structural funds receipts and FDI have generally been recognized in the historiography, another less acknowledged factor that contributed to Irish economic development was Britain's economic revival.[35] The dynamism of international financial services in the British economy benefited Irish developments in this area from the late 1980s, while British investment in Irish banking, financial services and retailing became increasingly important from the 1990s, in addition to an influx of British human capital (including returned Irish migrants with British work experience) in several sectors, facilitating the more rapid expansion of the economy during the Celtic Tiger period. Strong economic links to Britain were no longer a disadvantage to the Republic of Ireland in the way they had been between independence and EEC entry, since after 1979 Britain was no longer falling behind the rest of Europe.

Of the various theories advanced in the introduction to this volume, the 'micro-economy' is particularly useful for the period since EEC entry in 1973, when the Irish economy slowly began to catch up with the rest of Europe. Despite considerable diversity among micro-states globally, Armstrong *et al.* have found that those micro-states specializing in tourism, financial services and manufacturing performed exceptionally well in economic terms,[36] and this has particular salience in the case of the experience of the Republic of Ireland. The micro-economy model (as opposed to the dependency model where exogenous factors loom larger) in our view affords more agency to the role of the state in Irish economic development, in terms of both its successes and failures. As a small 'micro state' within the EEC, Ireland achieved relatively greater economic benefits from EEC entry than most other member states and its political influence within the EEC was greater than might be expected from such a small economy. Like Luxembourg, another high-performing micro-economy, small size was not a major disadvantage to the Republic of Ireland, which defies traditional assumptions in the literature on the disadvantages of smaller economies. Moreover, the state through various policy initiatives and institutions was in a stronger position to attract FDI following entry to the large EEC market. More often than not this could be undertaken on a targeted firm by firm basis, attracting major firms such as Intel, which through demonstration effects brought many other ICT firms into the state. Such a strategy was more feasible in a small micro-economy, where the entire resources of the state could be readily mobilized to support specific goals. Moreover, cohesive elites facilitated a greater degree of institutional and organisational coherence between employers, trade unions and government, as evident during the period of Social Partnership, between 1987 and 2007.[37]

However, micro-economies display particular vulnerabilities. Small and cohesive social elites are especially vulnerable to corruption and regulatory capture. Nowhere was this more evident than in the construction and development sector, where local government regulation of planning for development became notorious for political corruption, and this began to surface more clearly in the 1990s at both local and national level.[38] It has been revealed that 40 per cent of disclosed donations to the Fianna Fáil party between 1997 and 2007 came from builders and property developers.[39] The state's continual failure to police the banking system adequately has a history which long predates the Celtic Tiger. This tolerance of banking mal-practices is another unpalatable aspect of the Irish micro-state. The state rescued banks from catastrophic management decisions including the greatest corporate failure in the history of the state down to 1985, when the collapse of the Insurance Corporation of Ireland threatened to take down the entire banking system; the state intervened to relieve AIB of its ill-advised investment at great cost to the taxpayer. In subsequent decades it failed to regulate offshore tax evasion, bogus non-resident accounts and overcharging on foreign exchange transactions. While a Financial Regulator was finally appointed to police the financial sector in 2003, no punitive sanctions were imposed on any Irish bank in the following three years.[40] Such a lax and even indulgent regulatory regime, undoubtedly contributed to the subsequent banking crisis in 2008 and its scale was sufficient when debts were socialized by the state to undermine its fiscal regime. The fallout has illustrated the fatal strategy adopted by the government in dealing with the crisis.

Inappropriate government policies such as tax reliefs to appease property developers and builders further inflated the property sector to unsustainable levels. It has been observed that in micro-state economies, elites and vested interests are more capable of influencing policy in negative and selfish ways than in larger economies,[41] and this book has revealed that the Republic of Ireland broadly conforms to this pattern. This is the lesson that must be learned from the recent boom, which evidently was not learned in 1985. After decades of neo-liberal deregulation, it is now starkly apparent that banks and developers need to be closely monitored and regulated by the state, and this particular public watch dog needs to behave more like a rottweiler than a poodle.

If Ireland has benefited more than most countries from the expansion of the global economy since the 1980s, conversely it suffered more from the post-2007 global economic crisis. The downturn in the Irish economy was much more severe in 2007 than any other OECD country except Iceland, declining from a GNP growth rate of 4.5 per cent in 2007 to a contraction of minus 3.5 per cent in 2008. This contraction continued with a massive decline in GNP of minus 10.7 per cent in 2009,[42] reputedly the deepest and most rapid fall in any Western economy since the Great Depression.[43]

This survey of the economic history of independent Ireland has illustrated the central importance of economic policy in fostering development and regulating economic activity in a balanced way. It has demonstrated how the state was an important agent in promoting long-term economic development, especially in building up vital infrastructure, increasing the educational attainment of the workforce and attracting FDI to intensify industrialization, which remained relatively limited by European standards prior to the 1970s. The fact that Ireland exhibited many of the characteristics of a 'micro-state' made it easier for the government to mediate and coordinate institutions and individuals in support of government policies, so that the available factors of production could be exploited to better effect in helping the Republic of Ireland catch up with the rest of Europe. The gradual move away from protectionism between 1956 and 1973 marked a watershed in policy terms in which the state recognized the failure of the old model based on import substitution and sought to foster a more trade orientated formula for development, which included exploiting FDI to a greater degree. The utilization of the IDA to promote industrial development provides a centrally important example of how the state maximized FDI at arms length from vested interests; by the turn of the century foreign multinationals accounted for half the jobs in the manufacturing sector and one in five in services. The manufacturing sector had become internationalized, while aspects of the services sector had become a European entrepôt. Equally significant was the development of a social partnership model from 1987, which contributed to fiscal consolidation in the following decades. State policy fostered stellar improvement in educational attainment, not least in technical areas such as ICT, science and engineering (with some important interventions by the IDA in ensuring a greater degree of applied education and competiveness). In addition to these major achievements, Frank Barry has made the important point that the state utilized its EU regional aid to better effect than Greece, Spain and Portugal, for example, who spent their funding more on infrastructure such as roads, instead further developing education and human capital both before and after 1989.[44]

If these examples exemplify some of the beneficial capacities of a micro-economy to move things forward, in stark contrast the political elite were equally capable of regressive behaviour in delaying necessary reform, or taking a far too indulgent approach to sectional interests, most notably in the banking and construction sectors. From a historical perspective, expansionary fiscal policies to achieve short-term electoral advantage with flagrant disregard for long-term economic stability have long been a problematic feature of the Irish story going back to the 1970s. The obvious lessons from that era of Irish economic history were not learned during the Celtic Tiger years, when fiscal over-stimulation contributed to over heating the economy and an unprecedented property and banking boom, predictably followed by an even more dramatic property and banking bust, so that when the global recession struck in 2008 there was, in Barry's words, 'no stabilizing margin', and the state was consequently forced into a 'destabilising fiscal contraction'.[45]

The 'micro-state' nature of the Republic allowed vested interests to gain an undue influence on government, resulting in a combination of misplaced policy decisions, a lack of regulation and a misallocation of resources. In the short term this further fuelled economic growth, which was electorally popular, but created economic conditions which, in the longer-term, were unsustainable and ultimately destructive. The government, in other words, should have been dampening economic growth, preparing to soften the inevitable arrival of the downturn. All the delusional hubris of the Celtic Tiger vanished when the Irish banking crisis surfaced in late September 2008, and the ill-advised government bank guarantee effectively socialized one of the most expensive bank rescues in history, which has gradually exposed the unsustainable flaws at the core of the Irish economic model.

This book has demonstrated the important role the state has played in Irish economic development since 1922, more particularly when it has encouraged the creative and innovative capacity of the private sector. Despite periodic regressions (including the current crisis), the beneficial agency of the state in economic policy must take some of the credit for the general convergence of Irish living standards with the European norm since 1922. But it needs to learn from the mistakes of the recent past; further steps need to be taken so that the state is protected from regulatory capture by vested interests and the quality of expert advice available to government on economic matters needs to be radically improved across the public service.

Statistical appendix

Table 1 GDP per capita (Geary-Kamis Dollars, 1990 prices), for Irish Free State/Republic of Ireland, UK and 29 Western European countries (WEC), 1922–2008

Year	*Ireland*	*UK*	*29 WEC*	*Year*	*Ireland*	*UK*	*29 WEC*
1922	2,598	4,637	3,372	1966	5,080	9,585	8,686
1923	2,575	4,670	3,314	1967	5,352	10,049	8,936
1924	2,569	4,921	3,539	1968	5,770	10,410	9,355
1925	2,573	5,144	3,706	1969	6,089	10,552	9,825
1926	2,572	4,936	3,723	1970	6,199	10,767	10,195
1927	2,653	5,315	3,880	1971	6,354	10,941	10,465
1928	2,737	5,357	4,013	1972	6,663	11,294	10,860
1929	2,824	5,503	4,111	1973	6,867	12,025	11,416
1930	2,897	5,441	4,014	1974	7,042	11,859	11,611
1931	2,972	5,138	3,793	1975	7,316	11,847	11,521
1932	2,885	5,148	3,675	1976	7,302	12,115	11,983
1933	2,800	5,277	3,779	1977	7,795	12,380	12,289
1934	2,882	5,608	3,909	1978	8,250	12,828	12,621
1935	2,966	5,799	4,045	1979	8,366	13,167	13,041
1936	3,052	6,035	4,162	1980	8,541	12,931	13,197
1937	2,957	6,218	4,317	1981	8,716	12,747	13,188
1938	3,052	6,266	4,399	1982	8,821	12,955	13,270
1939	3,052	6,262	4,624	1983	8,740	13,404	13,491
1940	3,052	6,856	4,548	1984	9,056	13,720	13,794
1941	3,052	7,482	4,589	1985	9,306	14,165	14,113

Table 1 Continued

Year	*Ireland*	*UK*	*29 WEC*	*Year*	*Ireland*	*UK*	*29 WEC*
1942	3,052	7,639	4,544	1986	9,265	14,742	14,476
1943	3,052	7,744	4,542	1987	9,698	15,393	14,857
1944	3,052	7,405	4,361	1988	10,234	16,110	15,406
1945	3,019	7,056	3,806	1989	10,880	16,414	15,856
1946	3,052	6,745	3,628	1990	11,818	16,430	15,966
1947	3,092	6,604	3,824	1991	11,969	16,136	16,152
1948	3,230	6,746	4,039	1992	12,277	16,088	16,256
1949	3,404	6,956	4,319	1993	12,538	16,416	16,129
1950	3,452	6,939	4,579	1994	13,198	17,082	16,517
1951	3,544	7,123	4,816	1995	14,445	17,495	16,860
1952	3,642	7,091	4,963	1996	15,472	17,891	17,097
1953	3,747	7,346	5,186	1997	16,978	18,459	17,502
1954	3,794	7,619	5,437	1998	18,233	18,925	17,974
1955	3,920	7,868	5,740	1999	19,981	19,291	18,413
1956	3,897	7,929	5,962	2000	22,015	19,817	19,002
1957	3,914	8,017	6,181	2001	23,201	20,127	19,256
1958	3,870	7,966	6,282	2002	23,823	20,946	19,623
1959	4,038	8,240	6,530	2003	24,602	21,461	19,801
1960	4,282	8,645	6,896	2004	25,379	22,096	20,199
1961	4,508	8,857	7,203	2005	26,643	22,518	20,522
1962	4,636	8,865	7,483	2006	27,760	23,107	21,087
1963	4,821	9,149	7,767	2007	29,090	23,642	21,559
1964	4,986	9,568	8,167	2008	27,898	23,742	21,672
1965	5,051	9,752	8,441				

Source: 1922–2001, *OECD World Economy*, pp. 443–7. 2002–08, ggdc.net/maddison/index.htm

Table 2 Republic of Ireland GNP and GDP growth rates 1954–2006 (at 2006 constant prices)

Year	*GNP growth*	*GDP growth*	*Year*	*GNP growth*	*GDP growth*
1962	2.9	3.0	1987	2.2	2.2
1963	4.5	4.5	1988	1.4	2.3
1964	4.9	4.9	1989	4.0	4.6
1965	2.1	1.9	1990	5.9	6.7
1966	1.0	1.1	1991	2.0	1.8
1967	5.2	5.2	1992	2.8	3.5
1968	6.4	6.3	1993	2.5	2.1
1969	5.3	5.5	1994	6.5	6.0
1970	2.5	2.5	1995	7.5	8.8
1971	5.5	5.7	1996	7.6	8.0
1972	6.1	6.1	1997	10.2	11.4
1973	5.1	5.7	1998	7.4	8.1
1974	2.9	2.9	1999	8.6	10.5
1975	0.9	1.2	2000	9.2	9.0
1976	3.4	3.8	2001	4.2	5.8
1977	4.5	5.0	2002	3.3	6.3
1978	7.4	8.2	2003	5.6	4.5
1979	5.2	5.3	2004	4.0	4.2
1980	2.9	3.0	2005	4.9	5.9
1981	1.6	0.1	2006	6.5	5.8
1982	–1.6	–0.1			
1983	–1.6	–0.9			
1984	0.9	2.1			
1985	0.9	1.8			
1986	0.6	0.7			

Source: 1962–2006, Supplied from the ESRI Databank.

Table 3 Composition of Republic of Ireland Net Domestic Product for three-year intervals, 1947–2009

Year	*Agriculture as % of NDP*	*Industry as% of NDP*	*Services as % of NDP*
1947	32.3	21.2	46.5
1953	31.1	27.3	40.9
1956	27.8	29.7	44.0
1959	27.0	28.7	44.2
1962	23.8	31.4	45.5
1965	21.6	32.0	47.1
1968	19.7	34.8	47.1
1971	16.4	36.1	48.8
1974	15.9	39.0	51.7
1977	17.7	38.1	51.9
1980	10.3	40.9	57.4
1983	11.3	40.6	56.8
1986	9.0	38.4	58.0
1989	10.5	39.5	56.3
1992	9.0	37.2	59.7
1995	7.3	37.7	55.4
1998	4.6	42.5	54.0
2001	3.2	42.7	53.9
2004	2.5	37.7	59.8
2007	2.3	35.8	62.9
2009	1.7	33.4	64.9

Source: *Tables of national income and expenditure, 1938 and 1944–49. National income and expenditure 1960, 1969, 1975, 1982, 1989, 2004 , 2008, 2009.*

Note: No figure for national income was produced for 1950.

Table 4 Republic of Ireland balance of payments (£m) 1948–2010

Year	*Balance of payments*	*As % of GNP*	*Year*	*Balance of payments*	*As % of GNP*	*Year*	*Balance of payments*	*As % of GNP*
1948	–29.0	8.7	1969	–80.0	5.4	1990	–222.0	0.9
1949	–15.8	4.5	1970	–78.4	4.4	1991	208.5	0.8
1950	–34.3	9.9	1971	–78.1	3.9	1992	–111.0	0.4
1951	–66.5	18.0	1972	–53.7	2.2	1993	1,249.0	4.1
1952	–16.5	4.1	1973	–95.7	3.3	1994	953.0	2.9
1953	–16.6	3.2	1974	–293.4	9.0	1995	850.0	2.3
1954	–11.0	2.1	1975	–32.0	0.8	1996	1,177.0	2.9
1955	–42.9	7.8	1976	–146.2	2.9	1997	1,363.0	2.9
1956	–17.3	3.1	1977	–299.6	5.0	1998	1,247.0	2.3
1957	3.2	0.5	1978	–44.2	0.6	1999	233.0	0.4
1958	–6.2	1.0	1979	–1,025.9	12.3	2000	–484.0	0.7
1959	–17.9	2.8	1980	–1,037.9	10.5	2001	–270.0	0.4
1960	–3.9	0.6	1981	–1,594.7	13.4	2002	–145.0	0.2
1961	1.2	0.2	1982	–1,315.7	9.6	2003	–5,058.0	5.4
1962	–13.5	1.7	1983	–925.2	6.2	2004	–4,075.0	4.1

Tabele 4 (Continued)

Year	*Balance of payments*	*As % of GNP*	*Year*	*Balance of payments*	*As % of GNP*	*Year*	*Balance of payments*	*As % of GNP*
1963	–22.1	2.6	1984	–837.0	5.1	2005	–3,308.0	2.4
1964	–31.5	3.3	1985	–650.1	3.7	2006	–4,557.0	3.8
1965	–41.8	4.1	1986	–509.0	2.7	2007	–8,111.0	6.4
1966	–25.7	2.4	1987	239.0	1.2	2008	–6,595.0	5.4
1967	9.8	0.8	1988	437.0	2.1	2009	–3,821.0	3.8
1968	–25.8	2.0	1989	371.0	1.6	2010	–876.0	0.9

Source: 1948–70, *Statistical abstract 1950–72*. 1971–84, *Statistical abstracts 1972– 85*. 1985–2010, *Balance of international payments final quarter and years ending 1990, 1995, 1997, 1999, 2002, 2002, 2004, 2006, 2008, 2010.*

Table 5 Percentage composition of Irish Free State/Éire exports (value) by broad commodity groups, 1925–44

Year	*Live animals*	*Other agricultural products*	*Drink and tobacco*	*Textiles*
1925	40.5	34.6	14.8	4.7
1926	43.5	35.1	12.8	3.9
1927	41.9	36.5	11.9	4.5
1928	42.9	37.0	10.3	4.0
1929	42.8	33.8	10.8	3.9
1930	48.0	35.7	12.3	2.5
1931	51.4	27.0	13.5	2.5
1932	48.2	28.1	14.0	2.9
1933	41.5	29.4	19.4	4.7
1934	35.3	32.6	21.8	4.5
1935	37.8	32.4	19.8	4.6
1936	41.2	31.3	16.9	5.1
1937	44.6	27.8	15.5	5.5
1938	50.5	31.8	9.9	5.4
1939	54.2	27.9	9.0	4.5
1940	44.8	37.7	8.0	4.8
1941	25.8	47.4	15.8	4.3
1942	48.5	30.2	13.2	3.4
1943	49.6	27.8	10.0	6.1
1944	48.4	27.0	10.7	7.7

Source: *Trade and shipping statistics 1931–44.*

Note: excludes parcel post and re-exports.

Table 6 Composition of Republic of Ireland exports (value) by broad commodity groups, 1945–73 (percentage share)

Year	*Live animals*	*Other agricultural products*	*Drink and tobacco*	*Clothing and textiles*	*Machinery and manufactures*	*Chemicals*
1945	49.0	24.7	11.6	8.5	1.2	0.2
1946	52.3	23.1	10.4	7.4	1.0	0.6
1947	57.5	17.5	10.6	7.5	1.2	0.1
1948	47.1	25.3	9.2	6.9	5.9	0.1
1949	47.6	29.9	8.8	7.5	1.7	0.2
1950	41.9	35.0	7.1	9.7	1.5	0.3
1951	38.0	44.0	6.8	9.5	0.9	0.4
1952	33.7	52.8	6.3	5.9	0.6	0.7
1953	30.4	50.3	5.4	6.6	0.7	0.5
1954	38.9	38.7	5.3	6.7	2.3	0.6
1955	43.9	28.3	5.8	8.8	2.7	0.6
1956	45.7	25.7	6.7	9.7	1.6	0.6
1957	45.2	27.6	5.6	9.3	3.8	0.5
1958	40.0	33.2	5.5	7.8	2.7	0.6
1959	33.2	29.9	5.5	10.9	4.4	1.6
1960	32.0	31.3	5.1	10.7	4.1	3.5
1961	33.6	33.8	4.3	11.0	2.9	2.5
1962	30.0	34.8	4.7	12.2	3.6	2.5
1963	29.2	35.8	4.2	8.4	5.0	0.6
1964	32.2	31.4	3.8	8.5	5.9	0.9
1965	27.8	32.3	4.0	8.8	5.1	2.4
1966	24.3	33.8	3.8	9.1	5.6	3.1
1967	20.0	38.0	3.7	9.2	5.1	2.6
1968	18.7	34.3	3.8	10.7	6.3	4.1
1969	15.9	33.8	3.5	11.0	5.9	5.0
1970	14.3	34.1	3.5	11.3	7.1	4.6
1971	15.2	34.8	3.1	11.7	6.9	5.3
1972	14.9	32.4	2.8	11.2	9.9	6.0
1973	10.4	32.8	2.9	11.8	10.5	7.2

Source: *Statistical abstract 1951–52, 1953, 1958, 1962, 1965, 1967, 1970–71, 1972–73.*

Table 7 Agricultural and industrial exports of the Republic of Ireland as a percentage of all merchandise exports (value) 1974–89

Year	*Live animals*	*Other agricultural products*	*Drink and tobacco*	*Chemicals*	*Office and data equipment*	*Other machinery*	*Clothing, footwear and textiles*
1974	6.7	32.6	2.4	9.1	–	10.9	12.7
1975	9.0	37.8	2.3	7.9	–	11.7	9.9
1976	6.1	35.6	2.2	9.5	–	14.4	10.6
1977	6.1	31.9	1.6	9.7	4.9	8.0	8.9
1978	6.1	32.4	1.8	11.9	4.5	8.0	9.6
1979	3.3	31.5	1.9	13.0	5.3	10.8	9.1
1980	3.3	30.2	2.1	12.7	6.3	10.0	8.3
1981	3.7	27.1	2.8	13.4	9.8	12.2	8.2
1982	3.0	24.0	3.0	14.2	10.9	11.0	7.1
1983	3.4	21.7	2.6	13.9	13.8	9.8	6.3
1984	2.9	20.3	2.3	13.9	17.3	9.8	6.3
1985	2.6	20.0	2.4	14.4	18.7	9.9	5.2
1986	2.7	20.7	2.4	13.3	19.7	9.9	5.5
1987	1.6	23.3	2.2	12.2	20.9	9.7	5.0
1988	1.9	21.7	2.1	13.1	18.4	11.7	4.7
1989	1.3	20.6	2.0	14.3	19.9	10.8	4.2

Source: *Statistical abstract 1974–75, 1976, 1978, 1981, 1982–85,1988, 1990.*

Table 8 Percentage composition of mercantile exports (value) of the Republic of Ireland by broad commodity groups, 1990–2010

Year	*Agricultural products*	*Chemicals*	*Office and data equipment*	*Other machinery*	*Scientific apparatus*	*Drink and tobacco*
1990	19.9	15.9	19.3	12.0	2.8	2.3
1991	20.2	17.6	16.5	12.9	3.0	2.4
1992	22.1	19.2	15.6	11.3	2.8	2.3
1993	19.9	19.3	18.4	10.6	2.4	2.2
1994	18.6	20.8	17.7	12.3	2.1	2.0
1995	17.4	18.9	21.0	13.5	1.9	1.7
1996	13.6	22.1	21.4	13.6	2.5	1.7
1997	10.3	25.3	22.9	14.9	2.5	1.6
1998	8.6	31.7	22.6	14.8	2.4	1.3
1999	8.2	31.6	22.6	16.5	2.1	1.2
2000	7.1	32.6	23.4	17.2	2.0	1.1
2001	6.3	34.8	22.7	17.9	2.0	1.1
2002	6.2	41.7	18.5	16.9	2.2	1.1
2003	7.0	43.6	18.1	10.6	4.0	1.3
2004	7.2	44.4	15.9	11.3	4.5	1.2
2005	7.4	46.6	16.1	9.4	3.1	1.3
2006	8.1	45.7	16.2	10.5	2.7	1.6
2007	8.5	48.3	14.1	10.3	2.4	1.6
2008	8.2	51.2	10.8	10.4	3.2	1.4
2009	7.5	56.6	8.0	8.5	3.5	1.3
2010	7.8	59.4	3.7	9.3	8.6	1.3

Source: *Statistical abstract 1990, 1993, 1996. Statistical yearbooks 2001, 2002, 2004, 2005, 2006, 2007, 2008, 2009, 2010.*

Notes

Introduction

1 R. Crotty, *Irish agricultural production*, Cork, Cork University Press, 1966.
2 K. Kennedy, *Productivity and industrial growth: The Irish experience*, Oxford, Clarendon Press, 1971.
3 L. Cullen, *An economic history of Ireland since 1660*, London, Batsford, 1986, 2nd edition, pp. 171–97.
4 J. Meenan, *The Irish economy since 1922*, Liverpool, Liverpool University Press, 1970.
5 D. S. Johnson, *The interwar economy in Ireland*, Dublin, Economic and Social History of Ireland, 1989. L. Kennedy, *The modern industrialisation of Ireland, 1940–1988*, Dublin, Economic and Social History Society of Ireland, 1989.
6 J. J. Lee, *Ireland 1912–85, politics and society*, Cambridge, Cambridge University Press, 1989, pp. 511–39.
7 K. Kennedy, T. Giblin, D. McHugh, *The economic development of Ireland in the twentieth century*, London, Routledge, 1988.
8 C. Ó Gráda. *A rocky road: The Irish economy since the 1920s*, Manchester, Manchester University Press, 1997.
9 Adherents of this view include P. Honohan, B. Walsh, 'Catching up with the leaders: The Irish Hare', *Brookings papers on Economic Activity, 1*, 2002, pp.1–57. C. O'Grada, 'Is the Celtic Tiger a paper tiger?', *Quarterly Economic Commentary*, Dublin, Economic and Social Research Institute, 2002, pp. 51–62.
10 J. Fitzgerald, 'Understanding Ireland's economic success', Dublin, Economic and Social Research Institute, 1999, pp. 11–13. Honohan, Walsh, op cit., pp. 1–57.
11 C. Ó Grádá, K. O' Rourke, 'Irish economic growth, 1945–88', in N. Crafts, G. Toniolo (eds.), *Economic growth in Europe since 1945*, Cambridge, Cambridge University Press, 1996, pp. 388–427.
12 P. R. Krugman, 'Good news from Ireland: A geographical perspective', in A. W. Gray (ed.), *International perspectives on the Irish economy*, Dublin, Indecon, 1997, pp. 38–53. F. Barry, 'The Celtic Tiger era: Delayed convergence or regional boom', *Quarterly Economic Commentary, Summer 2002*, Dublin, Economic and Social Research Institute, 2002, pp. 1–7. F. Barry, 'Future Irish growth: Opportunities, catalysts, constraints', *Quarterly Economic Commentary, Winter 2005*, Dublin, Economic and Social Research Institute (ESRI), 2005, pp. 1–25.
13 F. Barry, 'The Celtic Tiger era: Delayed convergence or regional boom', in A. Bergin, D. Duffy, J. Eakins, C. MacCoille and D. McCoy (eds.), *Quarterly Economic Commentary, Summer 2002,* Dublin, ESRI, 2002, pp. 4–6.

14 D. O' Hearn, *The Atlantic economy: Britain, the US and Ireland*, Manchester, Manchester University Press, 2001, pp. 196–8.

15 J. K. Jacobsen, *Chasing progress in the Irish Republic: Ideology, democracy and dependent development*, Cambridge, Cambridge University Press, 1994, p.13, 68.

16 E. O' Malley, *Industry and economic development, the challenge for the latecomer*, Dublin, Gill and Macmillan, 1989, pp. 11–28, 215.

17 L. Mjøset, *The Irish economy in a comparative institutional perspective*, Dublin, National Economic and Social Council, 1992, pp. 6–8.

18 S. Ó Riain, *The politics of high-tech growth: Developmental network states in the global economy*, Cambridge, Cambridge University Press, 2004, pp. 32–43, 64–5.

19 Ó Grádá, O' Rourke, op. cit., p. 414.

20 E. O'Leary, 'Reflecting on the Celtic tiger: Before, during and after', *Irish Economic and Social History, 38*, 2011, pp. 73–89.

21 T. Garvin, *Preventing the future: Why was Ireland so poor for so long,* Dublin, Gill and Macmillan, 2004, pp. 8–24. J. Considine, R. Butler, 'Tom Garvin, Mancur Olson and Irish economic growth', Cork, Department of Economics, University College Cork, 2007, pp. 7–11, available from www.ucc.ie/en/economics/research/workingpapers-series/downloads/Documentfile,29192,en.pdf.

22 N. J. Smith, *Showcasing globalisation? The political economy of the Irish Republic*, Manchester, Manchester University Press, 2005, pp. 65–6. Also see C. Hay, N. J. Smith, 'Horses for courses? The political discourse of globalisation and European integration in the UK and Ireland', *West European Politics, 28*, 2005, pp. 124–58.

23 O'Leary, op. cit., p. 82. H. W. Armstrong, R. J de Kervenoal, X. Li., R. Read, 'A comparison of economic performance of different micro-states, and between micro-states and larger countries', *World Development, 26*, 1998, pp. 639–56. Ireland technically does not qualify for micro-state status as defined by Armstrong *et al.*, since it had a population somewhat higher than 3 million; however, such cut-offs are fairly arbitrary and many of the issues discussed have a salience to the Irish experience.

24 P. Kirby, *Celtic Tiger in collapse: Explaining the weaknesses of the Irish model*, Basingstoke, Palgrave Macmillan, 2010. K. Allen, *Ireland's economic crash: A radical agenda for change*, Dublin, The Liffey Press, 2009. For the most recent perspective with emphasis on the persistence of the crisis rather than its development in Irish economic history, see G. McCann, *Ireland's economic history: Crisis and development in the north and south*, London, Pluto Press, 2011.

1 From dependent free state to EEC member-state: economic policies 1922–73

1 F. Barry, 'Foreign investment and the politics of export profits tax relief 1956', *Irish Economic and Social History, 38*, 2011, p. 55. H. P. Smyth, *The B&I Line: A history of the British and Irish Steam Packet Company*, Dublin, Gill and Macmillan, 1984, p. 134. E. Kavanagh, 'Independence, conservatism and interest rate setting in Ireland', Political Studies Association of Ireland, Annual Conference, 2006, p. 7, available from www.psai.ie/conferences/papers2006/kavanaghe pdf.

2 C. Ó Gráda, 'Money and banking in the Irish Free State', in C. H. Feinstein (ed.), *Banking, currency and finance in Europe between the wars*, Oxford University Press, 1995, pp. 414–20.

3 L. Ó Broin, *No man's man, a biographical memoir of Joseph Brennan: Civil servant and first governor of the Central Bank*, Dublin, Institute of Public Administration, 1982, p. 137.

4 Ó Gráda, op. cit., pp. 414–33. J. Pratschke, 'The establishment of the Irish Pound: A backward glance', *Economic and Social Review, 1*, 1969–70, pp. 51–75. D. O'Mahony, *The Irish economy*, Cork, Cork University Press, 1967, pp. 75–98, 135–41.
5 R. Fanning, *The Irish Department of Finance*, Dublin, Institute of Public Administration, 1978, pp. 184–5.
6 M. E. Daly, *Industrial development and Irish national identity 1922–1939,* New York, Syracuse University Press, 1992, pp. 24–32.
7 B. Girvin, *Between two worlds: Politics and economy in independent Ireland*, Dublin, Gill and Macmillan, 1989, pp. 39–40.
8 Ibid., p. 35.
9 M. E. Daly, 'An Irish-Ireland for business?: The Control of Manufactures Acts, 1932 and 1934', *Irish Historical Studies, 24*, 1984, pp. 246–72.
10 D. S. Johnston, *The inter-war economy of Ireland*, Dublin, Economic and Social History Society of Ireland, 1989, p. 22.
11 K. Coleman, J. Considine, 'The no income tax campaign: Twenty-first century tax philosophy in 1920s Ireland', *Irish Economic and Social History, 33*, 2006, pp. 1–18.
12 D. Ferriter, *The transformation of Ireland, 1900–2000*, London, Profile Books, 2004, p. 314.
13 T. K. Daniel, 'Griffith on his noble head: The determinants of Cumann na nGaedheal economic policy, 1922–32', *Irish Economic and Social History, 3*, 1976, pp. 55–66.
14 M. Ó Riain, *'On the move': Coras Iompair Éireann 1945–1995*, Dublin, Gill and Macmillan, 1995, p. 18.
15 N. J. A. Smith, *Showcasing globalisation? The political economy of the Irish Republic*, Manchester, Manchester University Press, 2005, pp. 168–9. J. Kennelly, *The Kerry way: The history of Kerry Group, 1972–2000*, Dublin, Oaktree Press, 2001, pp. 14–17.
16 J. S. Meehan, *The Irish economy since 1922*, Liverpool University Press, 1970, p. 35.
17 C. Ó Gráda, *A rocky road: The Irish economy since the 1920s*, Manchester University Press, 1997, pp. 144–5.
18 M. E. Daly, *The first department: A history of the Department of Agriculture*, Institute for Public Administration, 2002, p. 537.
19 C. Ó Gráda, K. O'Rourke, 'Irish economic growth, 1945–88', in N. Crafts, G. Toniolo (eds), *Economic growth in Europe since 1945*, Cambridge, Cambridge University Press, 1996, pp. 391–421.
20 J. P. Neary, C. Ó Gráda, 'Protection, economic war and structural change: The 1930s in Ireland', *Irish Historical Studies, 27*, 1991, pp. 250–63. D. McMahon, *Republicans and Imperialists: Anglo-Irish relations in the 1930s*, New Haven, CT, Yale University Press, 1984, p. 63.
21 D. Fitzpatrick, *The two Irelands, 1912–1939*, Oxford, Oxford University Press, 1998, p. 152.
22 Fanning, op. cit., pp. 218–19, 257–8.
23 Smith, op. cit., p. 169.
24 Girvin, op. cit., pp. 89–91.
25 Daly, 'An Irish-Ireland for business?', op. cit., pp. 246–9. Barry, op. cit., pp. 54–73.
26 Daly, *Irish industrial development*, op. cit., p. 109.
27 C. Ó Gráda, *Ireland, a new economic history*, Oxford, Oxford University Press, 1994, p. 398.
28 Daly, *Irish industrial development*, op. cit., p. 65.
29 Neary, Ó Gráda, op. cit., p. 253. M. Daly, 'The Irish free state and the Great Depression of the 1930s: The interaction of the global and the local', *Irish Economic and Social History, 38*, 2011, pp. 19–36.

30 Ó Gráda, *Ireland, a new economic history*, op. cit., p. 421. K. O'Rourke, 'Burn everything British but their coal: The Anglo-Irish economic war of the 1930s', *The Journal of Economic History, 51*, 1991, pp. 357–66.
31 Ó Gráda, *Ireland, a new economic history*, op. cit., pp. 430–2.
32 *Commission of inquiry into banking, currency and credit, reports*, Dublin, Stationery Office, 1938, pp. 130–1.
33 A. J. Leddin, B. Walsh, *The macroeconomy of the Eurozone: An Irish perspective*, Dublin, Gill and Macmillan, 2003, p. 242.
34 R. Dunphy, *The making of Fianna Fáil power in Ireland 1923–1948*, Oxford, Oxford University Press, 1995, pp. 221–2. B. Evans, *Seán Lemass; democratic dictator*, Collins Press, Cork, 2011, pp. 134–41.
35 P. Rigney, *Trains, coal and turf: Transport in emergency Ireland*, Dublin, Irish Academic Press, 2010, pp. 1–3, 33, 48, 51, 59, 102. Passenger traffic is taken from B. F. Shields, 'An analysis of the financial and operating statistics of the Great southern Railways Co…1938–44' *Journal of the Statistical and Social Inquiry Society of Ireland, 17*, 1946–7, pp. 541–64.
36 Ferriter, op. cit., p. 388. D. Clarke, *Brown gold: A history of Bord na Mona and the Irish peat industry*, Dublin, Gill and Macmillan, 2010, pp. 53–4, 68.
37 T. Brown, *Ireland: A social and cultural history 1922–79*, London, Fontana, 1981, p. 176. R. Fisk, *In time of war: Ireland, Ulster and the price of neutrality*, Andrè Deutsch, London, 1983, p. 315.
38 Rigney, op. cit., p. 106.
39 K. Allen, 'Forging the links, Fianna Fáil, the trade unions and the emergency', *Saothar, 16*, 1991, pp. 48–56.
40 J. J. Lee, *Ireland 1912–1985: Politics and society*, Cambridge, Cambridge University Press, 1989, p. 233. R. J. Raymond, 'World War 2 and the foundation of Irish Shipping Ltd. 1941–1945', *Éire-Ireland, 19*, 1984, pp. 48–76.
41 R. J. Raymond, 'De Valera, Lemass and Irish economic development 1933–1948', in J. P. O'Carroll, J. A. Murphy (eds), *De Valera and his Times*, Cork, Cork University Press, 1983, pp. 113–33. Girvin, *Between two worlds*, op. cit., pp. 140–3, provides a sceptical critique of this argument.
42 M. Moynihan, *Currency and central banking in Ireland 1922–1960*, Dublin, Gill and Macmillan, 1975, pp. 310–5. Kavanagh, op. cit., pp. 6–16.
43 M. J. Shiel, *The quiet revolution: The electrification of rural Ireland 1946–1976*, Dublin, O'Brien Press, 1984, pp. 30–1.
44 B. Whelan, *Ireland and the Marshall Plan, Irish economic and social history, 19*, 1992, pp. 49–73.
45 R. J. Raymond, 'Ireland and the Marshall Plan', in P. J. Drudy (ed.), *The Irish in America: Emigration, assimilation and impact*, Cambridge, Cambridge University Press, 1985, pp. 295–329, 121.
46 O'Mahony, op. cit., pp. 181–2.
47 Ó Gráda, O' Rourke, op cit., pp. 400–1.
48 Lee, op. cit., pp. 312–13.
49 M. Hederman, *The road to Europe: Irish attitudes 1948–1961*, Institute of Public Administration, Dublin, 1983. D. J. Maher, *The tortuous path: The course of Ireland's entry into the EEC 1948–1974*, Institute of Public Administration, Dublin, 1986.
50 T. Geiger, 'Why Ireland needed the Marshall Plan but did not want it: Ireland the Sterling area and the European recovery programme, 1947–8', *Irish Studies in International Affairs, 11*, 2000, pp. 193–215.

51 B. Girvin, 'Irish agricultural policy, economic nationalism and integration in Europe', in B. Girvin, R. T. Griffith (eds), *The green pool and the origins of the common agricultural policy*, London, Lothian, 1995, pp. 239–59.
52 B. Girvin, 'Ireland and the Marshall Plan', in R. T. Griffith (ed.), *Explorations in OEEC history*, Paris, 1997, pp. 61–71.
53 T. K. Whitaker, *Protection or free trade: The final battle*, 2006, Dublin, Institute of Public Administration, 2006, pp. 7–8.
54 Whitaker, 'Financial turning points', op. cit., p. 91.
55 Ó Broin, op. cit., p. 163. Kavanagh, op. cit., p. 12.
56 Whelan, 'Ireland and the Marshall Plan', op. cit., p. 70.
57 P. Honahan, C. Ó Gráda, 'The Irish macroeconomic crisis of 1955–56', *Irish Economic and Social History*, *25*, 1998, pp. 52–80.
58 Kennedy *et al.*, op. cit., p. 63.
59 J. Meenan, *The Irish economy since 1922*, Liverpool, Liverpool University Press, 1970, p. 168.
60 S. Ó Riain, *The politics of high-tech growth: Developmental network states in the global economy*, Cambridge, Cambridge University Press, 2004, p. 174.
61 *Regional policy in Ireland: A review, NESC Report no. 4*, Dublin, National Economic and Social Council, pp. 20–3.
62 J. F. McCarthy, 'Ireland's turnaround: Whitaker and the 1958 plan for economic development', J. F. McCarthy (ed.), *Planning Ireland's future, the legacy of T. K. Whitaker*, Dublin, Glendale Publications, 1990, pp. 11–74.
63 Barry, op. cit., pp. 61–3.
64 B. Girvin, 'Economic policy, continuity and crisis in de Valera's Ireland, 1945–61', *Irish Economic and Social History, 38*, 2011, pp. 36–54.
65 Barry, op. cit., pp. 54–73.
66 Evans, op. cit., p. 207.
67 R. Fanning, 'Séan Lemass', in J. McGuire, J. Quinn (eds), *Dictionary of Irish biography*, RIA, Cambridge University Press, pp. 438–9.
68 T. K. Whitaker, 'From protection to free trade, the Irish experience', reprinted in T. K. Whitaker, *Interests*, Dublin, Institute of Public Administration, 1983, pp. 55–81. F. Barry, M. Daly, 'Mr Whitaker and industry: Setting the record straight', *The Economic and Social Review, 42*, 2011, pp. 159–63.
69 Fanning, *Department of Finance*, op. cit., pp. 509–11.
70 Leddin, Walsh, op. cit., pp. 87–8.
71 F. Barry, 'Politics and fiscal policy under Lemass: A theoretical appraisal', Dublin, Institute of International Integration Studies (discussion paper, no. 292), 2009, pp. 1–2.
72 L. Kennedy, *The modern industrialisation of Ireland 1940–1988*, Dundalk, Irish Economic and Social History Society, 1989, pp. 14–5.
73 Ó Gráda, O' Rourke, 'Irish economic growth', op. cit., p. 401. J. Bradley, 'The legacy of economic development: The Irish economy; 1960–1987', J. F. McCarthy (ed.), *Planning Ireland's future: The legacy of T. K. Whitaker*, Dublin, Glendale Publications, 1990, pp. 128–52. Leddin, Walsh, op. cit., pp. 88–9.
74 B. Eichengreen, *The European economy since 1945: Coordinated capitalism and beyond*, Princeton, NJ, Princeton University Press, 2007, pp. 32–4.
75 Ó Gráda, O' Rourke, 'Irish economic growth', op. cit., p. 415.
76 Roche, op. cit., p. 188.
77 Kennelly, op.cit., pp. 21–2.

78 W. Black, 'Industrial development and regional policy', in N. J. Gibson, J. E. Spencer (eds), *Economic activity in Ireland: A study of two open economies*, Dublin, 1977, pp. 40–2.
79 L. Kennedy, op. cit., p. 12.
80 D. McDonald, 'Issues in industrial development policy', in J. W. O'Hagan (ed.), *The economy of Ireland*, Dublin, Irish Management Institute, 1978, p. 271.
81 R. MacSharry, P. White, *The making of the Celtic Tiger: The inside story of Ireland's boom economy*, Dublin, Mercier Press, 2000, pp. 190–2.
82 Ibid., p. 273.
83 M. Cooper, J. Davis, *The Irish fertiliser industry: A history*, Dublin, Irish Academic Press, 2004, pp. 201–3, 266–70.
84 MacSharry, White, op. cit., pp. 299–302.
85 Black, op. cit., pp. 73–7.
86 A. O'Brien, *The politics of tourism development: Booms and busts in Ireland*, London, Palgrave Macmillan, 2011, pp. 75–95.
87 Smyth, op. cit., p. 222.
88 I. Furlong, *Irish tourism 1880–1980*, Dublin, Irish Academic Press, 2009, pp. 159–209.
89 D. J. Cogan, *The Irish services sector*, Dublin, Stationery Office, 1978, pp. 155–66.
90 F. Barry, 'Politics and economic policy making in Ireland', in J. Hogan, P. F. Donnelly, B. K. O'Rourke (eds), *Irish business and society*, Dublin, Oaktree Press, 2010, pp. 28–43.
91 Hederman, op. cit., p. 26, 131.
92 Maher, op. cit., pp. 72–5.
93 For the debate between free trade and protectionism, see T. K. Whitaker, *Protection or free trade: The final battle*, op. cit.
94 M. Fitzgerald, *Protectionism to liberalisation: Ireland and the EEC, 1957 to 1966*, Aldershot, Ashgate, 2000, pp. 106–7.
95 M. Fitzgerald, 'Ireland's relations with the EEC: From the treaties of Rome to membership', *Journal of European Integration, 7*, 2001, pp. 22–3.
96 Fitzgerald, *Protectionism to liberalisation*, op. cit., pp. 233–90.
97 Maher, op. cit., pp. 329–31.
98 M. J. Geary, *An inconvenient wait: Ireland's quest for membership of the EEC 1957–73*, Dublin, Institute of Public Administration, 2009, pp. 173–85.
99 B. Laffan, J. O'Mahony, *Ireland and the European Union,* Palgrave Macmillan, 2008, pp. 28–9.

2 A new frontier: the EEC/EU and economic governance: 1973–2011

1 J. O'Brennan, 'Ireland and the European Union: Mapping domestic modes of adaption and contestation', in J. Hogan *et al.*, *Irish business and society: Governing, participating and transforming in the 21st century*, Dublin, Gill and Macmillan, 2010, p. 380.
2 Ibid., pp. 380–7.
3 D. McAleese, 'Twenty-five years and growing', in R. O' Donnell (ed.), *Europe: The Irish experience*, Dublin, Institute of European Affairs, 2000, pp. 79–105. 1999–2008; *Department of Finance: Budgetary and economics statistics,* Dublin, Department of Finance, 2009.
4 G. McCann, *Ireland's economic history*, Pluto Press, London, 2011, p. 200.
5 R. MacSharry, P. White, *The making of the Celtic Tiger: The inside story of Ireland's boom economy*, Dublin, Mercier Press, 2000, pp. 107–15. Brennan, op. cit., p. 381.

6 Ibid., pp. 108–10.
7 F. Barry, J. Bradley, A. Hannan, 'The European dimension: The single market and the structural funds', in F. Barry (ed.), *Understanding Ireland's economic growth*, Dublin, 1999, pp. 99–117.
8 Ibid., p. 112.
9 B. Laffan, J. O'Mahony, *Ireland and the European Union*, Palgrave Macmillan, 2008, p. 49, 138.
10 E. O'Leary, 'Reflecting on the Celtic Tiger: Before, during and after', *Irish Economic and Social History*, 2011, pp. 83–4.
11 Laffan, O'Mahony, op. cit., pp. 32–3, 42.
12 Barry, Bradley, Hannan, op. cit., p. 100.
13 K. Kennedy, 'Reflections on the process of Irish economic growth', *Journal of the Statistical and Social Inquiry Society of Ireland, 30*, 2002, pp. 124–35. Barry, Bradley, Hannan, op. cit., p. 100, 106.
14 S. Ó Riain, *The politics of high-tech growth: Developmental network states in the global economy*, Cambridge, Cambridge University Press, 2004, p. 40.
15 *A review of industrial policy*, Dublin, NESC,1982, pp. 35–9. Lee, op. cit., pp. 531–2.
16 E. O' Malley, 'Revival of Irish indigenous industry', in T. J. Baker, D. Duffy, F. Shortall (ed.), *ESRI Quarterly Economic Commentary, April 1998*, Dublin, Economic and Social Research Institute, 1998, pp. 35–57.
17 D. O'Hearn, 'Macroeconomic policy in the Celtic Tiger: A critical reassessment', in C. Coulter, S. Coleman (eds), *The end of Irish history? Critical reflections on the Celtic Tiger*, Manchester, Manchester University Press, 2003, p. 38.
18 C. van Egeraat, 'The scale and scope of process R&D in the Irish pharmaceutical industry', *Irish Geography, 43*, 2010, pp. 35–6, 55–56.
19 C. Ó Gráda, *A rocky road: The Irish economy since the 1920s*, Manchester, Manchester University Press, 1997, p. 172. J. Fingleton, 'Competition and efficiency in the services sector', in J .W. O'Hagan (ed.), *The economy of Ireland*, Dublin, Gill and Macmillan, 1995, pp. 296–328.
20 P. Breathnach, 'The services sector', in B. Bartley, R. Kitchen (eds), *Ireland in the twenty-first century*, London, Pluto Press, 2007, pp. 146–57.
21 F. O'Toole, 'Competition policy, regulation and non-internationally traded services', in J. O' Hagan, C. Newman (eds), *The economy of Ireland: National and sectoral policy issues*, Dublin, Gill and Macmillan, 2005, pp. 188–212.
22 MacSharry, White, op. cit., pp. 299–302. *Regional policy in Ireland: A review*, Dublin, National Economic and Social Council, 1975, pp. 48–50.
23 Breathnach, op. cit., p. 151.
24 *Ireland: National development plan, 2000–2006*, Dublin, Stationery Office, 2000, p. 9.
25 E. Morgenroth, 'The national spatial strategy: Regional, urban and rural development', in E. Morgenroth, J. Fitzgerald (eds), *Ex-ante evaluation of the investment priorities for the National Development Plan, 2007–2013*, Dublin, Economic and Social Research Institute, 2006, pp. 75–98.
26 Lee, op. cit., pp. 465, 470.
27 P. Honohan, B. Walsh, 'Catching up with the leaders: The Irish Hare', *Brookings papers on Economic Activity, 1*, 2002, pp. 1–57, p. 5.
28 D. Keogh, *Jack Lynch: A biography*, Dublin, Gill and Macmillan, 2008, pp. 404–7.
29 Lee, pp. 488–9.
30 Ibid., pp. 501–2.
31 J. Bradley, 'The legacy of economic development: The Irish economy, 1960–1987', in J. F. McCarthy (ed.), *Planning Ireland's future: The legacy of T. K. Whitaker*, Dublin, Glendale Publications, 1990, pp. 128–52, 136.

32 Honohan, 'Fiscal adjustment', Barry (ed.), op. cit., p. 79. J. Considine, D. Duffy, 'Tales of expansionary fiscal contraction in two European countries: Hindsight and foresight', Cork, Department of Economics, University College Cork, 2007, p. 9, available from www.ucc.ie/en/economics/research/workingpaperseries/downloads/documentfile.38052.en.pdf.
33 *Proposals for plan, 1984–87*, Dublin Stationery Office, 1984, p. iii.
34 *Building on reality*, Dublin, Stationery Office, 1985, pp. 31–2.
35 Bradley, 'The legacy of economic development', op. cit., pp. 136–7.
36 MacSharry, White, op. cit., p. 60.
37 S. Collins, *Breaking the mould: How the PDs changed Irish politics*, Dublin, Gill and Macmillan, 2005, pp. 61–4.
38 Ibid., p. 231.
39 Honohan, 'Fiscal adjustment', Barry (ed.), op. cit., p. 81.
40 Hardiman, op. cit., p. 239.
41 MacSharry, White, op. cit., pp. 62, 75–7.
42 Considine, Duffy, op. cit., pp. 3–8, 10–1. A. de la Fuente, X. Vives, 'The sources of Irish growth,' in A. W. Gray (ed.), *International perspectives on the Irish economy*, Dublin, Indecon, 1997, pp. 112–34.
43 De la Fuente and Vives, op. cit., p. 125.
44 Honohan, 'Fiscal adjustment', Barry (ed.), op. cit., p. 82.
45 Collins, *Breaking the mould*, op. cit., p. 107.
46 S. Collins, *Spring and the labour story*, Dublin O' Brien Press, 1993, pp. 186, 203.
47 P. Sweeney, *Ireland's economic success: Reasons and lessons*, Dublin, New Island Books, 2008, op. cit., p. 47.
48 P. Honohan, B. Walsh, 'Catching up with the leaders: The Irish Hare', *Brookings papers on Economic Activity, 1*, 2002, pp. 1–57.
49 A. J. Leddin, B. Walsh, *The macroeconomy of the eurozone: An Irish perspective*, Dublin, Gill and Macmillan, 2005, p. 102.
50 *Commission on taxation*, op. cit., p. 155.
51 *A preliminary report on the sources of Ireland's banking crisis*, Dublin Department of Finance, 2010, p. 27.
52 M. Casey, *Ireland's malaise: The troubled personality of the Irish economy*, Dublin, Liffey Press, 2010, p. 73
53 Hardiman, op. cit., pp. 60–70.
54 Ibid., pp. 76–7.
55 C. Power, *Metamorphosis: Lessons from the formative years of the Celtic Tiger, 1979–1993*. Dublin, Oaktree Press, 2009, pp. 54, 138–43.
56 Hardiman, op. cit., pp. 75, 98–9, 175.
57 Ibid., pp. 146–7, 221–3.
58 Hastings *et al.*, op. cit., p. 12. Hardiman, op. cit., p. 223.
59 Hastings *et al.*, op. cit., pp. 18–21.
60 Ibid., pp. 31–3.
61 Hardiman, op. cit., pp. 234–9.
62 Hastings *et al.*, op. cit., pp. 145–67. W. K. Roche, 'Social partnership from Lemass to Cowen', *Economic and Social Review, 40*, 2, 2009, pp. 183–205.
63 T. Baker, 'The Irish economy: Then, now and next', in D. Duffy, J. Fitzgerald, K. Kennedy, D. Smyth (eds), *Quarterly Economic Commentary, Winter 1999*, Dublin, Economic and Social Research Institute, 1999, pp. 1–11.
64 P. R. Lane, 'Profits and wages in Ireland, 1987–1996', *Journal of the Statistical and Social Inquiry Society of Ireland, 27*, 5, 1998, pp. 229–32.
65 Kennedy, op. cit., p. 135.

66 O' Malley, 'Revival of Irish indigenous industry', op. cit., p. 54.
67 F. Barry, 'Social partnership, competiveness and exit from fiscal crisis', *Economic and Social Review, 40*, 2009, 1, p. 9.
68 Ibid., p. 9.
69 A. J. Leddin, 'The Philips curve and the wage-inflation process in Ireland', in S. Kinsella, A. J. Leddin (eds), *Understanding Ireland's economic crisis: Prospects for recovery*, Dublin, Blackhall Publishing, 2010, pp. 167–70.
70 Ibid., pp. 170–1.
71 Lane, op. cit., p. 230.
72 P. Tansey, *Ireland at work, economic growth and the labour market, 1987–1997*, Dublin, Oak Tree Press, 1998, pp. 200–2.
73 P. Teague, J. Donaghey, 'Why has Irish social partnership survived?', *British Journal of Industrial Relations, 47*, 2009, pp. 55–78.
74 N. Crafts, G. Toniolo, 'Aggregate growth, 1950–2005', in S. Broadberry, K. H. O'Rourke (eds), *The Cambridge economic history of modern Europe, volume 2, 1870 to the present*, Cambridge, Cambridge University Press, 2010, pp. 296–332.
75 Collins, *Breaking the mould*, op. cit., p. 108.
76 D. Palcic, E. Reeves, 'An economic analysis of privatization in Ireland 1991–2003', *Journal of the Statistical and Social Inquiry Society of Ireland, 24*, 2004, pp. 1–24.
77 *OECD reviews of foreign direct investment: Ireland*, Paris, OECD, 1994, p. 43.
78 F. Barry, 'Irish growth in a historical and theoretical perspective', in F. Barry *et al.* (ed.), op. cit., p. 31.
79 J. Kelly, M. Everett, 'Financial liberalisation and economic growth in Ireland', *Central Bank Quarterly Bulletin, Autumn 2004*, Dublin, Central Bank of Ireland, 2004, pp. 91–112.
80 McCann, op. cit., pp. 200–1.
81 Ó Gráda, op. cit., p. 173.
82 P. Massey, 'Is Irish utility regulation failing consumers?', in D. McCoy, D. Duffy, A. Bergin, S. Garrett, Y. McCarthy (eds), *ESRI Quarterly Economic Commentary, Winter 2004*, Dublin, Economic and Social Research Institute, 2004, pp. 1–18.
83 *OECD economic surveys, Ireland*, op. cit., pp. 26–8.
84 Leddin, Walsh, op. cit., p. 243.
85 Ó Gráda, op. cit., p. 65.
86 A. E. Murphy, 'The "Celtic Tiger": An analysis of Ireland's economic growth performance', Florence, European University Institute, Robert Schumann Centre for Advanced Studies (working paper RSCno.2000/16), 2000, pp. 8–9. Available from http://www.eui.eu/RSCAS/wp-texts/00.16.pdf (accessed 01/04/2010).
87 Ó Gráda, op. cit., p. 66.
88 P. Honohan, A Leddin, 'Ireland in EMU: More shocks, less insulation?', *Economic and Social Review, 37*, 2006, pp. 263–94.
89 Leddin, Walsh, op. cit., p. 482
90 Honohan, Leddin, op. cit., pp. 265–6.
91 A. E. Murphy, op. cit., p. 20.
92 Honohan, Leddin, op. cit., p. 286.
93 *A preliminary report on the sources of Ireland's banking crisis*, op. cit., p. 27.
94 N. J. Smith, *Showcasing globalisation? The political economy of the Irish Republic*, Manchester University Press, 2005, pp. 48–9, 134.
95 S. Ross, *The bankers: How the banks brought Ireland to its knees*, London, Penguin, 2009, pp. 8–33.

96 *The Irish banking crisis: Regulatory and financial stability policy, 2003–08; A report to the Minister for Finance by the Governor of the Central Bank*, Dublin, Central Bank of Ireland, 2010, p. 34.
97 Ibid., p. 35.
98 Ibid., p. 43.
99 Ross, op. cit., pp. 77–9.
100 *The Irish banking crisis: Regulatory and financial stability policy, 2003–08*, op. cit., p. 75.
101 M. Kelly, 'The Irish credit bubble', in S. Kinsella, A. Leddin (eds), *Understanding Ireland's economic crisis, prospects for recovery*, Dublin, Blackhall Publishing, 2010, pp. 57–87.
102 For a comparison of the Irish bailout with bank resource schemes in other countries, see L. Laven, F. Valencia, 'Systemic banking crisis databases, an update', IMF Working Paper WP/12/163, Washington DC, IMF, 2012, pp. 24–29.
103 The Icelandic bank bailout of 2008 accounted for 44 per cent of GDP compared to 41 per cent for Ireland, the fiscal cost of banking bailouts in Indonesia in 1997 and Argentina in 1990 exceeded 50 per cent of GDP. See Laven, Valencia, op cit., pp. 19–20.
104 M. Cooper, *How Ireland went bust*, Penguin Ireland, London, 2011, pp. 105, 123, 161, 173, 184, 385–8, 400.
105 K. Whelan, 'Policy lessons from Ireland's latest recession', *Economic and Social Review, 41*, 2, 2010, pp. 230–42.
106 P. Kirby, *Celtic Tiger in collapse: Explaining the weaknesses of the Irish model*, London, Palgrave Macmillan, p. 143.
107 Ibid., pp. 243–5.
108 Laffan, O'Mahony, op. cit., pp. 32, 138.
109 O'Brennan, op. cit., pp. 379, 387–8.

3 Nature's bounty: agriculture and natural resources

1 R. Crotty, *Irish agricultural production*, Cork, Cork University Press, 1966, pp. 111, 115.
2 J. O'Donovan, *The economic history of livestock in Ireland*, Cork, Cork University Press, 1940, pp. 423, 428. M. E. Daly, *The first department: A history of the Department of Agriculture*, Dublin, Institute of Public Administration, 2002, pp. 169–70.
3 For the background to the emergence of this trade, see D. S. Jones, *Graziers, land reform and political conflict in Ireland*, Catholic University Press of America, Washington, 1995.
4 T. Dooley, *'The land for the people': The land question in independent Ireland*, Dublin, University College Dublin Press, 2004, p. 60. K. Kennedy, T. Giblin, D. McHugh, *The economic development of Ireland in the twentieth century*, Routledge, London, 1989, p. 217.
5 G. Federico, *Feeding the world: An economic history of agriculture, 1800–2000*, Princeton, NJ, Princeton University Press, 2000, p. 155.
6 Dooley, op. cit., p. 60.
7 L. M. Cullen, *An economic history of Ireland since 1660*, London, Batsford, 1986, 2nd edition, pp. 171–2.
8 C. Guiomard, R. O' Connor, 'Agricultural output in the Irish Free State area before and after independence', *Irish Economic and Social History, 12*, 1985, pp. 89–97. Crotty, op. cit., p. 354. O'Donovan, op. cit., p. 441.
9 *Reports of the Commission on Agriculture, final report.* Dublin Stationery Office, 1924, pp. 27–31, 44–5.

10 *Farming since the famine, Irish farm statistics, 1847–1996*, Dublin, Central Statistics Office, 1997, p. 15.
11 D. S. Johnston, *The inter-war economy in Ireland*, Dundalk, Economic and Social History Society of Ireland, 1989, p. 11.
12 Daly, op. cit., p.155.
13 R. Ryan, 'Irish butter industry 1922–1939', *Irish Economic and Social History, 27*, 2001, pp. 32–47.
14 P. J. Sammon, *In the land commission: A memoir 1933–1978*, Dublin, Ashfield Press, 1997, p. 152.
15 Daly, op. cit., pp. 159, 163. J. J. Lee, 'From empire to Europe: The Irish state 1922–73', in M. Adshead, P. Kirby, M. Millar (eds), *Contesting the state: Lessons from the Irish case*, Manchester University Press, 2008, p. 38.
16 K. Kennedy, T. Giblin, D. McHugh, *The economic development of Ireland in the twentieth century*, Routledge, London, 1989, p. 212.
17 C. Ó Gráda, 'Irish agriculture north and south since 1900', in B. Campbell, M. Overton (eds), *Land, labour and livestock: Historical studies in European agricultural productivity*, Manchester University Press, 1991, pp. 441, 446–7.
18 Dooley, op. cit., pp. 190–1.
19 Daly, op. cit., pp. 181–2.
20 R. Ryan, 'Butter industry in Munster, 1884–1939', unpublished M. Phil Thesis, University College Cork, 2000, p. 161.
21 J. J. Lee, *Ireland 1912–85: Politics and society*, Cambridge, Cambridge University Press, 1989, pp. 184–6.
22 J. P. Neary, C. Ó Gráda, 'Protection, economic war and structural change: The 1930s in Ireland', *Irish Historical Studies, xxvii*, 107, 1991, pp. 250–63.
23 Daly, op. cit., pp. 170–80.
24 Guiomard, O' Connor, op. cit., p. 93. Livestock figure is inclusive of stock changes. Livestock products are comprised of milk and milk products, wool and eggs.
25 Daly, op. cit., p. 163.
26 B. Evans, 'The Irish smallholder, the state and compulsory tillage 1939–45', *Irish Economic and Social History, 36*, 2011, pp. 1–17. Daly, op. cit., pp. 225–6.
27 M. Cooper, J. Davis, *The Irish fertilizer industry: A history*, Dublin, Irish Academic Press, 2004, p. 148. C. A. Lewis, 'Recognition and development of the Irish draught horse', in M. McGrath, J. C. Griffith (eds), *The Irish draught horse: A history*, Cork, Collins Press, p. 160. P. Rigney, *Trains, coal and turf: Transportation in emergency Ireland*, Irish Academic Press, Dublin, 2010, p. 6.
28 C. Ó Gráda, *A rocky road: The Irish economy since the 1920s*, Manchester, Manchester University Press, 1997, pp. 16–7.
29 Crotty, op. cit., p. 159.
30 Kennedy *et al.*, op. cit., p. 204.
31 Daly, op. cit., pp. 248–52. Ó Gráda, op. cit., p. 16. J. Meenan, 'Irish agriculture policies in the last twenty years', in I. F. Baillie, S. J. Sheehy (eds), *Irish agriculture in a changing world*, Newcastle, Oliver & Boyd, 1971, p. 44.
32 H. G. Foster, 'Ireland's trade with Britain', Baillie, Sheehy, op. cit., p. 79. Rigney, op. cit., pp. 79–96, 170, 197, 200.
33 Daly, op. cit., pp. 284–5, 296–7, 312, 325.
34 R. J. Raymond, 'The Marshall Plan and Ireland, 1947–52', in P. J. Drudy (ed.), *The Irish in America: Emigration, assimilation and impact*, Cambridge, Cambridge University Press, 1985, p. 121.

35 M. Manning, *James Dillon: A biography*, Dublin, Wolfhound Press, 1999, pp. 296–302. M. Miley, 'Establishment and evolution of An Foras Talúntas', in M. Miley (ed.), *Growing knowledge: Fifty years of research and development in Irish farming and food*, Carlow, Teagasc, 2009, pp. 13–43.

36 A. Matthews, 'The state and Irish agriculture, 1950–1980', P. J. Drudy (ed.), *Ireland, land, politics and people*, Cambridge, Cambridge University Press, 1982, pp. 241–71.

37 Ó Gráda, op. cit., pp. 150–1.

38 Daly, op. cit., pp. 322–6.

39 Ibid., pp. 312–18.

40 M. J. Shiel, *The quiet revolution: The electrification of rural Ireland, 1946–1976*, Dublin, O' Brien Press, 1984, pp. 221–2.

41 P. Bolger, *The Irish co-operative movement: Its history and development*, Dublin, Institute of Public Administration, 1977, p. 234. M. Neenan, 'Agriculture in the new state', in P. L. Curran (ed.), *Towards a history of agricultural science in Ireland*, The Agricultural Science Association, Dublin, 1992, p. 120.

42 Crotty, op. cit., pp. 87, 215. J. Kennelly, *The Kerry way: The history of Kerry Group, 1972–2000*, Dublin, Oaktree Press, 2001, p. 6.

43 J. A. Walsh 'Adoption and diffusion processes in the mechanisation of Irish agriculture', *Irish Geography, 25*, 1992, pp. 33–53.

44 J. Bell, M. Watson, *A history of Irish farming 1750–1950*, Dublin, Four Courts Press, 2008, pp. 290–3. J. Blackwell, *Transport in the developing economy*, Dublin, ESRI, 1969, pp. 25, 61.

45 Ibid., pp. 46–8.

46 T. O'Neill, 'Tools and things: Machinery on Irish farms, 1700–1981', in A. Gailey, D. Ó Hogáin (eds), *Gold under the Furze: Studies in folk tradition*, Dublin, Glendale Press, 1982, p. 101. J. Neill-Watson, *A history of farm mechanisation in Ireland 1890–1990*, Farm Tractor and Machinery Trade Association, 1993, pp. 61–67, 72–84.

47 Walsh, op. cit., pp. 33–53.

48 Federico, op. cit., p. 168.

49 J. Feehan, *Farming in Ireland: History, heritage and environment*, Dublin, University College Dublin, 2003, pp. 194–5, 504.

50 M. Miley, 'Soils, grass and environmental research at Johnstown Castle', in M. Miley (ed.), *Growing knowledge. Fifty years of research and development in Irish farming and food*, Carlow, Teagasc, 2009, pp. 43–61. J. Murray, 'From grass to milk: The Moorepark story', Miley, op. cit., pp. 61–77. P. Smith, 'Leading progress in beef production', Miley, op. cit., pp. 77–89.

51 Kennelly, op. cit., p. 35.

52 D. A. Gilmour, 'Concentration of enterprises and spatial change in the agriculture of the Republic of Ireland', *Transactions of the Institute of British Geographers, 12*, 1987, pp. 204–16. D. A. Gilmour, 'The spatial structure of agricultural output in the Republic of Ireland', *Economic and Social Review, 8*, 1977, pp. 130, 141.

53 D. F. Hannan, P. Commins, 'The significance of small scale landholders in Ireland's socio-economic transformation', in J. H. Goldthrope, C. T. Whelan (eds), *The development of industrial society in Ireland*, Oxford, 1992, p. 85.

54 P. Commins, 'Land policies and agricultural development', Drudy, op. cit., p. 40.

55 S. J. Sheehy, 'The impact of EEC membership on Irish agriculture', *Journal of Agricultural Economics, 31*, 3, 1980, p. 300.

56 Ibid., pp. 300–5.

57 Feehan, op. cit., p. 505. R. Breen, 'Farm servanthood in Ireland, 1900–40', *Economic History Review, 36*, 1983, pp. 87–102.
58 Federico, op cit., p. 61.
59 P. O'Hara, *Partner's in production? Women, farm and family in Ireland*, Berghahn Books, New York, 1998, pp. 81–113.
60 Crotty, op. cit., pp. 160–3, 174–8, 186, 210.
61 Daly, op. cit., pp. 344–6. J. Meenan, 'Irish agricultural policies in the last twenty years', Baillie, Sheehy, op. cit., pp. 49–51.
62 Daly, op. cit., pp. 486–96.
63 Ibid., pp. 484–5. R. Fennell, 'The domestic market', op. cit., p. 106.
64 Fennell, op. cit., p. 100.
65 J. A. Walsh, 'Enterprise substitution in Irish agriculture: Sheep production in the 1980s', *Irish Geography, 22*, 1989, pp. 106–9.
66 Kennedy *et al.*, op. cit., p. 208.
67 D. MacAleese, 'Twenty five years a growing', in R. O' Donnell (ed.), *Europe: The Irish experience*, Dublin, Institute for European Affairs, 2000, pp. 79–105. N. Collins, 'Still recognisably pluralist? State–farmer relations in Ireland', in R. J. Hill, M. Marsh (eds), *Modern Irish democracy*, Dublin, Irish Academic Press, 1993, p. 106.
68 Daly, op. cit., pp. 507–10.
69 Federico, op. cit., p. 242.
70 A. Matthews, R. O' Connor, 'The food processing industry', in J. Bradley, J. Fitzgerald, R. A. Storey (eds), *ESRI medium term review, 1987–1992*, Dublin, Economic and Social Research Institute, 1987, p. 75.
71 Daly, op. cit., pp. 514–15. Quota levels were subsequently increased.
72 A. Matthews, 'Agriculture, rural development and food safety', J. O' Hagan, C. Newman (eds), *The economy of Ireland: National and sectoral policy issues*, Dublin, 2005, pp. 215–42. Feehan, op. cit., pp. 507–9.
73 J. A. Walsh, 'A regional analysis of enterprise substitution in Irish agriculture in the context of a changing common agricultural policy', *Irish Geography, 24*, 1991, pp. 10–23.
74 Ibid., p. 15.
75 *Compendium of agricultural statistics 1997. Compendium of agricultural statistics, 2007.*
76 J. A. Walsh, 'Regional analysis of enterprise substitution in Irish Agriculture', op. cit., p. 18.
77 A. A. Horner, J. A. Walsh, 'Regional aspects of agricultural production in Ireland, 1970–1980', *Irish Geography, 17*, 1984, pp. 95–101.
78 A. Matthews, 'Productivity growth in Irish agriculture', *Journal of the Statistical and Social Inquiry Society of Ireland, 29*, 2000, pp. 317–67.
79 Matthews, O' Connor, Bradley, *et al.*, op. cit., p. 76. J. A. Walsh, 'Regional analysis of enterprise substitution in Irish agriculture', op. cit., p. 18. *That was then, this is now: Change in Ireland 1949–1999*, Dublin, CSO, 2000, p. 122.
80 Federico, op. cit., p. 15.
81 J. J. Sexton, 'Trends in output, employment and productivity in Ireland, 1995–2005', Aylward, O' Toole, op. cit., pp. 28–34.
82 *Detailed assessment of Ireland's productivity performance, 1980–2005*, Dublin, Department of Enterprise, Trade and Employment, 2006, p. 12.
83 Matthews, 'Agriculture, rural development and food safety', op. cit., p. 217. Feehan, op. cit., p. 514.

84 *Farming since the famine, compendium of agricultural statistics, 1997.*
85 Gilmour, 'Land and people *c.* 1926', J. R. Hill, (ed.), *A new history of Ireland, vii, Ireland 1921–84,* Oxford, Oxford University Press, 2003, pp. 62–86.
86 J. P. Clinch, *Economics of Irish forestry: Evaluating the returns to economy and society,* Dublin, COFORD, 1999, pp. 1–3. B. Kearney, R. O' Connor, 'Economic issues in Irish forestry', *Journal of the Statistical and Social Inquiry Society of Ireland, 26,* 1993, pp. 170–209.
87 *Irish forestry policy,* Dublin, National Economic and Social Council, 1979, p. 31.
88 Clinch, op. cit., p. 2. Gilmour, 'Land and people *c.* 1983', in Hill (ed.), op. cit., p. 433.
89 *Irish forestry policy,* op. cit., p. 52.
90 Clinch, op. cit., p. 4. Kearney, O' Connor, op. cit., pp. 185–7.
91 Kearney, O' Connor, op. cit., p. 188.
92 Meenan, op. cit., p. 130. M. Ó Fathartaigh, 'Cumann na nGaedheal, sea fishing and west Galway, 1923–1932', *Irish Historical Studies, 36,* 2008, pp. 72–91.
93 Ó Fathartaigh, op. cit., pp. 87–8.
94 *Report to the Government of Ireland on the development of the sea fishing industries,* Rome, Food and Agriculture Organization of the United Nations, 1959, p. 1, 10.
95 Meenan, op. cit., p. 130.
96 Gilmour, *Economic activities in the Republic of Ireland,* op. cit., p. 135.
97 R. O' Connor, J. A. Crutchfield, B. J. Whelan, K. E. Mellon, *Development of the Irish sea fishing industry and its regional implications,* Dublin, Economic and Social Research Institute, 1980, pp. 3–7.
98 *Statistical Abstracts, 1931–48,* Dublin, Stationery Office; *Statistical Abstracts, 1960–84,* Dublin, Stationery Office.
99 O' Connor, Crutchfield, Whelan, Mellon, *Development of the Irish sea fishing,* op. cit., p. 5.
100 Gilmour, 'Land and people, *c.* 1983', Hill, (ed.), op. cit., p. 434.
101 *Bord Iascaigh Maraigh, annual report 2003,* Dublin, Bord Iascaigh Maraigh, 2004, p. 6
102 *Bord Iascaigh Maraigh, annual report 2002,* Dublin, Bord Iascaigh Maraigh, 2003, p. 7
103 *Bord Iascaigh Maraigh, annual report 2005,* Dublin, Bord Iascaigh Maraigh, 2006, p. 4
104 O' Connor *et al.*, op. cit., p. 18.
105 *Bord Iascaigh Maraigh, annual report 2003,* op. cit., p. 6 Dublin, Bord Iascaigh Maraigh, *Annual report 2004,* Dublin, Bord Iascaigh Maraigh, 2005,p. 9.
106 J. Fitzgerald, E. Morgenroth, *Ex-ante evaluation of the investment priorities for the National Development Plan, 2007–2013,* Dublin, Economic and Social Research Institute, 2006, p. 267.
107 *Agricultural Statistics,* 1954, 1960 and 1970. *Compendium of Agricultural Statistics,* 1997, 2003 and 2008.
108 *National farm survey, 2010,* Dublin, CSO, 2011.
109 A. Matthews, 'The agri-food sector', in J. O'Hagan, C. Newman (eds), *The economy of Ireland,* Dublin, Gill and Macmillan, 2011, p. 300.
110 J. A. Walsh, 'Agriculture in transition', in B. Bartley, R. Kitchin (eds), *Understanding contemporary Ireland,* London, Pluto, 2007, p. 162.
111 *Annual review of agriculture and food, 2004/5,* Teagasc NFS. CSO Statbank. Dramatic rises in Irish potato yields were noted between 1897 and 1951 from 2.2 tons per acre to 8.5 tons. *Farming since the famine: Irish farm statistics 1847–1996,* Dublin, CSO, 1997, p. 381.

112 *That was then, this is now: Changes in Ireland 1949–1999*, Dublin, CSO, 2000, p. 123. 1995–2010 data was posted by Alan Matthews on 9 March 2011, available from http://www.irisheconomy.ie/index.php/2011/03/09/rising-food-prices-and-farm-incomes/.
113 Crotty, op. cit., p. 104.
114 Daly, op. cit., p. 517.
115 *CSO farm structure survey 2007*. Kennedy *et al.*, op. cit., p. 218.
116 Crotty, op. cit., pp. 103, 222.
117 E. Crowley, 'The evolution of the Common Agricultural Policy and social differentiation in rural Ireland', *The Economic and Social Review, 34*, 3, 2003, pp. 65–85.
118 J. Walsh, 'Modernisation and marginalisation under the Common Agricultural Policy; Irish agriculture in transition', in T. Flognfeldt, R. Nordgreen (eds), *Proceedings of the xi International Seminar on Marginal Regions*, Lillehammer, Norway, 1992, p. 190.
119 G. Slevin, 'Is there a "new economy" in Ireland?', Dublin, Central Bank of Ireland, 2002 (Technical Paper 3/rt/02), p. 32. http://www.centralbank.ie/publication/Documents/3RT02.pdf.
120 G. Boyle, *National responses to the CAP reform proposals*, Dublin, National Economic and Social Council, 1991, pp. 17–18.
121 Ibid., pp. 19–21.
122 A. Matthews, 'The agri-food sector', op. cit., p. 301.
123 Ibid., pp. 295–7.

4 Late industrialization: from import substitution to foreign direct investment

1 For the history of industrial development in the century or more prior to partition see A. Bielenberg, *Ireland and the industrial revolution: The impact of the industrial revolution on Irish industry, 1801–1922*, London, Routledge, 2009.
2 *Census of industrial production 1926 and 1929*, Dublin, Stationery Office, 1930.
3 E. J. Riordan, *Modern Irish trade and industry*, London, Methuen, 1920.
4 S. Broadberry, 'The North European Depression of the 1920s', *Scandinavian Economic History Review, 32*, 1984, pp. 159–67.
5 A. Cannon, 'Arklow's explosive history: Kynoch, 1895–1918', *History Ireland*, Jan/Feb, 2006, pp. 30–5.
6 R. B. Weir, 'In and out of Ireland: The Distillers Co. Ltd and the Irish whiskey trade 1900–1939', *Irish Economic and Social History, 7*, 1980, pp. 45–65.
7 D. J Dwyer, 'The development and location of the textile industries in the Irish Republic', *Irish Geography, 4*, 1963, pp. 417–20.
8 R. C. Geary, 'Irish economic development since the Treaty', *Studies, xl*, 1951, pp. 403–5. M. E. Daly, *Industrial development and Irish national identity 1922–1939*, New York, Syracuse University Press, 1992, pp. 21, 41.
9 B. W. E. Alford, *W. D. and H. O. Wills and the development of the UK tobacco industry 1786–1965*, London, Methuen, 1973, pp. 385–90.
10 J. Press, *The footwear industry in Ireland 1922–1973*, Dublin, Irish Academic Press, 1989, p. 28.
11 A. Takei, 'The political economy of the Irish flour milling industry 1922–1945', in A. Bielenberg (ed.), *Irish flour milling: A History 600–2000*, Dublin, Lilliput Press, 2003, pp. 133–40.
12 M. E. Daly, *Industrial development and Irish national identity, 1922–1939*, New York, Syracuse University Press, 1992, pp. 42, 50, 53. Press, op. cit., p. 29.

13 Daly op. cit., pp. 42, 76–7.
14 *Saorstát Éireann official handbook*, Dublin, Stationery Office, 1932, p. 142.
15 S. R. Dennison, O. MacDonagh, *Guinness 1886–1939, from incorporation to the Second World War*, Cork, Cork University Press, 1998, pp. 160–1.
16 Dennison, MacDonagh, op. cit., p. 161. D. Ó Drisceoil, D. Ó Drisceoil, *The Murphy's story: The history of the Lady's Well Brewery*, Cork, Murphy's Brewery, 1997, p. 93.
17 Ó Drisceoil, Ó Drisceoil, op cit., pp. 100–1.
18 Dennison, MacDonagh, op.cit., pp. 176–8.
19 A. Bielenberg, *Locke's distillery: A history*, Dublin, Lilliput Press, 1993, pp. 72–3. M. Humphrey, 'An issue of confidence: The decline of the Irish whiskey industry in independent Ireland 1922–1952', *Journal of European Economic History, 23*, 1994, pp. 93–113.
20 M. Cooper, J. Davis, *The Irish fertiliser industry: A history*, Dublin, Irish Academic Press, 2008, pp. 139–43.
21 R. Ryan, 'The butter industry in Ireland, 1922–1939', *Irish Economic and Social History, 27*, 2001, pp. 36–7. J. Foley, 'The Irish dairy industry: A historical perspective', *Journal of the Society of Dairy Technology, 46*, 1993, pp. 124–38.
22 Foley, op. cit., pp. 141–3.
23 L. Shoen, 'The Irish free state and the electricity industry, 1922–37', in A. Bielenberg (ed.), *The Shannon scheme and the electrification of the Irish free state*, Dublin, Lilliput Press, 2002, pp. 28–48.
24 D. S. Johnson, *The interwar economy in Ireland*, Dundalk, Economic and Social History of Ireland, 1989, p. 24.
25 Schoen, op. cit., pp. 28–47. Johnson, op. cit., p. 24.
26 B. Girvin, *Between two worlds: Politics and economy in independent Ireland*, Dublin, Gill and Macmillan, 1989, pp. 89–91.
27 D. Clarke, *Brown gold: A history of Bord na Móna and the peat industry in Ireland*, Dublin, Gill and Macmillan, 2010, pp. 25–7.
28 Ibid., pp. 27, 32.
29 Daly, op. cit., pp. 65–73, 82–9. M. Foy, *The sugar industry in Ireland*, Dublin, Cómhluct Siúicre Éireann Teo, 1976, p. 40.
30 Girvin, op. cit., pp. 106–7.
31 J. J. Lee, *Ireland 1912–1985: Politics and society*, Cambridge, Cambridge University Press, 1989, pp. 616–17.
32 J. Meenan, *The Irish economy since 1922*, Liverpool, Liverpool University Press, 1970, p. 322.
33 Press, op. cit., p. 87.
34 J. Guerin, *A history of North Cork co-op*, Kanturk, North Cork Co-op, 2007, pp. 34–42.
35 Cooper, Davis, op. cit., p. 131.
36 Ryan, op. cit., pp. 38–9.
37 P. Bolger, *The Irish co-operative movement: Its history and development*, Dublin, Institute of Public Administration, 1977, p. 221.
38 S. A. Brophy, *The strategic management Of Irish enterprise 1934–1984*, Dublin, Smurfit, 1985, p. 231.
39 Dennison, MacDonagh, op. cit., pp. 249–57.
40 M. A. Nyhan, *Are you still below: A history of the Ford Marina plant*, Cork, Collins Press, 2007, pp. 55–67, 104.
41 E. O' Malley, *Industry and industrial development: The challenge for the latecomer*, Dublin, Gill and Macmillan, 1989, p. 65.
42 S. Hogan, *A History of Irish steel*, Dublin, Gill and Macmillan, 1980, pp. 19, 44.

43 L. Kennedy, *The modern industrialisation of Ireland, 1940–1988*, Dundalk, Economic and Social History Society of Ireland, 1989, p. 6.
44 K. Kennedy, T. Giblin, D. McHugh, *The economic development of Ireland in the twentieth century*, London, Routledge, 1988, p. 50.
45 Press, op. cit., pp. 75–7.
46 Nyhan, op. cit., p. 108.
47 C. Wills, *That neutral island: A cultural history of Ireland during the Second World War*, London, Faber & Faber, 2007, p. 142.
48 Hogan, op. cit., p. 47.
49 P. Rigney, *Trains, coal and turf: Transport in emergency Ireland*, Dublin, Irish Academic Press, 2010, pp. 79–89, 181–203.
50 J. Hearne ,'Industry in Waterford city 1932–1962', in W. Nolan, T. P. Power (eds), *Waterford history and society*, Dublin, Geography Publications, 1992, pp. 685–706. Brophy, op. cit., p. 232.
51 D. A. Gilmour, 'Land and people, *c.* 1926', in J. R. Hill (ed.), *A new history of Ireland, VII, Ireland 1921–84*, Oxford, Oxford University Press, 2003, pp. 62–86.
52 D. A. Gilmour, *Economic activities in the Republic of Ireland: A geographic perspective*, Dublin, Gill and Macmillan, 1985, p. 66.
53 T. Brown, *Ireland, a social and cultural history, 1922–1979*, London, 1981, p. 176. R. Fisk, *In time of war: Ireland, Ulster and the price of neutrality, 1939–45*, London, André Deutsch, 1983, p. 315. Ferriter, op. cit., p. 388. C. O'Grada, *A rocky road: The Irish economy since the 1920s*, Manchester, Manchester University Press, 1997, pp. 9, 138.
54 *Census of industrial production, 1926–29, 1931, 1938–1944, 1945–1947*, Dublin, Stationery Office.
55 T. K. Whitaker, 'Capital formation, saving and economic progress', *Journal of the Statistical and Social Inquiry Society of Ireland*, 1955–56, session 109, p. 192.
56 G. Fitzgerald, 'Mr Whitaker and industry', *Studies, 48*, 1959, pp. 145–7.
57 T. K. Whitaker, *Protection of free trade: The final battle*, Institute of Public Administration, 2006, p. 51.
58 Meenan, op. cit., p. 174. C. O' Riordan, *Development of Ireland's power system: 1957 to 1997*, Dublin, Eirgrid, 2000, pp. 4–8.
59 D. A. Gilmour, 'Land and people, *c.* 1983, in J. R. Hill (ed.), *A new history of Ireland, VII, Ireland, 1921–84*, Oxford, Oxford University Press, 2003, pp. 426–52.
60 Gilmour, *Economic activities*, op. cit., p. 53.
61 S. Galvin, 'The chemical industry in Ireland', *Chemistry in Action, 54*, 1998, p. 6. F. Barry, 'Some political economy lessons from Ireland's boom and bust', *Journal of Irish and Scottish Studies, 2*, 2009, p. 28.
62 Gilmour, *Economic activities*, op. cit., pp. 53, 127, 146.
63 Gilmour, 'Land and people *c.* 1984', in J. R. Hill (ed.), op. cit., p. 435.
64 J. Fitzgerald, E. Morgenroth, *Ex-ante evaluation of the investment priorities for the National Development Plan, 2007–2013*, Dublin, Economic and Social Research Institute, p. 205. O' Riordan, op. cit., pp. 7–11.
65 A. Matthews, 'The state and Irish agriculture: 1950–1980', in P. J. Drudy (ed.), *Irish Studies, 4, Ireland, Land, Politics and People*, Cambridge, Cambridge University Press, 1982, pp. 241–71.
66 M. E. Daly, *The first department: A history of the Department of Agriculture*, Dublin, Institute of Public Administration, 2002, p. 297.
67 Foley, op. cit., pp. 128–9. D. McCarthy, 'The Cadbury-Ireland (Ltd) factory, Rathmore', *Sliabh Luachra, Journal of Cumann Luchra, I*, 4, 1987, pp. 31–4.

68 Bolger, op. cit., p. 225.
69 Daly, *The first department,* pp. 357, 491.
70 M. McGrath, P. Somers, *Golden Vale remembered, 1948–2001*, Charleville, McGrath & Somers, 2006, p. 114.
71 Foley, op. cit., pp. 135–6.
72 McGrath, Somers, op. cit., pp. 142–3. P. Breathnach, 'The evolution of the spatial structure of the Irish dairy processing industry', *Irish Geography, 33*, 2000, pp. 166–84.
73 Kennelly, op. cit., pp. 68–70, 127.
74 E. B. Maguire, *Irish whiskey*, Dublin, Gill and MacMillan, 1973, pp. 369, 374, 381–2.
75 J. K. Jacobsen, *Chasing progress in the Irish Republic: Ideology, democracy and dependent development*, Cambridge, Cambridge University Press, 1994, p. 68. Gilmour, *Economic activities*, pp. 40–5.
76 Cooper, Davis, op. cit., pp. 198–203, 266–70.
77 F. Barry, M. Daly, 'Mr Whitaker and industry: Setting the record straight', *The Economic and Social Review, 42*, 2011, p. 166. S. Hogan, *A history of Irish steel*, Gill and MacMillan, Dublin, 1980, pp. 131–80.
78 W. Black, 'Industrial development and regional policy', in N. J. Gibson (ed.), *Economic activity in Ireland 1977*, Dublin, Gill and MacMillan, 1977, pp. 56, 71. T. P. Linehan, 'The structure of Irish industry', *Journal of the Statistical and Social Inquiry Society of Ireland, 20*, 1961–62, pp. 220–53.
79 N. J. Farley, 'Determinants of establishment size in Irish manufacturing industries: Some notes on the Irish case 1931–72', *Economic and Social Review, 6*, 1974, pp. 187–211.
80 F. Long, 'Foreign capital and development strategy in Irish industrialization 1958–70', *American Journal of Economic Sociology, 39*, 1980, pp. 137–50.
81 N. Brennan, P. Breathnach, 'The spatiality of Irish manufacturing linkages in the Celtic Tiger era', *Irish Geography, 42*, 2009, pp. 7–22.
82 R. MacSharry, P. White, *The making of the Celtic Tiger: The inside story of Ireland's boom economy*, Dublin, Mercier Press, 2006, pp. 187–9.
83 D. McAleese, 'Capital inflow and direct foreign investment in Ireland 1952–1970', *Journal of the Statistical and Social Inquiry Society of Ireland, 22*, 1971–72, pp. 63–105.
84 P. P. Walsh, C. Whelan, 'The importance of structural change in industry for growth', *Journal of the Statistical and Social Inquiry Society of Ireland, 29*, 2000, pp. 1–33.
85 Brennan, Breathnach, op. cit., p. 9.
86 M. Lawless, A. P. Murphy, 'Job gains and losses: Manufacturing and internationally traded services', *Central Bank Quarterly Bulletin, January*, 2008, pp. 91–104.
87 Walsh, Whelan, op. cit., p. 3.
88 O' Malley, op. cit., pp. 104–5.
89 B. Brunt, 'Manufacturing changes in the greater Cork Area 1980–84', *Irish Geography, 17*, 1984, pp. 101–8.
90 E. O' Malley, 'The revival of Irish indigenous industry 1987–1997', in T. J. Baker, D. Duffy, F. Shortall (eds), *ESRI Quarterly economic commentary April 1998*, Dublin, Economic and Social Research Institute, 1998, pp. 35–57.
91 S. Hallier, 'The distribution of productivity in Irish manufacturing, 1995–2003', in C. Aylward, R. O' Toole (eds), *Perspectives on Irish productivity*, Dublin, Forfás, 2007, pp. 402–6. Ó Gráda, op. cit., p. 111.
92 Press, op. cit., pp. 172–3.

93 O' Malley, *Industry and industrial development*, op. cit., pp. 105, 151.
94 Brunt, op. cit., pp. 102, 106.
95 Ó Drisceoil, Ó Drisceoil, op. cit., pp. 137–42.
96 Daly, *The first department*, p. 528.
97 J. Murray, *Glanbia: The story so far*, Kilkenny, Glanbia, 2007, pp. 65, 185–92, 265–9, 335, 366–7, 381–7, 486. J. Kennelly, *The Kerry way*, 2001, pp. 217–49.
98 J. Murray, op. cit., pp. 59, 65. Breathnach, op. cit., pp. 177, 181.
99 Kennelly, op. cit., pp. 273–289.
100 Newman, op. cit., p. 2. However, deterioration occurred within the competitiveness of the food and drink sector. A decline in the revealed comparative advantage for food and live animals as a whole, from 1.6527 (1997) to 1.11189 (2002), with declines of 0.87 in meat and meat preparation, and 1.6 in dairy products and birds' eggs occurred. See D. Addison-Smyth, (2005), 'Ireland's revealed comparative advantage', *Central Bank quarterly bulletin Spring 2005*, Dublin, Central Bank of Ireland, 2005, pp. 101–16.
101 E. Paus, *Foreign investment, development, and globalisation: Can Costa Rica become Ireland?*, Palgrave MacMillan, 2005, p. 89.
102 A. Matthews, 'The agri-food sector', J. O'Hagan, C. Newman (eds), *The economy of Ireland*, Gill & MacMillan, 2011, p. 295.
103 Brennan, Breathnach, op. cit., pp. 9–10.
104 G. Delaney, 'Electronics multinationals in the Cork region and Limerick/Shannon', *Irish Geography, 21*, 1988, pp. 101–3.
105 P. Murray, J. Wickham, 'Technocratic ideology and the reproduction of inequality: The case of the electronics industry in the Republic of Ireland', in G. Day (ed.), *Diversity and decomposition in the labour market*, Aldershot, Gower, 1982, pp. 179–210. Also see R. O'Brien, 'Technology and industrial development: The Irish electronics industry in an international context', in J. Fitzpatrick, J. Kelly (eds), *Perspectives on Irish industry*, 1985, pp. 197–255.
106 F. Barry, C. Van Egeraat, 'The decline of the computer hardware sector: How Ireland adjusted', *ESRI quarterly economic commentary, Spring 2008*, pp. 38–57. Delaney, op. cit., p. 102. P. Breathnach, C. Van Egeraat, 'The manufacturing sector', in B. Bartley, R. Kitchin (eds), *Understanding contemporary Ireland*, London, Pluto Press, 2007, pp. 128–45.
107 D. O'Hearn, 'Macroeconomic policy in the Celtic Tiger: A critical reassessment', in C. Coulter, S. Coleman (eds), *The end of Irish history? Critical reflections on the Celtic Tiger*, Manchester, Manchester University Press, 2003, p. 39.
108 N. Crafts, G. Toniolo, 'European Economic Growth, 1950–2005: An overview', London, Centre for Economic Policy Research, 2008 (discussion paper series, no. 6863), pp. 15–17.
109 N. Crafts, 'The Celtic Tiger in historical and international perspective,' in M. Mulreany (ed.), *Economic development 50 years on: 1958–2008*, Dublin, Institute of Public Administration, 2009, pp. 64–73.
110 F. Barry, 'FDI, transfer pricing and the measurement of R&D intensity', *Research Policy, 34*, 2005, pp. 673–81.
111 Brennan, Breathnach, op. cit., p. 10.
112 Paus, op. cit., pp. 93–103, 123.
113 Barry, Van Egeraat, op. cit., pp. 38–57. S. Grimes, 'Ireland's emergence as a centre for internationally traded services', *Regional Studies, 40*, 2006, pp. 1041–54.
114 Paus, op. cit., pp. 103–7
115 Barry, Van Egeraat, op. cit., pp. 38–57. Grimes, op. cit., p. 1046.

116 C. Van Egeraat, 'Spatial concentration in the Irish pharmaceutical industry: The role of government intervention and agglomeration economies', Maynooth, National Institute for Regional and Spatial Analysis, 2006 (working paper no. 28), pp. 10–15, available from http://www.nuim.ie/nirsa/research/documents/wp%2028%20chris%20 van%Egeraat.pdf.
117 Ibid., p. 15.
118 F. Barry, C. Van Egeraat, 'The Irish pharmaceutical industry over the boom period and beyond', *Irish Geography, 42*, 2009, pp. 23–44. C. Van Egeraat, 'The scale and scope of process R&D in the Irish pharmaceutical industry', *Irish Geography, 43*, 2010, pp. 35–58.
119 Addison-Smyth, op. cit., pp. 105–8.
120 Van Egeraat, op. cit., pp. 8–9.
121 Barry, Van Egeraat, 'The Irish pharmaceutical industry over the boom period and beyond', *Irish Geography, 42*, 2009, pp. 23–44.
122 Calculated from *Industrial production and turnover, March 2010–January 2011*, Dublin, Central Statistics Office, 2010–2011, pp. 6–7.
123 A series of articles by B. McCall gives a brief overview of construction developments from the 1940s onwards in *Construction*, July/August, 2004.
124 J. J. Sexton, 'Trends in output, employment and productivity in Ireland, 1995–2005', in C. Aylward, R. O' Toole (eds), *Perspectives on Irish productivity*, Dublin, Forfás, 2007, pp. 28–49.
125 P. Fink, *Late development in Hungary and Ireland*, Baden-Baden, Nomos, 2009.
126 F. McDonald, K. Sheridan, *The builders*, Dublin, Penguin, 2008, pp. 4–7, 16, 102–3, 237, 269, 275.
127 *National income and expenditure 2007*, Dublin, Central Statistics Office, 2008, p. 3.
128 *Eurostat yearbook 2010*, Brussels, Eurostat, 2011, p. 357.
129 *Statistical yearbook of Ireland 2009*, Dublin, Stationery Office, 2010, p. 29.
130 M. Soden, *Open dissent: An uncompromising view of the financial crisis*, Dublin, Blackhall Publishing, 2010, pp. 5, 119.
131 Department of Environment, Community and Local Government housing statistics, available from http://www.environ.ie/en/Publications/statisticsandRegularPublications/ Housingstatistics/FileDownload,15293,en.xls.
132 *Advisory group on unfinished housing development, emerging priority issues*, Dublin, Department of Environment Heritage and Local Government, 2010, p. 3, available from http://www.environ.ie/en/DevelopmentandHousing/Housing/News/MainBody,25485,en. htm.
133 *Europe in figures: Eurostat yearbook 2009*, Brussels, Eurostat, p. 77.
134 W. Keating, 'Measuring the economy-problems and prospects', *Journal of the Statistical and Social Inquiry Society of Ireland, 30*, 2000, p. 12.
135 G. Slevin, 'Is there a "new economy" in Ireland?', Central Bank of Ireland, Dublin, 2002 (technical paper 3/rt/01), p. 32. http:/www.centralbank.ie/publication/Documents/ 3RT02.pdf.
136 E. O' Leary, 'The convergence performance of Ireland among EU Countries, 1960–1990', *Journal of Economic Studies, 24*, 1/2, 1997, pp. 43–58.
137 Sexton, op. cit., p. 33.
138 P. Kirby, *Celtic Tiger in collapse: Explaining the weaknesses of the Irish model*, Basingstoke, Palgrave Macmillan, 2010, p. 7.
139 *Statistical portrait of the European Union 2007*, Brussels, European Commission, 2008, p. 49. Grimes, op. cit., p. 1044.

5 From good haircuts to bad bankers: the services sector in the Irish economy

1 D. S. Johnson, *The interwar economy in Ireland*, Dundalk, Economic and Social History Society of Ireland, 1989, p. 24. K. A. Murray, D. B. McNeill, *The Great Southern and Western Railway*, Wicklow, Irish Railway Record Society, 1976, pp. 80–106. D. A. Gilmour, *Economic activities in the Republic of Ireland: A geographic perspective*, Dublin, Gill and Macmillan, 1985, pp. 98, 162.
2 M. Ó Riain, *'On the move': Coras Iompair Éireann 1945–1995*, Dublin, Gill and Macmillan, 1995, p. 18. *Committee of inquiry into internal transport*, Dublin Stationery Office, 1957, p. 15.
3 P. Rigney, *Trains, coal and turf: Transport in emergency Ireland*, Dublin, Irish Academic Press, 2010.
4 J. Meenan, *The Irish economy since 1922*, Liverpool University Press, 1970, pp. 163–4. Ó Riain, op. cit., pp. 38–9, 52, 110–25, 150–62, 199, 360.
5 Ó Riain, op. cit., pp. 390, 404–18.
6 *National Development Plan 2007–2013*, Dublin, Stationery Office, 2006, p. 19.
7 B. Share, *The flight of the Iolar: The Aer Lingus experience 1936–1986*, Dublin, Gill & Macmillan, 1986, p. 38.
8 T. Garvin, *Judging Lemass*, Dublin, Royal Irish Academy, 2009, p. 165.
9 N. Weldon, *Pioneers in flight: Aer Lingus and the story of aviation in Ireland*, Dublin, The Liffey Press, 2002, pp. 100–7.
10 Gilmour, op. cit., p. 115.
11 D. Ó Drisceoil, D. Ó Drisceoil, *Fifty years have flown: The history of Cork Airport*, Cork, Collins Press, 2001, p. 88.
12 Ibid., pp. 157–8. A University College Cork study on the direct and indirect impact of Cork airport on its catchment area estimated that in 1995 the combined impact on local economic activity resulted in the provision of 702 full and part time jobs and the purchase of £5.08 million worth of goods and services. Airport visitors purchased a total of £137 million worth of goods and services in the catchment area, which sustained 3,600 full and part-time jobs. See E. Kavanagh, E. O' Leary, E. Shinnick, 'The role of airport infrastructure in regional development: The case of Cork Airport', in E. O' Leary (ed.), *Irish regional development: A new agenda*, Dublin, Liffey Press, 2003, pp. 181–201.
13 Gilmour, op. cit., p. 115. Weldon, op. cit., pp. 149, 166–7, 204–7, 243, 297–9.
14 A. Ruddock, *Michael O'Leary: A life in full flight*, Dublin, Penguin Ireland, 2007, pp. 22–3.
15 Ruddock, op. cit., pp. 31–2, 68–71. Weldon, op. cit., pp. 228–9.
16 Weldon, op. cit., pp. 229–99. M. Cooper, *Who really runs Ireland? The story of the elite who led Ireland from bust to boom ... and back again*, London, Penguin, 2010, p. 397. Ruddock, op. cit., pp. 86–9, 148.
17 M. Cronin, *Doesn't time fly? Aer Lingus: Its history*, The Collins Press, Cork, 2011, pp. 61, 159.
18 I. Furlong, *Irish tourism: 1880–1980*, Dublin, Irish Academic Press, 2009, pp. 39–47.
19 Furlong, op. cit., p. 63. E. Zuelow, *Making Ireland Irish: Tourism and national identity since the Irish civil war*, New York, Syracuse University Press, 2009, pp. xvi, 50–5.
20 C. Wills, *That neutral island: A cultural history of Ireland during the Second World War*, London, Faber & Faber, 2007, pp. 281–95.
21 K. Kennedy, T. Giblin, D. McHugh, *The economic development of Ireland in the twentieth century*, London, Routledge, 1988, p. 188.
22 *Statistical abstracts, 1944–1953*, Dublin, Stationery Office.

23 Furlong, op. cit., pp. 122, 164–7.
24 C. Ó Gráda, *A rocky road: The Irish economy since the 1920s*, Manchester, Manchester University Press, p. 172.
25 *Tourism policy*, Dublin, NESC, op. cit. pp. 102–3.
26 Zuelow, op. cit., pp. 145–8.
27 J. O'Hagan, M. Harrison, 'UK and US visitor expenditure in Ireland: Some economic findings', *The Economic and Social Review, 15*, 1984, pp. 195, 203–5.
28 Kennedy *et al.*, op. cit., p. 189.
29 Deegan, Dineen, op. cit., pp. 301–6.
30 Ibid., pp. 12–20, 101–11.
31 A. O'Brien, *The politics of tourism development: Booms and busts in Ireland*, Palgrave Macmillan, London, 2011, pp. 97–8, 107, 115, 118–27, 164, 190.
32 D. Gilmour, 'Republic of Ireland: An expanding tourism industry', in A. M. Williams, G. Shaw (eds), *Tourism and economic development*, John Wiley & Son, 1998, 3rd edition, pp. 221–41.
33 Deegan, Dineen, op. cit., pp. 313–14.
34 S. MacFeely, 'A statistical analysis of Irish domestic tourism', *Journal of the Statistical and Social Inquiry Society of Ireland, 36*, 2007, pp. 125–66.
35 *Budget 2006: Review of tax schemes, Vol. 1: Indecon review of property-based tax incentive schemes*, Dublin, Department of Finance, 2006, p. 81.
36 *Statistical abstracts*, 1963–1998, Dublin, CSO. *Statistical yearbooks*, 2007, 2010, Dublin, CSO.
37 MacFeely, op. cit., p. 171.
38 Ibid., pp. 130, 136.
39 M. Lynch Brennan, *The Irish Bridget: Irish immigrant women in domestic service in America, 1840–1930*, Syracuse University Press, 2009.
40 For the circumstances of domestic servants at the time of independence see M. Hearne, *Below stairs: Domestic service remembered in Dublin and beyond, 1880–1922*, Dublin, Lilliput Press, 1993. For the later period on household work see C. Clear, *Women of the house: Women's household work in Ireland 1926–1961*, Dublin, Irish Academic Press, 2000. For farm servants, see R. Breen, 'Farm servant-hood in Ireland 1900–40', *Economic History Review, 36*, 1983, pp. 87–102.
41 K. Spiller, D. Linehan,'"Beacons of modernity": Department stores, modernity and the urban experience in mid-twentieth century Ireland', *Irish Geography, 39*, 2006, pp. 143–58.
42 P. Costello, *Denis Guiney*, Dublin, University of Dublin Press, 2008, pp. 32–7.
43 M. Jones, 'Was this the first Chain store in Ireland? P. & J. Ryan Ltd. Ardnageeha, Charleville', *Charleville and District Historical Journal, 6*, 1992, pp. 33–7.
44 A. Findlater, *Findlaters: The story of a Dublin merchant family*, Dublin, Farmar, 2001, pp. 405–503.
45 A. Creighton, *The life and times of Arthur Henry*, Dublin, Blackwater Press, 1994, pp. 110–11. D. White, *A history of Musgrave: The first 125 years*, Cork, Musgrave, 2001, pp. 53–5.
46 White, op. cit., pp. 67–71.
47 Ibid., pp. 83, 108, 123.
48 Findlater, op. cit., p. 514.
49 White, op. cit., p. 43.
50 M. Casey, *Ireland's malaise: The troubled personality of the Irish economy*, Dublin, Liffey Press, p. 71.

51 M. Daly 'The return to the roads', in K. B. Nowlan (ed.), *Travel and transport in Ireland*, pp. 135–46. C. O'Flaherty, 'The problem of parking', *The institution of civil engineers of Ireland, 91*, 1965, pp. 206–65. A. Reynolds-Feighan, 'Accessibility, transportation, infrastructure planning and Irish regional policy: Issues and dilemmas', in E. O'Leary (ed.), *Irish regional development: A new agenda*, Dublin, Liffey Press, 2003, pp. 163–81.
52 A. Matthews, 'The agri-food sector', in J. O'Hagan, C. Newman (eds), *The economy of Ireland*, Dublin, Gill and Macmillan, 2011, p. 311.
53 R. J. Savage, *A Loss of innocence? Television and Irish society 1960–1972*, Manchester University Press, 2010.
54 B.R Mitchell, *European historical statistics*, London, Macmillan Press, p. 701.
55 J. Fitzgerald *et al.* (ed.), *ESRI Medium term review, 2008–2015*, Dublin, Economic and Social Research Institute, 2008, pp. 71, 86.
56 *Annual services inquiry, 1995, 1997, 1999, 2001*, Dublin, Stationery Office.
57 D. J. Cogan, *The Irish services sector: A study of productive efficiency*, Dublin, Stationery Office, 1978, pp. 97–8. Fitzgerald *et al.*, op. cit., p. 21.
58 D. Rae, L. Voigt, M. Wise, *Boosting competition in Ireland*, Paris, OECD, 2006, p. 10.
59 Ibid., p. 10.
60 F. Barry, D. Van Welsum, 'Services FDI and off-shoring into Ireland', Paris, OECD Directorate for Science, Technology and Industry paper, 2005, p. 14.
61 Barry, Van Welsum, op. cit., pp. 13–14. R. MacSharry, P. White, *The making of the Celtic Tiger: The inside story of Ireland's boom economy*, Dublin, Mercier Press, 2000, p. 330.
62 F. Reddan , *Ireland's IFSC: A story of global financial success*, Dublin, Mercier Press, 2008, pp. 84–5.
63 MacSharry, White, op. cit., p. 348.
64 P. Honohan, 'To what extent has finance been a driver of Ireland's economic success', in A. Barrett, I. Kearney, Y. McCarthy (eds), *Quarterly Economic Commentary Winter 2006,* Dublin, Economic and Social Research Institute, 2006, pp. 59–72.
65 Barry, Van Welsum, op. cit., p. 14.
66 *Future skills and research needs of the international financial services industry: A study for the expert group on future skills needs*, Dublin, Forfás, 2007, p. 40.
67 *International Trade and Investment Report 2004*, Dublin, Forfás, 2005, p. 19.
68 *Ireland, financial system stability assessment update*, Washington DC, IMF, 2006, pp. 8, 47.
69 *Future skills and research needs of the international financial services industry,* op. cit., pp. 40.
70 *International trade and investment report 2004*, op. cit., p. 19.
71 P. Breathnach, 'Globalisation, information technology and the emergence of niche transnational cities', *Geoforum, 31*, 2000, p. 481.
72 Barry, Van Welsum, op. cit., p. 15.
73 Breathnach, op. cit., p. 482.
74 MacSharry, White, op. cit., pp. 294–5.
75 *International Trade and Investment Report, 2005*, Dublin, Forfás, 2004, p. 21.
76 J. Mooney, C. O' Gorman, E. O' Malley, *Irish indigenous software industry: Application of Porter's Cluster Analysis*, Dublin, NESC, 1997, pp. 52–3. D. O'Hearn, 'Macroeconomic policy in the Celtic Tiger: A critical reassessment', in C. Coulter, S. Coleman (eds), *The end of Irish history? Critical reflections on the Celtic Tiger*, Manchester, Manchester University Press, 2003, p. 44.
77 *Service-type employment and regional development*, Dublin, NESC, 1977, pp. 104–5.
78 *International trade and investment report, 2005*, Dublin, Forfás, op. cit., p. 21.

79 D. O' Hearn, *The Atlantic economy: Britain, the US and Ireland*, Manchester, Manchester University press, 2001, pp. 182–3.
80 Clancy, Twomey, op. cit., pp. 2–4. *Shaping the future: A strategic plan for the development of the music industry in Ireland*, Dublin, Department of Arts, Sport and Tourism, 2003, pp. 16–19.
81 Ibid., pp. 30, 71.
82 *Price Waterhouse Coopers: Review of section 481 of the Taxes Consolidation Act 1997. Report to the Irish Film Board and the Department of Arts, Sport and Tourism*, Dublin, Department of Arts, Sport and Tourism, 2003, pp. 7–9, 14.
83 *The strategic development of the Irish film and television industry, 2000–2010. Final report of the Film Industry Strategic Review Group to the Minister for Arts, Heritage, Gaeltacht and the Islands*, Dublin, Department of Arts, Heritage Gaeltacht and the Islands, 1999, pp. 28, 56.
84 *International trade and investment report 2000*, Dublin, Forfás, 2001, p. 27.
85 T. Conefrey, J. D. Fitzgerald, 'The macro-economic impact of changing the rate of Corporation Tax', Dublin, Economic and Social Research Institute, 2009 (working paper, no. 273), p. 17.
86 *Balance of international payments, first quarter 1990, fourth quarter and year 1995 and fourth quarter and year 1997*, Dublin, CSO.
87 *Balance of international payments, fourth quarter and year ending, 1998–2010*, Dublin, CSO. *Balance of international payments, second quarter 2010*, Dublin, CSO.
88 *International trade and investment report, 2004,* op. cit., p. 24.
89 For precise definitions see *Balance of Payments 2008,* Dublin, CSO, 2009, p.16.
90 P. Lane, F. Ruane, 'Globalisation and the Irish economy', Dublin, Irish International Integration Studies Centre, Trinity College Dublin, 2006, p. 12.
91 *Service exports and imports, 2006 and 2007*, Dublin, CSO, 2008, pp. 4–5.
92 E. O'Leary, 'Sources of regional divergence in the Celtic Tiger', *Journal of the Statistical and Social Inquiry Society of Ireland, 31*, 2003, pp. 2–32.
93 D. S. Johnson, L. Kennedy, 'The two economies in Ireland in the twentieth century', in J. R. Hill (ed.), *A new history of Ireland, VII, Ireland, 1921–84*, Oxford, Oxford University Press, 2003, p. 480.

6 International trade and Irish economic development

1 B. Girvin, *Between two worlds: Politics and economy in independent Ireland*, Dublin, Gill and Macmillan, 1989, pp. 21–9.
2 M. E. Daly, *Irish industrial development and irish national identity, 1922–1939*, New York, Syracuse University Press, 1992, pp. 25, 29.
3 Ibid., pp. 39–40.
4 Girvin, op. cit., p. 36.
5 Daly, op. cit., p. 45.
6 F. Barry, 'Foreign investment and the politics of export profits tax relief 1956', *Irish Economic and Social History, 38*, 2011, p. 55.
7 D. McHugh, 'Trade growth and the role of demand: The experience of Ireland since 1947', *Journal of the Statistical and Social Inquiry Society of Ireland, 25*, Part II, 1984–5, p. 222.
8 M. O' Driscoll, 'The economic war and Irish trade policy: Irish–German commerce, 1932–9', *Irish Studies in International Affairs, 10*, 1999, pp. 72–83.
9 H.P. Smyth, *The B&I Line: A history of the British and Irish Steam Packet Company*, Dublin, Gill and Macmillan, 1984, pp. 95–121, 140, 149.

10 F. Forde, *The long watch: The history of the Irish mercantile marine in World War Two*, Dublin, Gill and Macmillan, 1981, pp. 1–2, 21, 34, 64, 94, 129. B. Peterson, *Turn of the tide: An outline of Irish maritime history*, Irish Shipping Ltd., Dublin, 1962, pp. 114–38. C. Ó Gráda, *A rocky road: The Irish Economy since the 1920s*, Manchester, Manchester University Press, 1997, p. 8.

11 Forde, op. cit., pp. 1–2, 21, 34, 64, 94, 129. Peterson, op. cit., pp. 114–38.

12 F. Forde, *Maritime Arklow*, Glendale Press, Dun Laoghaire, 1988, pp. 53, 286.

13 G. A. Duncan, 'The trade statistics of the Irish Free State', *Journal of the Social and Statistical Society of Ireland, 16*, 1937–8, 1937–8, p. 5.

14 *Trade and shipping statistics*, 1925–1944, Dublin, Department of Industry and Commerce, Statistics Branch.

15 M. Nyhan, 'Narration and memory, the experiences of the workforce of a Ford Plant', *Irish Economic and Social History, 33*, 2006, pp. 18–34. *Trade and shipping statistics*, 1925–1944, Dublin, Department of Industry and Commerce, Statistics Branch.

16 *Trade and shipping statistics*, 1925–1944, Dublin, Department. of Industry and Commerce, Statistics Branch.

17 H. A. Gilligan, *A history of the port of Dublin*, Gill and Macmillan, Dublin, 1988, pp. 166–87, 199–212. C. F. Smith, *The Shipping Murphy's: The Palgrave Murphy shipping line 1850–1926*, Dublin, Albany Press, 2004, p. 45. Smyth, op. cit., pp. 222–4.

18 Peterson, op. cit., pp. 152–7. Forde, *Maritime Arklow*, op. cit., pp. 164, 288. M. Leland, *That endless adventure: A History of the Cork Harbour Commissioners, Port of Cork*, Cork, 2001, pp. 187, 206.

19 J. Maddock, *Rosslare Harbour: Past and present*, Rosslare, Harbour Publications, pp. 77–80, 113.

20 B. Whelan, 'Ireland and the Marshall Plan', *Irish Economic and Social History, 19*, 1992, pp. 49–70.

21 Girvin, op. cit., p. 181.

22 Ibid., pp. 173–4.

23 D. McAleese, 'Do tariffs matter? Industrial specialization and trade in a small open economy', *Oxford Economic Papers, 29*, 1977, p. 117.

24 E. O'Malley, *Industry and economic development: The challenge for the latecomer*, Dublin, Gill and Macmillan, 1989, p. 73.

25 J. J. Lee, *Ireland 1912–85, Politics and Society*, Cambridge, Cambridge University Press, 1989, p. 358. F. Barry, J. Bradley, 'FDI and trade: The Irish host-country experience', *The Economic Journal, 107*, 1997, p. 1798.

26 T. K. Whitaker, 'From protection to free trade: The Irish experience', in T. K. Whitaker, *Interests*, Dublin, Institute of Public Administration, 1983, pp. 55–81.

27 Lee, op. cit., p. 353. H. G. Foster, 'Ireland's trade with Britain', in I. F. Baillie, S. J. Sheehy (eds), *Irish agriculture in a changing world*, Edinburgh, Oliver & Boyd, 1971, pp. 74–98.

28 *Statistical abstracts* 1951–1965, Stationery Office, Dublin.

29 Lee, op. cit., p. 187.

30 D. J. Cogan, *The Irish services sector: A study of productive efficiency*, Stationery Office, Dublin, 1978, pp. 119–27. For evidence on air freight volumes see B. Share, *The flight of the Iolar: The Aer Lingus experience 1936–1986*, Dublin, Gill and Macmillan, 1986, pp. 286–7.

31 D. J. Thornhill, 'The revealed comparative advantage of Irish exports of manufactures, 1969–1982', *Journal of the Statistical and Social Inquiry Society of Ireland, 25*, 1987–8, pp. 91–146. On late industrialization, see E. O'Malley, *Industry and economic development: The challenge of the latecomer*, Dublin, Gill and Macmillan, 1989.

32 P. J. O'Sullivan, 'An assessment of Ireland's export-led growth strategy via foreign direct investment: 1960–1980', *Weltwirtschaftliches Archiv, 129*, 1993, pp. 140–3.
33 E. Doyle, 'Export–output causality and the role of exports in Irish growth; 1950–1997', *International Economic Journal, 15*, 3, 1999, pp. 1–24.
34 S. J. Sheehy, 'The impact of EEC membership on Irish agriculture', *Journal of Agricultural Economics, 31*, 1980, pp. 305–6.
35 K. Kennedy, 'Reflections on the process of Irish economic growth', *Journal of the Statistical and Social Inquiry Society of Ireland, 30*, 2002, pp. 124–35.
36 F. Barry, J. Bradley, A. Hannan, 'The European dimension: The single aarket and the structural funds', in F. Barry (ed.), *Understanding Ireland's economic growth*, Dublin, 1999, p. 100, 106.
37 Ibid, p. 106.
38 W. Keating, 'Measuring the economy: Problems and prospects', *Journal of the Social & Statistical Society of Ireland, 30*, 2001, pp. 1–32.
39 D. O'Hearn, 'Macroeconomic policy in the Celtic Tiger: A critical reassessment', in C. Coulter, S. Coleman (eds), *The end of Irish history? Critical reflections on the Celtic Tiger*, Manchester, Manchester University Press, 2003, p. 44.
40 E. O'Leary, 'Reflecting on the Celtic Tiger: Before, during and after', *Irish Economic and Social History, 38*, 2011, pp. 74, 81.
41 Leland, op. cit., pp. 150–1, 206.
42 *IMF country report, Ireland, 2007* (no. 07/326*)*, Washington DC, IMF, 2007, pp. 15–16.
43 *International trade and investment report, 2005,* Dublin, Forfás, 2006, pp. 11–12.
44 M. Lawless, 'Destinations of Irish exports: A gravity model approach', *Journal of the Statistical and Social Inquiry Society of Ireland, 34*, 2009–10, pp. 4, 8.
45 N. Crafts, G. Toniolo, 'Aggregate growth, 1950–2005', in S. Broadberry, K. H. O'Rourke (eds), *The Cambridge economic history of modern Europe, Volume 2, 1870 to the present*, Cambridge University Press, 2010, pp. 326–7.
46 E. O' Malley, 'Revival of Irish indigenous industry, 1987–1997', in T. J. Baker, D. Duffy, F. Shortall (eds), *ESRI quarterly economic commentary, April 1998*, Dublin, ESRI, 1998, pp. 35–57.
47 *Irish Times*, 2 March 2012
48 *International trade and investment report, 2000,* Dublin, Forfás, 2001, p. 17. W. Keating, 'Measuring the economy', op. cit., p. 12.
49 *International trade and investment report, 2003,* Dublin, Forfás, 2004, p. 15.
50 Barry, Bradley, op. cit., p. 1798.
51 J. Meenan, *The Irish economy since 1922,* Liverpool University Press, 1970, pp. 71, 83. L. M. Cullen, *An economic history of Ireland since 1660*, London, Batsford, 1986, pp. 171–2.
52 *Statistical abstracts, 1937–50*, Dublin, Stationery Office.
53 M. J. MacCormac, 'Crisis in Ireland's balance of trade', *Studies, 159*, 1951, pp. 257–69.
54 K. A. Kennedy, T. Giblin, D. McHugh, *The economic development of Ireland in the twentieth century*, London, Routledge, 1988, p. 190
55 I. Furlong, *Irish tourism 1880–1980*, Dublin, Irish Academic Press, 2009, p. 209.
56 F. Barry, D. van Welsum, 'Services FDI and off-shoring into Ireland', Paris, OECD Directorate for Science, Technology and Industry paper, 2005, p. 14, available from http://www.oecd.org/dataoecd/14/0/3532060.pdf.
57 S. Grimes, 'Ireland's emergence as a centre for internationally traded services', *Regional Studies, 40*, 2006, pp. 1046–7. S. Grimes, M. White, 'The transition to internationally traded services and Ireland's emergence as a successful European region', *Environment and Planning, 37*, 2005, pp. 2169–88.

58 C. Newman, 'Manufacturing and internationally traded services', in J. O'Hagan, C. Newman (eds), *The economy of Ireland*, Gill and Macmillan, 2011, pp. 249–52.
59 C. Ó Gráda, 'From "frugal comfort" to ten thousand a year: Trade and growth in the Irish economy', R. Ryan, (ed.), *Writing in the Irish Republic: Literature, culture, politics 1949–1999*, Basingstoke, Macmillan, 2000, p. 265.
60 Ibid., pp. 274–5.
61 Eurostat, *Europe in figures: Eurostat yearbook, 2010*, Brussels,European Commission, 2010, pp .481–5.
62 H. W. Armstrong, R. Read, 'The phantom of Liberty?: Economic growth and the vulnerability of small states', *Journal of International Development, 14*, 2002, pp. 452–3. H. Armstrong, R. Read, 'Western European micro-states and EU autonomous regions: The advantages and size and sovereignty', *World Development, 23*, 1995, pp. 1229–45.

7 Investment and credit in Irish economic development

1 C. Ó Gráda, 'Money and banking in the Irish free state', in C. H. Feinstein (ed.), *Banking, currency and finance in Europe between the wars*, Oxford, Oxford University Press, 1995, pp. 428–31.
2 J. P. Neary, C. Ó Gráda, 'Protection, economic war and structural change: The 1930s in Ireland', *Irish Historical Studies, 27*, 1991, pp. 250–63.
3 Figures derived from C. Ó Gráda, *Ireland: A new economic history, 1780–1939*, Oxford, Oxford University Press, 1994, p. 440.
4 M. E. Daly, *Industrial development and Irish national identity*, New York, Syracuse University Press, 1992, p. 151. J. J. Lee, *Ireland 1912–85, politics and society*, Cambridge, Cambridge University Press, 1989, p. 190.
5 B. Girvin, *Between two worlds: Politics and economy in independent Ireland*, Dublin, Gill and Macmillan, 1989, pp. 91, 100.
6 Daly, op. cit. pp. 143–4.
7 T. K. Whitaker, 'Financial turning points', in T. K. Whitaker, *Interests*, Dublin, Institute of Public Administration, 1983, pp. 81–117. W. A. Thomas, *The stock exchanges of Ireland*, London, Francis Cairns, 1986, p. 172.
8 Figures calculated from T. K. Whitaker, 'Capital formation, savings and economic progress', *Journal of the Social Statistical Inquiry Society of Ireland, 109*, 1955–56, p. 38.
9 M. J. Shiel, *The quiet revolution: The electrification of rural Ireland, 1946–1976*, Dublin, O'Brien Press, 1984, pp. 150–3.
10 C. Ó Gráda, K. O' Rourke, 'Irish economic growth, 1945–88', in N. Crafts, G. Toniolo (eds), *Economic growth in Europe since 1945*, Cambridge, Cambridge University Press, 1996, pp. 388–427.
11 N. Hardiman, *Pay politics and economic performance in Ireland 1970–87*, Oxford, Oxford University Press, 1988, p. 228.
12 P. Sweeney, *Selling out? Privatisation in Ireland*, New Island, Dublin, 2004, p. 19. S. Ó' Riain, *The politics of high tech growth*, Cambridge, Cambridge University Press, 2004, pp. 55, 71–2, 93.
13 D. Palcic, E. Reeves, 'An economic analysis of privatisation in Ireland 1991–2003', *Journal of the Statistical and Social Inquiry Society of Ireland, 24*, 2004, p. 7.
14 M. Cooper, *Who really runs Ireland? The story of the elite who led Ireland from bust to boom ... and back again*, London, Penguin, 2010, pp. 378–81.
15 Palcic, Reeves, op. cit., p. 9.
16 Sweeney, op. cit., pp. 19, 162–3.

17 Ó Gráda, *Ireland: A new economic history*, op. cit., p. 365.
18 E. Kavanagh, 'Independence, conservatism and interest rate setting in Ireland', Political Studies Association of Ireland, Annual Conference, 2006, p. 7, available from http://www.psai.ie/conferences/papers2006/kavanaghe.pdf.
19 Ó Gráda, *Ireland: A new economic history*, op. cit., pp. 366–8.
20 *Commission of inquiry into banking, currency and credit, 1938, reports*, Dublin, Stationery Office, 1938, pp. 201–4.
21 Thomas, op. cit., p. 173, 192.
22 D. J. Cogan, *The Irish services sector, a study of productive efficiency*, Dublin, Stationery Office, 1978, p. 147. B. Ryan, *With a tap on the knee: Memoirs of a reluctant banker*, Dublin, MIS Books, 2001, pp. 67–8.
23 S. Ross, *The bankers: How the banks brought Ireland to its knees*, Dublin, Penguin, 2009, p. 9.
24 S. Carswell, *Anglo Republic: Inside the bank that broke Ireland*, Dublin, Penguin, 2011, pp. 5, 11. Ross, op. cit., pp. 40.
25 *Commission of inquiry into banking,* op. cit., p. 10.
26 A. T. Culloty, *Nora Herlihy, Irish Credit Union pioneer*, Dublin, Irish League of Credit Unions, 1990, pp. 35–6, 55–62.
27 A. A. Horner, 'Geographic diffusion in Ireland: The example of credit unions, 1958–82', in R. J. Bender (ed.), *Neue forschungen zur sozialgepgraphie von Irland*, Mannheim, 1984, pp. 191–219.
28 M. E. Daly, *The first department: A history of the Department of Agriculture*, Dublin, Institute of Public Administration, 2002, pp. 135–7.
29 K. Kennedy, T. Giblin, D. McHugh, *The economic development of Ireland in the twentieth century*, Routledge, London, 1989, p. 220.
30 S. J. Sheehy, 'The impact of EEC membership on Irish agriculture', *Journal of Agricultural Economics, 31*, 3, 1980, p. 300.
31 Whitaker, 'Capital formation', op. cit., pp. 188–9.
32 *Tables of national income and expenditure 1938 and 1944–49*, Dublin, Department of Industry and Commerce Statistics Branch.
33 A. E. Murphy 'The "Celtic Tiger": An analysis of Ireland's economic growth performance', Florence, European University Institute, Robert Schumann Centre for Advanced Studies (working paper RSC no. 2000/16, 2000), pp. 8, 13, available at http://www.eui.eu/RSCAS/wp-texts/00.16.pdf (accessed 01/09/2010).
34 Whitaker, 'Capital formation', op. cit., pp. 189, 202–3.
35 *Statistical abstracts, 1963, 1966, 1970, 1976*, Dublin, Stationery Office.
36 T. Baker, 'The Irish economy: Then, now and next', in D. Duffy, J. Fitzgerald, K. Kennedy, D. Smyth (eds), *Quarterly economic commentary, Winter 1999*, Dublin, Economic and Social Research Institute, 1999, pp. 1–11. C. Ó Gráda, 'Ireland in the 1950s', in M. Miley (ed.), *Growing knowledge: Fifty years of research and development in Irish farming and food*, Carlow, Teagasc, pp. 1–12.
37 F. Barry, 'The most FDI-intensive economy in Europe: Analysis of the Irish experience and current policy issues', in K. Liebscher *et al.* (eds), *Foreign direct investment in Europe: A changing landscape*, Cheltenham, Edward Elgar, 2007, pp. 347–57.
38 D. O' Hearn, *The Atlantic economy, Britain, the US and Ireland*, Manchester, Manchester University Press, 2001, pp. 170–2. M. O' Sullivan, *Ireland and the global question*, Cork, Cork University Press, 2006, p. 73.
39 O' Hearn, op. cit., p. 172.

40 Murphy, op. cit., pp. 13–14.
41 P. Krugman, 'Good news from Ireland, a geographic perspective', in A. W. Gray (ed.), *International perspectives on the Irish economy*, Dublin, Indecon, pp. 38–53.
42 N. Crafts, 'The Celtic Tiger in historical and international perspective', Warwick, Warwick University, 2008 (Warwick economic research papers, no. 867), pp. 2, 12.
43 D. O'Hearn, 'Macroeconomic policy in the Celtic Tiger: A critical reassessment', in C. Coulter, S. Coleman (eds), *The end of Irish history? Critical reflections on the Celtic Tiger*, Manchester, Manchester University Press, 2003, pp. 39–41.
44 H. Görg, F. Ruane, 'Aspects of foreign direct investment in Irish manufacturing since 1973: Policy and performance', *Journal of the Statistical and Social Inquiry Society of Ireland, 27*, 4, 1997, pp. 37–93.
45 *International trade and investment report, 2001*, Dublin, Forfás, 2002, p. 33.
46 Ibid., p. 32. *International trade and investment report, 2003*, Dublin, Forfás 2004, p. 34.
47 *International trade and investment report, 2003*, op. cit., p. 33. *International trade and investment report, 2004*, Dublin, Forfás, 2005, op. cit., p. 27.
48 *International trade and investment report, 2000,* Dublin, Forfás, 2001, p. 38.
49 P. Kirby, *Celtic Tiger in collapse: Explaining the weaknesses in the Irish model*, London, Palgrave Macmillan, 2010, p. 151.
50 *International trade and investment report, 2001*, op. cit., p. 38.
51 *International trade and investment report, 2003*, op. cit., p. 40. *International trade and investment report, 2005*, Dublin, Forfás 2006, p. 38.
52 *International trade and investment, 2005*, op. cit., p. 36.
53 Ibid, p. 36.
54 Cooper, op. cit., p. 252. *Balance of payments, final quarter and year ending 2008*, Dublin, CSO, 2009, p. 19.
55 *Private sector investment in Ireland*, Dublin, NESC, 1997, p. 31.
56 Kennedy *et al.*, op. cit., pp. 162–4.
57 J. Nugent, 'Corporate profitability in Ireland: Overview and determinants', *Journal of the Statistical and Social Inquiry Society of Ireland, 28*, 1, 1999, pp. 35–82.
58 Ibid., pp. 53–4.
59 Ibid., p. 50.
60 J. Kelly, M. Everett, 'Financial liberalisation and economic growth in Ireland', *Central Bank quarterly bulletin, Autumn 2004*, pp. 91–112.
61 Ibid, pp. 95–7.
62 P. Honohan, B. Walsh, 'Catching up with the leaders: The Irish Hare', *Brookings papers on Economic Activity, 1*, 2002, pp. 1–57.
63 *Private sector investment in Ireland*, op. cit., pp. 30–1.
64 *Private sector investment in Ireland*, op. cit., pp. 38–9. M. Soden, *Open dissent: An uncompromising view of the financial crisis*, Dublin, Blackhall Publishing, 2011, p. 148.
65 *The role of the financial system in financing the traded sectors*, Dublin, National Economic and Social Council, 1984, pp. 101–4.
66 *Efficiency gains of private sector credit growth in Ireland*, Paris, International Monetary Fund, 2007, p. 39.
67 On the global expansion of credit, see A. Greenspan, *The age of turbulence*, London, Penguin, pp. 510–1.
68 Kelly, Everett, op. cit., p. 95.
69 P. Honohan, 'To what extent has finance been a driver of Ireland's economic success', in A. Barrett, I. Kearney, Y. McCarthy (eds), *Quarterly economic commentary, Winter 2006*, Dublin, Economic and Social Research Institute, pp. 59–72.

70 Kelly, Everett, op. cit., p. 92.
71 *Misjudging risk: Causes of the systemic banking crisis in Ireland. Report of the Commission of Investigation into the banking sector in Ireland*, Dublin, Department of Finance, 2011, p. 24.
72 Kelly, Everett, op. cit., p. 16.
73 Ibid., p. 17.
74 P. R. Lane, 'Profits and wages in Ireland, 1987–1996', *Journal of the Statistical and Social Inquiry Society of Ireland, 27*, 1998, pp. 223–52.
75 Ibid.
76 Ross, op. cit., pp. 139–41.
77 Carswell, op. cit., pp. 29–31.
78 K, Allen, *Ireland's economic crash: A radical agenda for change*, Dublin, Oaktree Press, 2009.
79 R White, *Years of high income largely wasted*, Dublin, Davy Stockbrokers Report, 2010, p. 3.
80 Ibid., p. 1.
81 T. Fahey, D. Duffy, 'The housing boom', in T. Fahey, E. Russell, C. T. Whelan (eds), *The best of times? The social impact of the Celtic Tiger*, Dublin, 2005, pp. 123–38. D. Rae, P. van den Noord, 'Ireland's housing boom: What had driven it and have prices overshot?', *OECD Economics Department Working Papers*, Paris, OECD, 2006 (working paper no. 492), p. 5.
82 *Budget 2006, review of tax schemes, Vol. 1, Indecon review of property-based tax incentive scheme*, Dublin, Department of Finance, 2006, pp. 81–2, 221–2. Allen, op. cit., pp. 50–1. Cooper, op. cit., p. 106.
83 R. Kitchin, J. Gleeson, K. Keaveney, C. O' Callaghan, 'A haunted landscape: Housing and ghost estates in post-Celtic Tiger Ireland', NIRSA (working paper no. 59), Maynooth, National Institute for Regional and Spatial Analysis, 2010, http://www.nuim.ie/nirsa/research/documents/wp.59, pp. 22–5, 38.
84 J. Fitzgerald, 'The Irish housing stock: Growth in numbers of vacant dwellings', in A. Bergin, D. Duffy, S. Garrett, D. McCoy, Y. McCarthy (eds), *ESRI quarterly economic commentary, Spring, 2005*, Dublin, Economic and Social Research Institute, 2005, pp. 1–20.
85 Ibid., pp. 2, 12.
86 Ibid., pp. 17–18.
87 Kitchin *et al.*, op. cit., p. 36.
88 Ross, op. cit., p. 125.
89 M. Coleman, *Back from the brink: Ireland's road to recovery*, Dublin, Transworld, 2009, pp. 76–8. Lee, op. cit., p. 646. The irrational demand for property by Irish investors is also cited by Regling and Watson, *A preliminary report on the sources of Ireland's banking crisis*, Dublin, Department of Finance, 2010, p. 5.
90 Kitchin, *et al.*, op. cit., p. 35.
91 M. Kelly, 'The Irish credit bubble', in S. Kinsella, A. Leddin (eds), *Understanding Ireland's economic crisis: Prospects for recovery*, Dublin, Blackhall Publishing, 2010, pp. 57–87.
92 M. Kelly, 'On the likely extent of falls in Irish house prices', Dublin, University College Dublin, Centre for Economic Research (working paper series, 2007, WP07/01), pp. 10, 14.
93 Rae, van den Noord, op. cit., p. 13.
94 A. Kearns, M. Woods, 'The concentration in property-related lending: A financial stability perspective', *Central Bank Financial Stability Report, 2006*, Dublin, Central Bank of Ireland, 2006, pp. 133–44.

95 Allen, op. cit., p. 45.
96 *Residential property price index, May 2011*, Dublin, CSO.
97 Rae, van der Noord, op. cit., p. 5.
98 D. McWilliams, *The Pope's children: Ireland's new elite*, Dublin, Gill and Macmillan, 2006, pp. 84–5.
99 M. Kelly, 'The Irish credit bubble', op. cit., p. 59.
100 Kearns ,Woods, op. cit., pp. 135–6.
101 M. Cooper, *How Ireland went bust*, London, Penguin Ireland, pp. 173, 414.
102 P. Honohan, 'Resolving Ireland's banking crisis', *Economic and Social Review, 40*, 2, 2009, pp. 207–31.
103 Soden, op. cit., pp. 48–9.
104 Honohan, 'Resolving Ireland's banking crisis', op, cit., p. 217.
105 *The Irish banking crisis, regulatory and financial stability policy, 2002–2008: A report to the Minister for Finance by the Governor of the Central Bank*, Dublin, Central Bank of Ireland, 2010, p. 20.
106 Carswell, op. cit., pp. 29–31, 43–45.
107 *Misjudging risk: Causes of the systemic banking crisis in Ireland*, op. cit., pp. 31–34. Honohan, 'Resolving Ireland's banking crisis', op. cit., pp. 214 –17. Cooper, op. cit., p. 328. Soden, op. cit., pp. 48–9.
108 Carswell, op. cit., p. 49.
109 Cooper, op. cit., pp. 218–19.
110 *Misjudging risk*, op. cit., pp. 24, 33–35.
111 Carswell, op. cit., p. 70.
112 M. Kelly, 'The Irish credit bubble', op. cit., p. 60.
113 Ibid., pp. 123–30.
114 *Misjudging risk*, op. cit., p. ix.
115 Honohan, 'Irish banking crisis, pp. 223–5.
116 M. Kelly, 'The Irish credit bubble, pp. 61–2.
117 *EU/IMF programme of financial support for Ireland: Programme documents*, Dublin, Stationery Office, 2010, pp. 1–2.

8 A European outlier?: Demography and the labour force

1 L. Kennedy, *People and population change: A comparative study of population change in Northern Ireland and the Republic of Ireland*, Co-operation North, Dublin and Belfast, 1994, pp. 11–3, 27, 31.
2 D. A. Coleman, 'The demographic transition in Ireland in international context', in J. H. Goldthrope, C. T. Whelan (eds), *The development of industrial society in Ireland*, Oxford, Oxford University Press, 1993, p. 69.
3 Ibid., p. 69.
4 A Maddison, *The world economy*, Paris, OECD, 2006, pp. 422–3.
5 K. Kennedy, T. Giblin, D. McHugh, *The economic development of Ireland in the twentieth century*, London, Routledge, 1988, pp. 139–40.
6 Coleman, op. cit., p. 53.
7 C. Ó Gráda, *A rocky road: The Irish economy since the 1920s*, Manchester, Manchester University Press, 1997, pp. 194–5.
8 D. E. Bloom, D. Canning, 'Contraception and the Celtic Tiger', *Economic and Social Review, 34*, 2003, pp. 229–47.
9 B. Walsh, 'Demography and Irish economic growth: Past and future', in S. Kinsella, A. Leddin (eds), *Understanding Ireland's economic crisis: Prospects for recovery*, Dublin,

Blackhall Publishing, 2010, pp. 265–83. *Census 2011: Preliminary results,* Dublin, CSO, 2011, pp. 1, 10.

10 L. Kennedy, *People and population,* op. cit., pp. 13, 17, 28, 34, 47. Coleman, op. cit., pp. 53–67.

11 *Irish Times*, 26 February, 19 December, 2011.

12 R. Hamilton, 'Education, demographics and the Irish economic miracle', *Central Bank Quarterly Bulletin, 2,* 2003, pp. 103–30.

13 Bloom, Canning, op. cit., p. 232.

14 D.Baines, *Emigration from Europe 1815–1930,* Cambridge, Cambridge University Press, 1995, p. 4.

15 C. O'Grada, B. Walsh, 'The economic effects of emigration: Ireland', in B. Asch (ed.), *Emigration and its impact on the sending country*, Santa Monica, Rand, 1994, pp. 98, 124, 127, 135, 140.

16 Kennedy, op. cit., p. 22.

17 A. Bielenberg, 'Exodus: The emigration of Southern Irish Protestants during the Irish War of Independence and Civil War', *Past and present*, forthcoming, 2013.

18 J. J. Sexton, 'Emigration and immigration in the twentieth century, an overview', in J. R. Hill (ed.), *A new history of Ireland, VII, Ireland 1921–84,* Oxford, Oxford University Press, 2003, pp. 796–825. E. Delaney, *Demography, state and society: Irish migration to Britain 1921–1971*, Liverpool, Liverpool University Press, 2000, p. 45.

19 B. Walter, 'From flood to trickle: Irish migration to Britain 1987–2006', *Irish Geography, 41*, 2008, pp. 181–2.

20 E. Delaney, *The Irish in post-war Britain*, Oxford, Oxford University Press, 2007, pp. 17, 32, 42, 68. Ó Gráda, Walsh, op. cit., pp. 107, 137.

21 Delaney, op. cit., p. 201.

22 Ó Gráda, Walsh, op. cit., pp. 107–8, 123, 138–9.

23 P. Tansey, *Ireland at work: Economic growth and the labour market, 1987–1997*, Dublin, Oak Tree Press, 1998, op. cit., p. 69.

24 Ó Gráda, Walsh, op. cit., p. 106.

25 Ibid., p. 107. Sexton, op. cit., pp. 811–12.

26 J. J. Sexton, 'Emigration and immigration in the twentieth century', in Hill, op. cit., p. 814.

27 K. Kennedy, *Facing the unemployment crisis in Ireland*, Cork, Cork University Press, 1993, pp. 1–3.

28 L. Kennedy, op. cit., p. 54.

29 Accessed on 01/09/11 from www.cso.ie/px/pxeirestat/.

30 D. H. Aldcroft, *The European economy 1914–2000*, London, Routledge, 2004, p. 287.

31 *Census of population 1936, Vol. 7*, Dublin, Department of Industry and Commerce, Statistics Branch, p. 2.

32 B. Walsh, 'Labour participation and the growth of women's employment: Ireland 1971–1991', *Economic and Social Review, 24*, 1993, pp. 371–2, 397–9.

33 B. Cournède, 'Removing obstacles to employment for women in Ireland', *OECD Economics Department Working Paper*, Paris, OECD, 2006 (working paper no. 511), pp. 5–6. L. Kennedy, op. cit. pp. 50, 60.

34 J. O'Hagan, T. McIndoe-Calder, 'Population, employment and unemployment', J. O'Hagan, C. Newman (eds), *The economy of Ireland: National and sectoral policy issues*, Dublin, Gill and Macmillan, 2011, pp. 138–70.

35 *Statistical abstract 1931*, Dublin Stationery Office, 1932, p. 14.

36 F. Kennedy, *Cottage to creche: Family change in Ireland*, Dublin, Institute of Public Administration, 2000, p. 76.

37 Cournède , op. cit., p. 7.
38 K. Kennedy, 'Reflections on the process of Irish economic growth', *Journal of the Statistical and Social Inquiry Society of Ireland, 30*, 2002, pp. 124–35.
39 *Literacy in the information age: Final report of the international adult literacy survey*, Paris, OECD, 2000, p. 166.
40 Cni Laoire, 'Settling back? A biographical and life course perspective on Ireland's recent return migration', *Irish Geography, 41*, 2008, p. 195. R. C. Jones, 'Multinational investment and return migration in Ireland in the 1990s: A county level analysis', *Irish Geography, 36*, 2003, pp. 153–69.
41 *Census of population, 1926–2006*, Dublin, Stationery Office.
42 Walter, op. cit., p. 183. P. Mac Einri, 'Immigration: Labour migrants, asylum seekers and refugees', in B. Bartley, R. Kitchin (eds), *Understanding contemporary Ireland*, London, Pluto Press, pp. 236–48.
43 A. Barrett, A. Bergin, D. Duffy, 'The labour market characteristics and labour market impacts of immigrants in Ireland', *Economic and Social Review, 37*, 2006, p. 16.
44 S. Loyal, *Understanding immigration in Ireland: State, capital and labour in a global age*, Manchester, Manchester University Press, 2011, pp. 154–226.
45 *Skills needs in the Irish economy: The role of migration: A submission by the Expert Group of Future Skills Needs and Forfás to the Minister for Enterprise, Trade and Employment*, Dublin, Forfás, 2005, pp. 25–6.
46 Loyal, op. cit., pp. 184, 229.
47 *Census 2006, principal demographic results,* op. cit., p. 13.
48 *Skill needs in the Irish economy, the role of migration*, op. cit., p. 35.
49 Ibid., pp. 14–5, 48.
50 *Educational attainment thematic report 2009–2011*, Dublin, CSO, 2011.
51 Barrett *et al.*, op. cit., pp. 1–26.
52 Ibid., pp. 8–9.
53 Ibid., pp. 13–17.
54 *Annual competitiveness report, 2009*, op. cit., p. 16.
55 *Population and migration estimates, April 2009*, Dublin, CSO, 2009, p. 1.
56 D. S. Johnson, L. Kennedy, 'The two economies in Ireland in the twentieth century', in J. R. Hill (ed.), *A new history of Ireland, VII, Ireland 1921–1984,* Oxford, Oxford University Press, 2003, pp. 452–86.
57 L. Mjøset, *The Irish economy in a comparative institutional perspective*, Dublin, National Economic and Social Council, 1992, p. 261.
58 S. Ó Buchalla, *Education policy in twentieth century Ireland*, Dublin, Wolfhound Press, 1988, pp. 63, 69.
59 T. Garvin, *Preventing the future: Why was Ireland poor for so long*, Dublin, Gill & Macmillan, 2004, pp. 177, 196.
60 B. Eichengreen, *The European economy since 1945: Coordinated capitalism and beyond*, Princeton, NJ, Princeton University Press, 2007, pp. 24–6.
61 Ibid., pp. 169, 193.
62 Ó Buchalla, op. cit., p. 68.
63 F. Barry, 'Third level education, foreign direct investment and economic boom in Ireland', *International Journal of Technology Management, 38*, 3, 2007, pp. 198–219.
64 Garvin, op. cit., pp. 198–200.
65 Barry, 'Third level education', op. cit., p. 210.
66 Ibid., pp. 207–13.
67 A. Bergin, I. Kearney, 'Human capital, the labour market and productivity growth in Ireland', Dublin, ESRI, 2004 (working paper, no. 158.), p. 19.

68 Hamilton, op. cit., p. 113.
69 *Attainment thematic report 2009–2011*, Dublin, CSO, 2011.
70 Bergin, Kearney, op. cit., p. 1.
71 N. Crafts, G. Toniolo, 'Aggregate growth, 1950–2005', in S. Broadberry, K. H. O'Rourke (eds), *The Cambridge economic history of modern Europe, Vol. 2, 1870 to the present*, Cambridge, Cambridge University Press, 2010, pp. 308, 322–6.
72 J. Fitzgerald, A. Bergin, T. Conefrey, S. Diffney, D. Duffy, I. Kearney, S. Lyons, L. Malaguzi Valeri, K. Mayor, R. Tol, *ESRI medium term review 2008–15*, Dublin, ESRI, 2008, pp. 25–6.
73 Hamilton, op. cit., pp. 115, 120–21.
74 Ibid., pp. 114, 376.
75 *Annual competitiveness report, 2009*, op. cit., p. 15.
76 *Literacy in the information age: Final report of the international adult literacy survey*, Paris, OECD, 2000, p. 160. There is a question mark with regard to the accuracy of the foreign born component in Ireland.
77 N. Timoney, 'Labour and employment in Ireland in the era of the Celtic Tiger', in J. Hogan, P. Donnelly, F., O'Rourke, K. Brendan (eds), *Irish business and society*, Dublin, Oaktree Press, 2010, p. 13.
78 *PISA 2009 results, executive summary*, Paris, OECD, 2010, p. 8. C. Newman, 'Education: Market failure and government intervention', in J. O' Hagan, C. Newman (eds), *The economy of Ireland: National and sectoral policy issues*, Dublin, Gill and Macmillan, 2011, pp. 349–72.
79 Fitzgerald and Morgenroth, *Ex-ante evaluation of the National Development Plan*, op. cit., p. 9.
80 G. Boyle, 'A future driven by knowledge and innovation', in M. Miley (ed.), *Growing knowledge: Fifty years of research and development in Irish farming and food*, Carlow, Teagasc, 2008, pp. 193–4.
81 Newman, op. cit., p. 360.
82 Fitzgerald, Morgenroth, op. cit., p. 239.
83 F. Barry, J. Bradley, E. O' Malley, 'Indigenous and foreign industry, characteristics and performance', in F. Barry (ed.), *Understanding Ireland's economic growth*, London, Macmillan, 1999, pp. 45–70.
84 Fitzgerald, Morgenroth, op. cit., pp. 9, 241–4. Hewitt-Dundas, Roper, 'Ireland's innovation performance, 1991–2005', in A. Barrett, I. Kearney, M. O' Brien (eds), *ESRI quarterly economic commentary, Summer 2008*, Economic and Social Research Institute, Dublin, 2008, pp. 46–68.
85 Fitzgerald, Morgenroth, op. cit., p. 9, 244. N. Hewitt-Dundas, S. Roper, 'Ireland's innovation performance, 1991–2005', in A. Barrett, I. Kearney, M. O' Brien (eds), *ESRI quarterly economic commentary, Summer 2008*, Economic and Social Research Institute, Dublin, 2008, p. 47.
86 Eichengreen, op. cit., p. 88.
87 Barry, 'Ireland: Politics, institutions and post-war economic growth', *CESifo Forum, 1*, 2008, pp. 23–35.
88 N. Crafts, 'The Celtic Tiger in historical and international perspective', Warwick, Department of Economics, Warwick University (Warwick economic research papers, no. 867), p. 2.
89 Crafts, Toniolo, op. cit., pp. 297–332.
90 B. Walsh, 'The transformation of the Irish labour market: 1980–2003', *Journal of the Statistical and Social Inquiry Society of Ireland, 33*, 2003, p. 108.
91 Crafts, Toniolo, op. cit., pp. 297–332.
92 Ibid, pp. 297–332.

93 B. Walsh, 'Demography and Irish economic growth: Past and future', in Kinsella, Leddin, op. cit., p. 266.
94 Newman, 'Education: Market failure, op. cit., pp. 366–7.

Conclusion

1 D. S. Johnson, L. Kennedy, 'The two economies in Ireland in the twentieth century', in J. R. Hill (ed.), *A new history of Ireland, vii, Ireland, 1921–1984*, Oxford, Oxford University Press, p. 452. Johnson and Kennedy refer in this quote to the whole island.
2 J. G. Williamson, 'Economic convergence: Placing post-famine Ireland in comparative perspective', *Irish Economic and Social History, 21*, 1994, pp. 1–27.
3 K. Kennedy, T. Giblin, D. McHugh, *The economic development of Ireland in the twentieth century*, Routledge, London, 1988, pp. 117–21.
4 B. Girvin, 'Economic policy, continuity and crisis in de Valera's Ireland, 1945–61', *Irish Economic and Social History, 38*, 2011, pp. 37–41.
5 Kennedy *et al.*, op. cit., pp. 117–21.
6 C. O'Grada, K. O'Rourke, 'Irish economic growth, 1945–88', in N. Crafts, G. Toniolo (eds), *Economic growth in Europe since 1945*, Cambridge, Cambridge University Press, 1996, pp. 388–426.
7 Johnson and Kennedy, op. cit., p. 486.
8 N. Crafts, 'The golden age of economic growth in Western Europe, 1950–1973', *Economic History Review, 48*, 1995, p. 435.
9 A. Maddison, *The world economy*, Paris, OECD, 2006, pp. 446–7.
10 N. Crafts, G. Toniolo, 'Aggregate growth, 1950–2005', in S. Broadberry, K. H. O'Rourke (eds), *The Cambridge economic history of modern Europe, Volume 2, 1870 to the present*, Cambridge, Cambridge University Press, 2010, p. 301.
11 M. Cassidy, 'Productivity in Ireland: Trends and issues', *Central bank quarterly bulletin, Spring 2004*, Dublin, Central Bank of Ireland, 2004, p. 94.
12 N. Crafts, *Britain's relative economic performance 1870–1999*, London, Institute of Economic Affairs, 2002, p. 62.
13 R. Barrell, N. Pain, 'Foreign direct investment, technological change and economic growth within Europe', *The Economic Journal, 107*, 1997, p. 1776.
14 G. McCann, *Ireland's economic history: Crisis and development in the north and south*, London, Pluto Press, 2011, p. 163.
15 Crafts, op. cit., p. 46.
16 Crafts, Toniolo, op. cit., p. 318. The authors use GNP per hour worked in the Irish case, to remove the distorting effects of transfer pricing and profit repatriation of foreign multinational companies on Irish GDP data.
17 Ibid., pp. 306–13.
18 Cassidy, op. cit., p. 94.
19 P. Teague, J. Donaghey, 'Why has Irish social partnership survived?', *British Journal of Industrial Relations, 47*, 2009, p. 67.
20 P. Kirby, *Celtic Tiger in collapse: Explaining the weakness of the Irish model*, Basingstoke, Palgrave Macmillan, 2010, p. 37.
21 D. H. Aldcroft, *The European economy 1914–2000*, London, Routledge, 2004, p. 278.
22 K. A. Kennedy, 'Reflections on the process of Irish economic growth', *Journal of the Statistical and Social Inquiry Society of Ireland, 30*, 2001, pp. 124–7.
23 Crafts, op. cit., p. 61.

24 *Quarterly national household survey, educational attainment thematic report, 2011*, Dublin, CSO, p. 5.
25 A. Hyland, *Entry to higher education in Ireland in the 21st century*, Dublin, Higher Education Authority, 2011, p. 2
26 Crafts, Toniolo, op. cit., pp. 306–13.
27 *Educational attainment thematic report*, op. cit., p. 6.
28 H. Armstrong, R. Read, 'Western European micro-states and EU autonomous regions: The advantages and size and sovereignty', *World Development, 23*, 1995, p. 1230.
29 E. Delaney, *The Irish in post war Britain*, Oxford, Oxford University Press, 2007, p. 2.
30 D. O'Mahony, *The Irish economy*, Cork, Cork University Press, 1964, pp. 71–99.
31 See following by F. Barry: 'Irish growth in historical and theoretical perspective', in F. Barry (ed.), *Understanding Ireland's economic growth*, London, Macmillan, 1999, pp. 25–41. 'The Celtic Tiger era; delayed convergence or regional boom', in A. Bergin, D. Duffy, J. Eakins, C. MacCoille, D. McCoy (eds), *Quarterly economic commentary, Summer 2002*, Dublin, Economic and Social Research Institute, 2002, pp. 1–7. 'Future Irish growth: Opportunities, catalysts, constraints', in A. Barrett, S. Garrett, I. Kearney, D. McCoy (eds), *Quarterly economic commentary, Winter 2005*, Dublin, Economic and Social Research Institute, 2005, pp. 1–25.
32 F. Gould, 'The growth of public expenditure in Ireland 1947–77', *Administration, 29*, 1981, pp. 115–35.
33 L. Shoen, 'The Irish free state and the electricity industry, 1922–1927', A. Bielenberg (ed.), *The Shannon scheme and the electrification of rural Ireland*, Dublin, Lilliput, 2002, p. 29. M. Manning, M. McDowell, *Electricity supply in Ireland, the history of the ESB*, Dublin, Gill & Macmillan, 1984. M. Shiel, *The quiet revolution: The electrification of rural Ireland 1946–1976*, Dublin, O'Brien Press, 1984.
34 P. Honohan, B. Walsh, 'Catching up with the leaders: The Irish Hare', *Brookings papers on Economic Activity, 1*, 2002, pp. 1–57.
35 Crafts, op cit., p. 100.
36 H. Armstrong, R. J. de Kervenoal, X. Li, R. Read, 'A comparison of economic performance of different micro-states, and between micro-states and larger countries', *World Development, 26*, 1998, p. 651.
37 Teague, Donaghey, op. cit., pp. 55–78.
38 N. Collins, 'Corruption in Ireland: A review of recent cases', in N. Collins (ed.), *Political issues in Ireland today*, Manchester, Manchester University Press, 1999, pp. 73–74. N. Collins, *Understanding corruption in Irish politics*, Cork, Cork University Press, 2000, pp. 27–30. E. Byrne, *Political corruption in Ireland, 1922–2010: A crooked harp?*, Manchester University Press, Manchester, 2012.
39 D. Finn, 'Ireland on the turn? Political and economic consequences of the crash', *New Left Review, 67*, 2011, p. 20.
40 S. Carswell, *Something rotten: Irish banking scandals*, Dublin, Gill and Macmillan, 2006.
41 E. O'Leary, 'Reflecting on the "Celtic Tiger": Before, during and after', *Irish Economic and Social History, 38*, 2011, pp. 73–89. Armstrong *et al.*, p. 651.
42 *Ireland's five part crisis: An integrated national response*, Dublin, NESC, 2009, p. 11. 2007–2009: *Economic statistics, Department of Finance*, 2010, available from www.cso.ie/statistics/nationalgp.htm.
43 M. Cooper, *How Ireland went bust*, op. cit., p. 25. McCann, op. cit., p. 210.
44 F. Barry, 'Some political economy lessons from Ireland's boom and bust', *Journal of Irish and Scottish Studies, 2*, 2009, pp. 25–39.
45 Ibid., p. 35.

Bibliography

Official publications

National accounts

National income and expenditure 1960, Dublin, Stationery Office, 1961.
National income and expenditure 1969, Dublin, Stationery Office, 1971.
National income and expenditure 1975, Dublin, Stationery Office, 1976.
National income and expenditure 1982, Dublin, Stationery Office, 1983.
National income and expenditure 1989, Dublin, Stationery Office, 1990.
National income and expenditure 2004, Dublin, Stationery Office, 2005.
National income and expenditure 2006, Dublin, Stationery Office, 2006.
National income and expenditure 2007, Dublin, Stationery Office, 2007.
National income and expenditure 2008, Dublin, Stationery Office, 2008.
National income and expenditure 2009, Dublin, Stationery Office, 2009.
National income and expenditure 2010, Dublin, Stationery Office, 2010.
Tables of national income and expenditure 1938 and 1944–49, Dublin, Stationery Office, 1951.

Agriculture

Agricultural statistics 1934–56, Dublin, Stationery Office, 1960.
Agricultural statistics 1960, Dublin, Stationery Office, nd.
Agricultural statistics 1970, Dublin, Stationery Office, 1971.
Compendium of Irish agricultural statistics 1997, Dublin, Department of Agriculture, 1998.
Compendium of Irish agricultural statistics 2003, Dublin, Department of Agriculture, 2003.
Compendium of Irish agricultural statistics 2007, Dublin, Department of Agriculture, 2007.
Crops and livestock survey June 2009, final results, Dublin, CSO, 2010.
Farming since the famine: Irish farm statistics 1847–1996, Dublin, CSO, 1997.
Farm structure survey 2007, Dublin, CSO, 2008.
National farm survey 2010, Dublin, CSO, 2011.
Output, input and income in agriculture 2010, final estimates, Dublin, CSO, 2011.

Industry

Census of industrial production 1926 and 1929, Dublin, Stationery Office, 1933.

Services

Annual services inquiry 2001, Dublin, Stationery Office, 2003.
Annual services inquiry 2002, Dublin, Stationery Office, 2004.
Annual services inquiry 2003, Dublin, Stationery Office, 2005.
Annual services inquiry 2004, Dublin, Stationery Office, 2006.
Annual services inquiry 2005, Dublin, Stationery Office, 2007.
Annual services inquiry 2006, Dublin, Stationery Office, 2008.
Census of distribution 1933, Dublin, Stationery Office, 1936.
Census of distribution 1951–54, Dublin, Stationery Office, 1954.
Census of distribution 1956–59, Dublin, Stationery Office, 1962.
Census of distribution 1966, final report for retail trade, Dublin, Stationery Office, 1969.
Census of distribution 1971, summary results for retail and wholesale trade, Dublin, Stationery Office, 1977.
Census of distribution 1977, Vol. II, detailed results for retail establishments, Dublin, Stationery Office, 1983.
Census of services 1988, Vol. I, retail and wholesale trade, Dublin, Stationery Office,1990.
Tourism and travel quarterly, 2nd Q, 1989, Dublin, Stationery Office, 1989.
Tourism and travel quarterly, 1st Q, 1992, Dublin, Stationery Office, 1992.
Tourism and travel quarterly,1st Q, 1997, Dublin, Stationery Office, 1997.
Tourism and travel quarterly, 1st Q, 2003, Dublin, Stationery Office, 2003.
Tourism and travel quarterly, 1st Q, 2007, Dublin, Stationery Office, 2007.

Demography

Census of population 1926, Vol. II, occupations, Dublin, Stationery Office, 1932.
Census of population 1936, Vol. II, occupations, Dublin, Stationery Office, 1940.
Census of population 1946, Vol. II, occupations, Dublin, Stationery Office, 1953.
Census of population 1951, Vol. III Part 1, occupations, Dublin, Stationery Office, 1954.
Census of population 1961, Vol. III, occupations, Dublin, Stationery Office, 1964.
Census of population 1966, Vol. IV, occupations, Dublin, Stationery Office, 1969.
Census of population 1971, Vol. IV, occupations, Dublin, Stationery Office, 1975.
Census of population 1981, Vol. VII, occupations, Dublin, Stationery Office, 1986.
Census of population 1986, Vol. VII, occupations, Dublin, Stationery Office, 1993.
Census of population 1991, Vol. VI, occupations, Dublin, Stationery Office, 1993.
Census of population 2002, Vol. VI, occupations, Dublin, Stationery Office, 2003.
Census of population 2006, Vol. VIII, occupations, Dublin, Stationery Office, 2007.
Census of population 2006, principal demographic results, Dublin, Stationery Office, 2007.
Census of population 2006, principal socio-economic results, Dublin, Stationery Office, 2007.
Census of population 2011, preliminary results, Dublin, Stationery Office, 2011.
Population and migration estimates April 2009, Dublin, Stationery Office, 2009.

Investment and trade

Balance of international payments, quarter four and year ending 1990, Dublin, CSO, 1991.
Balance of international payments, quarter four and year ending 1995, Dublin, CSO, 1996.

Balance of international payments, quarter four and year ending 1997, Dublin, CSO, 1998.
Balance of international payments, quarter four and year ending 1999, Dublin, CSO, 2000.
Balance of international payments, quarter four and year ending 2001, Dublin, CSO, 2002.
Balance of international payments, quarter four and year ending 2002, Dublin, CSO, 2003.
Balance of international payments, quarter four and year ending 2004, Dublin, CSO, 2005.
Balance of international payments, quarter four and year ending 2006, Dublin, CSO, 2007.
Balance of international payments, quarter four and year ending 2008, Dublin, CSO, 2009.
Balance of international payments, quarter four and year ending 2010, Dublin, CSO, 2011.
External trade December 2010, Dublin, CSO, 2011.
International investment position 1998–2001, Dublin, CSO, 2002.
International investment position 2002, Dublin, CSO, 2003.
International investment position 2004, Dublin, CSO, 2005.
International investment position 2005, Dublin, CSO, 2006.
International investment position 2006, Dublin, CSO, 2007.
Foreign direct investment 2007, Dublin, CSO, 2008.
Trade and shipping statistics 1931, Dublin, Stationery Office, 1933.
Trade and shipping statistics 1938, Dublin, Stationery Office, 1939.
Trade and shipping statistics 1943–44, Dublin, Stationery Office, 1947.
Trade and shipping statistics 1951, Dublin, Stationery Office, nd.
Trade and shipping statistics 1956, Dublin, Stationery Office, nd.
Trade and shipping statistics 1962, Dublin, Stationery Office, nd.
Trade statistics February 2008, Dublin, CSO, 2009.

General

Statistical abstract 1937–38, Dublin, Stationery Office, 1938.
Statistical abstract 1947–48, Dublin, Stationery Office, 1949.
Statistical abstract 1951–52, Dublin, Stationery Office, 1953.
Statistical abstract 1953, Dublin, Stationery Office, 1954.
Statistical abstract 1956, Dublin, Stationery Office, 1957.
Statistical abstract 1958, Dublin, Stationery Office, 1958.
Statistical abstract 1961, Dublin, Stationery Office, 1961.
Statistical abstract 1962, Dublin, Stationery Office, 1962.
Statistical abstract 1965, Dublin, Stationery Office, 1965.
Statistical abstract 1966, Dublin, Stationery Office, 1966.
Statistical abstract 1967, Dublin, Stationery Office, 1967.
Statistical abstract 1970–71, Dublin, Stationery Office, 1972.
Statistical abstract 1972–73, Dublin, Stationery Office, 1976.
Statistical abstract 1974–75, Dublin, Stationery Office, 1977.
Statistical abstract 1976, Dublin, Stationery Office, 1978.

Statistical abstract 1978, Dublin, Stationery Office, 1981.
Statistical abstract 1981, Dublin, Stationery Office, 1985.
Statistical abstract 1982–85, Dublin, Stationery Office, 1986.
Statistical abstract 1988, Dublin, Stationery Office, 1988.
Statistical abstract 1990, Dublin, Stationery Office, 1990.
Statistical abstract 1993, Dublin, Stationery Office, 1993.
Statistical abstract 1996, Dublin, Stationery Office, 1997.
Statistical yearbook 2001, Dublin, Stationery Office, 2001.
Statistical yearbook 2002, Dublin, Stationery Office, 2002.
Statistical yearbook 2004, Dublin, Stationery Office, 2004.
Statistical yearbook 2005, Dublin, Stationery Office, 2005.
Statistical yearbook 2006, Dublin, Stationery Office, 2006.
Statistical yearbook 2007, Dublin, Stationery Office, 2007.
Statistical yearbook 2008, Dublin, Stationery Office, 2008
Statistical yearbook 2009, Dublin, Stationery Office, 2009
Statistical yearbook 2010, Dublin, Stationery Office, 2010.

Other

Quarterly national household survey, educational attainment thematic report 2011, Dublin, Stationery Office, 2012.
Residential property price index May 2011, Dublin, Stationery Office, 2012.
Saorstát Éireann official handbook, Dublin, Stationery Office, 1932.
That was then, this is now: Changes in Ireland 1949–1999, Dublin, Stationery Office, 2000.

Irish Government publications

National Competitiveness Council

Annual competitiveness report 2009, Vol. I, Benchmarking Ireland's performance, Dublin, National Competitiveness Council, 2009.

National Economic and Social Council (NESC)

A review of industrial policy, Dublin, NESC, 1982.
A strategy for development 1986–1990: Growth, employment and fiscal balance, Dublin, NESC, 1987.
Ireland's five part crisis: An integrated national response, Dublin, NESC, 2009.
Irish forestry policy, Dublin, NESC, 1979.
Private sector investment in Ireland, Dublin, NESC, 1997.
Regional policy in Ireland: A review, Dublin, NESC, 1975.
Service-type employment and regional development, Dublin, NESC, 1977.
The role of the financial system in financing the traded sectors, Dublin, NESC, 1984.
Tourism policy, Dublin, NESC, 1980.

Forfás

Detailed assessment of Ireland's productivity performance 1980–2005, Dublin, Forfás, 2006.

Future skills and research needs of the International Financial Services Industry: A study for the Expert Group on Future Skills Needs, Dublin, Forfás, 2007

International trade and investment report 2000, Dublin, Forfás, 2001.

International trade and investment report 2001, Dublin, Forfás, 2002.

International trade and investment report 2003, Dublin, Forfás, 2004.

International trade and investment report 2004, Dublin, Forfás, 2005.

International trade and investment report 2005, Dublin, Forfás, 2006.

Skills needs in the Irish economy: The role of migration: a submission by the Expert Group on Future Skills Needs and Forfás to the Minister for Enterprise, Trade and Employment, Dublin, Forfás, 2005.

The dynamics of the retail sector in Ireland, Dublin, Forfás, 1999.

Department of Finance/Central Bank

A preliminary report on the sources of Ireland's banking crisis, Dublin, Department of Finance, 2010.

Budget 2006, review of tax schemes, Vol. I, Indecon review of property-based tax incentive schemes, Dublin, Department of Finance, 2006.

Central Bank quarterly bulletin, Quarter 2, April 2011, Dublin, Central Bank of Ireland, 2011.

Department of Finance: Budgetary and economic statistics 2008, Dublin, Department of Finance, 2009.

Department of Finance: Budgetary and economic statistics 2009, Dublin, Department of Finance, 2010.

Misjudging risk: Causes of the systemic banking crisis in Ireland. Report of the Commission of Investigation into the banking sector in Ireland, Dublin, Department of Finance, 2011.

The Irish banking crisis, regulatory and financial stability policy, 2003–2008: A report to the Minister for Finance by the Governor of the Central Bank, Dublin, Central Bank of Ireland, 2010.

Department of Arts/Tourism

New horizons for Irish tourism: An agenda for action. Report of the Tourism Policy Review Group, Dublin, Department of Arts, Sports and Tourism, 2003.

Review of section 481 of the Taxes Consolidation Act 1997. Report by Price WaterhouseCoopers to the Irish Film Board and the Department of Arts, Sport and Tourism, Dublin, Department of Arts, Sport and Tourism, 2003.

Shaping the future: A strategic plan for the development of the music industry in Ireland, Dublin, Department of Arts, Sport and Tourism, 2003.

The strategic development of the Irish film and television industry, 2000–2010. Final report of the Film Industry Strategic Review Group to the Minister for Arts, Heritage, Gaeltacht and the Islands, Dublin, Department of Arts, Heritage, Gaeltacht and the Islands, 1999.

Department of Environment, Heritage and Local Government

Advisory group on unfinished housing development, emerging priority issues, Dublin, Department of Environment Heritage and Local Government, 2010. Available from http://www.environ.ie/en/DevelopmentandHousing/Housing/News/MainBody,25485,en.htm.

General

A time for change: Industrial policy for the 1990s. Report of the Industrial Policy Review Group (Culliton Report), Dublin, Stationery Office, 1992.
Building on reality 1985–87, Dublin, Stationery Office, 1985.
Commission of inquiry into banking, currency and credit 1938, reports, Dublin, Stationery Office, 1938.
Commission on Taxation report 2009, Dublin, Stationery Office, 2009.
Committee of inquiry into internal transport, Dublin, Stationery Office, 1957.
Developing sustainable tourism: Tourism development plan 1994–1999, Dublin, Bord Fáilte, 1994.
Economic development, Dublin, Stationery Office, 1958.
EU/IMF programme of financial support for Ireland: Programme documents, Dublin, Stationery Office, 2010.
First report of the Commission on Taxation: Direct Taxation July 1982, Dublin, Stationery Office, 1982.
National development plan: Productive sector operational programme 2000–2006, Dublin, Department of Enterprise and Employment, 2000.
National development plan, 2007–13, Dublin, Stationery Office, 2007.
Proposals for plan 1984–87, Dublin, Stationery Office, 1984.
Reports of the Commission on Agriculture, final report, Dublin Stationery Office, 1924.
The National Recovery Plan 2011–2014, Dublin, Stationery Office, 2010.

European Union (Eurostat)

Europe in figures: Eurostat yearbook 2002, Brussels, European Commission, 2002.
Europe in figures: Eurostat yearbook 2008, Brussels, European Commission, 2008.
Europe in figures: Eurostat yearbook 2010, Brussels, European Commission, 2010.

International organizations

International Monetary Fund

Ireland, financial system stability assessment update, Monetary and Financial Systems and European Departments, 2006.

Organisation for Economic Co-operation and Development

Literacy in the information age: Final report of the international adult literacy survey 2000, Paris, OECD, 2001.
OECD economic surveys 2008: Ireland, Paris, OECD, 2008.
OECD reviews of foreign direct investment: Ireland, 1994, Paris, OECD, 2005.
PISA 2009 results, executive summary, Paris, OECD, 2011.

d Nations

Report to the Government of Ireland on the development of the sea fishery industries, Rome, Food and Agriculture Organization of the United Nations, 1959.

Newspapers

Irish Times.

Secondary sources

Addison-Smyth, Diarmuid. 'Ireland's revealed comparative advantage', *Central Bank Quarterly Bulletin Spring 2005*, Dublin, Central Bank of Ireland, 2005, pp. 101–16.

Aherne, Alan, Kydland, Finn, Wynne, Mark A., 'Ireland's Great Depression', *Economic and Social Review, 37*, 2, 2006, pp. 215–45.

Aldcroft, Derek, H., *The European economy 1914–2000*, London, Routledge, 2004.

Alford, B. W. E., *W.D. and H.O. Wills and the development of the UK tobacco industry 1786–1965*, London, Methuen, 1973.

Allen, Kieran, 'Forging the links, Fianna Fáil, the trade unions and the emergency', *Saothar, 16*, 1991, pp. 48–56.

Allen, Kieran, *Ireland's economic crash: A radical agenda for change*, Dublin, Oak Tree Press, 2009.

Armstrong, Harvey W., de Kervenoal, R. J., Li, X , Read, R., 'A comparison of economic performance of different micro-states, and between micro-states and larger countries', *World Development, 26*, 1998, pp. 639–56.

Armstrong, Harvey W., Read, R., 'The phantom of Liberty?: Economic growth and the vulnerability of small states', *Journal of International Development, 14*, 2002, pp. 435–58.

Arrow, Kenneth, 'Economic growth policy for a small country', in Gray, Alan, W. (ed.), *International perspectives on the Irish economy*, Dublin, Indecon, 1997, pp. 1–8.

Baines, Dudley, *Emigration from Europe, 1815–1930*, Cambridge, Cambridge University Press, 1995.

Baker, Terry, 'The Irish economy: Then, now and next', in Duffy, David, Fitzgerald, John, Kennedy, Kieran and Smyth, D. (eds.), *Quarterly Economic Commentary, Winter 1999*, Dublin, Economic and Social Research Institute, 1999, pp. 1–11.

Barrell, Ray, Pain, Nigel, 'Foreign direct investment, technological change and economic growth within Europe', *The Economic Journal, 107*, 1997, pp. 1770–86.

Barrett, Alan, 'EU enlargement and Ireland's labour market', Bonn, Forschunginsuitut zur zukunft der arbeit, 2009 (discussion paper, no. 426).

Barrett, Alan, Bergin, Adele, Duffy, David, 'The labour market characteristics and labour market impacts of immigrants in Ireland', *Economic and Social Review, 37*, no.1, 2006, pp. 1–26.

Barry, Frank, 'Irish growth in historical and theoretical perspective', in Barry, Frank (ed.), *Understanding Ireland's economic growth*, Macmillan, London, Macmillan, 1999, pp. 25–41.

Barry, Frank, 'The Celtic Tiger era: Delayed convergence or regional boom', in Bergin, Adele, Duffy, David, Eakins, J., MacCoille, C., McCoy, Danny (eds), *Quarterly Economic Commentary, Summer 2002*, Dublin, Economic and Social Research Institute, 2002, pp. 1–7.

Barry, Frank, 'FDI, transfer pricing and the measurement of R & D intensity', *Research Policy, 34*, 2005, pp. 673–81.

Barry, Frank, 'Future Irish growth: Opportunities, catalysts, constraints', in Barrett, A., Garrett, S., Kearney, Ide, McCoy, Danny (eds), *Quarterly Economic Commentary, Winter 2005*, Dublin, Economic and Social Research Institute, 2005, pp. 1–25.

Barry, Frank, 'Third level education, foreign direct investment and economic boom in Ireland', *International Journal of Technology Management, 38*, 3, 2007, pp. 198–219.

Barry, Frank, 'Ireland: Politics, institutions and post-war economic growth', *CESifo Forum, 1*, 2008, pp. 23–35.

Barry, Frank, 'Politics and fiscal policy under Lemass: A theoretical appraisal', Dublin, Institute of International Integration Studies, Trinity College Dublin, 2009 (discussion paper no. 292).

Barry, Frank, 'Social partnership, competitiveness and exit from fiscal crisis', *Economic and Social Review, 40*, 1, 2009, pp. 1–14.

Barry, Frank, 'Some political economy lessons from Ireland's boom and bust', *Journal of Irish and Scottish Studies, 2*, 2009, pp. 25–39.

Barry, Frank, 'Politics and economic policy making in Ireland', in Hogan, John, Donnelly, Paul. F., O' Rourke, Brendan K. (eds), *Irish business and society*, Dublin, Oak Tree Press, 2010, pp. 28–43.

Barry, Frank, 'Foreign investment and the politics of export profits tax relief 1956', *Irish Economic and Social History, 38*, 2011, pp. 54–73.

Barry, Frank, Bradley, John, 'FDI and trade: The Irish host-country experience', *The Economic Journal, 107*, 1997, pp. 1798–881.

Barry, Frank,Van Welsum, Desiree, 'Services FDI and offshoring into Ireland', Paris, OECD Directorate for Science, Technology and Industry paper, 2005, available at: http://www.oecd.org/dataoecd/14/0/3532060.pdf.

Barry, Frank, Devereux, Michael B, 'A theoretical growth model for Ireland', *Economic and Social Review, 37*, 2006, pp. 245–62.

Barry, Frank, Van Egeraat, Chris, 'The decline of the computer hardware sector: How Ireland adjusted', in Barrett, Alan, Kearney, Ide, O' Brien, Martin (eds), *Quarterly Economic Commentary, Spring 2008*, Dublin, Economic and Social Research Institute, pp. 38–57.

Barry, Frank, Van Egeraat, Chris, 'The Irish pharmaceutical industry over the boom period and beyond', *Irish Geography, 42*, 1, 2009, pp. 23–45.

Barry, Frank, Daly, Mary E., 'Mr Whitaker and industry: Setting the record straight', *The Economic and Social Review, 42*, 2011, pp. 159–63.

Barry, Frank, Bradley, John, Hannan, Aoife, 'The European dimension: The single market and the structural funds', in Barry, Frank (ed.), *Understanding Ireland's economic growth*, London, Macmillan, 1999, pp. 99–117.

Barry, Frank, Bradley, John, O' Malley, Eoin, 'Indigenous and foreign industry: Characteristics and performance', in Barry, Frank (ed.), *Understanding Ireland's economic growth*, London, Macmillan, 1999, pp. 45–70.

Battilossi, S, Foremen-Peck, J., Kling, G, 'Business cycles and economic policy, 1945–2007', Broadberry, S., O' Rourke, K. H. (eds), *The Cambridge economic history of modern Europe, Vol. II, 1870 to the present*, Cambridge University Press, 2010.

Bell, Jonathan, Watson, Mervyn, *A history of Irish farming, 1750–1950*, Dublin, Four Courts Press, 2008.

Bergin, Adele, Kearney, Ide, 'Human capital, the labour market and productivity growth in Ireland', Dublin, Economic and Social Research Institute, 2004 (ESRI working paper no. 158).

Bielenberg, Andy, *Locke's distillery: A history*, Dublin, Liliput Press, 1993.
Bielenberg, Andy, *Ireland and the industrial revolution: The impact of the industrial revolution on Irish industry*, London, Routledge, 2009.
Bielenberg, Andy, 'Exodus: The emigration of Southern Irish Protestants during the Irish War of Independence and Civil War', *Past and Present* (forthcoming).
Black, W., 'Industrial development and regional policy', in Gibson, N. J., Spencer, J. E. (ed.), *Economic activity in Ireland: a study of two open economies*, Dublin, Gill and MacMillan, 1977.
Blackwell, J., *Transport in the developing economy*, Dublin, Economic and Social Research Institute, 1969.
Bloom, David E., Canning, David, 'Contraception and the Celtic Tiger', *The Economic and Social History Review, 34*, 3, 2003, pp. 229–47.
Bolger, Pat, *The Irish co-operative movement: Its history and development*, Dublin, Institute of Public Administration, 1977.
Boyle, Gerry, *National responses to the CAP reform proposals*, Dublin, National Economic and Social Council, 1991.
Boyle, Gerry, 'A future driven by knowledge and innovation', in Miley, Michael (ed.), *Growing knowledge: Fifty years of research and development in Irish farming and food*, Carlow, Teagasc, 2008, pp. 193–206.
Bradley, John, 'The legacy of economic development: The Irish economy, 1960–1987', in McCarthy, John. F. (ed.), *Planning Ireland's future: The legacy of T. K. Whitaker*, Dublin, Glendale Publications, 1990, pp. 128–52.
Bradley, John, Morgenroth, Edgar, 'Celtic Cubs? Regional manufacturing in Ireland', *ESRI Medium Term Review 1999*, Dublin, Economic and Social Research Institute, 1999, pp. 157–75.
Breathnach, Proinnsias, 'Globalisation, information technology and the emergence of niche transnational cities: The growth of the call centre sector in Dublin', *Geoforum, 31*, 2000, pp. 477–85.
Breathnach, Proinnsias, 'The evolution of the spatial structure of the Irish dairy processing industry', *Irish Geography, 33*, 2000, pp. 166–84.
Breathnach, Proinnsias, 'The services sector', in Bartley, Brendan, Kitchin, Robert (eds), *Understanding contemporary Ireland*, London, Pluto Press, 2007, pp. 146–57.
Breathnach, Proinnsias, Van Egeraat, Chris, 'The manufacturing sector', in Bartley, Brendan, Kitchin, Robert (eds), *Understanding contemporary Ireland*, London, Pluto Press, 2007, pp. 128–45.
Breen, Richard, 'Farm servant-hood in Ireland, 1900–40', *Economic History Review, 36*, 1983, pp. 87–102.
Brennan, Nicola, Breathnach, Proinnsias, 'The spatiality of Irish manufacturing linkages in the Celtic Tiger era', *Irish Geography, 42*, 2009, pp. 7–22.
Brophy, S. A., *The strategic management of Irish enterprise 1934–1984*, Dublin, Smurfit, 1985.
Brown, Terence, *Ireland, a social and cultural history, 1922–1979*, London, Fontana, 1981.
Browne, P. J., *Unfinished promise: Memories of Donogh O' Malley*, Dublin, Currach Press, 2008.
Brunt, Barry M., 'Manufacturing changes in the greater Cork Area 1980–1984', *Irish Geography, 17*, 1984, pp. 101–8.
Byrne, E. A., *Political corruption in Ireland 1922–2012: A crooked harp?*, Manchester, Manchester University Press, 2012.
Byrne, Julie, 'Ireland and the global financial crisis: Growth, volatility and financial development', *Journal of the Statistical and Social Inquiry Society of Ireland, 39*, 2010, pp. 166–86.

Cannon, A., 'Arklow's explosive history: Kynoch, 1895–1918', *History Ireland*, Jan–Feb 2006, pp. 30–6.

Carswell, Simon, *Anglo republic: Inside the bank that broke Ireland*, Dublin, Penguin, 2011.

Casey, Michael, *Ireland's malaise: The troubled personality of the Irish economy*, Dublin, Liffey Press.

Cassidy, Mark, 'Productivity in Ireland: Trends and issues', *Central Bank quarterly bulletin, Spring 2004*, Dublin, Central Bank of Ireland, 2004, pp. 83–105.

Clarke, Donal, *Brown gold: A history of Bord na Móna and the peat industry in Ireland*, Dublin, Gill and Macmillan, 2010.

Clear, Catríona, *Women of the house: Women's household work in Ireland, 1926–1961*, Dublin, Irish Academic Press, 2000.

Clinch, J. Peter, *Economics of Irish forestry: Evaluating the returns to economy and society*, Dublin, COFORD, 1999.

Cogan, D. J., *The Irish services sector: A study of productive efficiency*, Dublin, Stationery Office, 1978.

Coleman, D. A., 'The demographic transition in Ireland in international context', in Goldthrope, J. H., Whelan, C.T. (eds), *The development of industrial society in Ireland*, Oxford, Oxford University Press, 1993, pp. 53–77.

Coleman, Kieran, Considine, John, 'The No Income Tax campaign: Twenty-first century tax philosophy in 1920s Ireland', *Irish Economic and Social History, 33*, 2006, pp. 1–18.

Coleman, Marc, *Back from the brink: Ireland's road to recovery*, Dublin, Transworld, 2009.

Collins, Neil, 'Still recognisably pluralist? State–farmer relations in Ireland', in Hill, R. J., Marsh, M. (eds), *Modern Irish democracy*, Dublin, Irish Academic Press, 1993, pp. 104–23.

Collins, Neil, 'Corruption in Ireland: A review of recent cases', in Collins, Neil (ed.), *Political issues in Ireland today*, Manchester, Manchester University Press, 1999.

Collins, Neil, *Understanding corruption in Irish politics*, Cork, Cork University Press, 2000.

Collins, Stephen, *Spring and the labour story*, Dublin, O' Brien Press, 1993.

Collins, Stephen, *Breaking the mould: How the PDs changed Irish politics*, Dublin, Gill and Macmillan, 2006.

Commins, Patrick, 'Land policies and agricultural development', in Drudy, P. J. (ed.), *Irish studies, Vol. IV, Ireland: Land, politics and people*, Cambridge, Cambridge University Press, 1982, pp. 217–241.

Conefrey, Thomas, Fitzgerald, John. D., 'The macro-economic impact of changing the rate of corporation tax', Dublin, Economic and Social Research Institute, 2009 (working paper, no. 273).

Considine, John, Butler, Robert, 'Tom Garvin, Mancur Olson and Irish economic growth', Cork, Department of Economics, University College Cork, 2007, available: http://www.ucc.ie/en/economics/research/workingpapersseries/downloads/DocumentFile,29192,en.pdf.

Considine, John, Duffy, David, 'Tales of expansionary fiscal contraction in two European countries: Hindsight and foresight', Cork, Department of Economics, University College Cork. 2007, available: http://www.ucc.ie/en/economics/research/workingpapersseries/downloads/DocumentFile,38052,en.pdf

Cooper, Mark, Davis, John, *The Irish fertiliser industry: A history*, Dublin, Irish Academic Press, 2004.

Cooper, Matt, *Who really runs Ireland? The story of the elite who led Ireland from bust to boom ... and back again*, London, Penguin, 2010.
Costello, Peter, *Denis Guiney*, Dublin, University of Dublin Press, 2008.
Cournède, Boris, 'Removing obstacles to employment for women in Ireland', *OECD Economics Department Working Papers*, Paris, OECD, 2006 (working paper no. 511).
Crafts, Nicholas, 'The golden age of economic growth in Western Europe, 1950–1973', *Economic History Review, 48*, 1995, pp. 429–87.
Crafts, Nicholas, *Britain's relative economic performance, 1870–1999*, London, Institute of Economic Affairs, 2002.
Crafts, Nicholas, 'The Celtic Tiger in historical and international perspective', Warwick, Warwick University, 2008 (Warwick economic research papers, no. 867).
Crafts, Nicholas, 'The Celtic Tiger in historical and international perspective', in M. Mulreany (ed.), *Economic development 50 years on: 1958–2008*, Dublin, Institute of Public Administration, 2009, pp. 64–73.
Crafts, Nicholas, Toniolo, Gianni, 'European economic growth, 1950–2005: An overview', London, Centre for Economic Policy Research, 2008 (discussion paper no. 6863).
Crafts, Nicholas, Toniolo, Gianni, 'Aggregate growth, 1950–2005', in Broadberry, Stephen, O' Rourke, Kevin, H. (eds), *The Cambridge economic history of modern Europe, Vol. II, 1870 to the present*, Cambridge, Cambridge University Press, 2010.
Creighton, Arthur Henry, *The life and times of Arthur Henry*, Dublin, Blackwater Press, 1994.
Cronin, Mike, *Aer Lingus: Its history*, Cork, Collins Press, 2011.
Crotty, Raymond, *Irish agricultural production*, Cork, Cork University Press, 1966.
Crowley, Caroline, Walsh James. A., Meredith, David, *Irish farming at the millennium: A census atlas*, Maynooth, National Institute for Regional and Spatial Analysis, 2008.
Crowley, Ethel, 'The evolution of the Common Agricultural Policy and social differentiation in rural Ireland', *The Economic and Social Review, 34*, 2003, pp. 65–85.
Cullen, Louis. M., *An economic history of Ireland since 1660*, London, Batsford, 1986, 2nd edition.
Culloty, A. T., *Nora Herlihy, Irish Credit Union pioneer*, Dublin, Irish League of Credit Unions, 1990.
Daly, Mary. E., 'The return to the roads', in Nowlan, Kevin B. (ed.), *Travel and transport in Ireland*, Dublin, Gill and Macmillan, 1973, pp. 135–46.
Daly, Mary E., 'An Irish-Ireland for business?: The Control of Manufactures Acts, 1932 and 1934', *Irish Historical Studies, 25*, 1984, pp. 246–72.
Daly, Mary E., *Industrial development and Irish national identity, 1922–1939*, New York, Syracuse University Press, 1992.
Daly, Mary E., *The first department: A history of the Department of Agriculture*, Dublin, Institute of Public Administration, 2002.
Daly, Mary E., 'The Irish Free State and the Great Depression of the 1930s: The interaction of the global and the local', *Irish Economic and Social History, 38*, 2011, pp. 19–36.
Daniel, T. K., 'Griffith on his noble head, the determinants of Cumann na nGaedheal economic policy', *Irish Economic and Social History, 3*, 1976, pp. 55–66.
Deegan, Jim, Dineen, D. A., 'The tourism dimension to Irish economic development', in Ó Muircheartaigh, Fionnáin (ed.), *Ireland in the coming times: Essays to celebrate T. K. Whitaker's 80 Years*, Dublin, Institute of Public Administration, 1997, pp. 299–324.
De la Fuente, Angel, Vives, Xavier, 'The sources of Irish growth', in Gray, A. W. (ed.), *International perspectives on the Irish Economy*, Dublin, Indecon, 1997, pp. 112–32.

Delaney, Enda, *Demography, state and society: Irish migration to Britain, 1921–71*, Liverpool, Liverpool University Press, 2000.

Delaney, Enda, *The Irish in post-war Britain*, Oxford, Oxford University Press, 2007.

Delaney, Gerard, 'Electronics multinationals in the Cork region and Limerick/Shannon', *Irish Geography, 21*, 1988, pp. 101–3.

Delaney, Liam, 'Well-being under conditions of abundance: Ireland from 1990 to 2007', *Journal of the Statistical and Social Inquiry Society, 38*, 2009, pp. 205–20.

Dennison, S. R., MacDonagh, Oliver, *Guinness, 1886–1939: From incorporation to the Second World War*, Cork, Cork University Press, 1998.

Dooley, Terence, 'Land and politics in independent Ireland, 1923–48: The case for reappraisal', *Irish Historical Studies, 34*, 2004, pp. 175–98.

Dooley, Terence, '*The land for the people': The land question in independent Ireland*, Dublin, University College Dublin Press, 2004.

Doran, Justin, O' Leary, Eoin, 'External interaction, innovation and productivity: An application of the innovation value chain for Ireland', Cork, Department of Economics, University College Cork, 2010, available: http://www.ucc.ie/en/economics/research/workingpaperseries/downloads/wp10-eoin and justin.pdf

Doyle, Eleanor, 'Export-output causality and the role of exports in Irish growth: 1950–1997', *International Economic Journal, 15*, 3, pp. 1–24.

Doyle, Eleanor, Kavanagh, Catherine, 'Human capital and productivity in the Irish context', in Aylward, Ciaran, O' Toole, Ronnie (eds), *Perspectives on Irish productivity*, Dublin, Forfás, 2007, pp. 297–315.

Doyle, Eleanor, Gallagher, Liam. A., O' Leary, Eoin, 'Creating the Celtic Tiger and sustaining economic growth: A business perspective', in Duffy, David, Hore, J., MacCoille, Cathal, McCoy, Danny (eds), *Quarterly economic commentary, Spring 2002*, Dublin, Economic and Social Research Institute, 2002, pp. 63–79.

Duncan, G. A., 'The trade statistics of the Irish Free State', *Journal of the Statistical and Social Inquiry Society of Ireland, 16*, 1937–38, pp. 1–6.

Dunphy, Richard, *The making of Fianna Fáil power in Ireland, 1923–48*, Oxford, Clarendon Press, 1995.

Dwyer, D. J., Symons, L. J., 'The development and location of the textile industries in the Irish Republic', *Irish Geography, 4*, 1963, pp. 415–32.

Eichengreen, Barry, *The European economy since 1945: Coordinated capitalism and beyond*, Princeton, NJ, Princeton University Press, 2007.

Evans, Bryce, *Seán Lemass: Democratic dictator*, Collins Press, Cork, 2011.

Evans, Bryce, 'The Irish smallholder, the state and compulsory tillage 1939–45', *Irish Economic and Social History, 36*, 2011, pp. 1–18.

Everett, Mary, Kelly, John, 'Financial liberalisation and economic growth in Ireland', *Central Bank quarterly bulletin, Autumn 2004*, Dublin, Central Bank of Ireland, 2004, pp. 91–112.

Fahey, Tony, 'Trends in Irish fertility rates in comparative perspective', *Economic and Social Review, 32*, 2001, pp. 153–80.

Fahey, Tony, Duffy, David, 'The housing boom', in Fahey, Tony, Russell, Helen, Whelan, Christopher T. (eds), *Best of times? The social impact of the Celtic Tiger*, Dublin, Institute of Public Administration, 2007, pp. 123–38.

Fallon, Ivan, *The player: The life of Tony O' Reilly*, London, Hodder & Stoughton, 1994.

Fanning, Ronan, *The Irish Department of Finance*, Dublin, Institute of Public Administration, 1978.

Fanning, Ronan, 'Seán Lemass', in McGuire, James, Quinn, J. (eds), *Dictionary of Irish biography*, RIA, Cambridge University Press, 2009.

Farley, Noel. J., 'Determinants of establishment size in Irish manufacturing industries: Some notes on the Irish case 1931–72', *Economic and Social Review, 6*, 1974, pp. 187–211.

Federico, Giovanni, *Feeding the world: An economic history of agriculture, 1800–2000*, Princeton, NJ, Princeton University Press, 2000.

Feehan, J. *Farming in Ireland: History, heritage and environment*, Dublin, University College Dublin Press, 2003.

Fennell, R. 'The domestic market for Irish agricultural produce', in Baillie, I. F., Sheehy, S. J. (eds), *Irish agriculture in a changing world*, Newcastle-Upon-Tyne, Oliver & Boyd, 1971.

Ferriter, Diarmuid, *The transformation of Ireland*, London, Profile Books, 2006.

Findlater, Alex, *Findlaters: The story of a Dublin merchant family*, Dublin, Farmar, 2001.

Fingleton, John, 'Standards of competition in the Irish economy', *Journal of the Statistical and Social Inquiry Society of Ireland, 28*, IV, 1998, pp. 87–118.

Fingleton, John, 'Competition and efficiency in the services sector', in O' Hagan, John (ed.), *The economy of Ireland*, Dublin, Gill and Macmillan, 2005, pp. 296–328.

Fink, Philipp, *Late development in Hungary and Ireland*, Baden-Baden, Nomos, 2009.

Finn, Daniel, 'Ireland on the turn? Political and economic consequences of the crash', *New Left Review, 67*, 2011, pp. 5–41.

Fisk, Robert, *In time of war: Ireland, Ulster and the price of neutrality, 1939–45*, London, André Deutsch, 1983.

Fitzgerald, Garret, 'Mr Whitaker and industry', *Studies, 48*, 1959, pp. 138–50.

Fitzgerald, Garret, *All in a life: An autobiography*, Dublin, Gill and Macmillan, 1991.

Fitzgerald, John, 'The Irish housing stock: Growth in numbers of vacant dwellings', in Bergin, Adele, Duffy, David, Garrett, Shane, McCoy, Danny, McCarthy, Yvonne, (eds), *ESRI Quarterly Economic Commentary, Spring 2005*, Economic and Social Research Institute Dublin, 2005, pp.1–20.

Fitzgerald, John, 'Lessons from 20 years of cohesion', in Mundschenk, Susanne, Stierle, Michael, Stierle-von Schutz, Ulrike, Traistaru, Iulia (ed.), *Competitiveness and growth in Europe: Lessons and policy implications for the Lisbon strategy*, Cheltenham, Edward Elgar, 2006, pp. 66–101.

Fitzgerald, John, Morgenroth, Edgar, *Ex-ante evaluation of the investment priorities for the National Development Plan, 2007–2013*, Dublin, Economic and Social Research Institute, 2006.

Fitzgerald, John, Bergin, Adele, Conefrey, Thomas, Diffney, Sean, Duffy, David, Kearney, Ide, Lyons, Sean, Malaguzi Valeri, Laura, Mayor, Karen, Tol, Richard (eds), *ESRI Medium Term Review, 2008–2015*, Dublin, Economic and Social Research Institute, 2008.

Fitzgerald, Maurice, *Protectionism to liberalisation: Ireland and the EEC, 1957 to 1966*, Ashgate, Aldershot, 2000.

Fitzgerald, Maurice, 'Ireland's relations with the EEC: From the treaties of Rome to membership', *Journal of European Integration, 7*, 2001, pp. 11–24.

Fitzpatrick, David, *The two Irelands 1912–1939*, Oxford, Oxford University Press, 1998.

Foley, J., 'The Irish dairy industry: A historical perspective', *Journal of the Society of Dairy Technology, 46*, 1993, pp. 124–38.

Forde, Frank, *The long watch: The history of the Irish mercantile marine in World War Two*, Dublin, Gill and Macmillan, 1981.

Forde, Frank, *Maritime Arklow*, Dun Laoghaire, Glendale Press, 1988.

Foster, H. G., 'Ireland's trade with Britain', in Baillie, I. F., Sheehy, S. J. (eds), *Irish agriculture in a changing world*, Newcastle-Upon-Tyne, Oliver & Boyd, 1971, pp. 74–98.

Foy, Michael, *The sugar industry in Ireland,* Dublin, Cómhlucht Siúicre Éireann Teo, 1976.
Furlong, Irene, *Irish tourism:1880–1980,* Dublin, Irish Academic Press, 2009.
Galvin, Sharon, 'The chemical industry in Ireland', *Chemistry in Action, 54,* 1998, pp. 5–10.
Garvin, Tom, *Preventing the future: Why was Ireland poor for so long?,* Dublin, Gill and Macmillan, 2004.
Garvin, Tom, *Judging Lemass,* Dublin, Royal Irish Academy, 2009.
Geary, Michael, J., *An inconvenient wait: Ireland's quest for membership of the EEC, 1957–1973,* Dublin, Institute of Public Administration, 2009.
Geary, R. C., 'Irish economic development since the Treaty', *Studies, xl,* 1951, pp. 399–418.
Geiger, Till, 'Why Ireland needed the Marshall Plan but did not want it: Ireland, the Sterling area and the European Recovery Programme, 1947–8', *Irish Studies in International Affairs, 11,* 2000, pp. 193–215.
Gilligan, H. A., *A history of the port of Dublin,* Dublin, Gill and Macmillan, 1988.
Gilmour, D. A., 'The spatial structure of agricultural output in the Republic of Ireland', *Economic and Social Review, 8,* 1977, pp. 130–41.
Gilmour, D. A., *Economic activities in the Republic of Ireland: A geographic perspective,* Dublin, Gill and Macmillan, 1985.
Gilmour, D. A., 'Concentration of enterprises and spatial change in the agriculture of the Republic of Ireland', *Transactions of the Institute of British Geographers, 12,* 1987, pp. 204–16.
Gilmour, D. A., 'Republic of Ireland: An expanding tourism industry', in Williams, Allan M., Shaw, Gareth (eds), *Tourism and economic development,* London, John Wiley & Son, 1998, 3rd edition.
Gilmour, D. A., 'Land and people, *c.*1926', in Hill, J. R. (ed.), *A new history of Ireland, Vol. VII, Ireland, 1921–84,* Oxford, Oxford University Press, 2003, pp. 62–86.
Gilmour, D. A., 'Land and people, *c.* 1983', in Hill, J. R. (ed.), *A new history of Ireland, Vol. VII, Ireland, 1921–84,* Oxford, Oxford University Press, 2003, pp. 426–52.
Girvin, Brian, *Between two worlds: Politics and economy in independent Ireland,* Dublin, Gill and Macmillan, 1989.
Girvin, Brian, 'Irish agricultural policy and the green pool', in Girvin, Brian, Griffith, Richard T. (eds), *The green pool and the origins of the Common Agricultural Policy,* London, Lothian, 1995, pp. 239–59.
Girvin, Brian, 'Ireland and the Marshall Plan: A North Atlantic cargo cult', in Griffith, Richard T. (ed.), *Explorations in OEEC history,* Paris, OECD, 1997, pp. 61–71.
Girvin, Brian, 'Political culture, political independence and economic success in Ireland', *Irish Political Studies, 12,* 1997, pp. 48–77.
Girvin, Brian, 'Did Ireland benefit from the Marshall Plan? Choice, strategy and the national interest in a comparative context', in Geiger, Till, Kennedy, Michael (ed.), *Ireland, Europe and the Marshall Plan,* Dublin, Four Courts Press, 2004, pp. 182–220.
Girvin, Brian, *The emergency: Neutral Ireland 1939–45,* London, Macmillan, 2006.
Girvin, Brian, 'Economic policy, continuity and crisis in de Valera's Ireland, 1945–61', *Irish Economic and Social History, 38,* 2011, pp. 36–54.
Görg, Holger, 'Productivity spillovers from multinationals companies', in Aylward, Ciaran, O' Toole, Ronnie (eds), *Perspectives on Irish productivity,* Dublin, Forfás, 2007, pp. 241–9.
Görg, Holger, Ruane, Frances, 'Aspects of foreign direct investment in Irish manufacturing since 1973: Policy and performance', *Journal of the Statistical and Social Inquiry Society of Ireland, 27,* 1997, pp. 37–93.

Gould, F., 'The growth of public expenditure in Ireland 1947–77', *Administration, 29*, 1981, pp. 115–35.

Greenspan, Alan, *The age of turbulence*, London, Penguin, 2008.

Grimes, Séamus, 'Ireland's emergence as a centre for internationally traded services', *Regional Studies, 40*, 2006, pp. 1041–54.

Grimes, Séamus, White, Mark, 'The transition to internationally traded services and Ireland's emergence as a successful European region', *Environment and Planning, 37*, 2005, pp. 2169–88.

Guerin, Joe, *A history of North Cork co-op*, Kanturk, North Cork Co-operative, 2007.

Guiomard, Cathal, *The Irish disease and how to cure it: Common-sense economics in a competitive world*, Dublin, Oak Tree Press, 2005.

Guiomard, Cathal, O' Connor, R., 'Agricultural output in the Irish Free State area before and after independence', *Irish Economic and Social History, 12*, 1985, pp. 89–97.

Hallier, Stephaine, 'The distribution of productivity in Irish manufacturing, 1995–2003', in Aylward, Ciaran, O' Toole, Ronnie (eds), *Perspectives on Irish productivity*, Dublin, Forfás, 2007, pp. 402–6.

Hamilton, Rob, 'Education, demographics and the Irish economic miracle', *Central Bank quarterly bulletin, 2*, 2003, pp. 103–30.

Hannan, D. F., Commins, P., 'The significance of small scale landholders in Ireland's socio-economic transformation', in Goldthorpe, J. H., Whelan, C. T., (eds), *The development of industrial society in Ireland*, Oxford, Oxford University Press, 1992, pp. 79–104.

Hardiman, Niamh, *Pay, politics and economic performance in Ireland, 1970–1987*, Oxford, Clarendon Press, 1988.

Hastings, Tim, Sheehan, Brian Yeates, Padraig, *Saving the future: How social partnership shaped Ireland's economic success*, Dublin, Blackhall, 2007.

Hay, C., Smith, Nicola Jo-Anne, 'Horses for courses: The political discourse of globalisation and European integration in the UK and Ireland', *West European Politics, 28*, 2005, pp. 124–58.

Healy, John, *No one shouted stop!*, Achill, House of Healy, 1988.

Healy, Tom, Kennedy, Kieran A., 'Small-scale industry in Ireland', in Fitzpatrick, Jim, Kelly, John. H., (eds), *Perspectives on Irish industry*, Dublin, Irish Management Institute, 1985, pp. 47–93.

Hearne, John, 'Industry in Waterford city 1932–1962', in Nolan, William, Power, Thomas, P. (eds), *Waterford history and society*, Dublin, Geography Publications, 1992, pp. 685–706.

Hearne, Mona, *Below stairs: Domestic service remembered in Dublin and beyond, 1880–1922*, Dublin, Lilliput Press, 1993.

Hederman, Miriam, *The road to Europe: Irish attitudes 1948–1961*, Dublin, Institute of Public Administration, 1983.

Hewitt-Dundas, Nola, Roper, Stephen, 'Ireland's innovation performance: 1991–2005', in Barrett, Alan, Kearney, Ide, O' Brien, Martin (eds), *ESRI Quarterly Economic Commentary, Summer 2008*, Dublin, Economic and Social Research Institute, pp. 46–68.

Hogan, Sarsfield, *A history of Irish steel*, Dublin, Gill and Macmillan, 1980.

Honohan, Patrick, 'Fiscal adjustment and disinflation in Ireland: Setting the macro basis of economic recovery and expansion', in Barry, Frank (ed.), *Understanding Ireland's economic growth*, London, Macmillan, 1999, pp. 75–98.

Honohan, Patrick, 'To what extent has finance been a driver of Ireland's economic success', in Barrett, Alan, Kearney, Ide, McCarthy, Yvonne (eds), *Quarterly Economic*

Commentary Winter 2006, Dublin, Economic and Social Research Institute, 2006, pp. 59–72.

Honohan, Patrick, 'Resolving Ireland's banking crisis', *Economic and Social Review, 40*, 2, 2009, pp. 207–31.

Honohan, Patrick, Ó Gráda, Cormac, 'The Irish macroeconomic crisis of 1955–56: How much was due to monetary policy?', *Irish Economic and Social History, 25*, 1998, pp. 52–80.

Honohan, Patrick, Walsh, Brendan, 'Catching up with the leaders: The Irish Hare', *Brookings papers on Economic Activity, 1*, 2002, pp. 1–57.

Honohan, Patrick, Leddin, Anthony, J., 'Ireland in EMU: More shocks, less insulation', *Economic and Social Review, 37*, 2006, pp. 263–94.

Horner, A. A., 'Geographic diffusion in Ireland: The example of Credit Unions, 1956–82', in Bender, Rainer Joha (ed.), *Neure forschungen zur sozialgeographie von Irland*, Mannheim, 1984, pp. 191–219.

Horner, A. A., Walsh, James, A., 'Regional aspects of agricultural production in Ireland, 1970–1980', *Irish Geography, 17*, 1984, pp. 95–101.

Hourihan, Kevin, Spillane, Neil, 'Manufacturing change in Cork City, 1977–1986', *Irish Geography, 22*, 1989, pp. 13–21.

Humphrey, Madeline, 'An issue of confidence: The decline of the Irish whiskey industry in independent Ireland 1922–1952', *Journal of European Economic History, 23*, 1994, pp. 93–113.

Hyland, Aíne, *Entry to higher education in Ireland in the 21st century*, Dublin, Higher Education Authority, 2011.

Jacobsen, John Kurt, *Chasing progress in the Irish Republic: Ideology, democracy and dependent development*, Cambridge, Cambridge University Press, 1994.

Jacobson, David, Van Egeraat, Chris, 'Information exchange and the geography of production linkages: The microcomputer industry in Ireland and Scotland' (working paper no. 26, National Institute for Regional and Spatial Analysis, NUI Maynooth), 2005.

Johnson, David S., *The interwar economy in Ireland*, Dublin, Economic and Social History Society of Ireland, 1989.

Johnson, David S., Kennedy, Liam, 'The two economies in Ireland in the twentieth century', in Hill, J. R. (ed.), *A new history of Ireland, VII, Ireland, 1921–84*, Oxford, Oxford University Press, 2003, pp. 452–86.

Jones, Michael, 'Was this the first chain store in Ireland? P. & J. Ryan Ltd, Ardnageeha, Charleville', *Charleville and district Historical Journal, 6*, 1992, pp. 33–7.

Jones, Richard C., 'Multinational investment and return migration in Ireland in the 1990s: A country level analysis', *Irish Geography, 36*, 2003, pp. 153–69.

Jordan, Declan, O' Leary, Eoin, 'The roles of interaction and proximity for innovation by Irish high-technology business: Policy implications', in McCoy, Daniel, Duffy, David, Bergin, Adele, Garrett, Shane and McCarthy Yvonne (eds), *ESRI Quarterly Economic Commentary, Summer 2005*, Dublin, Economic and Social Research Institute, pp. 86–100.

Jordan, Declan, O' Leary, Eoin, 'Is Irish innovation policy working? Evidence from Irish technology business', *Journal of the Statistical and Social Inquiry Society of Ireland, 37*, 2008, pp. 1–43.

Kavanagh, Ella, 'Independence, conservatism and interest rate setting in Ireland', Political Studies Association of Ireland, Annual Conference 2006, available: http://www.psai.ie/conferences/papers2006/kavanaghe.pdf (accessed 1 June 2012).

Kavanagh, Ella, O' Leary, Eoin, Shinnick, Edward, 'The role of airport infrastructure in regional development: The role of Cork Airport', in O' Leary, Eoin (ed.), *Irish regional development: A new agenda*, Dublin, Liffey Press, 2003, pp. 181–201.

Kearney, B., O' Connor, R., 'Economic issues in Irish forestry', *Journal of the Statistical and Social Inquiry Society of Ireland, 26*, 1993, pp. 170–209.

Kearns, Allan, Woods, Maria, 'The concentration in property-related lending: A financial stability perspective', *Central Bank Financial Stability Report 2006*, Dublin, Central Bank of Ireland, 2006, pp. 133–44.

Keating, William, 'Measuring the economy: Problems and prospects', *Journal of the Statistical and Social Inquiry Society of Ireland, XXX*, 2000–01, pp. 1–32.

Kelly, Catherine, 'Tourism and heritage', in Bartley, Brendan, Kitchin, Robert (eds), *Understanding contemporary Ireland*, London, Pluto Press, 2007, pp. 170–80.

Kelly, Morgan, 'On the likely extent of falls in Irish house prices', Dublin, University College Dublin, Centre for Economic Research, Working Paper Series, 2007 (WP07/01).

Kelly, Morgan, 'The Irish credit bubble', in Kinsella, Stephen, Leddin, Anthony J. (eds), *Understanding Ireland's economic crisis: Prospects for recovery*, Dublin, Blackhall, 2010, pp. 57–87.

Kennedy, Finola, *Cottage to creche: Family change in Ireland*, Dublin, Institute of Public Administration, 2000.

Kennedy, Kieran. A., *Productivity and industrial growth: The Irish experience*, Oxford, Clarendon Press, 1971.

Kennedy, Kieran, A., *Facing the unemployment crisis in Ireland*, Cork, Cork University Press, 1993.

Kennedy, Kieran A., 'Reflections on the process of Irish economic growth', *Journal of the Statistical and Social Inquiry Society of Ireland, 30*, 2002, pp. 124–35.

Kennedy, Kieran, A., Giblin, T., McHugh, Deirdre, *The economic development of Ireland in the twentieth century*, London, Routledge, 1988.

Kennedy, Liam, *The modern industrialisation of Ireland, 1940–1988*, Dublin, Economic and Social History Society of Ireland, 1989.

Kennedy Liam, *People and population change: A comparative study of population change in Northern Ireland and the Republic of Ireland*, Dublin and Belfast, Co-operation North, 1994.

Kennelly, J. J., *The Kerry way: The history of the Kerry Group, 1972–2000*, Dublin, Oak Tree Press, 2001.

Keogh, Dermot, *Jack Lynch, a biography*, Dublin, Gill and Macmillan, 2008.

Kirby, Peadar, *Celtic Tiger in collapse: Explaining the weaknesses of the Irish model*, Basingstoke, Palgrave Macmillan, 2010.

Kitchen, Rob, Gleeson, Justin, Keaveney, Karen, O' Callaghan, Cian, 'A haunted landscape: Housing and ghost estates in post-Celtic Tiger Ireland', Maynooth, National Institute for Regional and Spatial Analysis, 2010 (working paper no. 59), available: http://www.nuim.ie/nirsa/researchdocument/swp59.

Krugman, Paul, 'Good news from Ireland: A geographical perspective', in Gray, Alan, W. (ed.), *International perspectives on the Irish Economy*, Dublin, Indecon, 1997, pp. 38–53.

Laffan, Brigid, O' Mahony, Jane, *Ireland and the European Union*, London, Palgrave, 2008.

Lane, Philip. R. 'Profits and wages in Ireland, 1987–1996', *Journal of the Statistical and Social Inquiry Society of Ireland, XXII*, V, 1998, pp. 223–52.

Lane, Philip R., Ruane, Frances, 'Globalisation and the Irish economy', Dublin, Irish International Integration Studies Centre, Trinity College Dublin, 2006.

Laugn, Luc, Valencia, Fabian, 'Systemic banking crisis database: An update', IMF Working Paper, WP/12/163, Washington DC, IMF, 2012.

Lawless, Martina, 'Destinations of Irish exports: A gravity model approach', *Journal of the Statistical and Social Inquiry Society of Ireland, 39*, 2010, pp. 1–23.

Lawless, Martina, Murphy, Alan, 'Job gains and losses: Manufacturing and internationally traded services', *Central Bank Quarterly Bulletin, January 2008*, Dublin, Central Bank of Ireland, Dublin, 2008, pp. 91–104.
Leddin, Anthony, 'The Philips curve and the wage-inflation process in Ireland', in Kinsella, Stephen, Leddin, Anthony (eds), *Understanding Ireland's economic crisis: Prospects for recovery*, Dublin, Blackhall, 2010, pp. 159–79.
Leddin, Anthony, Walsh, Brendan, *The macroeconomy of the Eurozone: An Irish perspective*, Dublin, Gill and Macmillan, 2003.
Lee, J. J., *Ireland 1912–85: Politics and Society*, Cambridge, Cambridge University Press, 1989.
Lee, J. J., 'From Empire to Europe: the Irish State, 1922–73', in Adshead, M., Kirby, P., Millar, M. (ed), *Contesting the state: Lessons from the Irish case*, Manchester, Manchester University Press, 2008, pp. 25–50.
Leland, Mary, *That endless adventure: A history of the of the Cork Harbour Commissioners*, Cork, Port of Cork, 2001.
Lewis, C. A., 'Recognition and development of the Irish draught horse', in McGrath, M., Griffith, J. C. (eds), *The Irish draught horse: A history*, Cork, Collins Press, 2005, pp. 146–67.
Linehan, Thomas P., 'The structure of Irish industry', *Journal of the Statistical and Social Inquiry Society of Ireland, 20*, 1961–62, pp. 220–53.
Long, Francis, 'Foreign capital and development strategy in Irish industrialization 1958–70', *American Journal of Economic Sociology, 39*, 1980, pp. 137–50.
Loyal, Steven, *Understanding immigration in Ireland: State, capital and labour in a global age*, Manchester, Manchester University Press, 2011.
Lynch-Brennan, Margaret, *The Irish Bridget: Irish immigrant women in domestic service in America, 1840–1930*, New York, Syracuse University Press, 2009.
McAleese, Dermot, 'Capital inflow and direct foreign investment in Ireland 1952–1970', *Journal of the Statistical and Social Inquiry Society of Ireland, 22*, 1971–72, pp. 63–105.
McAleese, Dermot, 'Do tariffs matter? Industrial specialization and trade in a small open economy', *Oxford Economic Papers, 29*, 1977.
McAleese, Dermot, 'Economic policy and performance: The Irish experience', *Journal of the Statistical and Social Inquiry Society of Ireland, 27*, 1998, pp. 3–15.
McAleese, Dermot, 'Twenty-five years a growing', in O' Donnell, Rory (ed.), *Europe: The Irish experience*, Dublin, Institute of European Affairs, 2000, pp. 79–105.
McCann, Gerard, *Ireland's economic history: Crisis and development in the north and south*, London, Pluto Press, 2011.
McCarthy, Diarmuid, 'The Cadbury-Ireland (Ltd) factory, Rathmore', *Sliabh Luachra, Journal of Cumann Luachra, 4*, 1987, pp. 31–4.
McCarthy, John F., 'Ireland's turnaround: Whitaker and the 1958 Plan for Economic Development', in McCarthy, John F. (ed.), *Planning Ireland's future: The legacy of T. K. Whitaker*, Dublin, Glendale Publications, 1990, pp. 11–74.
MacCormac, M. J., 'Crisis in Ireland's balance of trade', *Studies, 32*, 1951, pp. 257–69.
McDonald, D., 'Issues in industrial development policy', in O' Hagan, J. W. (ed.), *The economy of Ireland*, Dublin, Irish Management Institute, 2005.
McDonald, Frank, Sheridan, Kathy, *The builders*, Dublin, Penguin, 2008.
MacEinrí, Piarais, 'Immigration: Labour migrants, asylum seekers and refugees', in Bartley, Brendan, Kitchin, Robert (eds), *Understanding contemporary Ireland*, London, Pluto Press, 2007, pp. 236–49.
MacFeely, Steve, 'A statistical analysis of Irish domestic tourism', *Journal of the Statistical and Social Inquiry Society of Ireland, 36*, 2007, pp. 125–66.

McGrath, Michael, Somers, Peter, *Golden Vale remembered, 1948–2001*, Charleville, County Cork, McGrath & Somers, 2006.
McHugh, Deirdre, 'Trade growth and the role of demand: The experience of Ireland since 1947', *Journal of the Statistical and Social Inquiry Society of Ireland, 25*, 1984–5, pp. 221–38.
MacMahon, Deirdre, *Republicans and Imperialists: Anglo-Irish relations in the 1930s*, New Haven, CT, Yale University Press, 1984.
MacSharry, Ray, White, Paraic, *The making of the Celtic Tiger: The inside story of Ireland's boom economy*, Dublin, Mercier Press, 2000.
McWilliams, David, *The Pope's children, Ireland's new elite*, Dublin, Gill and Macmillan, 2005.
McWilliams, David, *The generation game*, Dublin, Gill and Macmillan, 2007.
McWilliams, David, *Follow the money: The Tale of the Merchant of Venice*, Dublin, Gill and Macmillan, 2009.
Maddison, Angus, *The world economy*, Paris, OECD, 2006.
Maddock, J., *Rosslare Harbour: Past and present*, Rosslare, Harbour Publications, 1986.
Maher, Denis. J., *The tortuous path: The course of Ireland's entry into the EEC*, Dublin, Institute of Public Administration, 1986.
Manning, Maurice, 'The farmers', in Lee, J. J. (ed.), *Ireland, 1945–70*, Dublin, Gill and Macmillan, 1979, pp. 48–60.
Manning, Maurice, *James Dillon: A biography*, Dublin Wolfhound Press, 1999.
Manning, Maurice, McDowell, Moore, *Electricity supply in Ireland: The history of the ESB*, Dublin, Gill and Macmillan, 1985.
Massey, Patrick, 'Is Irish utility regulation failing consumers?', in McCoy, Danny, Duffy, David, Bergin, Adele, Garrett, Shane, McCarthy, Yvonne (eds), *ESRI Quarterly Economic Commentary, Winter 2004*, Dublin, Economic and Social Research Institute, 2004, pp. 1–18.
Matthews, Alan, 'The state and Irish agriculture: 1950–1980', in Drudy, P. J. (ed.), *Irish studies, Vol. IV, Ireland: Land, politics and people*, Cambridge, Cambridge University Press, 1982, pp. 241–71.
Matthews, Alan, 'Productivity growth in Irish agriculture', *Journal of the Statistical and Social Inquiry Society of Ireland, 29*, 2000, pp. 317–67.
Matthews, Alan, 'Agriculture, rural development and food safety', in O' Hagan, John, Newman, Carol (eds), *The economy of Ireland: National and sectoral policy issues*, Dublin, Gill and Macmillan, Dublin, 2005, pp. 215–44.
Matthews, Alan, 'The agri-food sector', in O' Hagan, John, Newman, Carol, (eds), *The economy of Ireland*, Dublin, Gill and Macmillan, 2011.
Matthews, Alan, O' Connor, R., 'The food processing industry', in Bradley, J., Fitzgerald, J., Storey, R. A. (eds), *ESRI Medium-Term Review, 1987–1992*, Dublin, Economic and Social Research Institute, 1987.
Matthews, Alan, Newman, Carol, Thorne, Fiona, 'Productivity in Irish agriculture', in Alyward, Ciaran, O' Toole, Ronnie (eds), *Perspectives on Irish productivity*, Dublin, Forfás, 2007 pp. 116–30.
Meenan, James, *The Irish economy since 1922*, Liverpool, Liverpool University Press, 1970.
Meenan, James, 'Irish Agricultural policies in the last twenty years', in Baillie, I. F., Sheehy, S. J. (eds), *Irish agriculture in a changing world*, Edinburgh, 1971, pp. 44–73.
Miley, Michael, 'Establishment and evolution of An Foras Talúntais', in Miley, Michael (ed.), *Growing knowledge: Fifty years of research and development in Irish farming and food*, Carlow, Teagasc, 2008, pp. 13–43.

Miley, Michael, 'Soils, grass and environmental research at Johnstown Castle', in Miley, Michael (ed.), *Growing knowledge: Fifty years of research and development in Irish farming and food*, Carlow, Teagasc, 2008, pp. 43–61.

Mitchell, B. R., *European historical statistics, 1750–1975*, London, Macmillan, 1981.

Mjøset, Lars, *The Irish economy in a comparative institutional perspective*, Dublin, National Economic and Social Council, 1992.

Mooney, J., O' Gorman, C., O' Malley, Eoin, *Clusters in Ireland: The Irish indigenous software industry – An application of Porter's Cluster Analysis*, Dublin, National Economic and Social Council, 1997.

Morgenroth, Edgar, 'The National Spatial Strategy: Regional, urban and rural development', in Fitzgerald, John, Morgenroth, Edgar (eds), *Ex-ante evaluation of the investment priorities for the National Development Plan, 2007–2013*, Dublin, Economic and Social Research Institute of Ireland, 2006, pp. 75–98.

Moynihan, Maurice, *Currency and central banking in Ireland, 1922–1960*, Dublin, Gill and Macmillan, 1975.

Munck, Ronnie, *The Irish economy: Results and prospects*, London, Pluto Press, 1993.

Murphy, Antoin E., 'The "Celtic Tiger": An analysis of Ireland's economic growth performance', Florence, European University Institute, Robert Schumann Centre for Advanced Studies(working paper, RSC no. 2000/16, 2000), available: http://www.eui.eu/RSCAS/wp-texts/00.16.pdf (accessed 01/09/2010).

Murphy, Gary, 'The Irish Government, the National Farmers' Association and the European Economic Community, 1955–1964', *New Hibernia Review, 6*, 4, 2002, pp. 68–84.

Murphy, Gary, 'From economic nationalism to European Union', in Girvin, Brian, Murphy, Gary (eds), *The Lemass era: Politics and society in the Ireland of Seán Lemass*, Dublin, University College Dublin Press, 2005, pp. 28–48.

Murray, Joe, *Glanbia: The story so far*, Kilkenny, Glanbia, 2007.

Murray, Joe, 'From grass to milk: The Moorepark story', in Miley, Michael (ed.), *Growing knowledge: Fifty years of research and development in Irish farming and food*, Carlow, Teagasc, 2008, pp. 61–77.

Murray, K. A., McNeill, D. B., *The Great Southern and Western Railway*, Wicklow, Irish Railway Record Society, 1976.

Murray, P., Wickham, J., 'Technocratic ideology and the reproduction of inequality: The case of the electronics industry in the Republic of Ireland', in Day, G. (ed.), *Diversity and decomposition in the labour market*, Gower, 1982, pp. 179–210.

Neary, J. P., Ó Gráda, Cormac, 'Protection, economic war and structural change: The 1930s in Ireland', *Irish Historical Studies, 27*, 1991, pp. 250–63.

Neenan, M. 'Agriculture in the new state', in Curran, P. L. (ed.), *Towards a history of agricultural science in Ireland*, The Agricultural Science Association, Dublin, 1992, pp. 98–117.

Neill-Watson, J., *A history of farm mechanization in Ireland, 1890–1990*, Dublin, Farm Tractor and Machinery Trade Association, 1993.

Newman, Carol, 'The impact of globalisation and trade on the productivity performance of the Irish food manufacturing sector', Dublin, Irish International Integration Studies Centre, Trinity College Dublin, 2006 (discussion paper no. 180).

Newman, Carol, 'Education: Market failure and government intervention', in O' Hagan, John, Newman, Carol (eds), *The economy of Ireland: National and sectoral policy issues*, Dublin, Gill and Macmillan, 2011, pp. 349–72.

Ní Laoire, Catríona, '"Settling Back?": A biographical and life course perspective on Ireland's recent migration', *Irish Geography, 41*, 2009, pp. 195–210.

Nugent, Jim, 'Corporate profitability in Ireland: Overview and determinants', *Journal of the Statistical and Social Inquiry Society of Ireland, 38*, 1, 1999, pp. 35–82.

Nyhan, Miriam.A., 'Narration and memory, the experiences of the workforce of a Ford Plant', *Irish Economic and Social History,* 33, 2006, pp. 18–34.

Nyhan, Miriam A, *Are you still below: A history of the Ford Marina Plant*, Cork, Collins Press, 2007.

O'Brennan, John,'Ireland and the European Union: Mapping domestic modes of adaption and contestation', in Hogan, John, Donnelly, Paul. F., O' Rourke, Brendan K. (eds), *Irish business and society, participating and transforming in the 21st century*, Dublin, Oak Tree Press, 2010, pp. 379–97.

O'Brien, Anne, *The politics of tourism development: Booms and busts in Ireland*, Palgrave Macmillan, London, 2011.

O'Brien, Ronan, 'Technology and industrial development: The Irish electronics industry in an international context', in Fitzpatrick, J., Kelly, John (eds), *Perspectives on Irish industry*, Dublin, Irish Management Institute, 1985, pp. 197–255.

Ó Broin, Leon, *No man's man, a biographical memoir of Joseph Brennan: Civil servant and first Governor of the Central Bank*, Dublin, Institute of Public Administration, 1982.

Ó Buchalla, Séamus, *Education policy in twentieth-century Ireland*, Dublin, Wolfhound Press, 1988.

O'Connell, Larry, Van Egeraat, Chris, Enright, Pat, *The Irish dairy processing industry: An application of Porter's cluster analysis*, Dublin, National Economic and Social Council, 1997.

O'Connor, R., Crutchfield, J. A., Whelan, B. J., Mellon, K. E., *Development of the Irish sea fishing industry and its regional implications*, Dublin, Economic and Social Research Institute, 1980.

O'Donovan, John, *The economic history of livestock in Ireland*, Cork, Cork University Press, 1940.

Ó Drisceoil, Diarmuid, Ó Drisceoil, Donal, *The Murphy's story, the history of Lady's Well Brewery, Cork*, Cork, Murphy's Brewery, 1997.

Ó Drisceoil, Diarmuid, Ó Drisceoil, Donal, *Fifty years have flown: The history of Cork Airport*, Cork, Collins Press, 2011.

O'Driscoll, Mervyn, 'The economic war and Irish foreign trade policy: Irish–German commerce 1932–9', *Irish Journal in International Affairs, 10*, 1999, pp. 71–89.

Ó Fathartaigh, Mícheál, 'Cumann na nGaedheal, sea fishing and west Galway, 1923–32', *Irish Historical Studies, 36*, 141, 2008, pp. 72–91.

O'Flaherty, C., 'The problem of parking', *The Institution of Civil Engineers of Ireland, 91*, 1965, pp. 206–65.

Ó Gráda, Cormac, 'Irish agriculture north and south since 1900', Campbell, B., Overton, M. (eds), *Land, labour and livestock: Historical studies in European agricultural productivity*, Manchester, Manchester University Press, 1991.

Ó Gráda, Cormac, *Ireland, a new economic history, 1780–1939*, Oxford, Oxford University Press, 1994.

Ó Gráda, Cormac, 'Money and banking in the Irish Free State', in Feinstein, Charles H. (ed.), *Banking, currency and finance in Europe between the wars*, Oxford, Oxford University Press, 1995, pp. 414–33.

Ó Gráda, Cormac, *A rocky road: The Irish economy since the 1920s*, Manchester, Manchester University Press, 1997.

Ó Gráda, Cormac, 'From "frugal comfort" to ten thousand a year: Trade and growth in the Irish economy', in Ryan, Ray (ed.), *Writing in the Irish Republic: Literature, culture, politics 1949–99*, Basingstoke, Macmillan, 2000.

Ó Gráda, Cormac, 'Is the Celtic Tiger a paper tiger?', in Duffy, David, Hore, J., MacCoille, Cathal, McCoy, Danny (eds), *ESRI Quarterly Economic Commentary, Spring 2002*, Dublin, Economic and Social Research Institute, 2002, pp. 51–62.

Ó Gráda, Cormac, 'The Irish economy half a century ago', in Miley, Michael (ed.), *Growing knowledge: Fifty years of research and development in Irish farming and food*, Carlow, Teagasc, 2008, pp. 1–13.

Ó Gráda, Cormac, O' Rourke, Kevin, 'Irish economic growth, 1945–88', in Crafts, Nick, Toniolo, Giannai (eds), *Economic growth in Europe since 1945*, Cambridge, Cambridge University Press, 1996, pp. 388–427.

O'Hagan, John, Harrison, M., 'UK and US visitor expenditure in Ireland: Some economic findings', *The Economic and Social Review, 15*, 1984.

O'Hagan, John, McIndoe-Calder, Tara, 'Population, employment and unemployment', in O' Hagan, John, Newman, Carol (eds), *The economy of Ireland: National and sectoral policy issues*, Dublin, Gill and Macmillan, 2011, pp. 138–70.

O'Hara, P., *Partners in production? Women, farm and family in Ireland*, New York, Berghahn Books, 1998.

O'Hearn, Denis, *The Atlantic economy: Britain, the US and Ireland*, Manchester, Manchester University press, 2001.

O'Hearn, Denis, 'Macroeconomic policy in the Celtic Tiger: A critical reassessment', in Coulter, Carol, Coleman Shane (eds), *The end of Irish history? Critical reflections on the Celtic Tiger*, Manchester, Manchester University Press, 2003.

O'Leary, Eoin, 'The convergence performance of Ireland among EU countries: 1960–1990', *Journal of Economic Studies, 24*, 1, 1997, pp. 43–58.

O'Leary, Eoin, 'Regional income estimates for Ireland, 1995', *Regional Studies, 33*, 9, 1999, pp. 805–14.

O'Leary, Eoin,'Convergence of living standards among Irish regions: The roles of productivity, profit outflows and demography, 1960–1996', *Regional Studies, 35*, 3, 2001, pp. 197–205.

O'Leary, Eoin, 'Sources of regional divergence in the "Celtic Tiger": Policy responses', *Journal of the Statistical and Social Inquiry Society of Ireland, 32*, 2003, pp. 2–32.

O'Leary, Eoin, 'Reflecting on the "Celtic Tiger": Before, during and after', *Irish Economic and Social History, 38*, 2011, pp. 73–89.

O'Mahony, David, *The Irish economy*, Cork, Cork University Press, 1967.

O'Malley, Eoin, *Industry and economic development: The challenge for the latecomer*, Dublin, Gill and Macmillan, 1989.

O'Malley, Eoin, 'The revival of Irish Indigenous Industry 1987–1997', in Baker, T. J., Duffy, David, Shortall, Fergal (ed.), *ESRI Quarterly Economic Commentary, April 1998*, Dublin, Economic and Social Research Institute, 1998, pp. 35–57.

O'Malley, Eoin, Van Egeraat, Chris, 'Industry clusters and Irish indigenous manufacturing: Limits of the Porter view', *Economic and Social Review, 31*, 2000, pp. 55–79.

O'Malley, Eoin, McCarthy, Yvonne, 'New drivers of growth? Sectoral contributors to the Irish economy', in Barrett, A., Kearney, Ide, McCarthy, Yvonne (eds), *ESRI Quarterly Economic Commentary, Summer 2006*, pp. 30–62.

O'Neill, T., 'Tools and things: Machinery on Irish farms, 1700–1981', in Gailey, Alan, Ó Hogáin, Daithí (ed.), *Gold under the Furze: Studies in folk tradition*, Dublin, Glendale Press, 1982.

Ó Riain, Mícheal, *'On the move': Coras Iompair Éireann, 1945–1995*, Dublin, Gill and Macmillan, 1995.

Ó Riain, Seán, *The politics of high-tech growth: Developmental network states in the Global Economy*, Cambridge, Cambridge University Press, 2004.

O'Riordan, Cecil, *Development of Ireland's power system: 1927 to 1997*, Dublin Eirgrid, 2000.
O'Rourke, Kevin, 'Burn everything British but their coal: The Anglo-Irish economic war of the 1930s', *The Journal of Economic History, 51*, 1991, pp. 357–66,
O'Sullivan, Michael J., *Ireland and the global question*, Cork, Cork University Press, 2006.
O'Sullivan, P. J., 'An assessment of Ireland's export-led growth strategy via foreign direct investment: 1960–1980', *Weltwirtschaftliches Archiv, 129*, 1993, pp. 131–58.
O'Toole, Francis, 'Competition Policy, regulation and non-internationally traded services', in O' Hagan, John, Newman, Carol (eds), *The economy of Ireland: National and sectoral policy issues*, Dublin, Gill and Macmillan, 2005, pp. 188–215.
Olson, Mancur, *The rise and decline of nations: Economic growth, stratification and social rigidities*, New Haven, CT, Yale University press, 1982.
Orridge, Andrew W., 'The Blueshirts and the "economic war": A study of Ireland in the context of dependency theory', *Political Studies, 31*, 1983, pp. 351–69.
Palcic, Dónal, Reeves, Eoin, 'An economic analysis of privatisation in Ireland 1991–2003', *Journal of the Statistical and Social Inquiry Society of Ireland, XXIV*, 2004, pp. 1–24.
Paus, Eva, *Foreign investment, development and globalisation: Can Costa Rica become Ireland?*, London, Palgrave Macmillan, 2005.
Peterson, Basil, *Turn of the tide: An outline of Irish maritime history*, Dublin, Irish Shipping Ltd, 1962.
Power, Con, *Metamorphosis: Lessons from the formative years of the Celtic Tiger, 1979–1993*, Dublin, Oak Tree Press, 2009.
Pratschke, J., 'The establishment of the Irish Pound: A backward glance', *Economic and Social Review, 1*, 1969–70, pp. 51–75.
Press, J. P., 'Protectionism and the Irish footwear industry, 1932–39', *Irish Economic and Social History, 13*, 1986, pp. 74–89.
Press, J. P., *The footwear industry in Ireland 1922–1973*, Dublin, Irish Academic Press, 1989.
Quill, Patrick, Teahon, Paddy, 'Structural economic change in Ireland, 1957–2006: Statistics, context and analysis', *Journal of the Statistical and Social Inquiry Society of Ireland, 39*, 2010, pp. 110–44.
Rae, David, van den Noord, Paul, 'Ireland's housing boom: What had driven it and have prices overshot?', *OECD Economics Department working papers*, Paris, OECD, 2006 (working paper, no. 492).
Rafter, Kevin, *The Clann: The story of Clann na Poblachta*, Dublin, Mercier Press, 1996.
Raymond, Raymond J., 'De Valera, Lemass and Irish economic development: 1933–1948', in Murphy, J. A., O' Carroll, J. P. (eds), *De Valera and his times*, Cork, Cork University Press, 1983, pp. 113–34.
Raymond, Raymond J., 'World War 2 and the foundation of Irish Shipping Ltd 1941–1945', *Éire-Ireland, XIX*, 1984, pp. 48–76.
Raymond, Raymond J., 'The Marshall Plan and Ireland', in Drudy, P. J. (ed.), *Irish studies, Vol. IV*, Cambridge, Cambridge University Press, 1985, pp. 295–329.
Raymond, Raymond J., 'The Marshall plan and Ireland, 1947–52', in Drudy, P. J., (ed.), *The Irish in America: Emigration, assimilation and impact*, Cambridge, Cambridge University Press, 1985.
Reddan, Fiona, *Ireland's IFSC: A story of global financial success*, Dublin, Mercier Press, 2008.

Reynolds-Feighan, Aisling, 'Accessibility, transportation, infrastructure planning and Irish regional policy: Issues and dilemmas', in O' Leary, Eoin (ed.), *Irish regional development: A new agenda*, Dublin, Liffey Press, 2003, pp. 163–81.

Rigney, Peter, *Trains, coal and turf: Transport in emergency Ireland*, Dublin, Irish Academic Press, 2010.

Roche, William K., 'Social partnership: From Lemass to Cowen', *Economic and Social Review, 40*, 2, 2009, pp. 183–205.

Ross, Shane, *The bankers: How the banks brought Ireland to its knees*, London, Penguin, 2009.

Ruane, Frances, 'Resonances from economic development for current economic policy-making', in Mulreany, Michael (ed.), *Economic development 50 years on*, Dublin, Institute of Public Administration, 2009, pp. 122–44.

Ruddock, Alan, *Michael O'Leary, a life in full flight*, Dublin, Penguin Ireland, 2007.

Ryan, Bob, *With a tap on the knee: Memoirs of a reluctant banker*, Dublin, Mib Books, 2001.

Ryan, Raymond, 'Butter industry in Munster, 1884–1939', Unpublished M. Phil thesis, University College Cork, 2000.

Ryan, Raymond, 'The Butter industry in Ireland, 1922–1939', *Irish Economic and Social History, 27*, 2001, pp. 32–47.

Sachs, Jeffrey, 'Ireland's growth strategy: Lessons for economic development', in Gray, Alan W. (ed.), *International perspectives on the Irish economy*, Dublin, Indecon, 1997, pp. 54–63.

Sammon, P. J., *In the Land Commission: A memoir, 1933–1978*, Dublin, Ashfield Press, 1997.

Savage, R. J., *A Loss of innocence? Television and Irish society 1960–1972*, Manchester, Manchester University Press, 2010.

Schoen, Lothar, 'The Irish free state and the electricity industry, 1922–27', in Bielenberg, Andy (ed.), *The Shannon Scheme and the electrification of the Irish free state*, Dublin, Lilliput Press, 2002, pp. 28–48.

Seth-Jones, David, *Graziers, land reform and political conflict in Ireland*, Washington DC, The Catholic University of America Press, 1995.

Sexton, J. J., 'Emigration and immigration in the twentieth century: An overview', in Hill, J. R. (ed.), *A new history of Ireland, Vol. VII, Ireland, 1921–84*, Oxford, Oxford University Press, 2003, pp. 796–825.

Sexton, J. J., 'Trends in output, employment and productivity in Ireland, 1995–2005', in Alyward, Ciaran, O' Toole, Ronnie (eds), *Perspectives on Irish productivity*, Dublin, Forfás, 2007, pp. 28–49.

Sheehy, Séamus J., 'The impact of EEC membership on Irish agriculture', *Journal of Agricultural Economics, 31*, 1980.

Shiel, Michael J., *The quiet revolution: The electrification of rural Ireland, 1946–1976*, Dublin, O' Brien Press, 1984.

Shields, B. F., 'An analysis of the financial and operating statistics of the Great Southern Railways Company, 1938–1944', *Journal of the Statistical and Social Inquiry Society of Ireland, 17*, 1946–47, pp. 541–64.

Slevin, Geraldine, 'Is there a "new economy" in Ireland'?, Dublin, Central Bank of Ireland, 2002 (technical paper, 3/rt/02). http:/www.centralbank.ie/publication/documents/3RT02.pdf.

Smith, C. F., *The shipping Murphy's: The Palgrave Murphy shipping line 1850–1926*, Dublin, Albany Press, 2004.

Smith, Nicola Jo-Anne, *Showcasing globalisation? The political economy of the Irish Republic*, Manchester, Manchester University Press, 2005.

Smyth, H. P., *The B&I line:A history of the British and Irish Steam Packet Company*, Dublin, Gill and Macmillan,

Soden, Mike, *Open dissent: An uncompromising view of the financial crisis*, Dublin, Blackhall, 2010.

Spiller, Keith, Linehan, Denis, 'Beacons of modernity': Department stores, modernity and the urban experience in mid-twentieth century Ireland', *Irish Geography, 39*, 2, 2006, pp. 143–58.

Sweeney, Paul, *The politics of public enterprise and privatisation*, Dublin, Tomar, 1990.

Sweeney, Paul, *Selling out? Privatisation in Ireland*, Dublin, New Island Books, 2004.

Sweeney, Paul, *Ireland's economic success: Reasons and lessons*, Dublin, New Island Books, 2008.

Takei, Akihiro, 'The political economy of the Irish flour milling industry 1922–1945', in Bielenberg, Andy (ed.), *Irish flour milling: A history 600–2000*, Dublin, Lilliput Press, 2003, pp. 133–45.

Tansey, Paul, *Ireland at work, economic growth and the labour market, 1987–1997*, Dublin, Oak Tree Press, 1998.

Teague, Paul, Donaghey, Jimmy, 'Why has Irish social partnership survived?', *British Journal of Industrial Relations, 47*, 2009, pp. 55–78.

Thomas, William Arthur, *The stock exchanges of Ireland*, London, Francis Cairns, 1986.

Thornhill, D. J., 'The revealed comparative advantage of Irish exports of manufactures, 1969–1982', *Journal of the Statistical and Social Inquiry Society of Ireland, 25*, 1987–8, pp. 91–146.

Timoney, N., 'Labour and employment in Ireland in the era of the Celtic Tiger', in Hogan, John, Donnelly, Paul F., O' Rourke, Brendan K. (eds), *Irish business and society*, Dublin, Oak Tree Press, 2010, pp. 3–28.

Van Egeraat, Chris, 'Spatial concentration in the Irish pharmaceutical industry: The role of government intervention and agglomeration economies', Maynooth, National Institute for Regional and Spatial Analysis, 2006 (working paper no. 28), available: http://www.nuim.ie/nirsa/research/documents/wp%2028%20/chris%20van%Egeraat.pdf.

Walsh, Brendan, 'Labour participation and the growth of women's employment: Ireland 1971–1991', *Economic and Social Review, 24*, 1993, pp. 369–401.

Walsh, Brendan, 'The transformation of the Irish labour market: 1980–2003', *Journal of the Statistical and Social Inquiry Society of Ireland, 33*, 2004, pp. 83–115.

Walsh, Brendan, 'Demography and Irish economic growth: Past and future', in Kinsella, Stephen, Leddin, Anthony (eds), *Understanding Ireland's economic crisis: Prospects for recovery*, Dublin, Blackhall, 2010, pp. 265–83.

Walsh, James. A., 'Enterprise substitution in Irish agriculture: Sheep production in the 1980s', *Irish Geography, 22*, 1989, pp. 106–9.

Walsh, James A., 'A regional analysis of enterprise substitution in Irish agriculture in the context of a changing Common Agricultural Policy', *Irish Geography, 24*, 1, 1991, pp. 10–23.

Walsh, James A., 'Modernisation and marginalisation under the Common Agricultural Policy: Irish agriculture in transition', in Flognfeldt, T., Nordgreen, R., (eds), *Proceedings of the xi International Seminar on Marginal Regions,* Lillehammer, Norway, 1992.

Walsh, James A., 'Agriculture in transition', in Bartley, Brendan, Kitchin, Robert (eds), *Understanding contemporary Ireland*, London, Pluto Press, 2007, pp. 158–69.

Walsh, Patrick Paul, Whelan, Ciara, 'The importance of structural change in industry for growth', *Journal of the Statistical and Social Inquiry Society of Ireland, 29*, 2000, pp. 1–33.

Walter, Bronwen, 'From flood to trickle, Irish migration to Britain, 1987–2006', Irish Geography, *41*, 2008, pp. 181–94.

Weir, R. B., 'In and out of Ireland: The Distillers Co. Ltd and the Irish whiskey trade 1900–1939', *Irish Economic and Social History, 7*, 1980, pp. 45–65.

Weldon, Niall, *Pioneers in flight: Aer Lingus and the story of aviation in Ireland*, Dublin, Liffey Press, 2002.

Whelan, Bernadette, 'Ireland and the Marshall Plan', *Irish Economic and Social History, 19*, 1992, pp. 49–73.

Whelan, Karl, 'Policy lessons from Ireland's latest recession', *Economic and Social Review, 41*, 2, 2010, pp. 230–42.

Whitaker, T. K. 'Capital formation, savings and economic progress', in Whitaker, T. K., *Interests*, Dublin, Institute of Public Administration, 1983, pp. 19–55.

Whitaker, T. K., 'Financial turning points', in Whitaker, T. K., *Interests*, Dublin, Institute of Public Administration, 1983, pp. 81–117.

Whitaker, T. K., 'From protection to free trade, the Irish experience', in Whitaker, T. K., *Interests*, Dublin, Institute of Public Administration, 1983, pp. 55–81.

Whitaker, T. K., *Protection or free trade: The final battle*, Dublin, Institute of Public Administration, 2006.

White, Dan, *A history of Musgrave: The first 125 years*, Cork, Musgrave, 2001.

White, Rossa, *Years of high income largely wasted*, Dublin, Davy Stockbrokers, 2010.

Williamson, J. G., 'Economic convergence: Placing post-famine Ireland in comparative perspective', *Irish Economic and Social History, 21*, 1994, pp. 1–27.

Wills, Clair, *That neutral island: A cultural history of Ireland during the Second World War*, London, Faber & Faber, 2007.

Wrigley, Leonard, 'Ireland in economic space', in Lee, J. J. (ed.), *Ireland: Towards a sense of place*, Cork, Cork University Press, 1985, pp. 66–84.

Zuelow, Eric, *Making Ireland Irish: Tourism and national identity since the Irish Civil War*, New York, Syracuse University Press, 2009.

Index

Note: *Italic* page numbers indicate tables.

A rocky road: The Irish economy since the 1920s (Ó Gráda) 1
academic interest 1
Access to Finance Scheme 156
advertising, breweries 74
Aer Lingus 99–100, 101
Aer Rianta 100
age profile, farmers 67–8
agricultural and veterinary science, research institute 55–6
agricultural credit 148–9
Agricultural Credit Corporation (ACC) 12, 145, 148
agricultural employment, decline 22
Agricultural Institute 56
agricultural sector: 1960s 22; under-capitalization 56; cash costs 68; concentration and specialization 58; continued importance 191; continuity 69–70; crops planted *54*; dominance 189–90; effects of EEC entry 60–1; as employer 68–9; environmental protection 62; export dominance 126, 128–9; exports 60–1; female workers 173; and GDP growth 68; geographical concentration 62; Great Depression, 1929 51; income gap 58; investment 59, 60–1; labour 59; marketing 50–1; mechanization 57–8; output distribution *61*; output value 52; overview 49; percentage distribution of output *64*; policy and intervention 50; policy significance 12, 49; productivity 62–3; reduced support 61–2; role of women 59; science 58; Second World War 53–4; state support 56; US support 56; yields 67, 68
air freight 130
airline companies 99–101
airline deregulation 101, 104
airports 100
Allied Irish Bank, reckless lending 162
An Bord Bainne 22, 60, 81
An Bord Iascaigh Mhara (BIM) 65
An economic history of Ireland since 1660 (Cullen) 1
An Foras Talúntas 56, 184
An Foras Tionscal 19
Anglo-Irish Bank 162, 163
Anglo-Irish Free Trade Area Agreement 128
Anglo-Irish Trade Agreement 13, 24, 55, 76, 81, 130
Apple 88
Armstrong, H. 4, 195
army 96
autonomy 123
aviation 99–100
Avonmore 86

bacon 55
Bacon and Pigs Marketing Boards 52
bailouts 43
balance of payments 139, 140–1
balance of trade 139, 140–1
balance sheets 161
bank balance sheets 161
bank debts, government guarantees 43, 44
bank loans, to farmers 59
Bank of Ireland 9, 162
banking: government intervention 163; ineffective regulation 4; property bubble 162; rationalization 148; regulatory failure 44, 197
banking crisis 162, 199
bar 60
barley 63
Barrett, A. 178–9
Barry, F. 2–3, 28, 38–9, 181, 186, 195, 199

Beamish 74
Beddy Report 98
beef 60
Bergin, A. 183
bicycles 110
birth rate *166*, 166–8, 174, 187
Bloom, D. E. 167, 168
Blythe, E. 123
Bord Fáilte 102
Bord na Móna 80
borrowing 146
Boundary Commission 11
Boyle, G. 68
Brennan, J. 10, 14
breweries 74, 77, 86
Britain: agricultural sector 56; economic revival 196; food shortages 55; immigration to 170; importance as export market 23–4; tariffs 12; trade dependence 123, 194; trade relations 75
British companies 73
British deficiency payments 60
British markets, access to 84
British military withdrawal, effects of 96
British Ministry of Food 55
British National Debt 11
Buchanan report 23
budget deficit 31, 33
budgetary stance and government debt *32*
Building on Reality 33
Building Society Act 156
Business Expansion Scheme (BES) 116
business offshore process sector 114
butter 51, 52, 54–5, 81

Cabinet Committee on Economic Planning 16
call centres 114
calved heifer subsidy 60
Campbell, G. 10
Canning, D. 167, 168
capital acquisition 155–6
capital budget deficit 35
capital expenditure 17, 35
capital expenditure programme, revival 35
capital gains tax, reduction 35
capital investment 149
Capital Investment Advisory Committee 20
capital taxation 35
cars 110–11, 127
cash and carry 109
cash costs, agricultural sector 68
Catholicism, and fertility rates 168
cattle 49, 52–3, 60, 81
celibacy 165
Celtic Tiger 1, 2, 39, 87, 91, 104, 132, 156, 167, 171, 172, 177, 183, 188, 190, 194, 199
cement 73, 86
Central Bank 9, 16, 42–3
Central Statistics Office (CSO), establishment 17, 55
chain stores 106–7, 109–10
Chamberlain, N. 13
cheese 77, 81
chemical firms 29
chemicals 88, 90–1, 135
China/Hong Kong, imports from 138
chocolate 81
Civil War damages 11
Clann na Poblachta 146
classical economic theory 11, 155
clothing *see* textile industry
co-operative financial institutions 148
co-ops, move to plc status 86
Coal–Cattle Pact 13, 52
coal mining 78; *see also* mining
coalition government 1982–7, fiscal and monetary policy 146–7
cohesion funding 28
Coillte 64
Coleman, K. 160
Colley, G. 31
commercial development 93
Commission of Agriculture 50
Commission of Inquiry into Banking, Currency and Credit 14
Commission on Banking 148
Common Agricultural Policy (CAP) 25, 26, 60, 61–2
Common Fisheries Policy 25, 66
commuting 98
Company Development Programme 29
comparative historical context 1
competition, international 3
compulsory tillage orders 16, 53, 54
computers 87–9
Condensed Milk Company 74
Conefrey, T. 116
confectionery 10–11, 73
Confederation of Irish Industries, lack of influence 37
Congested Districts 50
construction sector 91–3, 95; commercial development 93; corruption 197; credit 158; and education 183; effects of boom 44; employment 93; encouraging 35–7; private sector credit growth 156; tax exemptions 4

containerization 127
contraception 167, 168
Control of Manufactures Acts 13, 19, 22, 75, 128, 149
convergence 145
convergence theory 2–3
Cooper, M. 153
Coras Iompair Éireann (CIE) 98, 99
Córas Tráchtála 128
Cork, port development 127, 133
corn 53
corporate reorganization 86–7
corporation tax 19–20, 28, 149–50
corruption 197
Costello, J. A. 19
Council of Education 181
Crafts, N. 39–40, 88, 133, 150, 183, 185, 186, 190–1, 193
creamery industry 74, 77, 81–2, 86
credit: agricultural 148–9; importance of 145
credit availability 91, 148, 156–7, 162
credit creation 156
credit guidelines 40
credit unions 148
crops 63
Crotty, R. 1, 49, 54, 67
Crowley, E. 68
Cullen, L. 1
cultural values, and economic development 4
Cumann na nGaedheal: economic intervention 11–12; economic policy 195; fiscal policy 11; fisheries policy 64–5; government investment 145; industrial policy 72, 73–4; land policy 50; support base 9; trade policy 123
Currency Commission, establishment 9–10
current budget surplus 35
current expenditure 35
current surplus 35
Customs Duties Act 75

dairy 50–1, 54–5, 56, 60, 61–2, 77, 81, 86
Dairy Disposal Company (DDC) 11, 74, 77
DART system 98
De Gaulle, C. 24
De Valera, E. 51
death rate *166*, 168, 169
debt guarantees 43, 44
decentralization 31
decoupling 62
deflationary policies 18
delayed convergence 2–3, 196
Delors programmes 28
demography 194; birth rates, death rates and natural increase *166*; overview 165; and retail 112; trajectory of economic growth 187–8
Department of Agriculture Butter Marketing Committee 52
Department of Finance: attitude to development 12; British influence 10; policy reform 21
Department of Industry and Commerce 10, 72, 73
Department of Supplies 125
dependency ratio 170, 175–6, *176*, 187
deposit guarantee 163
deregulation 40, 42, 101, 156–7, 197–8
development aid, manufacturing bias 30
development policy, from 1973 29
developmental state network 3
disposable income 112
distilling 74, 82
diversification 86–7
Dollar Exports Advisory Committee 128
domestic credit policy, Fianna Fáil 14
domestic demand 83
domestic property sector 158–60; *see also* construction sector
domestic saving 153
domestic service 105–6
domestic technology 106
Donaghey, J. 39
Dooley, T. 50
Doyle, E. 131–2
drug substance plants 90
Drumm, D. 162
Dublin: concentration of development 31; industrial employment 13–14; industry 71, 83; port development 127
Dublin Airport 100
Dukes, Alan 34
Dunlop 78
dwellings built *92*

economic collapse, 2008 1, 43
economic credibility 163–4
economic dependency 3
economic development, conceptualization 2
Economic Development (Whitaker) 21, 59
economic liberalization, EEC/EU 29
economic planning, introduction of 16
economic policy: British influence 11; centrality of 198; objectives 22

economic recovery, European factors 34
economic sovereignty, loss of 43–4
Economic War 12–13, 51, 52, 53, 77, 125
education 194; curriculum 180–1; investment 181; school leaving 183; secondary and tertiary-level *181*; technological 181–2; tertiary 181–3; vocational 179–80, 182
education reform 23
educational attainment 168, 178–9, 181, 182–3, 184, 187–8, 194
eggs 56
Eichengreen, B. 185
electrical engineering 88
electrical generation and distribution 74–5
Electricity Supply Board (ESB) 11, 40, 74–5
electronics 87–8, 89
electronics firms 29
Emergency Powers legislation 15, 53–4
emigration 165, 166, 169–71; destinations 170; migration rates *172*; and recession 171; returning migrants 171
employment: agricultural and fisheries *69*; agricultural sector 68–9; construction sector 93; domestic service 105–6; general clerical occupations 106; growth rates 79; of immigrants 177–8; industrial 73–4, 85, 192–3; non-commercial services 106; sectional distribution *191*; services sector 96, *97*, *107*, *108*, 119; tourism 104; transportable goods sectors *79*, *85*
employment creation 176
employment protection 186
employment rate 176, *177*
energy security 79–80; *see also* fuel supply
entertainment industry 115–16
entry criteria, single currency 41
environmental protection, agricultural sector 62
ESRI historical series 1
ethno-religious profile 170
euro 41–2, 133
Europe: agricultural sector 56; imports from 138; opportunities 24
European Agricultural Guidance and Guarantee Fund (FEOGA) 60
European Central Bank (ECB) 41, 43, 45
European Economic Community (EEC): applications 24–5; assistance 86; attractions of 20; benefits of membership 26; effects of entry 44–5; effects on agricultural sector 60–1; effects on fishing 66; effects on industry 84–5; effects on trade 131–2, 144; membership issues 25; significance of membership 25, 26
European Free Trade Association (EFTA) 20, 24, 128
European integration 4
European Monetary System (EMS) 41, 61
European Monetary Union (EMU) 41
European reconstruction, post Second World War 16
European Recovery Programme (ERP): agricultural sector 55; funding 16–18
European single currency 41–2
European Structural Funding 27
European Union: Irish relations with 45; support for construction 91; transfers 34
Evans, B. 20
ewe premium 60
exchange controls 40
exchange rate 42
Exchange Rate Mechanism (ERM) 41
excise duties 11
Expansionary Fiscal Contraction 34
expenditure, priorities 149
export orientation 85
Export Profits Tax Relief Scheme 128
exports: to Britain 78, 129; composition 126–7, 128–30, 131, 132, 133–5, *136*; diversification 28–9; geographic distribution *129*, *134*, *135*; growth 130; and growth 132–3; increase 140–1; industrial 130; industrial commodities *131*; invisible exports 141–3; services sector 116, *117*, 118–19, *142*
Exports Profits Tax Relief (EPTR) 19, 20, 128, 130
external borrowing 146

Fahey, T. 168
family farms 12
family size 167–8, 174
Fanning, R. 20
farm modernization scheme 68
farm sizes 50, 52, 58–9, 67, 68
farmers: age profile 67–8; difficulties 50
Federated Union of Employers 37
fertility: marital 165, 166–7; non-marital 168; total rate 168
fertilizer industry 74, 82–3
fertilizers 53–4
Fianna Fáil: agricultural policies 51–2, 53; economic policy 195; fiscal policy 14, 31,

33–4, 141; in government 12; government investment 145; governmental roles and responsibilities 13; industrial policy 75–6; monetary policy 14; trade policy 124
film industry 116
financial acceleration model 162
financial account balances *153*
financial institutions, private sector 147
financial markets, deregulation 40
financial policy 156
Financial Regulator 42–3, 197
financial services sector 113–14; deregulation 156–7; exports 116; foreign firms 114; private sector credit growth 156; regulation and supervision 42–3, 44
financial transfers 26, *27*, 28
Findlater's 107, 109
Fine Gael–Labour coalition: economic strategy 33; fiscal policy 31
Fine Gael, support for Fianna Fáil 33–4
First Programme for Economic Expansion 103
fiscal autonomy 9, 123
fiscal contraction 33
fiscal policy: Cumann na nGaedheal 11; expansionary 199; Fianna Fáil 14, 31, 33–4; Fine Gael/Labour coalition 31; for growth 31, 35; manufacturing bias 30
fiscal position, improvement 34–5
fisheries protection 25
fishing 64–7; employment *69*
Fitzgerald, G. 33
Fitzgerald, J. 2, 159, 182, 183
Fitzgerald, J. D. 116
Fitzgerald, M. 24, 79
Fitzpatrick, S. 148
flexibility, loss of 42
flour milling 73
food processing 81, 83, 84, 86, 87, 191
food shortages, Britain 55
food supplies, Second World War 15–16
footwear 73, 77–8, 86
Ford 77, 78, 127
foreign borrowing 31
foreign direct investment (FDI) *151*, 193–4; benefits 141; chemicals and pharmaceuticals 90–1; effects of EEC membership 28; encouraging 22, 149–50, 196–7; growth 136; high share 94; IDA role in 29–30; outward 152–3; from US 150
foreign investment 19, 75, 83, 84
forestry 63–4; acreage *65*; private and state-owned *66*
free trade 24–5, 28, 85
fuel supply 15, 55, 78–9; *see also* energy security

Gallaher's 73
Garvin, T. 4, 180
GDP: agricultural sector 68; effects of structural funding 28
Geiger, T. 18
general clerical occupations 106
General Tourist Development Fund 103
German firms 83
Germany, trade with 124
Girvin, B. 18, 190
Glanbia 86
glass industry 86
global economic crisis 198
globalization 4, 198
GNP, exports and imports 130
Görg, H. 152
government borrowing 146
government expenditure, 1983–2009 *36*
government intervention: industry 74–5; retail 110; *see also* agricultural sector
grassland 63
Great Depression, 1929 12, 51, 52–3, 75, 124, 198
Great Southern and Western Railway 97–8
Great Southern Railway (GSR) 11, 15, 98
green pound 61
Groceries Order 40, 110
Gross Added Value (GVA) growth, construction sector 91
Gross Domestic Fixed Capital Formation, percentage composition *157*
Gross Domestic Physical Capital Formation 153–4, *154*, 158
gross fixed capital formation, agricultural sector 59
group-trading system 109
growth: 1958–59 21; as distinct from development 3; and exports 132–3
growth rates 189–91
Guaranteed Trade Loans 145, 146
Guiney, D. 106
Guinness 74, 77

Hamilton, R. 182, 183
Harbour Act 127
Hardiman, N. 37
Haughey, C. 33
Hederman, M. 17–18

Hogan, P. 12
Honohan, P. 2, 19, 34, 156, 161–2, 163, 196
horses, agricultural sector 53–4, 57–8
hospitality industry 156
housebuilding *92*
houseworkers 105–6
housing prices 158–61, *161*
human capital 194; education as 182; growth of 182–3; immigrant 184; and immigration 178–9
Human Capital Index 182
hydro-electricity 74–5, 79–80

IBM 89
ideology 12, 13
immigrant–native wage differential 179
immigrant occupation gap 179
immigrants: occupational profile 186; relief of labour shortages 187
immigration 171, 176–9, 184, 194
import substitution industrialization (ISI) 76, 144, 195
imports: composition 127, 136–8; geographic distribution *129*, *139*, *140*; increase 140–1; percentage distribution *138*; post-Second World War 140–1; role in development 135–6; services sector 116–19, *117*, *142*; from UK 137–8
income 189–90
income gap, agricultural sector 58
income tax, reductions 35
incomes and savings 154–5
independence: effects of 96; expectations for industry 72
indirect taxation 11
industrial commodities, exports *131*
Industrial Credit Corporation (ICC) 145–6
industrial development: Campbell's concept 10; regional policy 23; state and private companies 14
Industrial Development Act 22
Industrial Development Authority (IDA) 19, 20, 85, 89, 114; changing role 22–3; export promotion 128; policy dominance 29–30; promotional activities 150; regional development 30–1; Services Industries Programme 115
industrial employment 13–14, 192–3
industrial exports 130
Industrial Grants Act 22
industrial policy: from 1973 29; initiatives 19
industrial relations 21–2
industrialization: overview 71; *see also* manufacturing
industrialization through protectionism 13
industry: British companies 73; British involvement 10–11; British presence 75; capital investment 83; contribution to economy 94; domestic demand 83; employment in 73, 85; expansion periods 93–4; expectations after independence 72; exports 78; foreign involvement 84–5; foreign sector 87; government intervention 74–5; high-end 89; loss of 88–9; post-First World War 72; regional 71, 83; reorganization 86–7; Second World War 77–8; self sufficiency 79–80; *see also* manufacturing
inflation: increasing 42; and wages 39
inflationary wage–price spiral 31
information technology-based industries 88, 132, 193, 194; attracting 182; exports 133–4; investment 150; service functions 141, 142; TFP growth 186–7
information technology, financial services sector 113
infrastructure development 91, 146, 195–6
installation aid 68
insurance 114
Insurance Corporation of Ireland 197
Intel 30, 88
intellectual property 117
inter-party government: agricultural sector 55; state investment 146
inter-party governments: 1947 16, 18, 19; 1954 18–19
interest rates, low 42
international competition, effects of 3
international economic initiatives: non-participation 18; participation 23–4
International Financial Services Centre (IFSC) 113–14
international recession, 1979 31–3
international trade: composition 143; diversification 124; economic impact 139–40; effect of US links 133; with Europe 133; geographic distribution 125, *126*; magnitude 142; overview 123; as percentage of GNP *143*; services sector 141–3, 144; vulnerability 144; *see also* exports; imports; trade
intervention system 61
investment 187, 193–4; agricultural sector 59, 60–1; British 10; capital investment 149; in education 181; export-oriented 22;

foreign 75; importance of 145; industry 83; multinational 30; overseas 152; portfolio investment 153; priorities 158; private sector 145; in property 160; public sector 146; and savings 155; Second World War 149; social infrastructure 146; state investment 145, 146, 195; and structural change 157; tourism 103, 104; transport 99; from US 132; *see also* foreign direct investment (FDI)
Investment in Education 181
invisible exports 141
Ireland 1912–85 (Lee) 1
Irish Agricultural Production (Crotty) 1
Irish Associated Creameries 51
Irish Banks Standing Committee 18–19, 147
Irish Congress of Trade Unions (ICTU) 37
Irish Council for Science, Technology and Innovation 184
Irish Dairy Board 22
Irish Distillers Group 82
Irish Export Board 128
Irish Financial Services Centre 34–5
Irish pound 10, 41, 195
Irish Punt 41
Irish Refining Company Ltd 80
Irish Research Council for Science, Engineering and Technology 184
Irish Research Council for the Humanities and Social Sciences 184
Irish Shipping 15
Irish Stock Exchange 155–6
Irish Sugar Company 14, 76
Irish Tourist Association 102
Irish Tourist Board 102
IT investment 30

Jacobsen, J. K. 3
jobs, creation and losses 28
Johnson, D. 1, 189, 190
joint-stock banks 147
Jones, R. C. 177

Kearney, I. 183
Kearns, A. 160
Keating, W. 94, 132, 136
Kelly, C. 104
Kelly, M. 160, 161, 163
Kennedy, K. 1, 38, 171, 175–6
Kennedy, L. 1, 21, 168, 172, 189, 190
Kerry 86–7
Kerrygold 81–2
Kitchin, R. 159, 160
Krugman, P. 150

labour: agricultural sector 59; demand for 172
labour costs 154–5
labour demand 176
labour force: entrants 168; overview 165; *see also* demography
labour migration, effects of 2
Labour Party 146
labour productivity 185–7
Laffan, B. 28
Land Act 1933 52
land annuities 51
Land Commission 52
land reclamation 55
land reform 12, 49–50, 51–2
language, as difficulty for immigrants 179
Lawless, M. 133, 186
leasing companies 156
Leddin, A. J. 21, 35, 39
Lee, J. 1, 160
Lemass, S. 15, 20, 75, 77, 100, 125
liberalization 20, 128–9, 144, 190, 196
licensing, financial services sector 113–14
life expectancy 165–6
limestone subsidy 55
Lisbon treaty, voting 45
literacy 183–4, 188
livestock 60; numbers 63; *see also* cattle; pigs and pig meat; sheep
livestock marts 60
livestock numbers *56*
livestock premia 62
living standards 22, 91, 189–90
Lloyd George, D. 123
loan purchase 163
local sourcing 76
Long-Term Recovery Programme 17
Loyal, S. 178

Maastricht criteria 34, 155
Mace 109
MacElligott, J. J. 123–4
MacEntee, S. 18
macroeconomic crisis, 1955–56 19
MacSharry reforms 62
Maddison, A. 190
Maddison's data 1
Maher, D. J. 17–18
man-made fibres 90
Manpower Consultative Committee 182
manufacturing 71, 83–4, 143, 155, 193; *see also* industrialization; industry
marketing, breweries 74
marriage 165, 168
married women, workforce participation 174–5

Marshall Aid 16
Marshall Plan 55
Matthews, A. 69–70
McCreevey, C. 35
McGilligan, P. 17
McGrath, J. 10
McWilliams, D. 160
meat exports 60
meat processing 81
meat, world market 49
mechanization, agricultural sector 57–8
Meenan, J. 1, 76
Merchants National Co-operative 109
micro-economy model 196–7, 198–9
micro-state model 4–5, 196–7, 199
migrants: education 178–9; returning 171
migration 167, 178, 195
migration rates *172*, *180*
milk 81
milk quotas 61–2, 86
Milne Report 98
Miloko co-operative society 81
mining 82; *see also* coal mining
Mjøset, L. 3, 179
monetary policy: Fianna Fáil 14; following EEC entry 40–2
mortgages 161
motor cars 110–11
motor trade 110–11
Moylan, Sean 179
multinational investment 30
multinationals 28–9, 115, 130, 132, 150, 193
Murphy, A. E. 41, 186
Murphy's 74, 86
Musgrave Bros 109
Musgrave, J. 109
music industry 115–16

National Asset Management Agency (NAMA) 163; value of loans transferred *163*
national debt 14, 146
National Development Plan, fishing 66
National Economic and Social Council (NESC) 38
National Enterprise Agency 37
National Income growth, 1958–63 21
National Institutes of Higher Education 181
National Linkage Programme 29
National Planning Board 33
National Spatial Strategy 31
National Understanding 37
National Wage Agreement 37
national wage agreements 37–8, 39
nationalist developmental policies 11
natural gas 80
natural increase *166*, 168
Neary, J. P. 52
neo-classical growth model 2
neo-corporatist institutions 21
neo-liberalism 33, 147, 196, 197–8
net domestic product (NDP), composition *192*
net services trade deficit 118
Nítrigin Éireann Teoranta (NET) 22
non-commercial services 106
non-tradable services 112–13
Northern Ireland, peace process 104
Nugent, J. 154–5

Ó Gráda, C. 1, 2, 12, 19, 41, 52, 144, 146, 167, 190
Ó Riain, S. 3, 115
oats 63
O'Brennan, J. 26
O'Brien, A. 23, 103
O'Donoghue, M. 31, 37
O'Donovan, J. 49
O'Hearn, D. 3, 115
O'Leary, E. 3–4, 94, 119, 132
O'Mahony, D. 17, 28
O'Malley, E. 3
oil 80, 127
oil crises 31–2, 37, 100, 141
Olson, M. 3–4
Organization for European Economic Cooperation (OEEC) 16, 149
O'Rourke, K. 2, 12, 146, 190
over-dependence 3, 24

P. & J. Ryan Ltd 106–7
peripheral regional economy 2–3
Pfizer 89
pharmaceuticals 89–91, 132, 135
pigs and pig meat 51, 52, 54, 56, 62
planned government deficit 31
planning 159–60
Players 73
policy: demography and growth 187; European and international influence 23–4; inappropriate 197; inter-war 9
policy errors 44
political instability, early 1980s 33
population density 169–70
population growth 187
population summary *169*
port development 127, 130, 133
portfolio investment 153
potatoes 63

poultry 56; numbers *63*
price supports, agricultural sector 52
private capital inflows 154–5
private companies, industrial development 14
private sector credit growth 156
private sector credit, percentage distribution *159*
privatization 40, 147
productivity: agricultural sector 62–3; services sector 119
Productivity and industrial growth: The Irish experience (Kennedy) 1
profits 193
Programme for Economic and Social Progress 40
Programme for Economic Expansion 59
Programme for National Recovery 38
Programme for Research in Third-Level Institutions 184
Progressive Democrats 33, 40
property market: boom 158–61; collapse 35, 43–4
protectionism 189; agricultural sector 51; dismantling 25; effects of 13–14; effects on agriculture 52–3; Fianna Fáil 12; indigenous industry 19–20, 22; industry 72, 75–6; move away from 128–9, 143; post-independence 10, 123–4; post-Second World War 80–1; Second World War 125
Protestant emigration 170
Public Capital Programme 17, 18, 146
public expenditure control 33, 34
public housing 21
public sector investment 146
pubs 112–13

Rae, D. 160
railways 11, 15, 97–9; lines and freight *99*
Railways Act 98
Ranks 73, 86
Raymond, R. J. 16
Read, R. 195
reading 184
recession 85–6, 171
recession, 1979 31–3
regional development 30–1
regional economy model 2, 195
regional policy: Industrial Development Authority (IDA) 23; revival 31
Regional Technical Colleges (RTCs) 182
regulation, agricultural sector 52
regulatory failure, banking 44, 197
remittances 11, 171
reorganization 86–7
research and development (R&D) 30, 89, 90, 184–5; expenditure *185*
research funding 184–5
retail 105, 106–12; percentages of sales *113*
retail establishments, numbers *111*
Retail Grocers, Drapers and Allied Trades Association 109
retail traders 109
Retailing Planning Guide 110
return migration 171, 176–7
revealed comparative advantage 130
risk aversion 156
road traffic 98, 99
rolling stock 98
Rosslare, port development 127
Royalties and Licence 117–18
Ruane, F. 34, 152
rural electrification 16, 146
rural organizations 55
Ryanair 101

sales 105
savings 154–5
school leaving 183
science 58, 184
Sea Fisheries Association 65
Second World War: agricultural sector 53–4; food supplies 15–16; industry 77–8; investment 149, 195; legacy of 16; protectionism 125; shortages 53, 125; tourism 102
Seed and Venture Capital Measures 156
self-service retail 109
self sufficiency, industry 79–80
services sector: anti-competitive forces 4; contribution to Net Domestic Product *118*; employment 23, 96, *97*, *107*, *108*, 119; expansion 187, 192–3; exports 116, *117*, 118–19, 141–3; female workers 174–5; foreign direct investment (FDI) 152; imports 116–19, *117*; imports and exports *142*; investment 30; non-commercial 106; non-tradable 112–13; overview 96; productivity 119; state intervention 23; tradability 116; trade deficit 118
Sexton, J. J. 91
Shannon Dam scheme 10
Shannon Free Airport Development Company 19
Shannon Free Zone 19
sheep 54, 60
shipping 124–5, 127
shortages 53, 125

single currency 41–2
Single European Act 26, 29
Single European Market 26, 28, 29, 132, 133, 152
skills 171, 179
Slevin, G. 94
slum clearance 145
Smith, N. J.-A. 4, 42
soap industry 10–11, 73
social expenditure 149
social inequalities 188
social infrastructure, investment 146
social partnership 34, 37, 38, 39, 196
software 89, 115, 132
Spar 109
stamp duty 35
State Capital Programme, expenditure 146
state enterprises 11
state intervention, Second World War 15
state investment 145, 146, 195
state-owned companies 14, 147
state, role in development 199
Strategy for Development 38
structural change 191
structural funding 28
subsidies, agricultural sector 52
sugar beet 50, 60, 63, 74
sugar industry 76
super levy system 61–2
supermarkets 109–10; numbers and sales *110*
Sweetman, G. 19

Tallaght Strategy 34
Tansey, P. 39, 171
Tariff Commission 123
tariffs 9, 12–13, 72, 76, 123–4
tax incentives 19
tax uniformity 30
taxation: capital taxation 35; corporation tax 114, 149–50; Exports Profits Tax Relief (EPTR) 19, 20, 128, 130; film industry 116; housing market incentives 158–60; income tax 35; indirect 11, 73–4; music industry 116; personal 39; preferential 35; and private investment 145; property market 160; property related 35; protests 38; reductions 35; software exports 115; tax reliefs 197
Teagasc 184
Teague, P. 39
technology, domestic 106
telecommunications 147
Telesis Report 29
television 112
textile industry 76, 79, 83, 86, 126–7, 172
The economic development of Ireland in the twentieth century (Kennedy *et al*) 1
The First Programme for Economic Expansion (white paper) 21
The Irish economy in the inter war years (Johnson) 1
The Irish economy since 1922 (Meenan) 1
The modern industrialization of Ireland (Kennedy) 1
The Rural Environment Protection Scheme (REPS) scheme 62
The Second Programme for Economic Expansion 21
Third Programme for Economic Expansion 21
tillage, area aid 62
tillage orders 53, 54
tillage subsidization policy 52
tobacco industry 10, 73
Toniolo, G. 39–40, 88, 133, 183, 185, 186, 190–1, 193
total factor productivity growth 61
Total factor Productivity (TFP) 185–7
tourism 23, 30, 101–4, 116, 171; earnings and spending *105*
tractors 57–8
tradability, of services 116
trade: dependence on Britain 143–4; diversification 124; following EEC entry 26; liberalization 128–9, 144, 190, 196; liberalization, European debate 20; promotion 85; relations with Britain 75; *see also* international trade
trade deficit 140–1
trade union bill, 1941 15
trade union–employer relations 21–2
trade union movement: fragmentation 37; revision of priorities 38
traditional industries, decline 38
transport 97–100; *see also* airline companies; railways
Transport Act 1986 40
transportable goods sectors: employment *79*, *85*; net outputs *84*
Treaty on the European Union 29
triadic relationships 3
Troubles, effects of 100
turf 15, 75–6, 78–9, 80
Turf Development Board (TDB) 76, 80

under-capitalization, agricultural sector 56
Underdeveloped Areas Act 19

Underdevelopment Areas Board 19
underemployment 171–2
unemployment 154, 171–2, *173*
unemployment benefit 186
United Distillers of Ireland 82
United Kingdom *see* Britain
United States: European Recovery Programme funding (ERP) 16–17; foreign direct investment (FDI) 150, 152; immigration to 170; investment 30, 132; role as supplier 128; support for agricultural sector 56; trade links 133
universities 181, 182
urban renewal 91
US sub-prime mortgage market 162

Van den Noord, P. 160
van Egeraat, C 30
vocational education 179–80
voluntary sector 38

wage bargaining 21–2, 39–40
wage differentials, immigrant-native 179
wage freeze 15
wage growth 37
wage moderation 38–9
wages 193
Walsh, B. 2, 21, 34, 35, 167, 186, 187, 196
Walsh, J.J. 10
War of Independence 11
Waterford Co-op 86
wheat 52, 60, 63
Whelan, K. 44
Whitaker, T. K. 20, 21, 59–60, 79, 149
White, R. 158
William Clarke & Sons 73
Wills 73
women: agricultural sector 59; life expectancy 165; sector participation *175*; workforce participation 167, 172–5, *174*, 187
Woods, M. 160
working age cohorts 168
working hours 176

yoghurt 86